FRANK LLOYD WRIGHT
COLLECTED WRITINGS

FRANK LLOYD WRIGHT
COLLECTED WRITINGS

Volume **1**

1894–1930

Edited by
Bruce Brooks Pfeiffer

Introduction by
Kenneth Frampton

Rizzoli/New York in association with The Frank Lloyd Wright Foundation

Acknowledgments

This book could not have been published without the extraordinary assistance of Margo Stipe, Indira Berndston, Penny Fowler, and Oscar Muñoz of The Frank Lloyd Wright Archives. Especially to Ms. Stipe I am grateful for patience and dedicated research. I also express gratitude to Berna Neal, Head Librarian of the Howe Architectural Library at Arizona State University, for providing material not in the archives collection. My gratitude also to Charles Miers, Michael Bertrand, Elizabeth White, Jane Cowen, and Simone Rene of Rizzoli and Brian Sisco of Harakawa-Sisco; to our representative, Steven Kroeter, and to Richard Carney, CEO of The Frank Lloyd Wright Foundation, for their support of the publication program between Rizzoli and the FLWF.

For nearly fifty years I have been associated with and virtually consumed by the life and work of Frank Lloyd Wright. I can in no way find words that describe my gratitude to him and to his wife, Olgivanna. It is to them that these volumes are dedicated. —B.B.P.

First published in the United States of America in 1992 by Rizzoli International Publications, Inc.,
300 Park Avenue South, New York, New York 10010
Copyright © 1992 The Frank Lloyd Wright Foundation
The drawings of Frank Lloyd Wright are copyright © 1992 The Frank Lloyd Wright Foundation

The following articles and essays published here for the first time are copyright © 1992 The Frank Lloyd Wright Foundation: The Architect and the Machine; Architect, Architecture, and the Client; A Philosophy of Fine Art; Concerning Landscape Architecture; The Print and the Renaissance; On Marriage; The Pictures We Make; In the Cause of Architecture: Purely Personal; The Plan for the Erection of a Model Building; The Line Between the Curious and the Beautiful; Who Said "Conservative?"; Confession; The Commercially Degenerate Architect

The publisher gratefully acknowledges *The Architectural Record* for generously granting permission to reproduce the following articles from the "In the Cause of Architecture" series. Reprinted with permission:

The Architect and the Machine (May 1927); Standardization, The Soul of the Machine (June 1927); Steel (August 1927); Fabrication and Imagination (October 1927); The New World (October 1927); The Logic of the Plan (January 1928); What "Styles" Mean to the Architect (February 1928); The Meaning of Materials—Stone (April 1928); The Meaning of Materials—Wood (May 1928); The Meaning of Materials —The Kiln (June 1928); The Meaning of Materials—Glass (July 1928); The Meaning of Materials—Concrete (August 1928); Sheet Metal and a Modern Instance (October 1928); The Terms (December 1928)

Printed in Mexico
Designed by Brian Sisco of Harakawa-Sisco

Library of Congress Cataloging-in-Publication Data
Wright, Frank Lloyd, 1867–1959.
      [Selections,   1992]
      The collected writings of Frank Lloyd Wright/edited by Bruce Brooks Pfeiffer.
        p.   cm.
    Includes index.
    Contents: v. 1. 1894–1930—v. 2. 1931–1932. including a reprint of his 1932 autobiography.
    ISBN 0–8478–1546–3 (HC : v. 1). —ISBN 0–8478–1547–1 (pbk. : v. 1). —ISBN 0–8478–1548–X (HC : v. 2). — ISBN 0–8478–1549–8 (pbk.: v. 2)
    1. Wright, Frank Lloyd, 1867–1959—Philosophy. I. Pfeiffer, Bruce Brooks. II. Wright, Frank Lloyd, 1867–1959. Autobiography.
NA737. W7A35 1992
720—dc20   91–40987
                                                        CIP

C O N T E N T S

PREFACE

Frank Lloyd Wright was as prolific a writer as he was a designer. He left us a prodigious amount of written material in the form of published books, articles, and essays, as well as manuscripts for an additional 265 articles and essays that were never published. During the next three years, The Frank Lloyd Wright Foundation and Rizzoli/New York will publish six projected volumes of his writings, arranged chronologically, under the title *The Collected Writings of Frank Lloyd Wright*. In addition to bringing back into print Wright's published works, these volumes will also include a large selection of previously unpublished articles and essays. Practically all of the material that was originally published between 1896 and 1959 is no longer in print. It seems essential now to present to the general public the vast collection of his writing and only appropriate to issue the first two volumes in this series on the auspicious date of June 8, 1992, the one hundred and twenty-fifth anniversary of the birth of Frank Lloyd Wright. His importance to us grows steadily, thirty-three years after his death, as the principles of his work and the humanity of his life's endeavors take on even greater value the more we look back on them and realize how visionary their content still is. Their relevance lies in Wright's advocacy of a more humane existence. That was the raison d'être of all he did and all he wrote.

Wright's ability to describe his architecture as well as his insights into American culture grew more lucid as his architectural work matured. His writings, like his buildings, were directed to the American citizen, not to the elite nor exclusively to professional architects. When he did address architects, it was usually to rebuke them, even to castigate them, for their lack of responsibility concerning the deeper significance of architecture.

When he opened his practice in 1893 and watched the gilder put the letters FRANK LLOYD WRIGHT ARCHITECT on the plate-glass door of his office, he thought to himself, "My God, what gall!" This admission, later in his life, of that moment when he was a twenty-six-year-old beginner in the profession, reveals his attitude toward architects and architecture. He saw, from the very start of his work, the architect as a great benefactor to humanity, the artist with the power to change, alter, influence, and direct the course of human life. To him that was an enormous responsibility, a sacred mission.

As radical as his work was, a complete break from the Victorian influences rampant in the nation at that time, and as controversial as his ideas were about importing European culture into America, he was not a starving young artist isolated from society and lacking commissions. His first work, a house for William H. Winslow of River Forest, built in 1893, was created for a conservative, upper-class businessman. Commissions for clients such as Winslow, as well as substantial commercial and religious works, came in steady succession over the next eighteen years.

In designing buildings for his clients, Wright responded to individual requirements with an architectural solution. The client presumably believed in him and in his work. But in his writings he was addressing a far greater audience, and on far broader terms: he pointed out the problems concerning the state of architecture in the nation, calling for people to wake up to the deeper meaning of the term "culture," with architecture as its spearhead. In many respects, he was writing a gospel. And as the son and grandson of ministers, his words often assume the character of a sermon. He admitted as much years later when talking to his young apprentices at his architectural school, the Taliesin Fellowship:

My family has been preaching since the days of Reformation in England. . . . Well now you mustn't let me preach to you. I don't want to. I don't want to be a preacher. It is in my blood, I can't help it, I get that way. Sometimes when I am talking on the platform I feel that sort of thing— I catch myself at it.

THE FRANK LLOYD WRIGHT ARCHIVES

A great many of the books, articles, and essays in *The Collected Writings* are now out of print and have been for a long time. The majority of them are to be found in The Frank Lloyd Wright Archives. All the unpublished manuscripts appearing in these volumes belong to the archives collection.

The Frank Lloyd Wright Archives are housed at Taliesin West in Scottsdale, Arizona. Taliesin West was the Southwest home and studio of Frank Lloyd Wright from 1938 until his death in 1959. It remains today the winter headquarters and main office of The Frank Lloyd Wright Foundation. Wright set up his architectural practice as a foundation in 1940, and he turned over all his drawings, manuscripts, books, periodicals, and future architectural earnings to the foundation. By far the most valuable holding within the archives is his collection of architectural drawings, covering the period from 1885 to 1959, and comprising a file of more than twenty-one thousand sheets of paper.

During his lifetime Wright several times relocated his architectural practice, which he first opened in Chicago in 1893, moved to Oak Park in 1897, and then to Wisconsin in 1911. His work on the Imperial Hotel in Tokyo required him to move to Japan in 1916. Returning to the United States in 1922, he settled in Los Angeles, only to depart the Southwest and return, finally, to Taliesin, his home and studio in Wisconsin, in 1924. For the last two decades of his life, from 1938 to 1959, he migrated annually between Wisconsin and Arizona. Looking back over a career that spanned nearly three-quarters of a century, it is indeed remarkable that he was able to keep the drawings collection intact. The correspondence files, manuscripts, rare books, and periodicals were mainly kept in Wisconsin, following the dissolution of his Oak Park Studio in 1911. In spite of the fact that there were two disastrous fires at Taliesin—one in 1914 and another in 1925—his drawings, papers, and documents were not damaged. On his eightieth birthday, during a breakfast party held for him in the large studio at Taliesin, he reminisced about the studio and the fire. He pointed to the doorway that led from the studio onto a breezeway and the house beyond. Each time the fire had been stopped at that doorway before it reached the studio. "It was as if God questioned my character," he told us, "but not my work." In 1961 all his papers were moved to Arizona, where the archives are permanently housed.

Wright saved everything: woodcuts depicting famous English cathedrals that his mother hung in his childhood bedroom and the libraries of his father and paternal grandfather—including books dating back to 1666—are part of the archives collection; letters dating from 1887 to 1959 make up a file of 103,000 records, or more than 289,000 documents; the manuscript collection numbers more than 600 individual files, including short essays and entire books (such as his autobiography). The mission of The Frank Lloyd Wright Archives is to preserve the work and ideas of Frank Lloyd Wright and to make the material available for research, publication, and exhibition. This publication of his collected writings furthers that objective.

These volumes include all of Wright's previously published manuscripts as they first appeared in print. His own special form of punctuation and use of capitals are likewise reproduced in facsimile (although, with extreme caution taken, selected spellings have been updated to avoid confusion or ambiguity). Readers will encounter innumerable so-called stylistic inconsistencies and idiosyncrasies in Wright's prose—of which he was well aware. Sometimes the choice of style was profound:

In an interview with broadcaster Mike Wallace:

Wallace: Do you go to any specific church?
Wright: Yes. I go occasionally to this one and sometimes to that one, but my church—I put a capital N on nature and go there. . . . You spell God with a G, don't you?
Wallace: I spell God with a G, you will spell it. . . .
Wright: I spell nature with an N, a capital.

And, in *The Living City* (1958):

I hardened into my own severest critic, I thought, and yet—sentences quoted by my critics to show my style just this side of "deplorable" I found right enough—in their way. They stand. I apologize. But I did find the affair with capitalization fantastic, far too capitalistic. . . . As for clichés, if so, I made the original of every cliche myself. —F. Ll. W.

The Collected Writings also includes numerous previously unpublished articles: transcripts for public deliveries, articles intended for publication, or extended drafts for articles published before or later in a different context. Manuscripts that do not substantially supplement Wright's published oeuvre, such as first drafts or minimally rewritten drafts, have not been included. Therefore, these volumes represent to a great degree the complete writings of Wright.

CHRONOLOGY

To present the writings in any sequence other than chronological (and by order of original publication or, in the case of unpublished works, of writing) would seem unnatural and forced, even though Wright himself constantly reached back into previous work he had done to breathe new life into it. Some articles, initiated at the turn of the century, he reworked fifty years later. Likewise in his architecture, there were plans from much earlier periods that he might redesign if he saw the original scheme was appropriate for a later application.

Wright's prodigious editing of his own work, be it on his drawings or on his manuscripts, was the result of his constant striving for perfection. Change appealed to him always—not for the sake of change itself, but rather as a means of improvement, amplification, and elucidation. Those who were close to him witnessed this continual, almost obsessive, desire to make changes. Whenever he returned to Taliesin after an extended absence, he would go from room to room rearranging furniture and frequently engaging everyone around him in construction projects that literally required rebuilding sections of the complex. When asked why all this commotion and energy spent on something that others perceived as beautiful and perfect in every way, he would reply, "I am seeing it all with a fresh eye now, and I can plainly see what I did wrong and how to make it better."

Because of the innumerable changes to the manuscripts requiring numerous revised drafts, the size of the collection is staggering. Researchers who study the collection invariably ask the same question when they see the amount of time Wright spent on his writings: "Where did he ever find the time to design over a thousand buildings and projects and still accomplish all of this work in writing?" Or vice versa, for that matter.

Other than the writings themselves, there is a collection of over 300 transcripts of his various public lectures as well as his private talks to the apprentices in the Taliesin Fellowship. These so-called "Fellowship Talks," 238 in all, took place over a period of nine years, from 1950 to 1959, when, following Sunday morning breakfast, he would speak on any number of subjects to his apprentices and guests. None of these talks is included in this series of publications. Wright's correspondence, too, has been excluded from this collection. Both those voluminous files, the transcripts and the letters, should someday find their way into print and provide even more insight into Wright's life and work.

The environment in which Wright was raised introduced him to the great poets, writers, and philosophers. He was raised a Unitarian in a family of ministers and educators. The young Wright was immersed in literature. A list in The Frank Lloyd Wright Archives of the books in his mother's library shows a heavy diet of Victorian writers, English poets, and the writings of the transcendentalists, Unitarians Emerson, Thoreau, and Wright's favorite American poet, Walt Whitman. He loved the English language, from Shakespeare to Blake to contemporary literature. When asked once why he never learned a "foreign" language, he replied, "Because I have spent my lifetime learning the one I was born to."

In addition to these early influences provided by American men of letters, he read others voraciously throughout his life, especially the work of Schiller, Goethe, Mazzini, Silvio Giselle, Prince Kropotkin, and Tolstoy. And he once remarked:

> As for inspiration from human nature there were Laotze, Jesus, Dante, Bach, Vivaldi, Palestrina, Mozart. Shakespeare was in my pocket for the many years I rode the morning train to Chicago. I learned, too, from William Blake (all of his work I read), Goethe, Wordsworth, Dr. Johnson, Carlyle (Sator Resartus at the age of fourteen), George Meredith, Victor Hugo, Voltaire, Rousseau, Cervantes, Nietzsche, Unamuno, Heraclitus, Aristotle, Aristosphanes.

This is not simply a book list; it is a record of those writers whom he read and absorbed not just once, in his youth, but continued to go back to, often reading their work aloud to his family and to his apprentices.

Wright was not without a fine sense of humor, and humor played a strong part in his selection of reading, chiefly his fondness for Mark Twain and O. Henry and, later in his life, for James Thurber. Many a Sunday evening, during the last decade of his life, he would read aloud stories by these writers to his apprentices in his living room at Taliesin.

A dominant characteristic of his genius was his power of absorption; ideas poured into him. Literature undeniably was a distinct source of nourishment throughout his life. Literature and historical writings not only influenced his way of thinking, but also affected his own inventive work.

A study of his writings reveals how his style changed and grew, how sometimes he became caustic, even bitter and sarcastic, especially as he wrote about the tragic fate of architecture in the United States. But like his architectural forms, which became simpler and more articulate, so, too, did his language. He referred to those forms and their various applications as "grammar," the analogy to language being obvious. In his architecture, building types expressed a "grammar" closely associated with each type. The early Prairie houses, in particular those of the cement plaster, or stucco—Willits, Hickox, Bradley, or Coonley—quickly developed a grammar of their own derived from the method of construction. The grammar was therefore not an application, not a surface "style," but an expression of form related to the function out of which it grew. Louis Sullivan stated that "form follows function." Early in his work, however, Wright qualified his own interpretation of that statement by maintaining that "form and function are one." The difference between the two viewpoints is larger than one might assume at first glance: if form follows function, it becomes, then, something applied, something that could be separated from function; but if form and function are one, then separation becomes impossible, or—if forced—as destructive as tearing the blossom from the stem or the branch from the tree. "Grammar" thus meant that special form feature characteristic of a particular genre of designs.

Wright worked as meticulously on his manuscripts as he did on the drawings for the buildings he designed. He edited himself ruthlessly, starting first with his handwritten manuscript and then attacking the typed copies. He clearly was determined to be as explicit in expressing himself with the written word as he was in expressing himself in stone, brick, or concrete.

Bruce Brooks Pfeiffer

INTRODUCTION

Amid the onrush of modernity, when innovation and obsolescence follow each other at ever closer intervals, we are, at last, turning back to Wright to look for that which we may have either missed or lost in the thirty-three years that have elapsed since his death. This collection of his writings, excluding correspondence, is a welcome complement to the recent twelve-volume publication of drawings held in the Taliesin archive.

Four rather slight essays separate Wright's first tentative formulations, as they appear in his 1894 address "The Architect and the Machine," from the epoch-making "The Art and Craft of the Machine," first presented at Jane Addams's Hull House in Chicago in 1901. In this last paper he will acknowledge his despair at first reading Victor Hugo's prophecy that architecture will be superseded by the printed word—by the advent of the rotary press, which, along with the teeming industrialized mass of Chicago, will constitute the very essence of the machine for Wright. Wright will conclude by reversing the logic and by arguing that only an intelligent application of machine production will be able to redeem the excesses of mechanization, that is to say, will be able to imbue the mercantile nineteenth-century capital city with the essence of a soul.

Three years later, in 1897, in his essay "Architect, Architecture, and the Client," Wright will arrive at the prerequisites of his new domesticity, already anticipating the labor-saving kitchen, with his ball-bearing machinism, some sixteen years before Christine Frederick will publish her *Ladies' Home Journal* articles as a book, her *Housekeeping with Efficiency* of 1913. In the same essay he will oppose free-standing radiators or free-standing anything for that matter, be it the furniture or the house itself. Indeed, Wright's new American home is largely couched at this time in negative terms, as a cleaning of the Augean stables. Thus, he will come out against pictures for their capacity to destroy the repose of the interior and against direct artificial lighting for much the same reason. He will repudiate the use of gilt in any form and advocate the use of natural wood and plaster, stained so as to convey a sense of sempiternal warmth, in conjunction with dried grasses or fresh flowers artfully displayed in well-appointed vases.

The ideological ramifications of all this will be elaborated at an abstract level in his address "The Philosophy of Fine Art," delivered at the Art Institute of Chicago four years later, where he will compare the laws of form to musical harmonics and go on to insist that true art must be based on conventionalization. Elsewhere he will rail against the fashionable "plan factory" architect and will assert, long before Le Corbusier, that architecture is largely a matter of organization, while its formal syntax must be derived from nature with a capital N. Given the primacy that he will attach to Nature at every conceivable juncture, seeing it as the embodiment of the godhead itself, it is altogether surprising that he will say so little that is specific about the art of landscapes, save for expressing his passing admiration for the gardens of Gertrude Jekyll.

That he will become an exceptionally experienced home builder during the first decade of this century is borne out by the thirty-three Prairie houses of widely varying size that he will realize between 1900 and 1910 and by the various innovatory devices that he will use in their construction, from the long-span steel beams of the Robie House to the construction of partitions from cement and plaster applied to both sides of metal lathing, from the application of reinforced concrete to domestic construction to the general use of built-in vacuum systems to the application of side-hung casement windows in specific opposition to the classical American preference for the guillotine sash window.

The outward swinging casement will be prominently featured in his first manifesto, "In the Cause of Architecture" published in *The Architectural Record* in May 1908. In this six-point manifesto Wright will argue for a domestic architecture characterized by simplicity, repose, economy, horizontal windows, discrete ornaments, built-in furniture, undressed natural materials, and the full integration of the building into its site.

Having thus established his basic precepts, Wright will formulate his concept of *constitutional ornament*, that is to say, ornament that is integrated into, rather than applied to, the fabric of a building: a preference for structural decoration rather than decorated structure, to cite the distinction coined by Auguste Perret. At the same time, after mounting a categorical attack on the barbarism of the Renaissance, he will admit to being profoundly influenced by the Japanese print.

These are the twin themes that he will return to in his next two essays: first, in the polemical pro-Gothic introduction with which he will open the 1910 Wasmuth volumes, *Ausgeführte Bauten und Entwürfe von Frank Lloyd Wright*; second, in his homage to Japanese civilization that first appears with his initial essay on the Japanese woodblock print, *The Japanese Print*. This essay will afford him a further occasion on which to elaborate his views as to the nature of the decorative:

> The ultimate value of a Japanese print will be measured by the extent to which it distills, or rather exhales, this precious quality called "decorative." We generally do not quite understand what that means and are apt to use the term slightingly—especially when compared with "art," which has supposedly some other and greater mission. I—speaking for myself—do not know what other mission it legitimately could have, but I am sure of this at least, that the rhythmic play of parts, the poise and balance, the respect the forms pay to the surface treated, and the repose these qualities attain to and impart and which together constitutes what we call good decoration, are really the very life of all true graphic art whatsoever. In the degree that the print possesses this quality, it is abidingly precious; this quality determines—constitutes its intrinsic value.[1]

This was by no means Wright's last word on Japanese culture, for he will write three further introductory essays between 1912 and 1927 and later still he will indulge in the annual fall ritual of the so-called "print party" at the Taliesin Fellowship, in which he will habitually display his print collection. For Wright, the Japanese print remained the ethical shibboleth with which he would always be able to attack the pompier bourgeois taste for the Renaissance. Moreover, much like the role played by the Purist canvas in the architecture of Le Corbusier, the print, for Wright, was an icon that embodied the essence of an entire civilization.

The received historical accounts of Wright's career to date have tended, for inexplicable reasons, to ignore two seminal creations of the late Prairie period. The first of these is the design for a prototypical subdivision submitted for the City Club of Chicago competition of 1913, the principles of which were summed up by Wright three years later in an essay that appeared in the competition publication, *City Residential Land Development*, edited by Alfred B. Yoemens and published in May 1916. The second remarkable achievement was the Imperial Hotel in Tokyo, under construction from 1916 to 1922, and its even more miraculous survival of the Kanto earthquake disaster of 1923.

Wright's 1913 "city-in-miniature" is a hypothetical urban synthesis of all the prototypical Prairie forms that he had evolved between his Francisco Terrace apartments in Chicago of 1895 and his Midway Gardens, opened in Chicago in 1914, including such key pieces as the Larkin Building (1904), Unity Temple (1906), the City National Bank, Mason City (1909), the various Prairie houses of the period, and the quadruple block plan—comprising four houses, each with different aspects and pinwheeling about a central core—and even his first sketches for Aline Barnsdall's Olive Hill Theater.

In principle, all these types are somehow incorporated into Wright's prototypical park-city that was far more cogent and discretely scaled in its various dispositions than anything attained in the realized garden city prototypes of the period, such as Letchworth in England. Moreover it was an imminently realizable vision of middle-class civility that has unfortunately never been attained in America or elsewhere. Wright's subsequent deurbanization theory, beginning with *The Disappearing City* of 1932, veers toward a rather abstract vision dominated by mechanization. In retrospect this seems to have been the last moment when the form of a specific urbanity could still be imagined just prior to the apocalypse of motopia. It was Wright's Oak Park critique of Daniel Burnham's monumental "city beautiful" Chicago plan of 1909.

Wright's diminutive neighborhood unit was an apotheosis of American Progressivism, directly related to the Chicago School of urban sociology and educational reform, to the revisionist social consensus shared by such intellectuals as Jane Addams, John Dewey, Thorstein Veblen, and Charles Hortens Cooley, whose book *Social Organization* had been published in 1909. Wright's City Club plan is organized in such a way as to facilitate the maintenance of Cooley's primary social groups, the family, the kindergarten, and the neighborhood unit. Evidently indebted to Jens Jensen and the Chicago park system, Wright's "park-city" was designed to facilitate a pattern of social interaction that would be capable of compensating for the loss of the small town. This mythic "city-miniature" was thus intended to serve as a socially integrative settlement pattern in which worker's low-rise, high-density collective housing would be mixed in with quadruple-block houses, grouped in clusters of four, the whole being inextricably woven together, like a carpet, particularly in respect to its socio-cultural, educational, and recreational facilities. The aim was to raise the level of the society through a process of spatial acculturation. It was perhaps the last reformist effort, as Roger Cranshawe has remarked, to transcend the hegemony of industrialized capitalism through bourgeois moral reform, and it is no surprise that the church in Wright's plan, significantly called a temple, is strictly nondenominational.[2]

Apart from the obituaries written on the occasion of Louis Sullivan's death in 1924, Wright's incidental writings for the years 1922 to 1925 are almost exclusively devoted to the achievement of the Imperial Hotel, which was in so many ways a homecoming for Wright in that it was a Xanadu built by a Westerner who had been profoundly influenced by Japanese culture. In his essay "The New Imperial Hotel" of 1923, Wright will make it only too clear how different his garden-hotel type was from the standard American "office-hotel" and how, with its 1,000-seat theater and 300-seat cabaret, it was intended to function as much as a general cultural center as a luxury residence. In this and other essays dedicated to the hotel he will constantly remark on this unprecedented combination of occidental and oriental types and on the difficulty of achieving such a synthesis, particularly given the precise but idiosyncratic character of the typical Japanese craftsman and the rather awkward labor-intensive methods employed by the Japanese building industry. Elsewhere he will rail against the Japanese weakness for the steel-framed Yankee skyscrapers, many of which were destroyed in the 1923 earthquake. He will express his frustration over their distressing penchant for Western-style, neo-Renaissance emporia. The achievement of the spectacularly anti-seismic Imperial Hotel gave further proof, as though any were needed, of Wright's consummate skill as a builder, his ever-present inventiveness in dealing with unprecedented conditions—such as his prompt abandonment of steel plumbing halfway through construction, when he learned of its propensity to rust out in the Tokyo climate, or his equally ingenious but scandalous use of cheap Oya lava stone for fairfaced revetment. In this regard he will attribute to his hotel the Japanese term *shibui*, indicative of a quality that while at first resisted by society comes to be increasingly valued.

As far as his compulsive writing was concerned, Wright was never more revealing nor at the same time more diffuse and repetitive as in the numerous articles that he wrote for the editor of *The Architectural Record*, M. A. Mikkelson, the essays appearing more or less consecutively in 1927 and 1928, once again under the omnibus title "In the Cause of Architecture." While Wright was unduly rhetorical by nature, the main cause of the repetition on this occasion arose from the fact that the first year was a dry run to be followed by a final version, comprising nine installments that were published in 1928.

The main themes of these articles were by now somewhat predictable, such as the imperative to master the machine and the need to ground tectonic form in natural law. The term "Usonia," meaning the U.S.A., first coined by Wright in 1925, reappears here with increasing frequency, in the light of Wright's advocacy of standardized modular construction, this being seen as a future guarantor of Usonian democracy. Wright will liken this approach to weaving and to the warp and woof of an oriental rug, a metaphor also employed by Sullivan in accounting for the brick-faced construction of his Midwestern banks. Wright will follow this by stressing the varying constitutive and expressive capacities of different materials and at this juncture he will begin to introduce, if not a new theme, then certainly a new discourse on the potential of relatively unprecedented materials and processes, such as wood veneer, plate-glass electroglazing, steel, sheet metal, and various kinds of modern joining and finishing techniques. Wright will go out of his way to classify both terra-cotta and concrete as conglomera; that is, as nontectonic material.

In the first of the essays for the 1928 series, entitled "The Logic of the Plan," Wright will argue that the architect must prove his ability at the level of the ground plan or not at all (shades here of Le Corbusier's "the plan is the generator" of 1923), and he will go on to contend that the basic tectonic principle of the work as a whole is immediately readable from the plan. Thus, just as Unity Temple was an *in situ* concrete building, the Avery Coonley residence was destined to be framed in wood, and the Larkin Building had a plan that could only be realized through the use of brick.

In the later essays of the 1928 series, numbers VI, VII, and VIII, Wright will begin to formulate the component parts of his emerging Usonian aesthetic. Thus, he will pass from the crystalline potential of glass to his first theoretical justification of the textile-block system, and finally to the penultimate and most important essay of the series, devoted to sheet metal, wherein we will encounter what is surely his most vivid description of a work—his 1924 proposal for the National Life Insurance offices in Chicago:

> The exterior walls, as such, disappear—instead are suspended, standardized sheet-copper screens. The walls themselves cease to exist as either weight or thickness. Windows become in this fabrication a matter of a unit in the screen fabric, opening singly or in groups at the will of the occupant. All windows may be cleaned from the inside with neither bother nor risk. The vertical mullions (copper shells filled with non-conducting material) large and strong enough only to carry from floor to floor and project much or little as shadow on the glass may or may not be wanted. Much projection enriches the shadow. Less projection dispels the shadows and brightens the interior. These protecting blades of copper act in the sun like the blades of a blind.
>
> The unit of two feet both ways is, in this instance, emphasized on every alternate vertical with additional emphasis on every fifth. There is no emphasis on the horizontal units. The edge of the various floors being beveled to the same section as is used between the windows, it appears in the screen as such horizontal division occurring naturally on the two-foot unit lines.
>
> Being likewise fabricated on a perfect unit system, the interior partitions may all be made up in sections, complete with doors, ready to set in place and designed to match the general style of the outer wall screen.
>
> These interior partition-units thus fabricated may be stored ready to use, and any changes to suit tenants may be made over night with no waste of time and material.
>
> The increase of glass area over the usual skyscraper fenestration is only about ten per cent (the margin could be increased or diminished by expanding or contracting the copper members in which it is set), so the expense of heating is not materially increased. Inasmuch as the copper mullions are filled with insulating material and the window openings are tight, being mechanical units in a mechanical screen, this excess of glass is compensated.

The radiators are cast as a railing set in front of the lower glass unit of this outer screen wall, free enough to make cleaning easy.[3]

It is interesting to note that Wright conceived of the internal treelike cantilevered structure of this proposal in two different forms, in the first instance as a composite cantilever and in the second as a twin-stem structure with symmetrically cantilevered floors, linked by a bridge-span between the points of contraflexure. The essential continuity and articulation of Wright's magnum opus—his masterly S. C. Johnson Wax Administration Building of 1936—is already anticipated here in a dramatic synthesis of structural and membraceous form.

Repudiating the categories of style and composition and asserting in their place character and organic rhythm, Wright will end the 1920s defining beauty as a natural order, "Whether of the mind or the body, because we are Nature ourselves in this sense." He will add to this the corollary that the curious is merely a disorder in nature, and with this aphorism he will distance himself from the European avant-garde and assert his own cause conservative in the deepest sense. Wright enters the 1930s unemployed and embittered, and his essays dating from early 1930 are little more than diatribes against all and sundry, against the profession, the AIA, and Henry Russell Hitchcock, who just over a decade later will produce his classic study of Wright's work, *In the Nature of Materials.*

Kenneth Frampton
Columbia University

1. Frank Lloyd Wright, *The Japanese Print: An Interpretation* (Chicago: Ralph Fletcher Seymour, 1912).
2. Roger Cranshawe, "Frank Lloyd Wright's Progressive Utopia," *Architectural Association Quarterly X*, no. 1 (1978), pp. 3–9.
3. Frank Lloyd Wright, "In the Cause of Architecture: Sheet Metal and a Modern Instance," *The Architectural Record*, October 1928.

FRANK LLOYD WRIGHT
A BIOGRAPHICAL SKETCH
1894–1930

Frank Lloyd Wright was twenty-seven years old when he wrote his first essay on architecture, which he read to a group in Evanston, Illinois, in 1894. His own architectural practice was barely one year old. His first work was just completed, a house for William H. Winslow in River Forest, Illinois, built in 1893. The design of that house soon brought him international acclaim. It stands today as testimony to his precocious mastery of the art. His subsequent buildings were not always as seminal. He even built some "period" houses that seem totally inconsistent with the design for Winslow. These include a Georgian Colonial house for George Blossom, in the same year that he was beginning his serious writings, a Dutch Colonial house for Frederick Bagley, and an English Tudor house for Nathan G. Moore, all in the Chicago area. But these were obviously specified requests; Moore, for example, pointedly stipulated that he did not want the type of house that his young architect-to-be had done for William Winslow, reasoning that he did not want to sneak down the back streets to avoid being laughed at!

Other papers were written and delivered by Wright during the 1890s—and not published until now—but by 1901, when he delivered the lecture "The Art and Craft of the Machine" at Hull House, in Chicago, at the instigation of Jane Addams, his work in architecture had deeply matured. The steady progession of buildings he was completing in and around Chicago and its suburbs was heralding a new era in architecture.

At first Wright referred to his work as the "New" architecture, emphasizing its break with the past, with period styles and time-worn traditions. He would adopt the word *organic* to qualify his work. He used the adjective in his first essay in 1894, and he further defines it in his first essay for *The Architectural Record* in 1908. Throughout his life he would continually seek a better definition for it, until he came upon the simple formula that qualifies a building as "organic" if it is appropriate to its place, to its time, and to its users.

In the fall of 1909 Wright suddenly closed the Oak Park Studio and left for Berlin to work on a monograph of his architecture to be published by Ernst Wasmuth. For sixteen years the studio had been a thriving establishment, with several notable draftsmen and architects working for him. It was estimated that a new set of working drawings was turned out by the studio every six weeks. But the request from Wasmuth allowed Wright to rationalize leaving his home and practice.

His departure for Europe was prompted by an equally sudden change in his personal life. He had fallen in love with Mamah Borthwick Cheney, the wife of one of his Oak Park clients. Abandoning his wife and six children—she likewise abandoned her husband and children—Wright fled with Cheney to Berlin. She accepted a teaching position, and he began work on the monograph. Choosing not to weather a bleak winter in Germany, Wright relocated in Florence, sent for his son Lloyd and draftsman Taylor Woolley, and continued to make the ink drawings required by Wasmuth. Soon Mamah also left Berlin, and the two of them took up residence in Fiesole, near Florence. Wright's personal actions had provoked a scandal difficult for the American public to comprehend, much less forgive. And on their return to America, Wright and Cheney retreated once more—this time to southwestern Wisconsin, where he built his home and studio, Taliesin, on the land of his family ancestors. He pleaded for a divorce, but his wife, Catherine, refused to grant him one.

By 1913 the "prairie house" era in his architecture was completed. Midway Gardens, a restaurant and beer garden planned and built on Chicago's south side revealed an entirely different approach to architecture and a new avenue into design; he created all the interior design elements, including sculpture, mural paintings, furniture, tableware, chinaware, and carpets. This commission was soon followed by the Imperial Hotel in Tokyo.

Wright first visited Japan in 1905 with his wife, Catherine, and two of his clients, Mr. and Mrs. Ward W. Willits. Again in 1913 he made a voyage to Japan, accompanied on this second trip by Mamah Cheney. The purpose of his first trip was rest and respite after the arduous ordeal of building the Larkin Company administration headquarters in Buffalo.

But for the voyage in 1913, he had a definite aim in mind: to secure the commission of the Imperial Hotel. As early as 1911 people were at work to get him the job, namely Frederick Gookin,[1] a noted authority on Japanese prints and a close friend of Wright's. They had worked together on an exhibition of Hiroshige prints at Chicago's Art Institute in 1908, and although of very different temperaments, they complemented each other perfectly and worked together in harmony and shared respect. Gookin also had important contacts in Japan, among them the manager of the Imperial Hotel, Aisaku Hayashi. In a letter to Wright, Gookin mentions the new hotel commission:

My dear Wright:
Do you remember that when I saw you last I asked you how you would like to design a new building for the Imperial Hotel at Tokyo? Well, I wrote a long letter to Mr. Hayashi urging him that you were the right man for him to select as his architect. Today I have a letter from him in reply and this is what he says: "Many thanks for your opinion of Mr. Wright. I shall write him shortly after completing a rough plan according to my idea. If he would not be too radical and would work under reasonable terms he would be the first one." I presume therefore that you will also hear from him before a great while, and I sincerely hope this may lead to your getting the commission. Somehow it seems to me that this would be a great opportunity for you to do a stunning thing. Would it not be possible to retain the feeling and spirit of Japanese architecture and yet construct a building that would be compatible according to the standard and requirements of travellers from the rest of the world? If you could do this you would build a building that would be an object lesson to Japanese and Europeans and Americans alike.[2]

On his 1913 voyage, as well as on the 1905 trip, Wright spent considerable time and money on Japanese works of art, particularly on the prints of *ukiyo-e* artists Harunobu, Kiyonaga, Utamaro, Sharaku, Hokusai, and Hiroshige. Japanese folding screens of the Momoyama and Edo periods were also avidly sought by him, along with kakemono, bronzes, ceramics, and textiles. Later in his life he would expand his horizon into the arts of China and Korea. But Japanese art was his first love, especially the woodblock print.

Returning to the States the same year, he wrote to Darwin D. Martin, his client and patron, for whom he had designed the Larkin Building and a fine, large residence in Buffalo, New York: "My dear Mr. Martin—I have just got into the office (an hour ago). The planning of the Imperial Hotel is 'up to me.'"[3]

The following year, with the commission for the hotel secured, Wright was struck by tragedy while he was in Chicago at work on Midway Gardens. A servant at Taliesin locked the doors to the house during lunch, spread gasoline around the entrance, and set the residence ablaze, axing the victims as they tried to flee through the burning exit. Mamah Cheney and her two children were slain, along with four others—apprentices and workmen. Wright rushed back from Chicago, arriving early in the evening to find a charred, smoking ruin of the living quarters of Taliesin and seven bodies lain out on the grass in the garden court.

Shortly after the tragedy Wright received a letter from a person totally unknown to him, Miriam Noel, expressing her sympathy about the tragedy and asking to meet him. Weakened and depressed, he was singularly drawn to this sympathetic voice outside his circle. Together they launched a relationship that was to last ten years. Sensitive and artistic herself, she was also addicted to drugs and alcohol. The relationship quickly soured. She accompanied him on his trips to Japan from 1916 to 1922, but secluded herself, except for outbursts of violent temper. To the extreme burden of building a hotel in a foreign city and in a foreign language was added the constant insecurity of a personal life that had become a daily torment for both of them.

Taliesin was rebuilt. The commission from the hotel provided the funds with which Wright continued to collect Japanese art, and at the same time he collected for other Americans: the William Spauldings of Boston, Howard Mansfield of The Metropolitan Museum of Art in New York City, Sally Casey Thayer, whose collection would eventually be given to the Spencer Museum at the University of Kansas, and Gookin at the Art Institute of Chicago.

With the completion of the major part of the Imperial Hotel in 1922, Wright returned to the States to take up work for Aline Barnsdall in Los Angeles. Barnsdall was heir to a Pennsylvania oil fortune and had first met Wright in Chicago in 1914. Her passion was the theater, and she moved to Los Angeles where she intended to set up a community theater and drama workshop. Her colony was to include a large drama theater, a motion-picture theater, residences for actors and directors, shops, and Barnsdall's own home. None of the theater projects materialized. But her house, Hollyhock House, and two other residences were finally, after much deliberation and difficulty, built. With Miriam at his side, Wright did not need another tempestuous relationship in his life. But Barnsdall provided just that: she was mercurial, demanding, changing, anxious about her projects; altering her requirements, siding with her contractor against her architect, and ever fearful of being taken advantage of because of her money. No other client gave him such trouble nor caused him such pain and grief over building projects.

In 1922 Catherine finally granted him the divorce he had pleaded for twelve years earlier. The next year, hoping that marriage would assuage Miriam's temper and bolster her sense of security, Wright married her. Notwithstanding, matters worsened; any kind of normal life together proved impossible, and six months later they separated.

While working in Los Angeles on the projects for Barnsdall, he began experimenting with a new construction technique employing concrete blocks. Long considered the gutter product of the building industry, the blocks presented Wright with the very same answer to twentieth-century methods of which he wrote earlier in "The Art and Craft of the Machine." Here the machine, the mold, could produce a material of great poetry and beauty, as he proved in four houses he built between 1923 and 1924: the Millard, Freeman, Ennis, and Storer residences. With the Barnsdall works and the block houses, Wright felt he would be able to launch a new career in greater Los Angeles. But Californians seemed to prefer accepted styles, and Wright soon realized that the area held no future for him.

By 1924 he was back at Taliesin, separated from Miriam, and at work on new commissions, including the National Life Insurance Company, Nakoma Country Club, and the Gordon Strong Automobile Objective. But none of these projects was built. He opened his studio to several Europeans and Japanese, among them Dione and Richard Neutra (he had met Neutra at Louis Sullivan's funeral) from Vienna, Sylva and Werner Moser from Zurich, and Nobu and Kameki Tsuchiura from Tokyo. Rudolph Schindler had worked at Taliesin earlier, but had left by this time. In November 1924 Eric Mendelsohn came for an extended visit. Taliesin was becoming quite international, but there was no architectural work coming in. Dione Neutra recollected that on Christmas Eve of 1924, "We sat in the presence of the greatest architect of the twentieth century, who had no work, while architects of lesser quality were garnering great commissions."

In November 1924 Wright had been in Chicago visiting his friend, the painter Jerome Blum. Together they took in a matinee performance of the Russian ballerina Karsinova. Shortly after they were seated in the box, a young woman was seated in the remaining chair. She had black hair, worn loosely at the sides, and tied into a bun in the back. Wright observed her aristocratic bearing and thought she might be a Russian princess. Blum immediately recognized her as Olgivanna Lazovich Hinzenberg, a former pupil of G. I. Gurdjieff, whom he had met at a dinner in New York sometime earlier. Wright was introduced to her, but she admitted that she was not familiar with his work. Born into a patrician family in Montenegro, educated in Czarist Russia, and for the past several years studying with Gurdjieff at Fontainbleau-Avon, she further explained that she was not aware of the work of American architects in general.

They quickly fell in love, but both of them were waiting for divorces, he from Miriam Noel, and she from her husband who had come to Chicago to try to take away her daughter, Svetlana. Three months later she agreed to come to Taliesin to stay, a difficult decision for a person of her upbringing. The next four years, until they were married in August 1928, were horrendously difficult for them. In the spring of 1925 Taliesin was again destroyed by fire, the living quarters burned to the ground after an electrical storm started a fire in faulty wiring. Rebuilding Taliesin plunged Wright again into debt, and no architectural commissions of any significance were coming his way. Without doubt this was the result of his controversial personal life, which was viewed as immoral—the more so when a daughter was born to Wright and Olgivanna in 1925. On the advice of some of their friends, in the summer of 1926 they motored from Taliesin to Minneapolis, where they rented a summer cottage and, under assumed names, went into hiding.

There he began writing his autobiography, at Olgivanna's instigation. The following year an auction of his Japanese prints in New York helped to get him out of debt and pay for the rebuilding of Taliesin. But Noel's lawsuits and payments and the expenses of constant travel ate deeply into his earnings, and he was forced to turn Taliesin and its collections over to the banks. Wright was again a wanderer.

Most of the next year was spent in New York, where they lived with his sister, Maginel Wright Barney, an illustrator of children's books. The next year work came in the form of a request by the McArthur family to consult on the design of the Arizona Biltmore Hotel. While living in Phoenix, from February to April 1928, Wright met Dr. Alexander Chandler, founder of the town south of Phoenix that bears his name and owner of a large hotel in downtown Chandler. Chandler proposed that Wright design a new resort hotel in the desert outside of Chandler, up against the south slopes of South Mountain. For the next several months Wright worked on the project, San Marcos-in-the-Desert, first in Phoenix and later in La Jolla, California.

On August 25, 1928, in a quiet ceremony outdoors in the garden of an inn, Wright and Oglivanna were married in Rancho Santa Fe, California. The prospect of new work, along with the formation of "Frank Lloyd Wright, Inc." by former clients and friends, made possible once more their return to Taliesin.

As the winter of 1929 began, Chandler invited Wright to come back to the Arizona desert to prepare the working drawings for the San Marcos resort. Wright and his family, along with several draftsmen he hired for this new work, arrived in the desert and there built temporary quarters out of box boards and canvas. They called their camp Ocotillo.[4]

Another commission, from former client and friend William Norman Guthrie, brought Wright to New York for the design of an apartment tower adjacent to Guthrie's church, St. Mark's in the Bouwerie. It seemed as though with new work coming in now, including a large residence for his cousin Richard Lloyd Jones of Tulsa, Oklahoma, Wright was getting back on his feet financially. However fate was to deal another blow: the stock market crash of October 1929 brought all the projects and the commissions to a halt. Only the house for cousin Richard went on. Wright turned now to his writings and to the preparation of an exhibition of his work that would tour the United States and Europe.

1. Gookin was originally a banker who became, as a collector of Japanese art in the 1880s, one of the nation's foremost authorities of *ukiyo-e* woodblock prints. Gookin's knowledge of Japanese art later secured him the position of curator at the Art Institute in Chicago for the remainder of his long life.
2. Letter from Gookin to Wright, October 16, 1991. The Frank Lloyd Wright Archives.
3. Letter from Wright to Martin, June 11, 1913. University of New York at Buffalo.
4. Ocotillo, or "candle flame," is a cactus with long slender spires of green topped by brilliant red blossoms. It prompted the name of the desert camp roofed in white canvas, whose triangular flaps on the sides were dyed flame red.

THE ARCHITECT AND THE MACHINE

In 1893 the twenty-six-year-old Wright opened his architectural practice. His design for the William H. Winslow house in River Forest, his first commission, clearly revealed a new direction in residential architecture. One year later, with the Winslow house constructed, he brought the principles he used to design the building to the speaker's platform.

There is nothing in the Frank Lloyd Wright Archives that sheds any light on the origins of this speaking engagement. His accomplishments in architecture were certainly no closeted secret, and the steady commissions he was granted proved that his new architecture, albeit with some exceptions, was well received. Rather, he perceived his work in architecture as a mission: public speaking, to him, was but another way of promulgating that mission.

On the typewritten copy of this essay, Wright wrote, "Read to the University Guild, Evanston, Illinois, 1894." Although the essay bears no title on the first page, on its folder is printed the title "The Architect and the Machine."[1] However, the text of the essay deals exclusively with the design of the home and highlights the difference between mere "houses" and homes. It is noteworthy that as early as 1894, Wright introduced ideas that he argued for all his life and finally distilled sixty years later in the book The Natural House. *In 1954 he further qualified the distinction between house and home by writing, "I believe a house is more a home by being a work of Art."[2] [Unpublished speech]*

THE MORE TRUE CULTURE A MAN HAS, THE MORE SIGNIFICANT his environment becomes to him. The end and aim of all good education is to make man more alive to everything, or in other words to make everything more keenly alive to him, to make "sermons in stones, and symphonies in running brooks" an everyday possibility.[3]

It is a great thing to really live, and we only live by the insight to keep in touch with the beauty of our own little world within the great world—for every man's home should be that to him. I want to show you that bricks and mortar may lie to you, that everything in the front parlor may be calling every other thing bad names, not only that, but calling you bad names to your very face, that you have given house room, unwittingly perhaps, to criminals, inebriates, and idiots that harm you by association with them, just as association with true things help you.

Many people nowadays are content to live in "houses" instead of homes, hiding behind the plea of small means, which can never wash their sins away, for "home" means more than money and the smaller means sometimes show the very best results. To understand that houses, pictures, furniture, and books are either false or true in the same sense that you are taught that a thing is good or bad morally is to simply recognize the fact that truth means harmony and falsity means discord. That is exactly what harmony does mean, truth of relation in all parts one to another and is the same in the house, character, or the picture. Therefore, it is not so much a matter of taste, as of knowledge and cultivation. Although one's instincts may be true and lead to a recognition of the right thing instinctively, it is hardly safe to lean on these instincts very heavily unless they are supported and justified by cultivated knowledge. The expression "Oh well, that's a matter of taste" had better be exchanged for "Yes, that is a matter of education."

Many people seem to think (though I suspect it is because they do not think) that an "artistic" house is more or less of a "fake" anyway and is a fussy impractical and expensive thing at the best, fit only for the consideration of silly women, or those who would put on airs. With a comfortable sort of satisfaction with their superior worldly sort of common sense, they invest money in a "house" that is the most impractically practical sort of a box and looks as though it had been cut from cardboard with a pair of scissors and whitewashed for luck. On the other hand, your so-called artistic house has been quite as bad in the other direction and has degenerated to a mass of deformities, curlicues, and Jim Crow ornament that make the whole thing a meaningless freak, whose only office is to fall to pieces as rapidly as possible in order that nature may regain her equilibrium. Unfortunately we are so accustomed to seeing these things day in and day out that we finally accept them because they are the fashion without analyzing them; and when confronted with a quiet, thoughtful piece of work, the very absence of the bad qualities of the fashionable thing offends us and we wonder how any man could waste money on a thing like that, why he did not get into line. Straightaway we begin to see things weak about him that had not appeared to us

before, and even shake hands with him in a critical sort of way. All of which goes to show that while we have made some advance along the lines of other arts, home building is yet in a very crude state and though in reality the most important of the arts, the least understood.

I should like to give you a set of golden rules for house building that would forever settle the matter for you as some "plan-books-for-one-dollar" do, but I should play the "fool who rushes in where angels fear to tread," to your amusement perhaps and my own confusion no doubt. But certain well-established principles are within our reach.

First, it should appear to be a part of the site and not a foreign element set up boxwise on edge to the utter humiliation of every natural thing in sight. It should be simple, containing as few rooms as will meet the conditions under which you live, and right there is a good time to consider improvement in your former habit of living in the interest of simplicity. There is nothing like a good, easy, homelike plan to influence you in these very things, to take the starch out of the stiff collar of your everyday life and substitute something comfortable for it. The better houses of today are those with a living room, which is sometimes the living room and several other rooms in one, with a large fireplace and sunny exposure. Beside this, a reasonable hallway and a small reception room or social office to relieve the living room of formal elements not wanted in the family circle, the dining room, and working department complete the first floor. It is the "ensemble" of these rooms that requires careful study, for the more simple the conditions become, the more careful you must be in the working out of your combinations in order that comfort and utility may go hand in hand with beauty as they inevitably should. Rooms with great open staircases have come to be regarded as ostentatious and vulgar, for a utilitarian feature is paraded to the discomfiture and draughty conditions of the whole house. It is advisable to subordinate, and even in some instances disconnect, the stairway from the main rooms, emphasizing its entrance and locating it with careful consideration.

Proportion is the great thing in this fundamental work, cut within the cloth at your disposal.

It means certain harmonious relationships between the various rooms, that all may contribute to easy utility and quiet beauty to the end.

Avoid all things which have no real use or meaning and make those which have especially significant; for there is no one part of your building that may not be made a thing of beauty in itself as related to the whole.

Consistency from first to last will give you the result you seek and consistency alone. Not sensation, not show, not meaningless carpenter work and vulgar decoration, but quiet thoughtful consistency throughout brings this harmony to be a factor in your daily lives, and it is good for sore eyes and tired nerves.

Your fireplace no longer need be an inconsequential piece of wooden furniture, planked against a blank wall, with about as inviting an aspect as the coal hod or a pair of tongs and quite as deciduous in character, but may be a substantial thing of beauty that you feel is solidly incorporated in your building and you may burn cordwood and toast your feet at the genuine article for almost the same price. So consider this well in your plan.

Make your kitchen fit to live in and have all the little conveniences and necessities well arranged, for they lessen the petty friction of life that gradually makes things creak and groan. Get everything on "ball bearings" where you can. It means brains more than money. Your philosophy of life will be reflected in all these things, to your shame or to your credit. They are silent, though eloquent, indexes of your personal quality and character.

But your second floor is perhaps a truer index. Why should your second floor be less carefully planned than this first floor! Are you to pay more respect to the neighbors than to yourself, then perhaps your underclothing is shabby when your hat and coat are fine. Finish your house consistently throughout and adopt a sober gait in the beginning that you can come in with at the finish. The second floor is too often what is left over from the first.

The closet craze is also an abuse of the advantages of this floor, and housewives erroneously gauge convenience by the number and size of dark places in which to pack things out of sight and ventilation. The more closets you have, the more you will have to have, and as ordinarily used they are breeders of disease and poor housekeeping. Wardrobes, if you will, and light airy closets, but as few dark pockets as you can get along with.

Sleeping rooms should be as pleasant as the living rooms and should be so arranged that the second floor is a natural development of the first, in the order that partitions may be carried through from below and the frame of the building knit together vertically, as well as horizontally.

Treat your servants as you treat your friends—with consideration. Give them good sleeping rooms at least, if not plumbing of their own, and a pleasant little dining room or sitting room, for you gain in more ways than one by doing so.

Houses are built today on too narrow gauge a plan with a petty economy that does not economize further than to get the contractor paid in the first instance at as low a figure as possible, and then money is freely spent afterward to atone for the things you could not economically do in the first place. There is more penny-wise and pound-foolish economy in the building line than any other, and alleged good businessmen are usually the ones who slit their own throats the widest when they begin to deal with its propositions. Not your broad-minded businessman of today with experience and culture, but the man of yesterday who has nothing more than a record for narrow-minded economy of the boomerang type. If you cannot build a house and build it right, why don't not build it, for you are not ready and will regret it. I do not advocate richness nor the luxury that surfeits but rather a serene simplicity that is content with little, so long as that little is good.

It would take days to consider the various phases of the plan of a modern dwelling with its possibilities of heating, ventilating, plumbing, sewerage, and the multiplicity of details going to make its sum, and I might as well drop it within these meager limits and take up its exterior treatment.

The average desire seems to be to build something which will rear on its hind legs and paw the air in order that you may seem more important than your neighbor, with the average result that you look more uncomfortable and foolishly pretentious and uninteresting. What right has man in the name of law to outrage Nature by setting at defiance all her teachings, which mean to him the best he can ever hope to get out of life?

Go to Nature, thou builder of houses, consider her ways and do not be petty and foolish. Let your home appear to grow easily from its site and shape it to sympathize with the surroundings if Nature is manifest there, and if not, try and be as quiet, substantial, and organic[4] as she would have been if she had the chance. In other words, give the matter some intelligent thought, backed by artistic feeling if you can command it, then go to the woods for your color schemes and not to the ribbon counter at "Field's."[5]

I might enter here into a discussion of the various merits of the various styles of "house" building, but would end with saying that it matters very little what "style" your house was as long as it was built like home and with a true consideration for harmony. There should be as many types of homes as there are types of people, for it is the individuality of the occupants that should give character and color to the building and furnishings. Some people are already intelligent enough to recognize that manners, speech, and clothing becoming to some people would not become them; others, I am happy to say, recognize that same element in making their homes. Mere fashion in house building is confined more and more to the rank of the "nouveau riche" and the lighter-weight social element. A house that has "character" stands a good chance of growing more valuable as it grows older and public opinion is educated, whereas the house built in the prevailing mode, "Colonial" or what not, is soon flat and stale, to be pitied for having outlived its popularity with little else to recommend it. A comparatively poor investment. The fear of being made ridiculous or of making a mistake is among people who have no minds of their own one cause of the poverty-stricken aspect of their homes from the standpoint of genuine character and tone; better to have the courage of your convictions and live in your house, even if it does not win the applause of the gallery, than to live in a borrowed one that does not fit you.

Simplicity and repose are ideals to cleave to, and you can make no mistake in striving in earnest for these blessed qualities, for if you succeed in reaching them it will mean a benediction to you, your children, and society, and you will not have lived altogether in vain even if you have nothing else to recommend you; but you will never reach them unless you have many qualities that necessarily recommend you.

Do not think that simplicity means something like the side of a barn, but rather something with graceful sense of beauty in its utility from which discord and all that is meaningless has been eliminated. Do not imagine that repose means taking it easy for the sake of a rest, but rather taking it easily because perfectly adjusted in relation to the whole, in absolute poise, leaving nothing but a feeling of quiet satisfaction with its sense of completeness. These are the qualities that measure the true value of a work of art from the highest standpoint, and wonderfully fine qualities they are to live with from day to day. They are worth all the money man ever paid to get them. They creep into your building schemes as you work at harmonizing the elements of your home, the handling of the material, the construction of the windows, doors, walls, roof, with the various conditions and possibilities in proportion and combination. They are there only when integrity is there, when your work is honest, true to itself in other words, and the day will come when the universal average of intelligence will be high enough to make it a thing of disrepute and a menace to the good morals of the community to build on any other basis. It is the duty of every man to raise the character and tone of his own home in this respect to the highest point his capabilities permit. There is no place for him to hide from this responsibility except in ignorance, and in these days of educational advantages ignorance of moral responsibility is characterized as crime. The same principles that work in home building apply with equal force in home furnishing, and I have tried to show you that they are the same as the principles of character building. Let your home have the air of being lived in, and I assure you that it will not have this air unless you really do live in it in the best sense of the term.

Do not save any of it for company unless it is that little social office alluded to before, and make this as inviting as possible with just as few gold chairs with seats to look at and not to sit on as the law allows. This room is a necessary evil, as yet I regret to admit. What is good enough for you is good enough for your company if they are worth inviting. Do not make things look fixed or as though posing for effect—and so like a book of etiquette, I might run on with a series of "don'ts" as long as the section therein devoted to table manners. Let me warn you, however, against the prevailing vulgarity of declining a good thing because it is common, or because the so and so's have it, for it is a sure mark of a mean mind and a love not of the good there is in the thing itself, but a greed of petty distinction as selfish as it is contemptible. Wipe out all the "fixed"-up effects you can find and substitute natural ones that contribute in some way to the comfort and beauty of your apartment considered as a room to live in. The old front parlor is seldom seen now off the vaudeville stage, and society is a number of points ahead on that account.

The most satisfactory apartments are those in which most of the furniture has been built in as a part of the original scheme; much of the money foolishly paid for expensive furniture would be better spent in this way, as it is the only means of arriving at the very best results. The healthful color schemes possible in interiors at a cost of little more than the brains and stains are something wonderfully beautiful. Color has a tremendous influence on our moods and cannot be too carefully considered. Use soft warm tones in preference to blues, grays, and cold pinks, for they are more wholesome to live with and better adapted in most cases to good decoration.

As to further decoration, never have any unless you understand it thoroughly and are satisfied that it means something good in the scheme as a whole, for you are in most cases better off without it. Decoration can tell your friends lots of things that you do not know and would not like if you did. It is of no use to you unless you do understand and appreciate it. It would not be sufficient justification for you to have it just because it looked rich or because somebody else had it.

Remember that we truly own only what we can absorb and appreciate—not one jot more.

Then there is the matter of draperies. So many women insist upon making everything stuffy with all sorts of curtains, and their windows are tricked out in a mass of millinery without rhyme or sanitary reason. They say it does not seem like home to them without it, and there is a confession you can never get beyond. In this connection a word about bric-a-brac. Do not buy things of this description unless you know that they are good. The only object in possessing them is to live in touch with their beauty and profit by an interest in it. If they mean nothing more than expensive things that cost you dear, kick them out—or perhaps you might as well let them stay for they cannot do you harm for home in its high sense is little above the level of the bargain counter to you.

Too many houses are like notion stores, bazaars, and junk shops. It is really distressing to find the homes of people who should know better intemperate in this regard, for it is a species of inebriety that does one little credit, unless conditions outside of homemaking enter, as they sometimes do.

Consider first your general scheme and then fill in as much fine detail as it will stand, remember that an excessive love of detail to the confusion of the whole has ruined more good things than any one human shortcoming from the standpoint of fine art or fine living, and is hopelessly vulgar beside.

An architect's never-ending fight for a recognition of this is one of the most irksome plagues of his practice. The average mind will look at the thing for and by itself and say, "I do not like that" without considering the part that it is harmoniously playing in the general scheme. If he were weak in this regard the result would be that your homes would be a petty agglomeration of features, and on this basis parts that would each please in themselves confound each other as a whole.

The cheap furniture to be had in the market now is for the most part vicious because our remarkable scientific possibilities are bent to turning out clear imitations of the old hand-carved type. The less superfluous furniture about your rooms the better. Furniture which is true to itself can be had,

William H. Winslow House. River Forest, Illinois. 1893. FLLW Fdn FA#9305.0008

but is expensive as yet, for these things work from the top downward. Good hangings and wallpapers are more plentiful as more advance has been along these lines than any other, owing to the Associated Artists,[6] Liberty stuffs,[7] and William Morris, not to mention beautiful stuffs and colors in plain material.

Splendid things in pictures and photographs are available on every hand in good frames. Rather one good thing, one really fine thing, be it useful beauty or beautiful use, than wagonloads of the merely rich.

I believe implicitly in the good influence of flowers in the home, growing plants preferably or

arrangements of flowers in simple vases, even branches of twigs, dried weeds with their seedpods make beautiful things to look at, if arranged with a sympathetic touch. If a man has twenty cents for the family meal, he had best invest three cents of that in a flower; for the glass in the middle of the table the family will be better fed in the long run.

But what I want you to feel tonight is the vital importance of all this concerning yourselves, the part it should play in your lives and particularly in the lives of little children.

For the same reason that we teach our children to speak the truth, or better still, live the truth, their environment ought to be as truly beautiful as we are capable of making it. Making it beautiful again simply means a due consideration of the same elements in the makeup of their home surroundings, that we consider so minutely in their moral training. We try to make them feel the great value of simplicity and dignity in their daily conduct, and quite likely we are at the same time teaching them to sing or play music that amounts to nothing more than trashy noise, a species of nervous affectation.

We teach them the value of consistency and let them live and breathe in houses in which the relation of nearly every object is inconsistent with every other object. We believe that peace and gentle harmony should prevail among little brothers and sisters, when the floors, walls, and ceilings round about them are at war and every form and color is quarreling viciously with its immediate neighbor.

The sum total of "house" and all the things in it with which we try to satisfy the requirements of utility and our craving for the beautiful is atmosphere, good or bad, that little children breathe as surely as the plain air.

While you are making such a fuss over sewer, gas, ventilation, and good nickel-plated plumbing, why not ventilate the more vital atmosphere of your children's house a little and give them a chance to recognize the true and the beautiful when they see it?

How can we expect a child's intuition to remain clean and accurate when we teach him to respect and cherish the absolute falsehood or meaningless elaboration with which he is surrounded nine cases out of ten. And what a pity that tender associations should be permitted to develop and cling about things which are in themselves unworthy. I have seen so much evidence of this in my architectural practice. Furniture and pictures handed down from father to son, which were as utterly false to themselves and their environment as any criminal and just as worthy of destruction, yet they must remain as members of the family when a funeral and decent burial in the backyard would much benefit society generally and the possessors particularly.

When a thing is good from a standpoint of fine art, you may be sure that vital laws and organic requirements were not disregarded in its makeup; they were either intuitively felt or carefully taken into account; and whether it is a building, painting, or rug, its expression can only be beautiful and helpful when the rudiments of common honesty have been observed in its construction. You may never violate or ignore normal tendencies inherent in the law of the thing itself.

1. A portion of the text was published in *Frank Lloyd Wright on Architecture*, as "Architecture and the Machine," edited by Frederick Gutheim (New York: Duell, Sloan and Pearce, 1940), p.3.
2. Frank Lloyd Wright, *The Natural House* (New York: Horizon Press, 1954), endpapers.
3. The original use of a similar phrase appears in *As You Like It*, Act II, Scene I: "and this our life, exempt from public haunt, finds tongues in trees, books in the running brooks, sermons in stone and good in everything." It no doubt has been paraphrased by numerous people and Wright's immediate source, if this is a direct quote, is so far unidentified.
4. This is the first use of the term *organic* by Wright. He later defined it in May 1914; see *In the Cause of Architecture: Second Paper*.
5. Marshall Field Retail Store of Chicago.
6. Associated Artists was a leading New York interior design firm founded by Candace Wheeler (1829–1923), a pioneer of the Arts and Crafts movement in the United States, and Louis Comfort Tiffany (1848–1933) in 1879.
7. Presumably Liberty of London, a retail store founded in 1875 by textile designer Arthur Lasenby Liberty.

ARCHITECT, ARCHITECTURE, AND THE CLIENT

I *have to believe that the time is not so very far distant when the "American Home" will be really owned by the man who paid for it. It will belong to its site and to the country. It will grow naturally in the light of a finer consideration for the modern opportunity which is a more practicable truth and beauty. An American home will be a product of our time, spiritually and physically. It will be a great work of art, respected the world over, because of its integrity, its real worth.* —Frank Lloyd Wright, *"Architect, Architecture, and the Client"*

In this article of 1896, which, like his first essay, was prepared for a lecture Wright gave to the University Guild of Evanston, Illinois, the ideas he wrote about two years earlier are now more clearly expressed. Six years later, in 1902, he revised the text slightly and presented it to the Chicago Women's Club as a lecture entitled "The Modern Home As a Work of Art." [Unpublished speech, excerpts later published in On Architecture, *1940]*

IT IS WITH PAINFUL MISGIVING THAT THE ARCHITECT, AS Artist, deserts his drawing board and bricks and mortar to play the part of preacher. The nature of his work is far removed from expression, few of him have been "dramatized" by the elocutionists nor yet had time to wander by the oceanside with the histrionic pebble in his mouth. So my misgiving, I confess, is a form of fear that I shall trespass your right to be amused by asking you to think without that stimulus.

Architecture is an Art and though this time-worn, overworked subject, Art, is one usually connected with effrontery and irreverent assumption, perhaps arrogant, too, will be my attempt to assert its practical nature.

"Art," in the now popular sense of that term, has a practical value only to the shopkeeper. His word to conjure with in connection with trash: a commercial parasite; a social sham. Granting that familiarity can still breed contempt in this commercial age, then Art has indeed struck the bottom of the pit of intimacy and dragged the name of the beautiful to disrepute.

"Artistic," adjective or noun, has been tortured out of all semblance to its originally useful self, unfeelingly abused by Architect and commoner alike, stigmatized by evil associations, until roused at last, let us cast it out.

At least for the uses of this hour let us try to establish a more highly useful significance for this word "Art," a word that stands as the very name of the "Beautiful."

The most complete poetical genius in literary conception simply succeeds in saying over and over again, that "Art is."

We have all heard that Art is truth. Tolstoy tells us that "Art is the infection by one man of another with the feelings experienced by the infector." Emerson that "Art is life." Victor Hugo that "Art and Nature are two slopes of the same fact." And that "Art is the region of equals." Mr. Whistler, in common with Victor Hugo, that "Art is limited to the infinite and the beginning, and ending there cannot progress."[1]

Experience would seem to teach that Art is but an evanescent glimmer of the unknowable that strikes and flits like the fitful lightning flash, and if we continued for hours with the best that poets the world over have given, we should know in the end as much as our "Father Adam" knew.

We can no more say what Art is with definite comprehension than we can say what God is, and the nearest approach to that Victor Hugo made when he defined God as the universe extended.

We will never know, and why should we care to cut out the head of the drum to see from whence the sound comes? Fortunately for us, the head of this drum is beyond our social meddling instincts. Such speculation is in the nature of attempts to secure perpetual motion: fascinating, maybe, but futile.

We can know more definitely what art is to us. Art, as far as we are concerned, is a living expression of our actual lives in that realm beyond the reach of science we call "Beauty."

It is a manifestation to us in terms either of form, sound, thought, or color, or of all of these, of some individualized truth that hints to our poor condition—the sublime.

Our "poor condition" just now is ultra-commercial. It is a sophomorically scientific condition that declares head transcends heart and that a metaphysician of the deepest dye may perform for us the offices a wayward artist-soul performed in the time that was; a condition that would forget that elusive child of mystery, the "Artist" altogether.

Science overreaches. Science herself proves that although we may see great things yet unseen, hear things yet unheard, reckon one day with an infinite number of dimensions in place of three that serve now; still there is, and will always be, the forever unknowable force we call "life" itself.

In that force Art dwells for us a *creative power*, and all man's scientific grasp will never draw the veil aside, a fact Science herself recognizes. Art is at one with the Absolute to whom Science is utility maid. Science, the superb servant, has enabled the artist to seek "inner significance" in new light, in new fields, and to make application of the truths sought for in the "life force unknowable" with greater certainty and finer focus. Science has been creeping up, putting tools into modern artist hands that haven't yet learned to use them and opening new possibilities inconsistent with preconceived Art ideals.

Sectarian Art and Artist blindly resent this "presumption," and confusion is upon the house.

The conflict between Religion and Science we may see repeated in a divorce of Art and Science. The harmony in the first instance has been found absolute; it will be found that Science and Art too have no ground for quarrel, even though sectarian Art and Artist disappear as sectarian Christianity is disappearing.

Science, with no such intention on her part, emancipated the Artist and has provided him with a magnificent metaphysical technique on a scale that is for the moment confusing and appalling to him. When he learns to use this new equipment in light, yet too strong for him, we will have an Art beside which the old masters will seem fragmentary and crude.

Listen to Victor Hugo: "Inasmuch as the rivalry of intelligences is the life of the beautiful; O poets! the first rank is ever free. Let us remove everything which may disconcert daring minds and break their wings. Art is a species of valor. To deny that men of genius yet to come may be the peers of the men of genius of the past, would be to deny the ever-working power of God."

And let us believe that the Art of today will know no less of the creative power of the ideal than ever before, but it will be better governed, more synthetic than it ever was.

The practical value of Art on this, its true basis, it seems idle to call in question. To our natures it is what *Pyro* or *Eikonogen* is to the sensitized dry plate, with intellect for the restraining, film-strengthening element that gives good useful printing power to the negative. The greatest developer of what is best in mankind.

The commercial mind will grasp at it as something with a mighty money equivalent, once realizing its relation to growth and consequent happiness. The butcher, the baker, and candlestick maker will dwindle to comparative insignificance.

"Art," then, in the sense that we should see it, is to be revered and fostered as the creative power which gives the "practical" true, "practicability." Something to feel ennobling enthusiasm for and to work for.

Whatever may be the point and application of Art in general, I can only walk and talk in the path of my chosen work. There I may reduce to little immediates of life and give practical point in feeble detail to this great power in the aggregate. But an instance of good or evil import in Architecture is typical throughout the Arts. It is but the medium of expression that changes, the derangement.

Great Architecture in the old sense no longer exists for us. Centuries ago when the shifting types were invented in the quaint town of Gutenberg,[2] Architecture received a mortal blow, and its grand old frozen music began to fade away, to dissolve into rivulets of literature, first trickling, then flowing over the civilized world until inundation was complete.[3] Flowing still, it is a rising flood that buries ever deeper beneath its reflective surface the primitive necessities of concentration that gave to the cathedral of old its glory.

And the book is becoming to you and to me what the cathedral was to the Middle Ages. It embalms for us in type the qualifications of our time.

The quickening of thought and impulse that record our highest and best today is found in that precious storehouse, the book. Biographies and poems, most helpful of records, are most available in books.

But if great Architecture in the old sense no longer exists, in domestic Architecture today we have finer possibilities and a measure of "salvation."

The power of the types will have translated the beauty of the cathedral to the homes of the people: a broadening of the base on which the growing beauty of the world rests.

These homes in themselves will be biographies and poems instead of slanderers and poetry crushers, appealing to the center of the human soul through perceptive faculties as potent as those that made the book. It will become the Architect's higher province to translate the better thought and feeling of this time to the terms of environment that make the modern home, to nourish the root where before he garnished the branch.

Our home from general scheme to smallest detail of furnishing, from mass outline to a footstool or profile of wooden molding can give of the life-blood of a master spirit, and that fact imposes the obligation that it shall have it to give.

This matter of environment is capable of reflecting with a far more intimate influence on spiritual growth and physical well-being than cathedrals and palaces, the fineness or the coarseness of human fiber: so there should be as many types of house as there are types of people and as many differentiations of the types as there are different people.

It is the Architect's duty and his privilege to conserve these interests in the light of the individuality of the homemaker for whom he is chosen interpreter.

The opportunity to characterize men and women in enduring building material for their betterment and the edification of their kind is really one of the world's fine opportunities. A great responsibility. An Architect has had a rare chance to read the souls of man and woman when he has finished building a home. What they are, what they hope to be, is all there in highlight to be easily read. Traces of the influence of former environment that go to make their likes and dislikes are a never-ending, continually shifting sidelight on this subject.

If he is master of his technique, a far more momentous matter than brush and pigment, or tone and fingering, he can characterize in a building those who are to live in it. He may throw himself between the client and the work and shield him, he may reveal him, he may interpret the better side of him or a side of him that appeals to his imagination and give him something to grow to. Or he may commercially give him what he wants and let him go at that. Yet how in the face of the finer opportunity, the confusion and convulsive clinging to the letter of the beauty of other times sets the whole art world by the ears, and works havoc with the finer possibilities of this situation.

Most of our friends (some of ourselves) are, when it comes to Architecture, Art, and Decoration, masquerading in borrowed finery: borrowed of another epoch that cannot honestly fit them. The fashions and fads of any typical street grit the teeth of one so foolish as to take the matter seriously. Colonial and Renaissance, the château and châtelet. Anything that one can feel quite sure happened sometime, somewhere, and was not ridiculous, anything that is not our own, that is not American. Witness these ribald and inebriate freaks of fashion bedecked with painful deformities; the father of a respectable growing family would quite as soon paint his dress shirt scarlet and stand in the middle of the road and yell as to own some of these if he knew what relation they bore to sound architectural conduct. And the ugly carpenter-built mansion with the mansard roof, an arrogant menace to the nature of all things holy, and (though somewhat better) this staring, wedding-cake artificiality of the Colonial pretense now measured by the mile, or the borrowed affectation of simplicity which our imported English domestic architecture so heavily imposes. Simplicity cannot be borrowed. Murder will out!

Then the affected scene-painting of your château, your "classic" villas.

And the Classic? How the beauty-sophisticated Greek would shudder with impotent disgust if he could see the chaste proportions of his work mummified in your whitewashed imitations of his legitimately beautiful creations. The householder who longs for classic porticos or colonnades should be made to wear a tunic or toga by ordinance.

Get inside and it is more comfortable and sanitary than anything the world has yet seen. Science has accomplished that. Artistically it is an affectation inconsistent with any fine physical state.

Furniture and fixtures everywhere—furniture and fixtures, then again more furniture and more fixtures with touches of deciduous bric-a-brac to give an excuse for still more furniture and stupid ornamentation.

Blame the market if you will, but words fail to express proper contempt for the meaningless average householder's stuff—from the gold chair which is solid mahogany underneath to the deadly piano machine and machine-carved over-wrought state of things generally. The slick and shiny aspect of the "beautiful" things, the glassy woodwork and floors. The "cold molasses" aspect of "piano-finished" furniture, truly horrible.

The "chronic" efflorescence of hangings, apoplectic roses bulging from the walls, pears, melons, and grape clusters on tapestry chair seats and miles on miles of nervously overwrought window millinery competing with hysterical portieres.

Rugs laid askew (anything on the bias is so "artistic") or a quarreling collection of small "Oriental" pieces on slippery surfaces, enabling one to get about as gracefully as ducks upon the ice.

The more there is of it the more it all becomes a degeneration we are pleased to call "rich"; though the more there is of it the less you feel it, as its very clumsy obesity sinks all to "innocuous desuetude."

Vulgarity itself: the "one touch of nature that makes the whole world kin."[4] Beyond question it is thoroughly impractical.

The only American thing about it that it is "conglomerate."

This confused condition arises because conditions have changed: we have changed. And the old handicrafts ideal has not changed. There is some truth to fit our condition in all previous states of Fine Art expression, but it is to be found in the spirit of the previous Art as related to conditions that existed then, and it is not to be found in the manifest letter bodily appropriated in this fashionable folly.

Common sense should teach us to study these old forms of beauty in relation to the times that produced them, and to apply the knowledge gained that way to betterment of ourselves rather than to make ourselves ridiculous by tricking out in something that belonged to someone else. Bridget is necessarily only a joke when she wears her fashionable mistress's lovely gown, although it betoken in her a worthy longing for the beautiful. And in this matter—we are Bridget.

This abominable state of affairs will last as long as Art continues to be an antique commodity. Art is hawked about the streets by "representative" Artists after the manner of street peddlers to be stuck on by some hapless victim with the feeling that it ought to be admired; admired because reputed to be beautiful; no one willing to confess the lack of responsive uplift, for fear of betraying a lack of "culture."

The public has suffered long enough; let us hope to some good end.

We can at least be honest with ourselves as a preliminary to a better condition and can discourage the folly of sending our young men abroad to grow up in artistic hothouses that they may wilt and shrivel uselessly when transplanted to the soil they should have grown in, indigenous, in order to bear good fruit. Let them go abroad to widen their horizons when strong enough to assimilate not merely absorb.

We will never be respectable in art so long as artists persist in sacrificing the little individuality they have to the past. Our artistic enthusiasm is imported.

Perhaps we necessarily pass through this provincial stage: must we have these epidemics of fashion and "classicism" to finally clear the cobwebs from our brains before we can see straight into things again?

Centuries of fictitious education have removed us from our human birthright in Art.

The finer possibilities of the present situation—What are they? In good morals, good business or good art there is one consideration never to be violated without absolute loss of value, and it is "honesty."

To be honest commonly means to be undisguised, frankly showing purpose, free from deceit and hypocrisy. Every work of art that amounted to anything was all that first and whatever else it was afterward. To call the present state of things dishonest is harsh, but if we were calling things by their right names, that is what we would call it.

When dishonesty is not intentional, as such we modify the term, but the harm is done nevertheless.

And that, broadly speaking, is the first finer pos-

sibility of the present situation, common honesty, and who will question its practical nature? Not the commercial mind nor the scientific, nor yet the artistic mind—certainly not the prophetic mind—but where the matter becomes difficult is in determining honesty in building, decoration, and furniture.

The qualities in things like buildings, their furniture and decoration, have the misfortune to be subjective, therefore elusive to the grasp of the commercial objective mind by common consent, but why so?

Is it not a simple matter for a practical man to say to himself, I wish to make an abiding place for the woman that I love and the little ones that will grow about us?

There is more to me and to her, and will be I hope still more to them than eating, drinking, and sleeping. I know there are possibilities in the way of putting things together that are to my eyes or sense of fitness what music is to my ear or sense of sound.

True harmony is a good thing, why not the greatest thing in life, and there shall be as much as possible of it in ourselves.

Why shouldn't all uses have forms of beauty? It seems reasonable. Nature's work is so.

Say to yourself: my condition is artificial. So I cannot copy Nature and I will not slavishly imitate her, but I have a mind to control the shaping of artificial things and to learn from Nature her simple truths of form, function, and grace of line.

Nature is a good teacher. I am a child of hers, and apart from her precepts cannot flourish. I cannot work as well as she, perhaps, but at least can shape my work to sympathize with what seems beautiful to me in hers.

You would succeed if you took that humble attitude—at least in that nature would teach you first that "form" follows "function" and is never a matter of fashion or caprice unless by accident.

You would see that Nature's things seem to belong where they are put and to grow from their site and are not set up box-wise on edge to the utter humiliation of every natural thing in sight.

That Nature tones things to harmonize with the whole and doesn't seek to push some things out at expense to all the rest. Nature would show you

Isadore Heller House. Chicago, Illinois. 1896. Perspective. Ink on paper, 23 x 9". FLLW Fdn#9606.005

that all arrangement is organic and therefore complete in itself, and your work would have the repose which only a sense of completeness can give.

The atmosphere of your house would be quiet, restful, a subdued glow of conventionalized tones from woods and fields, restful surfaces, simple forms, thorough-going construction, and broad ease.

Granting you the insight of the poet that every really practical man somewhere in himself is: what graces and tenderness too Nature would teach you to touch this restful breadth with, adding quiet wealth to quiet surface, as she adds interest infinitely

without any sacrifice of true simplicity. She would teach you that crudity is not simplicity—that an affectation of "naivete" is puerile, that organic unity alone is noble and truly simple.

Organize this common ideal of unity in your heart and brain, look for someone to translate your general desire to technical terms of brick, wood, and plaster—an architect.

Believing in the possibilities of all these things as fine influence in character building—admitting therefore a truth whose force seems little understood—that they are exponents of character. You

shouldn't take much for granted when you enter this field. You should assume an independent thinking attitude in this matter. Before you give yourself to an architect, study him in the light of his work, his training, and his ideals.

And anyone building a home should make up his mind concerning all this before approaching any architect with his proposition; satisfied on these points he should give himself up to his architect and trust him as he would any other eminent professional specialist.

Fortunate architect with such a client. Let us

charitably assume the client equally fortunate.

Architect and client on this basis have little to tie to in the way of precedent.

They truly are in a dangerous position for they are likely to outrage conventional propriety of well-meaning members of the body politic. They will feel, think, and act with the best at their command. Their work will take shape on the strength of the conditions actual, with what grace and beauty in solution their nature-taught sense of the eternal fitness of things will furnish them. The building of a house on this basis means rebirth of countless refractory materials, by countless refractory processes, by means of refractory methods and men; conditions all warped by tradition and deformed by false ideals, though with glimmers of intelligence still, to cheer and make possible the honest building.

Let us follow you as the various problems of householder and homemaker in the face of the present conditions, come to your hand, and try to catch a glimpse of the finished work: your circumstances we assume are moderate as befits your type.

You want to live where your individuality will have a chance to grow free and strong, recognizing that perfect freedom is perfect obedience to perfect laws, as his Maker intended and not merely too many "laws."

You would live where your personality would count at its best.

Your circumstances, say, are humble, your means limited. But you say to yourself: "As far as I go, I shall go well. What I cannot have genuinely within my province to possess (not merely in dollar sense but in the broader sense of capacity to own and appreciate), I will not have at all. My home may be a poor thing, but after all my own."

Remember that we can own only what we can assimilate and appreciate, no more. Many wealthy people are little more than the janitors of their possessions for the benefit of those who more truly own them.

Then you cut your desires to essentials and consider the arrangement of your future dwelling as a place to live in. You make few concessions to this home considered as a place for other people to live in, for you must realize that your friends, if they are your friends, care for you and the closer they could get to you as you live, the more satisfied they would be. You would set up few artificialities to glaze over your defects and form the glittering groove so essential to the mushroom-like life of society, so called, to run in. No concessions would you make to the vulgarity of the struggle for popular preferment. Your acquaintances, as such, might be many. Your friends, few.

So in shaping any general arrangement of your ground plan you would naturally lay great stress upon the living room, as it is called—the heart of your house—almost your whole house, with other necessities arranged in relation to that as the dominant feature. The kitchen, not large but conveniently appointed and fitted with the little niceties of arrangement that put things on ball bearings and lessen the petty friction of everyday life.

The dining room, if any, a bright, cozy, cheerful place you involuntarily enter with a smile, not larger than the necessities of this family and current guests required, perhaps a sunny alcove of the living room.

Were you studious and your children too, you would have a quiet little library. Your entrance hall you would make large enough to be becoming as an approach to these and like a warm shake of the hand to those who entered there.

For the sake of your acquaintance, I am sorry to say, you would perhaps want to add (depending upon where you elected to live) a small social-office to protect your living room, though you surely would regret the necessity and think of it shamefacedly and do what you could to put some warmth and life into that place, too.

Your servants would not be tucked away under a hot roof with bath accommodations in the basement, but be treated with a good airy room on the ground floor and a bathroom there too. Moreover, depending on the site you would be apt to make your kitchen very small, but as completely appointed as a chemist's laboratory. You would give the servants a little dining and sitting room on the ground floor opening to the rear porch if you could.

All this you would make as self-contained as possible in general arrangement; that is, you have no outside steps to become dangerous in winter, your veranda so arranged as to be enclosed and not be a common walkway for those coming and going to the house.

Neither would you destroy the benefaction of a sunlit room by putting porch roofs against your walls. Area and cellar ways would disappear and combine with rear kitchen entrance in such a way as to protect both, affording an entrance to the icebox and a way to the cellar from the kitchen.

Below ground your cellar would become a storehouse well ordered and complete, that you might not live from hand to mouth in ordinary shiftless fashion, but might stock your cellar in the interest of a dignified economy and make it possible to care for it without loss. You would have appliances to care for ashes and coal that would be automatic, noiseless, and dust proof, for they are to be had in this age of mechanical contrivance. And your bathroom—at least that could necessarily be truly modern. Our appliances in plumbing are matchless.

That is the substance of all your demands on the ground floor. The proportion, substantial character, and the beautiful interest these might have would enlarge or diminish according to available funds, but the quality of thought and rare discrimination manifest there would be the same always.

It would scarcely be possible for you to separate the building and furnishing of your house, for nature taught you a higher ideal of unity than that. The money that is foolishly paid for expensive, highly finished furniture you incorporate with the house building. You would want very few pieces of furniture and want those in keeping with your home.

You would consider everything in the nature of a hanging fixture a weakness and naked radiators an abomination.

Much window millinery and draping of stuffs you could not tolerate. This work now becomes a matter of elevation, proportion, and expression. The artist in you must work even more closely in touch with your science as the complex meaningless outlines of conventional work are discarded and proportions that sympathize with the site and conditions are outlined from the plan determined before, by no means an easy matter, this. Say a roof is raised that is indeed a shelter and so quietly graceful as to soften, like a benediction, between the rasping roofs of convention. No dormers nor any excrescences. No saw-tooth upheavals to mar the perfection of its simplicity. For the interior is too consistently arranged and the roof too consistently fitted to the interior to require it. A delight to any decent carpenter to build such a roof. The roof a solace to its environment. The building as whole you see as a part of its site. You cannot imagine it away. It seems to have grown there where it is to be.

Perhaps you would make the walls of brick

that the fire touched to tawny gold or muddy tan, the choicest of all earth's hues—they do not rise rudely above the sod as though shot from beneath by a catapult, but recognize the surface of the ground on which they stand, gently spreading there to a substantial base that makes the building seem to stand more firmly in its socket in the earth and to carry with a profile of grace the protection of its sheltering eaves.

The porch, that curse of the American home, has become an extension or a semi-detached pavilion, accessible from hall or living room or by covered way. It is a summery, good-time place, that leaves the sunshine free to grow the roses in pale cheeks within the house in winter.

The windows, not all perhaps, arranged in regular order, but adapted each to its room and its purpose, indicative of good cheer and brightness within.

And all is simple in organic sense, and consistent, and strongly individual, because you in shaping it have had the right spirit toward the problem. The technical skill may be found, (a relatively simple matter) in this day and generation. Your result is sure to be a native creation, called to exist by a high demand for truth and beauty. No doubt the "gallery" will hiss and the over-cultivated "she" of the colonial and "he" of the château will smile a complacent smile and pass on their fashionable way.

But let us go in. This man who respects nature, we see, is a lover of flowers and growing things, because, to be a normally growing thing is to be beautiful, and while his piece of ground is small, he arranges and subdivides that too with a sympathetic eye and hand to harmonize with his plan, so that his building and his ground are not finally separable, one from the other; you scarcely know where ground leaves off and building begins. So we approach nearer the heart of this gently developing scheme and wait for the door to open.

You may be sure it is a simple door. And a broad and hospitable door; a door indicative of character and broad ease within, stripped of affectation. No varnish there nor much elaborate "hardware."

It opens, we enter, and an atmosphere of quiet strength and well-ordered repose envelops us, refreshes us, and gives us confidence in the personality of the "owner," assures us of depth, warmth, and simplicity.

The hall, as we look about it, gives us a thrill of welcome: it is high in key, red, perhaps, if such color deserves so crude a name.

No pictures are hung in effigy upon the walls, no naked radiators are in evidence, but softened, grateful heat in season wells gently from the window ledges. Nothing mars the complete arrangement of a room complete in every sense. The walls are rich, mellow surfaces of color, simply edged, framed and marked by emphasizing bands of wood—how lovely this wood to the touch, grateful [sic] to the eye, in reality the beauty of the wood, silken and soft it is with the sheen of a flower petal. How unlike the shining, clammy wood of fashionable treatment. The stairs lead, we suspect, out of yonder suggestive opening and are closed off by glass doors—perhaps—a concession to the climate, yet refreshing too—leaving our invitation undisturbed in the direction of the living room.

How cleverly this interior is arranged for hospitable use and soothing influence. Now we see that its furniture is "built in" in complete harmony, nothing to arrange, nothing to disturb: room and furniture an "entity." No glaring fixtures, there, but light, incorporated in the wall, which sifts from behind its surface opening appropriately in tremulous pattern, as sunlight sifts through leaves in the trees; and underfoot this thick soft rug of dignified weave provided for in thickness of the flooring. All so permanently organized, seeming to fit so well, we feel somehow that it is right we should be there.

Charming glimpses of inner restfulness, of inner harmony we catch from further on, and our wonderment increases as we see the living room. In truth it is a "living" room, to live with those who live in it, and how thoroughly you feel the flush of joyful respect for such evidence that people do sometimes really live their lives. Surely this is no mere performance. How broad it is—and quiet. Yet how pleasant, too; amiable in suggestion. The broad sunlit windows, the divans underneath, with broad restful backs and seats. The fireplace? The heart of the whole and of the building itself.

The floor is bordered about with waxed wood to match the waxed walls and centered with some heavy native weave of quiet color and durable texture, stretched in flush with the floor, in itself a rich but easily removable, substantial surface.

No prints or pictures intrude upon attention here, but the walls so quiet in the perfection of their framing finish and mystery of color are backgrounds for the pictures living there. How much more important, significant, these living, moving pictures become, emphasized and bettered by the gentle harmonious breadth around about.

Do not imagine that "pictorial" art is banished there. It is cherished and respected too highly to let it become inert or quarrelsome or common. A broad oak surface, with shelf above and simple dark framed surface over, contains yet conceals choice things for rare entertainment, when mood requires their use. Impression fresh and keen, suited to the mood this architectural portfolio holds with an appropriate setting just above for any one of them or perhaps two or the best the world affords, in print or etching, paint or watercolor. As music is provided for—"built in"—so is painting.

Ambitious scale in oil and color this man consigns to the professional setting the "art gallery" where happily it belongs as oratorio belongs to the audience hall.

Gold frames all gone.

White mats staring from the walls all gone.

The expense of these was spent upon the walls.

The peace of "quiet" descended on this house.

No fixtures staring overwrought intrude there, but part considered with the whole, the ceiling or the walls illuminated at will, without a light itself in sight. The warmth again wells gently from the high broad window ledges here.

Decoration? Yes, if may be, fresh flowers in beautiful vases in the niche provided over there; rare arrangement of dried grasses and weeds and seed pods in surface setting over here. A place for all and all contributing to grace.

Jardinieres and vases are no curious disgraces here. Protected, to interest on suitable occasion, not distract by habit.

And this indescribable texture that gives the wall its bloom. As we come nearer we see that

Warren Hickox House. Kankakee, Illinois. 1900. FLLW Fdn FA#0004.0004

exquisite pattern is there with polychromatic play and glimmer practiced with a cunning hand. With sympathetic eye and mind some mural painter has crowned the dignity of the masonry fireplace with brilliant color scheme of decorative significance. Fable or charming allegory? But ever in obedience to the whole, preserving the surface yet possessed of all the interpretive power of the consummate Artist mind.

The sculptor too has worked in touch with all we see, and he too has struck the keynote of this merit in some quiet bas-reliefs that grace and lend germane poetic interest to bookcases enframed within the walls.

"Architect," "painter," "sculptor," "poet," "homemaker" working together in full accord to swell the modern harmony. The greater demand, the freer use, have made it possible for them to min- ister to such growth as this at the fountainhead, the house without prohibitive price.

And then we see a surface near the entrance way, where the minute pattern of the wall drops out at intervals, in twos and threes, becoming natu- rally a delicate wood screen above a keyboard, built-in bookcases, etc., front below, and know that music is incorporated too, as it permeates the walls, the structure of the room, and seems a piece with all the rest.

Practical this is. It is to linger here and be min- istered to by ease so natural, as sweet sounds minis- ter to the ear.

Yes, here one may see that Nature taught this man well. All is a piece with all the rest. Joy, to see. No turbid air of "magnificent-expense," but wealth of beauty, natural, calm, and gratefully chaste.

Expensive? Yes, in time and forethought and

ARCHITECT, ARCHITECTURE, AND THE CLIENT

strong executive will, but no more in money than many a "he" or "she" of the complacent smile invests in claptrap for their furnishing.

So we might go on, but we should be saying the same thing over and over again. After all, you see by now, it is only a higher ideal of unity than known before that steam and electricity and modern processes have made possible to us if we would only see it and apply it.

To possess this practical harmony, a daily influence in our lives—to have the fruit of rare souls, the best the world affords in prints and etching, photographs or gravure, to have for beloved guests in their books, justly famous men; to hear at home the choicest music; in short to be companionable with this vast spiritual wealth, the accumulated cream of centuries of creative effort, and to enjoy a degree of bodily comfort withal that a king or baron of old never dreamed of attaining. It is yours almost for the asking.

Our riches are but the measure of our appreciation, our capacity to understand and then enjoy the depth of stored-up wealth that lies waiting for your heart's mind is beyond any comprehensive measure.

I have to believe that the time is not so very far distant when the "American Home" will be really owned by the man who paid for it. It will belong to its site and to the country. It will grow naturally in the light of a finer consideration for the modern opportunity which is a more practicable truth and beauty. An American home will be a product of our time, spiritually and physically. It will be a great work of art, respected the world over, because of its integrity, its real worth. Detractors it may have, they cannot shake it, for it will be "builded upon a rock," the rock of an organic integrity.

Who will question its practical nature?

To unify the spirit and the letter,

To eliminate antagonism of body and the soul,

To breathe into all things corporeal the spirit of life, to make two blades of grass grow where one grew before; that is the practical mission of art in our country if it has any mission as such.

1. Whistler's actual quote is, "So Art is limited to the infinite, and beginning there cannot progress." A number of references in this lecture make it clear that Wright was very familiar—and basically in agreement—with Whistler's 1885 "Ten O'Clock" address from which this quote is taken. The speech, first published in 1888, is reprinted in James McNeill Whistler, *The Gentle Art of Making Enemies* (New York: Dover, 1967).
2. Wright misattributed the name Gutenberg to a town. Johann Gutenberg (c.1400–1468) was the German inventor of movable type, the Gutenberg Bible being generally considered his work.
3. An admirer of Victor Hugo's, Wright often quoted or paraphrased him. This argument—that the demise of architecture was the result of the invention of the printing press—is presented at length in the chapter "The One Will Kill the Other" in Hugo's *The Hunchback of Notre-Dame.*
4. Wright's quote is a paraphrase of Whistler (paraphrasing Shakespeare), who boldly identifies the "one touch of nature [that] makes the whole world kin" as "vulgarity" in the "Ten O' Clock" lecture. The original phrase is from *Troilus and Cressida,* Act III, Scene III, line 175.

A PHILOSOPHY
OF FINE ART

This essay was prepared for delivery to the Architectural League of the Art Institute of Chicago in 1900. Whereas most of Wright's essays and articles are concerned with architecture and its place in the culture of the United States, this treatise addresses the broader topic of the fine arts: painting, sculpture, and architecture.

Wright describes the act of "conventionalizing" the forms of nature, as opposed to imitating them. As an architectural example, he points to the Egyptian architects' manner of translating the lotus flower into the capital of a stone column: "Of all Art, whatsoever, perhaps Architecture is the Art best fitted to teach this lesson, for in its practices this problem of 'conventionalizing' Nature is worked out at its highest and best."

This sense of "Nature" as a source of inspiration and study recurred continually in Wright's articles, addresses, and conversations during the next fifty years. As he once noted: "I am fond of saying, and I feel when I use the word 'Nature,' that nature is all the body God has by which we may become aware of Him, understand His processes, and justify the capital we put on the word God."[1] [Unpublished speech[2]]

"THE SIMPLICITY OF LIFE LIES IN ONE'S SPIRIT AND ATTITUDE of mind." It is the expression in the surroundings of one's life, of one's spirit, one's attitude of mind that is realized by means of the Arts. To have an adequate idea of the part Art plays in shaping the characters of men and what it does for the work men do is to know this expanding—"blossoming"—quality in man's nature that reaches upward to the spiritual sun for expression, as the Life principle[3] in the plant reaches toward the more evident, but less real sun.

Carlyle gave us a phrasing of a truth, that (thanks to his good mother) should ring in every boy's head until he grasps its vital meaning and then (thanks to his good wife) be kept still ringing there. Let it serve as a text in connection with our subject:

"The Ideal is within thyself, thy condition is but the stuff thou art to shape that same Ideal out of."

Carlyle meant that the "practical" is not one thing and the Beautiful another thing; that there is no beauty which can be superficially worn—it is within and of the thing itself or not at all. Although the "very pretty" and "practical" may never "mix" in some minds, there is no real life where they are not made one. There is not, nor ever was, room in right living for the ugly. Ugliness in anything is the incarnation of sin, and sin is death—ugliness is death. The elimination of the Beautiful! There is no death but that.

Personally I have small respect for the mere human animal and no enthusiasm for homilies upon the purity of the social state emanating from those whose personal belongings are nasty with ignorance, whose homes are a fashionable tangle of meaningless things, and whose persons are freaks of fashion. The homes of America need application of intelligent interest, which is rare, if they are to have an artistic [value], and therefore let it be, in a spiritual sense, the "airing" that will make them fit for the souls to grow in.

A child born in the artificial environment of a city home has a small chance. The atmosphere he breathes there is bad, because he is impressed from birth with fashion and sham, not ceremoniously alone, but actually, in the expression of almost everything he touches—this is so because the expression of everything that touches him depends for its integrity upon the power of men to put into these artificial things the loveliness one finds in the woods and wildflowers, which is neither more nor less than the truth and harmony of Nature—and that power in this age is, to say the least, sickly. There are spiritual needs in human character building to be served, and the sort of beauty that satisfies their growth is as organic and clean a revelation of natural conditions as a dynamo—an engine, or a battleship—but these needs seem to go unsatisfied, if they die not, unknown in the life of the average citizen today. As a rule, the more money spent in attaining this reflection of one's spirit—one's attitude of mind—in one's surroundings, the more painful the result, until the maximum is reached in the homes of the very rich; they are poisonous. The greater the material opportunity, the less true poetry, the less helpful significance results. It was my ill fortune to be shown through the palace of one of Chicago's great captains of industry, a short time ago. His pride in his belongings was immense, and he submitted that nothing in Italy could hold a candle to the magnificence of it all—but he was simply paying a half million dollars to advertise to posterity the fact that he was neither scholar nor gentleman. There was no single beautiful touch to mitigate the horror of the *tout-ensemble* (shout and scramble). This refreshing experience was repeated a short time ago in the home of a trust magnate who reveled in the sort of thing caricatured in the funny pa-

pers and that I had always supposed overdrawn—but the funny papers were feeble and kind compared to the hopeless vulgarity of the reality. Such homes are the result of a lust for possession, not an expression of sympathetic love for the Beautiful, and this lust is as conspicuous in the homes of New York's 400 as in the homes of their more clumsy Chicago imitators. Such perversion is contaminating to a degree we dimly realize and concerns us all.

The atmosphere of all this, from the limit of the "nouveau riche" to the homes of the more modest citizens in varying degree, is rank and unwholesome. A country boy has a better chance than his city brother. Who could imagine an Abraham Lincoln the product of such conditions, who lived his early life in touch with nature, in the fields, with the trees: and such as his artificial surroundings were, from the cabin to the simple dignity of his home in Springfield, they had at least the homely truth of the genuine? He grew withal his elemental grandeur the tenderest lover that ever wooed humanity. Who could fit the trappings of the White House to his character? I have never seen a monument that was becoming to him, unless it might be Saint-Gaudens's[4] statue in Lincoln Park—and then someone would have to "kindly remove the chair."

I know there are people who seem to have the faculty of making things lovely with the simplicity and freshness one finds in woods and wildflowers, who perhaps fail to pay their bills promptly, or send checks to charity and the church, but this may be after all but a seeming or else they have fallen heir to something which does not originate with them. I am persuaded that such perversion is the work of misfortune, if the faculty be genuine and has the royal ring of truth. Nevertheless, there is something to be done with the complacent, self-righteous sinner who, thinking his title to good citizenship is clear when he has paid his bills and sent his check to church and charity, sits at home in the midst of ugliness as a pillar of society, pointing heavenward, but who is, in point of fact, with neither form nor plan, like a rubble-stone foundation, among weeds, without a superstructure—solid perhaps, but "what for?" For the foundations of a soul are suited only to the superstructure of that soul and to no other. To rear the edifice God intended upon a good foundation is the indispensable business of civilization. "The degree of vision that dwells in a man is the correct measure of the man!" The sensibilities by which this vision is given and attuned to the life of man become atrophied if not degraded, so that we are content to take life at second hand, by rule, by vote (hence the increasing army of lawyers), or, worse than all, by habit. In fact, life seems to be a large matter of habit that soothes itself sentimentally with tradition in trite customs, moving in spasmodic waves of fashion!

But what is beautiful you say? That there is no standard is notorious; you may say that what is beautiful to me may not be beautiful to another and it is true—partially. There is a school of aesthetics which declares that if a man finds a row of stovepipe hats along the top of the cornice of his building beautiful, why, that is a privilege of his that should be respected; and so indeed, that same man has a legal right to paint his dress shirt front red and get into the middle of the road and "yell" if he chooses.

Both these things in this superlative degree we find ridiculous, from the standpoint of Fine Art, or fine conduct, although as we define the degrees, detection becomes more difficult until we push the thing beyond the zone of our own degree of intelligence. Anything without that particular zone, we subject to suspicion and even hatred, while, as a matter of fact, our appreciations would appear as absurd to a still finer intelligence as the row of chimney-pot hats or the blazing shirt front seems to ours. If there is something whereby the Beautiful may be apprehended as such, when the fine instructive love for the Beautiful which should be our natural birthright has been perverted by so-called education, we all want to know what it is. Nothing is of equal importance educationally.

There are laws of the Beautiful as immutable as the laws of elementary physics, and the work of art sifted by them and found wanting cannot be good for the growth of a soul, because all tendencies, either of form, line, or color, have a distinct significance. It is inevitable that a combination of forms, lines, and color should express something. That needs no demonstration. And as these tendencies are arranged and harmonized expression is gained, or modified, but never lost. A discord is an expression, in a sense, an expression of the devil! But the sort of expression we seek is that of harmony, or the good otherwise known as the true, otherwise known as the Beautiful, and it is folly to say that if the ear can distinguish a harmonious combination of sounds, the eye cannot distinguish a harmonious combination of forms or lines. For in the degree that the ear is sensitive to sound, it can appreciate the qualities of harmony in tones; and why in a larger degree should not the eye receive and appreciate the expression of harmonies in form, line, and color?

Rhythmical combinations of tone have portrayed the individualities of great souls to us, a Handel, a Beethoven, or a Wagner! And while no musical rule of three could compass their art or sound the depth of their genius, there are definite laws of harmony and construction common to their art and to all of them (leaving aside individual interpretation) and they are well-known, and well-taught. But similar rules governing the expression of feelings more catholic and useful still, as expressed in pictures, buildings, and statues, have scarcely been formulated and are still referred to as "matters of taste." Aside from the fact that expressions may be but the color of some man's soul, such expressions, to be works of Art, must convey an ideal of the conditions they seek to satisfy, because of the simple fact that such expressions arise from a spiritual need and nothing less will satisfy it. And so a Beethoven might color such tone revelations with his own soul. A Sargent might paint a hundred portraits without a signature, and the moment we see the work we might recognize it as Sargent's. But no less, for all that, each portrait [would] be a revelation of the individual soul of the subject, and this revelation would be accomplished through the medium of pigments, colors, and canvas instead of sound put together with Sargent's brains and feelings, and insofar he was true to the limitations imposed upon him by his pigments and canvas and to the degree he made his arrangement of colors and lines express the nature of the sitter, the result would be a work of Art. The directions his interpretation took, the materials he found in that human soul to portray, he might merely character-ize and possess little more than the insight of the great craftsman, or he might idealize them with the insight of the true poet, according to his own fiber, and be truly great as an Artist. Now all the while as in musical composing would be a conventionalizing process going on ever here. To have imitated the natural modeling and position of the subject photo-graphically in order to give a realistic topography of features and form would have been little and have required but manual dexterity and a mechanic's eye. There was the conception first and then the revelation of the conception. The Artist in any medium must first "see" with a prophetic eye, and then to reveal the vision he must handle his brush-es, pigment, and canvas with a sympathy that re-spects the limitations of the material and the process and makes both eloquent together. But eloquent before all, as brushwork, in paint, on canvas, mak-ing a delightful circumstance of that condition that raises the mere unrelated materials to the organic entity of a flower laden with fragrance of a human soul. Conditions conventionalize, but Art immor-talizes the conventionalization. So as a flat principle, one thing a work must be in any medium whatso-ever to be a work of Art is true to conditions of its existence. A painting must be a thing made with a brush, dipped in paint and applied to canvas; wherein this fact becomes a delightful circum-stance, it is not a piece of literature to tell a story, regardless of the conditions of its structure. And if you see a picture in which perhaps a cow is looking out at you "real," so "lifelike," rather buy the cow, for the picture in all human probability is worthless. A picture should be more than an imitation of a real object and more than a pretended hole in the wall through which you see a story about something, or the winter in summer, or the summer in winter! There are many degrees of this and none are beau-tiful. *Breaking Home Ties,*[5] and its vast kith and kin are not Art.

A musical composition is a thing of tone combinations in rhythmical progression, more or less modulated, suggestive poetically of phases of feeling, but when you read in your program at the concert that this or that particular passage represents the triumphant arrival of the passionate lover and picture his travels in search of his lady, who finally is located in a balcony with yellow hair worn in long braids, in shimmering blue, and a dialogue en-sues, be careful. For if the composer tried it, he was not an artist, and if he didn't, the man who said he did, or who wrote the program, is an artist with the reverse English. The programs are written to enter-tain the hopelessly objective mind, but they are an insult to the finer feelings of an intelligent audience. Theodore Thomas[6] himself knew better. Be con-tent to let the harmonies you hear color your moods and excite or soothe your imagination. Yield your temperament to your composer, but re-frain when you hear anything like the pattering of hoofs, the crowing of the cock, the firing of can-non, the twittering of birds, or the wailing of the damned—or revolt! And remember there are mod-ified degrees of this, not so easy to detect, but all of which mark the vulgarity of a pretender in the realm of Art.

And so in sculpture—perhaps the *ne plus ultra* of *E Pluribus Unum* of the thing we are discussing is represented in the Rogers Groups,[7] literal pho-tographs of scenes, that might make paintings, but which are simply absurd as sculpture. For sculpture has possibilities and limitations of its own, which we have no time to discuss, and to disregard them is always death to the pretended work of Art. All the classics which are living in our hearts today are tru-ly "Sculpture"—the Venus, the Winged Victory, and a long list—but the Art of painting has made sad inroads on modern sculpture. "Literature" has cursed both the painter and sculptor.

These general principles apply with even more relentless force in Architecture and are invio-lable in the decorative Arts. But we have no time for instances. I have chosen this fundamental phase of Art—the phase which deals with the conven-tionalization of natural things, revealing the inner poetry of their Nature, because it may bring a great lesson to us in the process of Civilization.

We marvel with a tinge of envy at the simple inevitableness with which the Life principle in so slight a thing as a willow wand, for instance, will find fullness of expression as a willow tree—a glorious sort of completeness—with that absolute repose which is of destiny fulfilled. Inevitably, the secret of the acorn is the glory of the oak. The fretted cone arises as the stately pine. Finding the fullness of a destined life in its untrammelled expression, simply, beautifully, naturally, we worship at the shrine of Nature and go to her for inspiration, to learn why we have laid upon us an artificiality that blights and oftentimes conceals ourselves and in the course of time and education deforms perhaps past recognition the fulfillment of the Life principle implanted in us. We walk in the cool, calm shade of the trees, and they say to us as they said to Emerson long ago, "Why so hot my little man?" And we wonder, why, indeed, so hot!

We feel and find in Nature always, an accord of form and function with Life principle, from zero to infinity, that seems to halt with our domestication of the infinite. There is some rare thing in this domesticating process of ours that society sets aside, and, striving for the freedom we love in Nature, we gain much friction and more discord for our pains. And so the wisest of savants, the deepest of the deep philosophers, and the noblest poets have gone to Nature for her secrets, hoping to find there the gist of this maddening, perplexing problem of Life, for it has become a problem for the human creature. A problem fashioning countless creeds, splitting philosophy into endlessly contending schools, dividing society into discordant, warring classes and grinding helpless humanity on the "rock of the ages," Civilization itself. But, however much we love the oak and pine in a state of nature in pristine freedom, their freedom is not for us. It does not belong to us now, however much the relic of barbarism within us may yearn for it. Civilization means for us a conventionalizing of our original state of nature, and it is here that the work of the Arts is inevitable, unless the light of the race is to go out. For Art is the great conservator of the finer sensibilities of a people. It is their only prophecy, the only light by which this conventionalizing process we call Civilization is to make its institutions eventually harmonious with the conditions of our life. I wish I might use another word than "conventionalizing," to convey the idea of this magic process, for only an artist or one with some genuine artistic training, will realize precisely what that means. To know a thing, what we can call knowing, a man must first love the thing, sympathize with it. So the Egyptians "knew" the Lotus and translated the Lotus to the dignified stone forms of their Architecture: this was the Lotus "conventionalized!" The Greeks "knew"and idealized the Acanthus in stone translations. This was the Acanthus conventionalized. Of all Art, whatsoever, perhaps Architecture is the Art best fitted to teach this lesson, for in its practices this problem of "conventionalizing" Nature is worked out at its highest and best. The Art of building is the great representative Art of Civilization when it comes to be understood, and music perhaps is next. A work of Architecture is a great coordination with a distinct and vital organism, but it is in no sense naturalistic—it is the highest, most subjective, conventionalization of Nature known to man, and at the same time it must be organically true to Nature when it is really a work of Art. To go back to the Lotus of the Egyptians (we may see in this mere detail of Art the whole principle), if Egypt had plucked the flower as it grew and had given us merely an imitation of it in stone, it would have died with the original—but in turning it to stone and fitting it to grace a column capital, the Egyptian artist put it through a rare and difficult process, wherein its natural character was really revealed and intensified in terms of stone, gaining for it an imperishable significance, for the Life principle of the flower is translated to terms of building stone to satisfy the Ideal of a real "need." This is Conventionalization, and it is Poetry. As the Egyptian took the Lotus, the Greek his Acanthus, to idealize the function of the capital, and as we may take any natural flower or thing, Civilization may take the natural man to fit him for his place in this great piece of Architecture we call the Social State, and today, as centuries ago, still it is the Artist's prophetic eye that must reveal, idealize, and conventionalize his natural state harmoniously with his Life principle. It cannot be otherwise. All the sheer wisdom of science, the cunning of politics—and the prayers of religion—can but stand and wait for the revelation. We say that God is Love—well Art is the very Genius of Love! But this elemental conventionalizing process is both difficult and dangerous in Art, for without the inspiration of the true artist the life of the flower is sacrificed, leaving a husk in place of the living thing. So in society this element of Civilization is even more dangerous and difficult, for instead of a leaf, we have a plant with a soul, and without the inner light of the true Artist, the life of the man is sacrificed, and society has an automaton where she should gain a noble, Democratic Citizen.

The Socialist would bow his neck in altruistic submission to the "harmonious whole"—his conventionalization would be like the poor craftsman's attempt to conventionalize his flower with the living character of the flower left out.

The Anarchist would pluck the flower as it grows and use it as it is for what it is—he is realistic with the essential reality left out.

The Plutocrat justifies his existence by his ability, owing to fortunate cabal [sic] to appropriate the flower to his own use after the craftsman has given it life and character and keeps the craftsman too by promising him his flower back—if he behaves well.

The Aristocrat does virtually the same thing, but on the strength of propinquity or heredity. But the true Democrat takes the human flower as it grows, and in the spirit of using the means at hand he puts Life into his conventionalization—preserves the individuality of the flower which is its life—

getting from it a living expression of its essential character, fitted perfectly to its place, without loss of vital significance.

When education has become prophetic, and Art again the prophet of the natural means by which we are to progress—we will possess this tool of Civilization as it now possesses us. When this dangerous conventionalizing force of the social state has been grasped and idealized, truthfully, we will find that this force is not antagonistic to the individualistic instinct in man, but is capable of bringing an adequate life to the individual, wherein the outward expression of the inner man will be a revelation of his inner Life and purposes.

1. Talk delivered to the Taliesin Fellowship, December 30, 1956. The Frank Lloyd Wright Archives #1014.178.
2. The lengthy essay published in *On Architecture* under the title of "A Philosophy of Fine Art" is really the essay that follows this, "The Architect." For reasons unknown, Wright and Gutheim choose to add several paragraphs of "A Philosophy of Fine Art" to "The Architect," but retained the title of the former.
3. This is the first appearance of the term *Life principle* by Wright, a phrase he used repeatedly to describe the organic structure underlying all forms that aspire to live.
4. American sculptor Augustus Saint-Gaudens (1848–1907).
5. A reference to a painting of a young man leaving home, done in 1890 by Thomas Hovendon and exhibited at the 1893 Columbian Exposition. Wright seems to have felt particularly strongly about the sentimentality of this painting as he refers to it again in *The Japanese Print*, in which he speaks of the vulgar pretense and banality of it and "its vast kith and kin."
6. Christian Friedrich Theodore Thomas (1835–1905). German-American conductor of the Chicago Symphony Orchestra (1891–1905).
7. "Rogers groups," groups of statuary created by John Rogers (1829–1904). Most of the "Rogers groups" were miniatures averaging around 20–22 inches high, all very literal representations. Subjects ranged from Civil War groups to scenes from Rip van Winkle and Shakespeare to genre scenes.

THE ARCHITECT

In Wright's second address to the Architectural League in June 1900, he decried the fate of American architecture. He blamed its lack of integrity directly on the pressures commerce was exerting over the architect. According to this paper, the profession of architecture had begun degenerating before the the turn of the century and was continuing in its misguided pursuit of direction. The address not only attacks this degeneration, but lays the groundwork for what Wright considers a solution based on the proper education of the architect.

Speaking to the Taliesin Fellowship fifty years later, Wright remembered the gentlemen of the profession as he had known them in his youth, men such as John Wellborn Root and Daniel Burnham. He admitted that their work was "classical," but noted that to them architecture was a fine and noble career. In his talks of the 1950s, he again described the typical architectural firm as a "plan-factory," in which publicity men and brokers hawked for commissions while the "boys in the back room" turned out designs. [Published in The Brickbuilder, *June 1900, without illustrations]*

A VITAL POINT OF DIFFERENCE BETWEEN A PROFESSIONAL man and a man of business is that money making to the professional man, should, by virtue of his assumption, be incidental; to the businessman it is primary.

Money has its limitations. While it may buy quantity, there is something beyond it and that is quality.

When the practice of a profession touching the Arts is assumed, certain obligations to the public concerning quality and beyond money making are also assumed, and without their faithful discharge the professional man degenerates to the weakest type of social menial in the entire system—an industrial parasite.

An architect practices a Fine Art as a profession with the Commercial and the Scientific of his time as his technique. Men are his tools.

In the age of "quantity" there is a growing tendency on the part of the public to disregard the architect in favor of the plan-factory magnate, or architectural broker, and there is consequent confusion in the mind of the young architect of today and of tomorrow as to the sound constitution of his ideal if that ideal is to be consistent with the "success" every man of him hopes to achieve. This confusion exists and naturally enough because the topography of his field of action has changed. It has changed to such an extent that in the letter at least the antique professional standard he may not recognize if he would. But the spirit of practice in the old field is still sound to the core; the spirit that made of the professional man a champion of finer forces in the lives of his own people.

The influence chiefly responsible for this change and most easily recognized is that of Science commercialized.

The tremendous forward march of scientific attainment with attendant new forces and resources—cultivation of the head at cost to the heart, of mind and matter at the expense of the emotions—has nevertheless given to him new and masterful tools that demand of him their proper use and have taken from him temporarily his power to so use them.

Because he has failed to realize and grasp his situation in its new bearings, he is not quite like his brother, the artist—a "thing afraid" of organization and its symbol, the machine. But the architect, the master of creative effort whose province it was to make imperishable record of the noblest in the life of his race in his time, for the time being has been caught in commercial rush and whirl and hypnotized into trying to be commercial himself. He has dragged his ancient monuments to the market places, tortured them with ribs of steel, twisted and unstrung them, set them upon pins, and perforated them until he has left them not a rag!

He has degenerated to a fakir. A fakir who flatters thin business imbecility with "Art architecture shop fronts" worn in the fashion of the old "dickie" or panders to silly women his little artistic sweets. His "Art is upon 'the town' to be chucked beneath the chin by every passing gallant, coaxed within the drawing room of the period and there betrayed as a proof of culture and refinement."[1]

Do you wonder at the prestige of the plan-factory when Architecture has become a commodity? A thing to be applied like a poultice or a porous plaster? Do you wonder that Architecture becomes of less and less consequence to the public and the architect has small standing except as he measures his success by the volume of business he transacts?

Divorced from Fine Art, the architect is something yet to be classified, though he is tagged with a license in Illinois. So is the banana peddler and the chiropodist.

Do you wonder that "the people" demand that he be at least a good businessman, a good salesman, as something that they can understand and appreciate—when the commodity he is selling has been dead to them so long as to be unrecognizable, except by virtue of association with the dim past and therefore not quite respectable even yet to do without something of the sort.

That commodity is as dead to the salesman as to the buyer, and to the fact that the thing is more easily handled dead than alive, the salesman, captain of industry though he be, owes his existence.

In business it is in the stock pattern that fortunes are made.

So in Architecture, it is in the ready-made article that the money lies, altered to fit by any popular "sartorial artist"—the less alteration the greater the profit—and the architect.

The present generation of the successful architect has been submerged, overwhelmed by the commercialism of the time. He has yielded to the confusion and feverish demand of the moment and has become a high-grade salesman of a high-priced imported article. His duty to the public as professional man laid aside, if it was ever realized, and merely because the public was ignorant of its claim and willing to buy even if the paint came off and the features peeled.

What has been gained by his feverish haste to offer his Art on the altar of commercial sacrifice has been quantity at the expense of quality—a general depreciation of architectural values and a corruption of the birthright of the "buyers."

In consequence Architecture today has not even commercial integrity, and the architect as he practices his profession is humiliated and craven.

Robbed by his own cowardice and mediocrity of his former commanding position in the Arts, he hesitates between stalking his victim outright or working wires—otherwise his friends—for the "job," as his opportunity is now styled.

He joins the club and poses, or hanging to the coattails of his friends he teases for the "jobs" they may carry in their pockets, his mouth sticky and his hands dirty, pulling and working for "more." Then he starves in the lower ranks of a doubtful aristocracy unless he comes by influence in other than architectural ways—by inheritance, by marriage or by politics. Does a sale of property appear in a trade journal? Immediately the owner is besieged by ten "first-class architects" suing for the privilege of submitting "samples free of charge," assuring the owner meanwhile that he would be granting a personal favor in permitting them to do so and if the samples were not what he wanted they would love each other nonetheless. Or his friend drops in shortly after the owner decides to build and incidentally mentions so-and-so as a good fellow and a winning architect. His wife perhaps has had influence brought to bear before he gets home, and while against the principles of the architect to work for nothing, yet the combination is of such a friendly nature as to form a special case and "sketches" in this instance, in place of "samples," are finally submitted to all intents and purposes as before, but a little higher in the social scale inasmuch as the method is less rude and abrupt.

The latest development is the hiring of a professional promoter by the year to drum up "trade"— mine and countermine the social system with pitfalls for the unwary to be ensnared for the practice of his principal. And talk to the best of him concerning "professional" advertising, making capital of himself in subtle telling ways—poor devil, the naivete of some of him would wring the tear of pity from Commerce herself. How many architects would live (and they are just the number that *should* live) if they depended upon the work that came to them because of intelligent, critical appreciation of actual qualifications or work performed? There would be a good many, but probably about seven percent of the profession. There is usually the maneuver, the pull; sometimes methods more open, but no more weak and shameful.

Because this matter of Architecture itself has become of little moment to the average client, Architecture as a Fine Art is really out of it and for the present Architecture is a commodity, a case of friendly favor and interference or a matter of "fashion."

The fact that all this has become so generally accepted as good form, is proof of the architect's danger and the damnable weakness of his position.

Another feature of his present plight is that not wholly respecting himself (how can he?) he is apt to be a hypersensitive individual, and like other unfortunates who depend upon preeminence of personality to get in the way of "the choosers," he is interested in pretty much everything as long as he counts, and at that as number one; none of his bloom or luster is to be rubbed off by contact. So, concerted effort in matters touching the welfare of his profession is rare among him.

Perhaps this is in the nature of the proposition.

There are intelligent architects who argue that only the selfish few give value to Art, the highlights only give value to the pattern of the fabric, but I believe it is because of warp and woof, undertone and motive that he has any value as a "highlight" and that type of individualism is one of the superstitions he must shed before he comes to his own.

The architect, so called today, is struggling in general depression in the level of his Art owing to the unknown character of the country patiently awaiting his exploration, prophesied by the past but of which no map may yet be made and of which no chart has been provided by the schools.

He is complacent inanity personified and counts not at all, or blinded by the baser elements of commerce, choked by greed, goaded by ambition for "success" of the current type, the feverish unrest common to false ideals racks his bones and wastes his substance until he finally settles, dazed and empty, in his muddy tracks, which amounts, I suppose, to giving the people what they want.

For the generalization of the situation, then, the architect is rapidly becoming accepted as a middleman or broker with the business instinct and ability, but who cannot have business integrity because of the nature of his self-imposed occupation. He sells the public ready-made imported Architecture that he himself buys in a "job-lot" of unfortunates in a "home" which he establishes to protect them from a condition which he himself has developed and fostered. This Architecture is applied to his client's condition as a poultice or porous plaster would be applied to his aching back and is accepted with a clamor for "more" through lack of acquaintance with the real thing, lack of an ideal, and of educational force in the profession itself. Meanwhile the younger aspirant for better things is either assimilated by the winners, plucked and shoved behind the scenes with the unfortunate, or settles down to give the people what they want, which simply means producing more of the type the plan-factory fashions.

An example of a once noble profession prostituted by [a] "commercial knight of untiring industry," abandoned to her fate by the "architect" in quotation marks, who shrugs his shoulders, looks aghast and contributes innocuous expectation of her ability "to pull out" (and pull him out too) to the general blight.

And why this network of cross-purposes?

Is it because the architect is now confronted with a condition which they say demands a combination of two of him and a corps of trained experts where before one was absolute?

Is it because he is now in a position that demands that an intricate commercial machine be perfected to carry into effect an idea?

Or is it because Architecture is a great thing in small hands, and Ideals, noble theories, if you will, "the rails of the track on which the car of Progress runs" have fallen to disrepute?

"Give me a great thought," cried the dying Herder, "that I may refresh myself with it."

He was of the stuff from which an architect is made.

The regeneration of Architecture does not lie in the hands of classicists or fashion mongers of the East or the West.

Their work is almost written at its length with no spark of life, and but a shroud of artistic respectability will cling to it half a century hence.

It is but archaeological dry bones bleaching in the sun!

America will regard it as crude—Chicago even now regards her county courthouse as something weak and servile, an insult to the people who entrusted to chosen ones the fruit of honest toil and were betrayed to perpetuate the degenerate Art of a degenerate people.

The American nation has a heart and backbone of its own and is rapidly forming a mind of its own.

It has not yet been taught self-expression except in the matter of dollars and cents, and recently of war. Presently Light, Grace, and Ethics, true to as virile an individuality as history has known will come as naturally to her as the breath of life that is already hers, and then, O, ye Stuffed Prophets of Plethoric "Success," will she look with pride upon the time that you bedizened her with borrowed finery; pierced her ears for borrowed ornaments; taught her to speak with a lisp and mince in her gait? No! Your very success was your undoing and her disgrace.

In her new code no one man will be entrusted with the amount of work that occasioned the "plan-factory." As no Rockefeller may rise to a legitimate point of vantage that would justify the control of such a vast share of the earth's resources, how unspeakably vulgar and illegitimate will it be for one man to undertake in the Fine Arts more than he can characterize in noble fashion as a work of Art!

The plan-factory is the product of a raw commercial state, perhaps a necessary evil to be passed through as we pass through the dark before day.

Perhaps the epidemic of Renaissance, French, Dutch, and English that encumbers the land was a contagious malady such as little children bring from school. Soonest over soonest mended.

It is argued that we are witnessing the same development in Architecture that we see is legitimate enough as means to an end in trade, as the Department Store and the Trust. But it is not in Architecture a development but a reflection or reflex action that is passing but causing painful confusion. It is making of Art a network of cross-purposes, but temporarily.

We are witnessing the inroads of trade upon ground it can never hold for there is underlying, undying distinction between Art and Trade as there is between Science and Religion. Perfect harmony in reality exists between the principles of Art and the principles of Commerce as we are coming to see it in Religion and Science, the one strengthening and confirming the other. Yet the principles governing trade, although harmonious with Art, may never govern her, as the Subjective will never be governed by the Objective.

The one is of the principle of Life, the other a matter of its fruit.

Art will reign as long as Life and greater than ever her prestige when the harmony between Commerce, Science, and Art is better understood.

It is this Harmony, this Commercialism, that the younger architect should strive to understand and appreciate, for it is the measure of his technique in his new field. But he should strive to understand it as a Master not as a Huckster; to poetize and deify it as an instrument in his hands.

He should help his lame, halt, and blind profession again to its place by respecting his Art and respecting himself; by making the solution of problems that come fairly his way such as will compel the recognition that there is no commercial dignity without that kind of Art; that will make the man of business see that a Greek temple made over to trade is an unhallowed joke and that he is the butt when genuine dignity and beauty might be his for less money; that will make the householder realize that if he would live in a Louis XV environment he is but a step removed from the savage with a ring in his nose; and make it felt that Architecture is not a matter of the scene painting of periods nor a mere matter of scene painting in any sense whatever.

Give back the slogan "a good copy is better than a poor original" to those whose desire for "success" outmeasured their capacity to perform and who framed it in self-defense.

"A poor thing but mine own" is better stuff for men when coupled with reverence and honesty and carries the fundamental principle of harmonious independence graven over the gate of the new country promised of old.

The architect should help the people to feel that Architecture is a destroyer of vulgarity, sham, and pretense, a benefactor of tired nerves and jaded souls, an educator in the higher ideals and better purposes of yesterday, today, and tomorrow.

Such an art only is characteristic of the better phase of Commercialism itself and is true to American independence and America's hatred of cant, hypocrisy, and base imitation.

When once Americans are taught in terms of building construction like the principles so dear to them at their firesides, the architect will have arrived!

But his own education is a matter of the greatest concern. We all catch a glimpse of the magnificent awaiting him, but how to prepare him is a more difficult matter.

It is for the higher Law and more Freedom in his architectural school that we plead, not Anarchy—a deeper sense of the significance to his Art of Nature! Manly independence! And vigorous imagination! A truer reverence for his precedent.

He should learn methods of attack; have cultivated in him the quality that gets at an architectural proposition from the inside outward for and by itself. He should be a thinking quantity when he leaves school. Standing on his own legs, such as they are, with ears and eyes wide open, receptive, eager, and enthusiastic; his faculties sharpened by metaphysical drill, his heart wide open to beauty, whether of a specific brand or no; and a worker first, last, and all the time a worker; his mind alive to opportunity knowing the direction in which it lies, gauging his own fitness in relation to it; farsighted enough to decline the opportunity that he was unfitted to undertake if it should come to him (and many such do come to all architects); courageous enough to decline it and wait for one "his size." And when it came he would make it count without making his client pay too much for a share of his education in the field.

He would gain experience and strength and build up solidly if slowly and the respect and confidence would in time be his that would make his personality a power for the architectural good of his country. His experience is to be gained only by solving problems for and by themselves.

Advice never built a character worth the name, though advice is good.

So an architect may practice Architecture extensively with book and precedent and die without experience, without a character.

The man who has worked out the salvation of a summer cottage on his merits, held the conditions in rational solution, and expressed them in terms of wood and plaster with beauty germane to the proposition has more valuable experience than he who builds a city with the pomp and circumstance of established forms.

A more intimate knowledge of conditions he is to be called upon to serve are what the student needs in his school. The classic is well as far as the elemental principles that make ancient architecture live as Fine Art are the burden of study; the letter valuable only as extraneous phenomena by means of which these elements in their time were made manifest. But the problems of today, the problems of transportation, warehousing, city building are his problems. Elevated railway systems and freight stations, manufactories, grain elevators and office buildings, the housing of highly organized industries, monumental in power and significance, stripped and trained to the bone for action. The housing of a people—nervous, intellectual, receptive, and progressive.

Architecture is essentially the art of organization, and her sons should be prophetic generals in this period of crystallizing social forces.

The architect may poetize and deify a more magnificent period of the world's progression than has yet been his opportunity.

And the stock has almost sold out.

Let the young student come to the front.

I have no quack nostrum for the sudden cure of the architect's complacent inertia nor his commercial delirium and know of no shortcut for him as he is coming on.

The education of the architect should commence when he is two days old—"three days is too much"—and continue until he passes beyond, leaving his experiments by the wayside to serve his profession as warning signs or guideposts.

The kindergarten circle of sympathetic discernment should be drawn about him when he is born, and he should be brought into contact with Nature by prophet and seer until abiding sympathy with her is his. He should be a true child of hers, in touch with her moods, discerning her principles and harmonics until his soul overflows with love of Nature in the highest and his mind is stored with a technical knowledge of her forms and processes.

Braced and stayed by that, he should move into the thick of civilization to study man and his methods in the things that are his and the ways thereof taking his averages and unraveling seeming inconsistencies shoulder to shoulder with his fellow men as one with them.

Meanwhile, as his discipline he should acquire the technical skill of the mill, forge, and try-pit of commerce in the light of Science; study the beauty of the world as created by the hand of man, as his birthright and his advantage; finding his passion and delight in various initial steps of composition with the encouraging guidance of a catholic-minded nature-wise and loving Master.

A master that would permit him to honor his precedent too much to sacrifice it to the stagnation or perversion of his own natural opportunities; who would hold with him that to "copy" was to cultivate a weakness, to draw from the cast an abomination; that mere imitation, beginning or ending, is forever contemptible and in the Fine Arts impossible. A master who would unconsciously imbue him with the sense of honor that recognized the same right of a man to the work of his brain as to the work of his hands that he might in turn hand it on to his public. Nor would there be confusion in his master's mind as to the fact that Architecture is a creative Art or nothing and that to take his place he must have technical discipline of the highest order, but his technique would never drive his Art nor would he ever mistake its place for his own.

In short, a master that would make the distinction between Fine Art and Fine Artisanship plain.

Now he is taught certain architectural phraseology of form and color dubbed "grammar" by his professors, and much foreign technique.

If teaching him that minutes and modules of the architraves and cornice of one type in certain measure make Greek and of another type in combination make Roman and when they corrode each other the result is "Renaissance"—there he is taught "grammar."

I imagine it to be a more difficult matter to teach him the "grammar" of Goth and Moor, but Architecture has no business primarily with this "grammar," which at its best, I suppose, might mean putting the architectural together correctly, but as taught means putting the architectural together as predetermined by fashion of previous races and conditions.

So the young student is eternally damned by the dogmas of Vignola and Vitruvius, provided with a fine repertoire of stock phrases as architectural capital and technique enough to make them go if he is let alone and conditions are favorable which he never is and they never are.

He comes to think these fine phrases and this technique are Architecture and sells both in judicious mixture to the "buyers" as such with the circumstance of the "scholar" and the "classical," and he would be shocked if told that he is a swindler.

He is sent out a callow, complacent fledgling, sure of his precedent, afraid of little but failure to "succeed," puffed up with architectural "excelsior" and wadded with "deafening," to become soaked and sodden in the field, hopelessly out of shape.

The architect primarily should have something of his own to say or keep silent.

There are more legitimate fields of action for him than the field of Architecture.

If he has that something to say in noble form, gracious line, and living color, each expression will have a "grammar" of its own, using the term in its best sense, and will speak the universal language of Beauty in no circumscribed series of set architectural phrase as used by people in other times, although a language in harmony with elemental laws to be deduced from the Beautiful of all peoples in all time.

This elemental law and order of the Beautiful is much more profound than the accepted grammatical of phrase in Architecture as Nature is deeper than Fashion.

Let the young student add to his wisdom the strength and wisdom of past ages, that is his advantage. But let him live his own life nor mistake for the Spirit the Letter.

I would see him relieved of the unnatural educational incubus that sowed the seed of the plan-factory and nurtured the false ideals that enable it to exist.

I would see him relieved of architectural lock-jaw not by prying the set teeth of his Art apart with a crowbar nor by cracking its jaws with a sledge hammer, but by a realization that life was given the architect that Architecture may grow and expand naturally as a noble Fine Art and as becomes a free-hearted, vigorous young people.

It may be that the very cosmopolitan nature of our nation will prevent a narrow confirmation of any one type.

I hope that we are destined to greater variety in unity than has yet existed in the Art of a great people.

The very strength of individuality developed in a free nation and the richness of our inheritance will find expression in more diverse and splendid ways than could be expected of a more narrowly nurtured race. Yet it will find expression in an Art that is indigenous and characteristic as an Architecture measured by the laws of Fine Art, the hardy grace of the wildflower perhaps rather than the cultivated richness of the rose, a further contribution to the Art of the world—not a servile extraction!

The architect has a hard road to travel and far to go.

He should know what he is to encounter in the field and be trained to meet it by men who have faced it in all its ugly significance with unconquerable soul and clear vision.

He should understand that to go into the field penniless with a family to support means the ultimate addition of one more craven to the ranks, unless some chance saves him or his fortitude is of the stuff that will see his wife and children suffer for ideals that may seem ridiculous and are to the average mind incomprehensible.

If he goes single-handed he must be content to walk behind, to work and wait.

The work to be done by the young architect entering the lists would better be done by him whose board and lodging is assured for life and whose communication with his base of supplies is not apt to be cut off.

He is going into a country almost abandoned to the enemy.

Yet the hardy pioneer who takes his architectural life in hand and fares boldly forth in quest of his Ideal, not scorning hard tack for food nor a plank for a bed,

Withal a soul like the bird,
Who pausing in her flight,
Awhile on boughs too slight,
Feels them give way beneath her and yet sings,
Knowing that she hath wings;

is perhaps the stuff from which the missionary we need is to come; the spirit that conquered Western wilds and turned them to fallow fields transmuted to the realm of Art a boy with the heart of a king; the scent of the pine woods deep in his nostrils, sweetness and light in his soul—the erudition of the world at his fingers' ends. Will the flickering Art spirit of this age produce him? If he is the stuff that architects are made of he is not to be discouraged by limitations.

The limitations within which an artist works do grind him and sometimes seem insurmountable, yet without these very limitations there is no Art. They are at once his problems and his best friends—his salvation in disguise.

In the Arts every problem carries within its own solution and the only way yet discovered to reach it is a very painstaking way—to look sympathetically within the thing itself, to proceed to analyze and sift it, to extract its own consistent and essential beauty, which means its common sense truthfully idealized.

That is the heart of the Poetry that lives in Architecture.

That is what they should teach the young architect in the schools, beginning early. But the schools will have to be taught before they will ever teach him.

His scientific possibilities and demands have outrun his handmade Art as planned for him in the school curriculum. He is without lettered precedent as he stands today on the threshold of great development in the industrial direction of the world.

A highly organized, complex condition confronts him.

He will understand it, learn the secret of its correspondencies and their harmonics and work with them, not against them. For his Art is of Life itself, it will endure.

Life is preparing the stuff to satisfy the coming demand, and the architect will know the capacities of modern methods, processes, and machines and become their master. He will sense the significance to his Art of the new materials that are his, of which steel is but one.

He will show in his work that he has been emancipated from the meager unit established by brick arch and stone lintel, and his imagination will transfigure to new beauty his primitive Art.

He will realize that the narrow limitations of structure outlined in his precedents are too mean and small to be longer useful or binding and that he is comparatively a free man to clothe new structural conditions in the living flesh of virile imagination.

He will write large in beautiful character the song of steel and steam—

Lord thou hast made this world below the
    shadow of a dream
And taught by time I take it so—exceptin' always steam.
Romance! Those first-class passengers they
    like it very well
Printed and bound in little books, but why
    don't poets tell?
I'm sick of all their quirks and turns, the loves
    and doves they dream.
Lord! Send a man like Bobbie Burns to sing
    the song of steam.
To match with Scotia's noblest speech yon orchestra sublime,
Whereto—uplifted like the Just—the tail rods
    mark the time,
The crank-throws give the double bass, the
    feed pump sobs and heaves;
And now the main eccentrics start their quarrel on the sheaves
Her time—her own appointed time the rocking link-head bides,
Till—hear that note—the rods return whings
    glimmering through the guides,
They're all away, true beat, full power, the
    clanging chorus goes.
Clear to the tunnel where they sit, my purring
    dynamos.

Interdependence absolute, foreseen, ordained, decreed,

To work ye'll note at any tilt on any rate of speed,

From skylight lift to furnace bars, backed, bolted, braced, and stayed

And singing like the Morning Stars for joy that they are made,

While, out o' touch of vanity the sweating thrust block says:

Not unto us the praise, or man—not unto us the praise.

Now all together, hear them lift their lessons, theirs and mine;

Law, Order, Duty and Restraint, Obedience, Discipline.

Mill, forge and try-pit taught them that when roaring they arose,

And th' while I wonder if a soul was gied them wi' the blows,

Oh for a man to weld it then in one trip-hammer strain

Till even first-class passengers could tell the meanin' plain.[2]

The architect will weld that strain and build that song in noble line and form.

He will write that record for all time.

He may last to "judge her line or take her cure," but he may say that he too has lived and worked, whether he has done well or ill, he will have worked as a man and given a shoulder to his fellows climbing after.

1. James McNeill Whistler (1834–1903). Introduction to the "Ten O' Clock" lecture, 1885. See footnote 1, page 38.
2. Wright makes reference to this same "hymn" in "The Print and the Renaissance," in which he identifies it as the work of an M. Andrews.

CONCERNING LANDSCAPE ARCHITECTURE

This address, read to the Fellowship Club, a ladies civic organization in Oak Park, Illinois, concerns land-scape architecture—in particular, how its principles might be applied to the town of Oak Park, where Wright lived and worked from 1889 to 1909. The stiff formality of à la mode landscaping is severely criticized; in-stead Wright advocates the grouping of foliage "as it naturally grows best to show its full beauty as a lilac, a syringa, an elm, an oak, or a maple." He despised the standard practice of what is called "foundation plant-ing," or surrounding the entire periphery of a house with bushes and shrubs planted against a wall. His own landscape plans show a more plastic, unconstrained "freehand" treatment—gathering groups of plant materi-als together, but always providing a supporting open space, like a pause in the midst of a conversation.

It is interesting to note that Wright refers to Gertrude Jekyll (1843–1932) in this essay. The English landscape architect, a contemporary of Wright's, was working a revolution in landscape architecture in England as he was in architecture in America. Her designs for informal, more natural gardens gave us what we refer to today as the "English garden," in contrast to the stiff formality of the "Renaissance garden." That Wright was keenly aware of her work attests to the fact that he was by no means isolated, that indeed he had a broad knowledge of contemporary movements, events, and publications. [Unpublished speech]

LADIES AND GENTLEMEN: YOUR CHAIRMAN HAS VERY graciously suggested that it might be well for me on this occasion to explain why I tried to make a scene when the village fathers decided to give our little town a shave, shampoo, and haircut and show wherein lay the philosophy that would have a peaceful, law-abiding village remain a jungle wherein people were known to lose themselves and wander about until starved to death; where no man could walk from his house to the train without hav-ing all the courage taken out of his collar and shirt front by the dampness of his way, along which way neither wooden sidewalks nor wood block pave-ments could thrive; where the sun was an unfamil-iar sight and little children grew thin and pallid like potato sprouts in a back cellar.

And indeed I feel that an apology is forthcom-ing. I had an idea, however, in the back of my head, and will try to show you what it was, leaving you to draw your own conclusions as to its moral or my own foolishness.

To begin with, I am always suspicious of the professional tree-man, as I have learned to be of most people whose whole lives are spent along some one line without regard to other lines of thought or work. We see a tendency in such people always, unless they are genuine artists inspired with a never-failing love of nature and strong in character and moral fiber, to grow away from certain normal qualities inherent in their work to a longing for new sensations, for curious effects, freaks, or too highly disciplined results.

Ignorance is dangerous but over-cultivation along narrow lines is much more dangerous still, because it usually has prestige, which ignorance lacks. Now, English landscape architecture is saddled with the most glaring evidence of this degeneracy—for it is just that. Magnificent yew and splendid box trees trimmed into animal shapes, barrels with roosters crowing on their tops, a railroad train running along the top of a hedge, are some of the most absurd, and this element is manifest in instances less and less striking until we can scarcely say where the genuine artist leaves off and his decay begins. The standard rose or the dwarf mulberry, together with all curious torture and forced treatments, evidence it.

We have a striking instance higher up in our own country in Louis Tiffany, the great decorator, who has given us so much that is exquisitely beautiful. In his case, it is the color sense that suffers. Blue, unless atmospheric, and green, unless translucent, are naturally discords. Tiffany, working in color all his life begins to tire of normal color effects and feels for new sensations and finds them on the ragged edge of discords, and his later work can please no healthy eye. Moreover, this had its effect on the fashionable world, and not very long ago how many of our wives and daughters just adored blue and green combinations in hats and gowns—the more violent, the more fashionable they were. So it is, wives and daughters, with your husbands, how many of them like their old cheese after dinner, their meat hung until "gamey" in flavor. I have dined at epicure's tables where the meats were as gamey as old rope-fat—and the cheese, well, the less said about it, the better.

Now, what is this but the same decay of the normal sense, the breaking down of the normal appetite, which is inevitable it seems, in long continued over-use of the senses—whether a sense of form, color, taste or touch? And much evidence of this tendency in human nature is beyond mention in polite society.

The importance to us in all this lies in the fact that a great deal of practice in trimming and planting trees (for one thing) today is the direct result of the precedents which were established in the past by over-cultivation of this sort. I am not foolish enough to attribute these things to Chicago and the West on the high plane of degeneracy, for poor old Chicago hasn't had cultivation enough in these things to be suspected of it, but unfortunately, neither has she cultivation enough to know it when she sees it, so it comes to her as tradition, and she accepts it with vigor and enthusiasm and thinks it great!

Go down to South Park and see the man rowing a boat all hens and chickens—the presidential chair—floral beds in which the plants are all trimmed to shape as hard as moldings. To execute some fell design, rows of standard roses, bursting from the top of their sticks, mulberries made to weep by clever tricks, and the curious trimming of trees—the trimming of trees to perverted ideals—just as woman trims her form to a perverted ideal—all of which has its origin in decadence and abuse.

Now, in this country, there is a sound healthy sentiment for these things, which has not been contaminated with this desire for meaningless artifice and respects a tree for its inherent grace of character rejecting any treatment which does not preserve it and emphasize it. You see, your professional gardener in these things has, as a rule, no creative mind but abundance of precedent, and when you call him in, he can tell you right away how these things ought to be done, for he has seen it done before, and you may get abuse for skill or you may not.

Now, in this school of which I speak, landscape architecture has a decidedly architectural basis—that is an architectural plan in arrangement and division, which provides for massing and grouping of foliage according to its true nature—that is, as it naturally grows best to show its full beauty as a lilac, a syringa, an elm, an oak, or a maple.

And it would be a criminal offence to make a maple grow like an elm, or in any way to mar or disturb the natural tendency of these things. The formality necessary to harmonize these growing things with man's surroundings is sought and found in the architectural nature of the plan, the division, the enclosure, the arrangement. It is no longer permitted to reach into and mar the natural grace of foliage, and this would seem like common sense, for the variety and interest—the chance for man's individuality to work itself out in these things is even greater than when the trees themselves are sacrificed to a fashionable perversion. A charming book by an English woman, Gertrude Jekyll, called *Home and Garden*[1], shows very well this attitude toward our subject, and it should be in every library.

In regard to Oak Park: a certain profusion of foliage characterized the village. I remember well that I came to Oak Park to live for no other reason than that, and the remarkable character of the foliage on the old Blair lot. I don't think the boldest among us would aver that Oak Park was anything but ugly architecturally—I do not ask you to take my word for this, consult a higher authority—but that ungracious circumstance was erased and modified by foliage, by trees which many of Oak Park's early citizens contributed, and I believe the late Mr. Austin imported Mr. Blair, a Scotch landscape gardener with a true feeling for nature, to help develop that side of the town, and his work remains today one of the chief beauties of the village.

Unfortunately, much of this early work was done to get shade quickly, and the trees were planted too close together, lining the streets with windrows [sic] of splendid foliage. Forest Avenue was positively a green vault in summer, to be looked into like the nave of a cathedral, and this effect would seem to be the natural result of the growth of trees, which had no room to develop except to the sides. It might have been better had the trees been so planted as to develop perfect specimens, but the present arrangement properly treated and handled has a charm of its own, provided the streets do not become too dark and damp.

Something had to be done in some quarters, doubtless, and what the minority feared was that it would be done in such a way as to leave rows of bare boles alternating with telephone and electric light poles, robbing benighted house fronts of their saving grace and taking away from the village the privacy and domestic charm, which intervening masses of foliage low down on lower limbs insured. This in many cases has happened, and the village is just that much more set and stiff therefore, I suppose, more "thrifty" than before.

Speaking of Oak Park's feeling for nature, I presume we might say that Oak Park—like Jerome K. Jerome's[2] Germany—likes the country but prefers it as the lady thought she would the noble savage, "more dressed."

Among trees, the Oak Park favorite should be the Lombardy poplar. Disorderly natures may sing the charm of the rugged oak, the spreading chestnut, or the waving elm; to Oak Parkers, all such, with their willful untidy ways, are eyesores. The Lombardy poplar grows where it is planted, and as it is planted. It has no improper, rugged ideas of its own. It does not want to wave nor spread itself. It just grows straight and upright as a proper Oak Park tree should grow, and so let us root out all other trees and replace them with Lombardy poplars. Let us talk no more nonsense about untrammeled nature. In Oak Park, nature has got to behave herself and not set a bad example to the children.

I suppose eventually the sober citizen who hates fuss, will plant his rose trees seven on the north side and seven on the south side, and if they fail to grow up all the same size and shape, they will worry him until he will lie awake. Every flower he will tie to a stick. This interferes with his view of the flower, but he will have the satisfaction of knowing that it is there and that it is behaving itself.

Then let us have those delightful little German lakes, lined with zinc, that we can take up once every week, to carry into the kitchen to be scoured.

Then let us rail around the grass plots and put a china dog in the center of each. A china dog never digs holes in the lawn, nor scatters the flower beds. He too will stay where you put him. You can have a blue dog or a pink dog, or, for a little extra, you may have a double-headed dog.

It is truly a tidy little land—is Oak Park.

But all joking aside:

I think intelligent communities are coming to realize more and more that he who meddles with aesthetic things, owes a duty to others as well as to himself, and to know that this is especially the case when the result is to stand conspicuously before the public eye. Everything that ever was undertaken is a good work or a bad one. If it plainly shows that its builders did not even try to make it good, it is only more inexcusably bad. We are not naive savages. We know that if a man is hungry for food or for beauty, our obligation is the same and we must give him the best that opportunity allows. When we insist that our neighbors shall daily look on barrenness or deformity just because we happen to hold a deed to the property, and fill what was before at least decent empty space with shapes of ugliness, we are bad citizens and brutal neighbors.

Someone has said that to build a hideous house is to indulge in the worst form of selfishness, and I am not sure that he exaggerates much, unless it is more selfish to cut down trees on one's lot which the neighborhood loves and admires. Truly you "own" the result; but it belongs also to the neighbor, and the artist, and to the town at large, interests quite as important as your own.

Indeed, in Art we have a legal right to befool ourselves, but there is a standard in Art as there is a standard in conduct. Most of us, I think, accept Christ as the standard in conduct, but few of us have learned to translate that standard to the beautiful ways of doing things, which we call Art and which determine our surroundings, and influence us through our environment even more than does the cultivated conduct of good society—though indeed the two are not to be widely separated. You will find the environment reflecting unerringly the society. If the environment is stupid and ugly, you may safely count upon that as the substratum of its society.

1. *Home and Garden* was first published in 1900.
2. English writer Jerome Klapka Jerome (1859–1927) is probably best known for his 1889 best-seller *Three Men in a Boat (To Say Nothing of the Dog),* a delightful piece about a rowing holiday on the Thames. Wright is no doubt referring to the sequel of 1900, *Three Men on the Bummel,* in which Jerome describes a German tour.

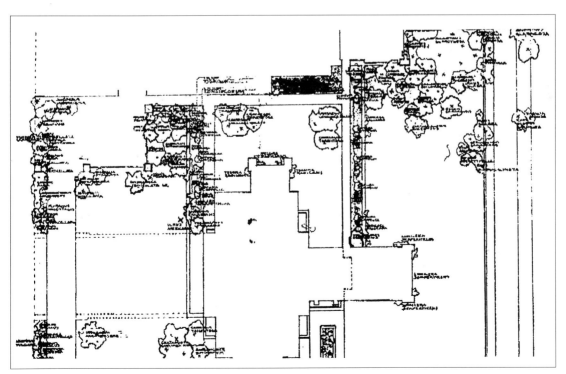

Francis W. Little House. Peoria, Illinois. 1900. Landscape Plan. Ink on tracing linen, 12 x 18". FLLW Fdn#0009.018

THE ART AND CRAFT
OF THE MACHINE

When Wright wrote and delivered this paper at Chicago's Hull House in March 1901, the influence of the English Arts and Crafts movement was making itself felt in American design circles. He maintained that it was the sort of movement that harked back to an era that had vanished, and it was therefore anachronistic and futile for American architecture and interior design; moreover, it glorified handiwork and handicraft at a time when industry was opening up new horizons, new techniques, and new methods for architecture and the decorative arts. The machine, to Wright's way of thinking, could be an invaluable tool in the hand of the artist and free him from the laborious and expensive handiwork that was not relevant to the twentieth century. The importance of this thesis never deserted him.

"The Art and Craft of the Machine" is a most elusive and enigmatic essay. It recurs in different forms throughout Wright's manuscript collection file, sometimes simply edited, sometimes completely rewritten. Wright seems to have worked on this text so many times that even he lost track of which version he was using. When he referred to reading from the 1901 version in his Princeton lectures (1930), for example, the paper he inserted was totally rewritten, bearing little resemblance to the original.

To many Wright scholars, this paper is often regarded as his first great manifesto. But the earlier manuscripts, unpublished until now, suggest this essay was really a carefully crafted summation of ideas and concepts he had been presenting to the public for a number of years. While the earlier pieces focused on the specific characteristics of the "American home" and what it should be and why, in "The Art and Craft of the Machine" Wright emphasizes the capabilities and potential of the machine itself in the hands of the artist:

Is it not more likely that the medium of artistic expression itself has broadened and changed until a new definition and new direction must be given the art-activity of the future, and that the Machine has finally made for the artist, whether he will yet own it or not a splendid distinction between the Art of old and the Art to come? A distinction made by the tool which frees human labor, lengthens and broadens the life of the simplest man, thereby the basis of the Democracy upon which we insist.

[Speech, later published without illustrations in the catalog of the fourteenth annual exhibition of the Chicago Architectural Club, March 1901]

AS WE WORK ALONG OUR VARIOUS WAYS, THERE TAKES shape within us, in some sort, an ideal—something we are to become—some work to be done. This, I think, is denied to very few, and we begin really to live only when the thrill of this ideality moves us in what we will to accomplish. In the years which have been devoted in my own life to working out in stubborn materials a feeling for the beautiful, in the vortex of distorted complex conditions, a hope has grown stronger with the experience of each year, amounting now to a gradually deepening conviction that in the machine lies the only future of art and craft—as I believe, a glorious future; that the machine is, in fact, the metamorphosis of ancient art and craft; that we are at last face to face with the machine—the modern Sphinx—whose riddle the artist must solve if he would that art live—for his nature holds the key. For one, I promise "whatever gods may be"[1] to lend such energy and purpose as I may possess to help make that meaning plain; to return again and again to the task whenever and wherever need be; for this plain duty is thus relentlessly marked out for the artist in this, the Machine Age, although there is involved an adjustment to cherished gods, perplexing and painful in the extreme the fire of many long-honored ideals shall go down to ashes to reappear, phoenix-like, with new purposes.

The great ethics of the machine are as yet, in the main, beyond the ken of the artist or student of sociology; but the artist mind may now approach the nature of this thing from experience, which has become the commonplace of his field, to suggest, in time, I hope, to prove, that the machine is capable of carrying to fruition high ideals in art—higher than the world has yet seen!

Disciples of William Morris cling to an opposite view. Yet William Morris himself deeply sensed the danger to art of the transforming force whose sign and symbol is the machine, and though of the new art we eagerly seek he sometimes despaired, he quickly renewed his hope.

He plainly foresaw that a blank in the fine arts would follow the inevitable abuse of new-found power and threw himself body and soul into the work of bridging it over by bringing into our lives afresh the beauty of art as she had been, that the new art to come might not have dropped too many stitches nor have unraveled what would still be useful to her.

That he had abundant faith in the new art his every essay will testify.

That he miscalculated the machine does not matter. He did sublime work for it when he pleaded so well for the process of elimination its abuse had made necessary, when he fought the innate vulgarity of theocratic impulse in art as opposed to democratic, and when he preached the gospel of simplicity.

All artists love and honor William Morris.

He did the best in his time for art and will live in history as the great socialist, together with Ruskin the great moralist: significant fact worth thinking about, that the two great reformers of modern times professed the artist.

The machine these reformers protested, because the sort of luxury which is born of greed had usurped it and made of it a terrible engine of enslavement, deluging the civilized world with a murderous ubiquity, which plainly enough was the damnation of their art and craft.

It had not then advanced to the point which now so plainly indicates that it will surely and swiftly, by its own momentum, undo the mischief it has made, and the usurping vulgarians as well.

Nor was it so grown as to become apparent to William Morris, the grand democrat, that the machine was the great forerunner of Democracy.

The ground plan of this thing is now grown to the point where the artist must take it up no longer as a protest: genius must progressively dominate the work of the contrivance it has created; to lend a useful hand in building afresh the "Fairness of the Earth."

That the Machine has dealt Art in the grand old sense a death blow, none will deny.

The evidence is too substantial.

Art in the grand old sense—meaning Art in the sense of structural tradition, whose craft is fashioned upon the handicraft ideal, ancient or modern;

an art wherein this form and that form as structural parts were laboriously joined in such a way as to beautifully emphasize the manner of the joining: the million and one ways of beautifully satisfying bare structural necessities, which have come down to us chiefly through the books as "Art."

For the purpose of suggesting hastily and therefore crudely wherein the machine has sapped the vitality of this art, let us assume Architecture in the old sense as a fitting representative of Traditional art and Printing as a fitting representation of the Machine.

What printing—the machine—has done for architecture—the fine art—will have been done in measure of time for all art immediately fashioned upon the early handicraft ideal.

With a masterful hand, Victor Hugo, a noble lover and a great student of architecture, traces her fall in *Notre-Dame*.

The prophecy of Frollo, that "the book will kill the edifice," I remember was to me as a boy one of the grandest sad things of the world.

After seeking the origin and tracing the growth of architecture in superb fashion, showing how in the Middle Ages all the intellectual forces of the people converged to one point—architecture—he shows how, in the life of that time, "whoever was born poet became an architect. All other arts simply obeyed and placed themselves under the discipline of architecture. They were the workmen of the great work. The architect, the poet, the master summed up in his person the sculpture that carved his façades, painting which illuminated his walls and windows, music which set his bells to pealing and breathed into his organs"—there was nothing which was not forced in order to make something of itself in that time, to come and frame itself in the edifice.

Thus, down to the time of Gutenberg, architecture is the principal writing—the universal writing of humanity.[2]

In the great granite books begun by the Orient, continued by Greek and Roman antiquity, the Middle Ages wrote the last page.

So to enunciate here only summarily a process, it would require volumes to develop; down to the fifteenth century the chief register of humanity is architecture.

In the fifteenth century everything changes.

Human thought discovers a mode of perpetuating itself, not only more resisting than architecture, but still more simple and easy.

Architecture is dethroned.

Gutenberg's letters of lead are about to supersede Orpheus' letters of stone.

The book is about to kill the edifice.

The invention of printing was the greatest event in history.

It was the first great machine, after the great city.

It is human thought stripping off one form and donning another.

Printed, thought is more imperishable than ever—it is volatile, indestructible.

As architecture it was solid; it is now alive; it passes from duration in point of time to immortality.

Cut the primitive bed of a river abruptly, with a canal hollowed out beneath its level, and the river will desert its bed.

See how architecture now withers away, how little by little it becomes lifeless and bare. How one feels the water sinking, the sap departing, the thought of the times and people withdrawing from it. The chill is almost imperceptible in the fifteenth century, the press is yet weak, and at most draws from architecture a superabundance of life, but with the beginning of the sixteenth century, the malady of architecture is visible. It becomes classic art in a miserable manner; from being indigenous, it becomes Greek and Roman; from being true and modern, it becomes pseudo-classic.

It is this decadence which we call the Renaissance.

It is the setting sun which we mistake for dawn.

It has now no power to hold the other arts; so they emancipate themselves, break the yoke of the architect, and take themselves off, each in its own direction.

One would liken it to an empire dismembered at the death of its Alexander, and whose provinces become kingdoms.

Sculpture becomes statuary, the image trade becomes painting, the canon becomes music. Hence Raphael, Angelo, and those splendors of the dazzling sixteenth century.

Nevertheless, when the sun of the Middle Ages is completely set, architecture grows dim, becomes more and more effaced. The printed book, the gnawing worm of the edifice, sucks and devours it. It is petty, it is poor, it is nothing.

Reduced to itself, abandoned by other arts because human thought is abandoning it, it summons bunglers in place of artists. It is miserably perishing.

Meanwhile, what becomes of printing?

All the life, leaving architecture, comes to it. In proportion as architecture ebbs and flows, printing swells and grows. That capital of forces which human thought had been expending in building is hereafter to be expended in books; and architecture, as it was, is dead, irretrievably slain by the printed book; slain because it endures for a shorter time; slain because human thought has found a more simple medium of expression, which costs less in human effort; because human thought has been rendered volatile and indestructible, reaching uniformly and irresistibly the four corners of the earth and for all."

Thenceforth, if architecture rise again, reconstruct, as Hugo prophesies she may begin to do in the latter days of the nineteenth century, she will no longer be mistress, she will be one of the arts, never again *the* art; and printing—the Machine—remains "the second Tower of Babel of the human race."

So the organic process, of which the majestic decline of Architecture is only one case in point, has steadily gone on down to the present time, and still goes on, weakening of the hold of the artist upon the people, drawing off from his rank poets and scientists until architecture is but a little, poor knowledge of archeology, and the average of art is reduced to the gasping poverty of imitative realism; until the whole letter of Tradition, the vast fabric of precedent, in the flesh, which has increasingly confused the art ideal while the machine has been growing to power, is a beautiful corpse from which the spirit has flown. The spirit that has flown is the spirit of the new art, but has failed the modern artist, for he has lost it for hundreds of years in his lust for the *letter,* the beautiful body of art made too available by the machine.

So the Artist craft wanes.

Craft that will not see that "human thought is stripping off one form and donning another," and artists are everywhere, whether catering to the leisure class of old England or ground beneath the heel of commercial abuse here in the great West, the unwilling symptoms of the inevitable, organic nature of the machine, they combat, the hell-smoke of the factories they scorn to understand.

And, invincible, triumphant, the machine goes on, gathering force and knitting the material necessities of mankind ever closer into a universal automatic fabric; the engine, the motor, and the battleship, the works of art of the century!

The Machine is Intellect mastering the drudgery of earth that the plastic art may live; that the margin of leisure and strength by which man's life upon the earth can be made beautiful, may immeasurably widen; its function ultimately to emancipate human expression!

It is a universal educator, surely raising the level of human intelligence, so carrying within itself the power to destroy, by its own momentum, the greed which in Morris' time and still in our own time turns it to a deadly engine of enslavement. The only comfort left the poor artist, sidetracked as he is, seemingly is a mean one; the thought that the very selfishness which man's early art idealized, now reduced to its lowest terms, is swiftly and surely destroying itself through the medium of the Machine.

The artist's present plight is a sad one, but may he truthfully say that society is less well off because Architecture, or even Art, as it was, is dead, and printing, or the Machine, lives?

Every age has done its work, produced its art with the best tools or contrivances it knew, the tools most successful in saving the most precious thing in the world—human effort. Greece used the chattel slave as the essential tool of its art and civilization. This tool we have discarded, and we would refuse the return of Greek art upon the terms of its restoration, because we insist now upon a basis of Democracy.

Is it not more likely that the medium of artistic expression itself has broadened and changed until a new definition and new direction must be given the art-activity of the future, and that the Machine has finally made for the artist, whether he will yet own it or not, a splendid distinction between the Art of old and the Art to come? A distinction made by the tool which frees human labor, lengthens and broadens the life of the simplest man, thereby the basis of the Democracy upon which we insist.

To shed some light upon this distinction, let us take an instance in the field naturally ripened first by the machine—the commercial field.

The tall modern office building is the machine pure and simple.

We may here sense an advanced stage of a condition surely entering all art for all time; its already triumphant glare in the deadly struggle taking place here between the machine and the art of structural tradition reveals "art" torn and hung upon the steel frame of commerce, a forlorn head upon a pike, a solemn warning to architects and artists the world over.

We must walk blindfolded not to see that all that this magnificent resource of machine and material has brought us so far is a complete, broadcast degradation of every type and form sacred to the art of old; a pandemonium of tin masks, huddled deformities, and decayed methods; quarreling, lying, and cheating, with hands at each other's throats—or in each other's pockets; and none of the people who do these things, who pay for them or use them, know what they mean, feeling only—when they feel at all—that what is most truly like the past is the safest and therefore the best; as typical Marshall Field,[3] speaking of his new building, has frankly said: "A good copy is the best we can do."

A pitiful insult, art and craft!

With this mine of industrial wealth at our feet we have no power to use it except to the perversion of our natural resources? A confession of shame which the merciful ignorance of the yet material frame of things mistakes for glorious achievement.

We half believe in our artistic greatness ourselves when we toss up a pantheon to the god of money in a night or two, or pile up a mammoth aggregation of Roman monuments, sarcophagi, and Greek temples for a post office in a year or two—

the patient retinue of the machine pitching in with terrible effectiveness to consummate this unhallowed ambition—this insult to ancient gods. The delicate, impressionable facilities of terra-cotta becoming imitative blocks and voussoirs of tool-marked stone, badgered into all manner of structural gymnastics, or else ignored in vain endeavor to be honest; and granite blocks, cut in the fashion of the followers of Phidias, cunningly arranged about the steel beams and shafts, to look "real"— leaning heavily upon an inner skeleton of steel for support from floor to floor, which strains beneath the "reality" and would fain, I think, lie down to die of shame.

The "masters"—ergo, the fashionable followers of Phidias—have been trying to make this wily skeleton of steel seem seventeen sorts of "architecture" at once, when all the world knows—except the "masters"—that it is not one of them.

See now, how an element—the vanguard of the new art—has entered here, which the structural-art equation cannot satisfy without downright lying and ignoble cheating.

This element is the structural necessity reduced to a skeleton, complete in itself without the craftsman's touch. At once the million and one little ways of satisfying this necessity beautifully, coming to us chiefly through the books as the traditional art of building, vanish away—become history.

The artist is emancipated to work his will with a rational freedom unknown to the laborious art of structural tradition—no longer tied to the meagre unit of brick arch and stone lintel, nor hampered by the grammatical phrase of their making—but he cannot use his freedom.

His tradition cannot think.

He will not think.

His scientific brother has put it to him before he is ready.

The modern tall office-building problem is one representative problem of the machine. The only rational solutions it has received in the world may be counted upon the fingers of one hand. The fact that a great portion of our "architects" and "artists" are shocked by them to the point of offense is as valid objection as that of a child refusing wholesome food because his stomach becomes dyspeptic from over-much unwholesome pastry— albeit he be the cook himself.

We may object to the mannerism of these buildings, but we take no exception to their manner nor hide from their evident truth.

The steel frame has been recognized as a legitimate basis for simple, sincere clothing of plastic material that idealizes its purpose without structural pretense.

This principle has at last been recognized in architecture, and though the masters refuse to accept it as architecture at all it is a glimmer in a darkened field—the first sane word that's been said in Art for the Machine.

The Art of old idealized a Structural Necessity—now rendered obsolete and unnatural by the Machine—and accomplished it through man's joy in the labor of his hands.

The new will weave for the necessities of mankind, which his Machine will have mastered, a robe of ideality no less truthful but more poetical, with a rational freedom made possible by the machine, beside which the art of old will be as the sweet plaintive wail of the pipe to the outpouring of full orchestra.

It will clothe Necessity with the living flesh of virile imagination, as the living flesh lends living grace to the hard and bony human skeleton.

The new will pass from the possession of kings and classes to the everyday lives of all—from duration in point of time to immortality.

This distinction is one to be felt now rather than clearly defined.

The definition is the poetry of this Machine Age, and will be written large in time; but the more we, as artists, examine into this premonition, the more we will find the utter helplessness of old forms to satisfy new conditions, and the crying need of the machine for plastic treatment—a pliant, sympathetic treatment of its needs that the body of structural precedent cannot yield.

To gain further suggestive evidence of this, let us turn to the Decorative Arts—the immense middle ground of all art now mortally sickened by the Machine—sickened that it may slough the art ideal of the constructural art for the plasticity of the new art—the Art of Democracy.

Here we find the most deadly perversion of all—the magnificent prowess of the machine bombarding the civilized world with the mangled corpses of strenuous horrors that once stood for cultivated luxury—standing now for a species of fatty degeneration simply vulgar.

Without regard to first principles or common decency, the whole letter of tradition—that is, ways of doing things rendered wholly obsolete and unnatural by the machine—is recklessly fed into its rapacious maw until you may buy reproductions for ninety-nine cents at "The Fair" that originally cost ages of toil and cultivation, worth now intrinsically nothing—that are harmful parasites befogging the sensibilities of our natures, belittling and falsifying any true perception of normal beauty the Creator may have seen fit to implant in us.

The idea of fitness to purpose, harmony between form, and use with regard to any of these things, is possessed by very few, and utilized by them as a protest chiefly—a protest against the machine!

As well blame Richard Croker[4] for the political iniquity of America.

As "Croker is the creature and not the creator" of political evil, so the machine is the creature and not the creator of this iniquity; and with this difference—that the machine has noble possibilities unwillingly forced to degradation in the name of the artistic; the machine, as far as its artistic capacity is concerned, is itself the crazed victim of the artist who works while he waits, and the artist who waits while he works.

There is a nice distinction between the two.

Neither class will unlock the secrets of the beauty of this time.

They are clinging sadly to the old order and would wheedle the giant frame of things back to its childhood or forward to its second childhood, while this Machine Age is suffering for the artist who accepts, works, and sings as he works, with the joy of the *here* and *now!*

We want the man who eagerly seeks and finds, or blames himself if he fails to find, the beauty of this time; who distinctly accepts as a singer and a prophet; for no man may work while he waits or wait as he works in the sense that William Morris' great work was legitimately done—in the sense that most art and craft of today is an echo; the time when such work was useful has gone.

Echoes are by nature decadent.

Artists who feel toward Modernity and the Machine now as William Morris and Ruskin were justified in feeling then, had best distinctly wait and work sociologically where great work may still be done by them. In the field of art activity they will do distinct harm. Already they have wrought much miserable mischief.

If the artist will only open his eyes he will see that the machine he dreads has made it possible to wipe out the mass of meaningless torture to which mankind, in the name of the artistic, has been more or less subjected since time began; for that matter, has made possible a cleanly strength, an ideality and a poetic fire that the art of the world has not yet seen; for the machine, the process now smooths away the necessity of petty structural deceits, soothes this wearisome struggle to make things seem what they are not, and can never be; satisfies the simple term of the modern art equation as the ball of clay in the sculptor's hand yields to his desire—comforting forever this realistic, brain-sick masquerade we are wont to suppose art.

William Morris pleaded well for simplicity as the basis of all the art. Let us understand the significance to art of that word—SIMPLICITY—for it is vital to the Art of the Machine.

We may find, in place of the genuine thing we have striven for, an affectation of the naive, which we should detest as we detest a full-grown woman with baby mannerisms.

English art is saturated with it, from the brand-new imitation of the old house that grew and rambled from period to period to the rain-tub standing beneath the eaves.

In fact, most simplicity following the doctrines of William Morris is a protest; as a protest, well enough, but the highest form of simplicity is not simple in the sense that the infant intelligence is simple—nor, for that matter, the side of a barn.

A natural revulsion of feeling leads us from the meaningless elaboration of today to lay too great stress on mere platitudes, quite as a clean sheet of paper is a relief after looking at a series of bad drawings—but simplicity is not merely a neutral or a negative quality.

Simplicity in art, rightly understood, is a synthetic, positive quality, in which we may see evidence of mind, breadth of scheme, wealth of detail, and withal a sense of completeness found in a tree or a flower. A work may have the delicacies of a rare orchid or the stanch fortitude of the oak, and still be simple. A thing to be simple needs only to be true to itself in organic sense.

With this ideal of simplicity, let us glance hastily at a few instances of the machine and see how it has been forced by false ideals to do violence to this simplicity; how it has made possible the highest simplicity, rightly understood and so used. As perhaps wood is most available of all homely materials and therefore, naturally, the most abused— let us glance at wood.

Machinery has been invented for no other purpose than to imitate, as closely as possible, the wood carving of the early ideal—with the immediate result that no ninety-nine-cent piece of furniture is salable without some horrible botchwork meaning nothing unless it means that art and craft have combined to fix in the mind of the masses the old hand-carved chair as the *ne plus ultra* of the ideal.

The miserable, lumpy tribute to this perversion which Grand Rapids alone yields would mar the face of art beyond repair; to say nothing of the elaborate and fussy joinery of posts, spindles, jig-sawed beams and braces, butted and strutted, to outdo the sentimentality of the already over-wrought antique product.

Thus is the woodworking industry glutted, except in rarest instances. The whole sentiment of early craft degenerated to a sentimentality having no longer decent significance nor commercial integrity; in fact all that is fussy, maudlin, and animal, basing its existence chiefly on vanity and ignorance.

Now let us learn from the Machine.

It teaches us that the beauty of wood lies first in its qualities as wood; no treatment that did not bring out these qualities all the time could be plastic, and therefore not appropriate—so not beautiful, the Machine teaches us, if we have left it to the machine that certain simple forms and handling are suitable to bring out the beauty of wood and certain forms are not; that all wood carving is apt to be a forcing of the material, an insult to its finer possibilities as a material having in itself intrinsically artistic properties, of which its beautiful markings is one, its texture another, its color a third.

The machine, by its wonderful cutting, shaping, smoothing, and repetitive capacity, has made it possible to so use it without waste that the poor as well as the rich may enjoy today beautiful surface treatments of clean, strong forms that the branch veneers of Sheraton and Chippendale only hinted at, with dire extravagance, and which the Middle Ages utterly ignored.

The machine has emancipated these beauties of nature in wood; made it possible to wipe out the mass of meaningless torture to which wood has been subjected since the world began, for it has been universally abused and maltreated by all peoples but the Japanese.

Rightly appreciated, is not this the very process of elimination for which Morris pleaded?

Not alone a protest, moreover, for the machine, considered only technically, if you please, has placed in artist hands the means of idealizing the true nature of wood harmoniously with man's spiritual and material needs, without waste, within reach of all.

And how fares the troop of old materials galvanized into new life by the Machine?

Our modern materials are these old materials in more plastic guise, rendered so by the Machine, itself creating the very quality needed in material to satisfy its own art equation.

We have seen in glancing at modern architecture how they fare at the hands of Art and Craft; divided and subdivided in orderly sequence with rank and file of obedient retainers awaiting the master's behest.

Steel and iron, plastic cement, and terra-cotta.

Who can sound the possibilities of this old material, burned clay, which the modern machine has rendered as sensitive to the creative brain as a dry plate to the lens—a marvelous simplifier? And this plastic covering material, cement, another simplifier, enabling the artist to clothe the structural frame with a simple, modestly beautiful robe where before he dragged in, as he does still drag, five different kinds of material to compose one little cottage, pettily arranging it in an aggregation supposed to be picturesque—as a matter of fact, millinery, to be warped and beaten by sun, wind, and rain into a variegated heap of trash.

There is the process of modern casting in metal—one of the perfected modern machines, capable of any form to which fluid will flow, to perpetuate the imagery of the most delicately poetic mind without let or hindrance—within reach of everyone, therefore insulted and outraged by the bungler forcing it to a degraded seat at his degenerate festival.

Multitudes of processes are expectantly awaiting the sympathetic interpretation of the mastermind; the galvano-plastic and its electrical brethren, a prolific horde, now cheap fakirs imitating real bronzes and all manner of the antique, secretly damning it in their vitals.

Electro-glazing, a machine shunned because too cleanly and delicate for the clumsy hand of the traditional designer, who depends upon the mass and blur of leading to conceal his lack of touch.

That delicate thing, the lithograph—the prince of a whole reproductive province of processes—see what this process becomes in the hands of a master like Whistler. He has sounded but one note in the gamut of its possibilities, but that product is intrinsically true to the process, and as delicate as the butterfly's wing. Yet the most this particular machine did for us, until then in the hands of Art and Craft, was to give us a cheap, imitative effect of painting.

So spins beyond our ability to follow tonight, a rough, feeble thread of the evidence at large to the effect that the machine has weakened the artist; all but destroyed his handmade art, if not its ideals, although he has made enough miserable mischief meanwhile.

These evident instances should serve to hint, at least to the thinking mind, that the Machine is a marvelous simplifier; the emancipator of the creative mind, and in time the regenerator of the creative conscience. We may see that this destructive process has begun and is taking place that art might awaken to that power of fully developed senses promised by dreams of its childhood, even though that power may not come the way it was pictured in those dreams.

Now, let us ask ourselves whether the fear of the higher artistic expression demanded by the Machine, so thoroughly grounded in the arts and crafts, is founded upon a finely guarded reticence, a recognition of inherent weakness or plain ignorance!

Let us, to be just, assume that it is equal parts of all three, and try to imagine an Arts and Crafts Society that may educate itself to prepare to make some good impression upon the Machine, the destroyer of their present ideals and tendencies, their salvation in disguise.

Such a society will, of course, be a society for mutual education.

Exhibitions will not be a feature of its programme for years, for there will be nothing to exhibit except the shortcomings of the society, and they will hardly prove either instructive or amusing at this stage of proceedings. This society must, from the very nature of the proposition, be made up of the people who are in the work—that is, the manufacturers—coming into touch with such of those who assume the practice of the fine arts as profess a fair sense of the obligation to the public such assumption carries with it, and sociological workers whose interest are ever closely allied with art, as their prophets Morris, Ruskin, and Tolstoy evince, and all those who have as personal graces and accomplishment perfected handicraft, whether fashion old or fashion new.

Without the interest and cooperation of the manufacturers, the society cannot begin to do its work, for this is the cornerstone of its organization.

All these elements should be brought together on a common ground of confessed ignorance, with a desire to be instructed, freely encouraging talk and opinions, and reaching out desperately for anyone who has special experience in any way connected to address them.

I suppose, first of all, the thing would resemble a debating society, or something even less dignified, until someone should suggest that it was time to quit talking and proceed to do something, which in this case would not mean giving an exhibition, but rather excursions to factories and a study of processes in place—that is, the machine in processes too numerous to mention, at the factories with the men who organize and direct them, but not in the spirit of the idea that these things are all gone wrong, looking for that in them which would most nearly approximate the handicraft ideal; not looking into them with even the thought of handicraft, and not particularly looking for craftsmen, but getting a scientific ground plan of the process in mind, if possible, with a view to its natural bent and possibilities.

Some processes and machines would naturally appeal to some, and some to others; there would undoubtedly be among us those who would find little joy in any of them.

This is, naturally, not child's play, but neither is the work expected of the modern artist.

I will venture to say, from personal observation and some experience, that not one artist in one hundred has taken pains to thus educate himself. I will go further and say what I believe to be true, that not one educational institution in America has as yet attempted to forge the connecting link between Science and Art by training the artist to his actual tools, or, by a process of nature-study that develops in him the power of independent thought, fitting him to use them properly.

Let us call these preliminaries then a process by which artists receive information nine-tenths of them lack concerning the tools they have to work with today—for tools today are processes and machines where they were once a hammer and a gouge.

The artist today is the leader of an orchestra, where he once was a star performer.

Once the manufacturers are convinced of due respect and appreciation on the part of the artist, they will welcome him and his counsel gladly and make any experiments having a grain of apparent sense in them.

They have little patience with a bothering about in endeavor to see what might be done to

A. K. McAfee House (Project). Kenilworth, Illinois. 1894. Perspective. Watercolor and watercolor wash on art paper, 29 x 10".
FLLW Fdn#9407.001

make their particular machine medieval and restore man's joy in the mere work of his hands—for this once lovely attribute is far behind.

This proceeding doubtless would be of far more educational value to the artist than to the manufacturer, at least for some time to come, for there would be a difficult adjustment to make on the part of the artist and an attitude to change. So many artists are chiefly "attitude" that some would undoubtedly disappear with the attitude.

But if out of twenty determined students a ray of light should come to one, to light up a single operation, it would have been worthwhile, for that would be fairly something; while joy in mere handicraft is like that of the man who played the piano for his own amusement—a pleasurable personal accomplishment without real relation to the grim condition confronting us.

Granting that a determined, dauntless body of artist material could be brought together with sufficient persistent enthusiasm to grapple with the Machine, would not someone be found who would provide the suitable experimental station (which is what the modern Arts and Crafts shop should be)—an experimental station that would represent in miniature the elements of this great pulsating web of the machine, where each pregnant process or significant tool in printing, lithography, galvano-electro processes, wood and steel working machinery, muffles and kilns would have its place and where the best young scientific blood could mingle with the best and truest artistic inspiration, to sound the depths of these things, to accord them the patient, sympathetic treatment that is their due?

Surely a thing like this would be worthwhile—to alleviate the insensate numbness of the poor fellows out in the cold, hard shops, who know not why nor understand, whose dutiful obedience is chained to botch work and bungler's ambition; surely this would be a practical means to make their dutiful obedience give us something we can all understand, and that will be as normal to the best of this machine age as a ray of light to the healthy eye; a real help in adjusting the *Man* to a true sense of his importance as a factor in society, though he does tend a machine.

Teach him that that machine is his best friend—will have widened the margin of his leisure until enlightenment shall bring him a further sense of the magnificent ground plan of progress in which he too justly plays his significant part.

If the art of the Greek, produced at such cost of human life, was so noble and enduring, what limit dare we now imagine to an Art based upon an adequate life for the individual?

The machine is his!

In due time it will come to him!

Meanwhile, who shall count the slain?

From where are the trained nurses in this industrial hospital to come if not from the modern arts and crafts?

Shelley says a man cannot say—"I will compose poetry." "The greatest poet even cannot say it, for the mind in creation is as a fading coal which some invisible influence, like an inconstant wind awakens to transitory brightness; this power arises from within like the color of a flower which fades and changes as it is developed, and the conscious portions of our nature are unprophetic either of its approach or its departure"; and yet in the arts and crafts the problem is presented as a more or less fixed quantity, highly involved, requiring a surer touch, a more highly disciplined artistic nature to organize it as a work of art.

The original impulses may reach as far inward as those of Shelley's poet, be quite as wayward a matter of pure sentiment, and yet after the thing is done, showing its rational qualities, are limited in completeness only by the capacity of whoever would show them or by the imperfection of the thing itself.

This does not mean that Art may be shown to be an exact Science.

"It is not pure reason, but it is always reasonable."

It is a matter of perceiving and portraying the harmony of organic tendencies; is originally intuitive because the artist nature is a prophetic gift that may sense these qualities afar.

To me, the artist is he who can truthfully idealize the common sense of these tendencies in his chosen way.

So I feel conception and composition to be simply the essence of refinement in organization, the original impulse of which may be registered by the artistic nature as unconsciously as the magnetic needle vibrates to the magnetic law, but which is, in synthesis or analysis, organically consistent, given the power to see it or not.

And I have come to believe that the world of Art, which we are so fond of calling the world outside of Science, is not so much outside as it is the very heart quality of this great material growth—as religion is its conscience.

A foolish heart and a small conscience.

A foolish heart, palpitating in alarm, mistaking the growing pains of its giant frame for approaching dissolution, whose sentimentality the lusty body of modern things has outgrown.

Upon this faith in Art as the organic heart quality of the scientific frame of things, I base a belief that we must look to the artist brain, of all brains, to grasp the significance to society of this thing we call the Machine, if that brain be not blinded, gagged, and bound by false tradition, the letter of precedent. For this thing we call Art is it not as prophetic as a primrose or an oak? Therefore, of the essence of this thing we call the Machine, which is no more or less than the principle of organic growth working irresistibly the Will of Life through the medium of Man.

Be gently lifted at nightfall to the top of a great downtown office building, and you may see how in the image of material man, at once his glory and menace, is this thing we call a city.

There beneath, grown up in a night, is the monster leviathan, stretching acre upon acre into the far distance. High overhead hangs the stagnant pall of its fetid breath, reddened with the light from its myriad eyes endlessly everywhere blinking. Ten thousand acres of cellular tissue, layer upon layer, the city's flesh, outspreads enmeshed by intricate network of veins and arteries, radiating into the gloom, and there with muffled, persistent roar, pulses and circulates as the blood in your veins, the ceaseless beat of the activity to whose necessities it all conforms.

Like to the sanitation of the human body is the drawing off of poisonous waste from the system of this enormous creature; absorbed first by the infinitely ramifying, threadlike ducts gathering at their sensitive terminals matter destructive to its life, hurrying it to millions of small intestines, to be collected in turn by larger, flowing to the great sewer, on to the drainage canal, and finally to the ocean.

This ten thousand acres of fleshlike tissue is again knit and interknit with a nervous system marvelously complete, delicate filaments for hearing, knowing, almost feeling the pulse of its organism, acting upon the ligaments and tendons for motive impulse, in all flowing the impelling fluid of man's own life.

Its nerve ganglia!—the peerless Corliss tandems whirling their hundred ton fly-wheels, fed by gigantic rows of water-tube boilers burning oil, a solitary man slowly pacing backward and forward, regulating here and there the little feed valves controlling the deafening roar of the flaming gas, while beyond, the incessant clicking, dropping, waiting—lifting, waiting, shifting of the governor gear controlling these modern Goliaths seems a visible brain in intelligent action, registered infallibly in the enormous magnets, purring in the giant embrace of great induction coils, generating the vital current meeting with instant response in the rolling cars on elevated tracks ten miles away, where the glare of the Bessemer steel converter makes a conflagration of the clouds.

More quietly still, whispering down the long, low rooms of factory buildings buried in the gloom beyond, range on range of stanch, beautifully perfected automatons, murmur contentedly with occasional click-clack, that would have the American manufacturing industry of five years ago by the throat today manipulating steel as delicately as a mystical shuttle of the modern loom manipulates a silk thread in the shimmering pattern of a dainty gown.

And the heavy breathing, the murmuring, the clangor, and the roar!—how the voice of this monstrous thing, this greatest of machines, a great city, rises to proclaim the marvel of the units of its structure, the ghastly warning boom from the deep throats of vessels heavily seeking inlet to the waterway below, answered by the echoing clangor of the bridge bells growing nearer and more ominous as the vessel cuts momentarily the flow of the nearer artery, warning the current from the swinging bridge now closing on its stately passage, just in time to receive in a rush of steam, as a streak of light, the avalanche of blood and metal hurled across it and gone, roaring into the night on its glittering bands of steel, ever faithfully encircled by the slender magic lines tick-tapping its invincible protection.

Nearer, in the building ablaze with midnight activity, the wide white band streams into the marvel of the multiple press, receiving unerringly the indelible impression of the human hopes, joys, and fears throbbing in the pulse of this great activity, as infallibly as the gray matter of the human brain receives the impression of the senses, to come forth millions of neatly folded, perfected news sheets, teeming with vivid appeals to passions, good or evil; weaving a web of intercommunication so far-reaching that distance becomes as nothing, the thought of one man in one corner of the earth one day visible to the naked eye of all men the next; the doings of all the world reflected as in a glass, so marvelously sensitive this wide white band streaming endlessly from day to day becomes in the grasp of the multiple press.

If the pulse of activity in this great city, to which the tremor of the mammoth skeleton beneath our feet is but an awe-inspiring response, is thrilling, what of this prolific, silent obedience?

And the texture of the tissue of this great thing, this Forerunner of Democracy, the Machine, has been deposited particle by particle, in blind obedience to organic law, the law to which the great solar universe is but an obedient machine.

Thus is the thing into which the forces of Art are to breathe the thrill of ideality! A SOUL!

1. From *Invictus*, by Willian Ernst Henley.

2. From this paragraph, through the next twenty–three paragraphs Wright has paraphrased Victor Hugo's "The One Will Kill the Other" from *The Hunchback of Notre-Dame*.

3. Marshall Field (1834–1906), a Chicago merchant, commissioned both Henry Hobson Richardson and the firm of D.H. Burnham and Co. to design his stores. Richardson's wholesale store of 1885 is a building many critics consider to be one of the greatest of the nineteenth century. Field's comment, therefore, probably relates to the later Burnham building. Richardson's untimely death at the age of 48 in 1886 forced Field to choose a new architect.

4. Richard Croker (1841–1922) a New York politician of Irish birth, who rose to Tammany leadership in the mid-1880s.

THE VILLAGE BANK SERIES

The dates given to this project are ambiguous. Wright published the design in The Brickbuilder *magazine in 1901, but later assigned the date of 1894 to an early scheme of this mono-material building. The 1901 date is probably more accurate. There is, however, a manuscript in the archives—believed to be the original text—with Wright's handwritten note at the top, "Script to go with design for a bank building." In* The Brickbuilder *the building is described as a brick structure, but word for word the text is the same, except for the description of the brick, where the manuscript reads:*

> *The building is cast as a monolith in cement, the mold being constructed of wood, with waterproof paper linings; plaster molds combined with the wood where surfaces are ornamented, suitable joints being provided to take care of shrinkage, and perforated metal covers imbedded in the cement at proper intervals. These joints would occur at structural lines of the building and not appear as a feature of the design in this case, although they might well do so. Or, if for some strange reason this is not deemed conservative, terra-cotta and brick, or brick and bronze, would answer excellently well.*

> *In France, Auguste Perret's building projects in cast concrete began in 1903 with the construction of an apartment house at 25b rue Franklin, in Paris. The French architects and builders of reinforced concrete buildings faced the problem of the steel support structure becoming susceptible to rust because of the porous nature of poured concrete. For this reason, builders often surfaced the concrete with other, nonporous materials. In his version of the bank as a monolithic structure in concrete, Wright let the cast concrete become the aesthetic of the building, much as he would do, even more eloquently, in Unity Temple three years later. [Published with three illustrations in* The Brickbuilder, *August 1901]*

WHILE THERE IS PROBABLY LITTLE ROMANCE ABOUT A bank—less poetry in the bray of Sancho Panza's substantial, positive gray donkey than in the sound of Rosinante's spirited neighing—yet the community likes to feel that this same bank is there to stay. It is, in fact, the town strongbox, and it is a temple to the God of Money, as modern temples go. In its temples, though they perform the function of modern mercantile machines, the community would find the lack of some attempt at ideal enrichment intolerably offensive. Just what this ingrained human love of ornament is, is not clear—not yet. Though

Monolithic Bank (Project). 1894. Perspective. Ink on art paper, 18 x 11". FLLW Fdn#9408.001

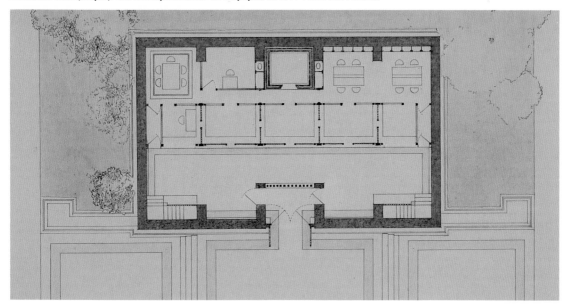

Monolithic Bank (Project). 1894. Plan. Ink on art paper, 22 x 12". FLLW Fdn#9408.003

this love is more indiscriminate than ever, more easily satisfied with meretricious gewgaws and meaningless signs and symbols, we may be thankful that we still possess it, for back of it are probably the only instincts that make life bearable or desirable.

This design has taken shape with some conception of the dignified character of the mercantile machine, and some concession to the time-honored love of ornament, with a monumental and significant simplicity arbitrarily associated in the popular mind, perhaps, with a tomb or a mausoleum. Most mausoleums are neither monumental nor significant, unless they are monuments to the well-meaning ignorance of their builders, and significant of a cold, stupid horror of death. The whole genus "monument," as we build it in our cemeteries, rests upon a false basis—a memorial is better.

The plan is intended to satisfy the necessities of the average banking business in a direct way, without waste space or waste motion. The entrance (and it is the only entrance) is barred with bronze gates closing over bronze doors, one of which would remain open during banking hours; as both bear the legend of the bank, one would always be in place to advertise its function. This matter of advertising, as usually practiced, seems better adapted to the handling of a three-ring circus than the handling of a dignified institution.

Within these doors there is a vestibule of glass and bronze, and the customer is compelled, by the swinging of the doors, to enter at one side and leave at the other. The public is thus thrown directly to the tellers and clerks. The cashier is located to the left, although the plan might better be reversed to keep the custom of moving to the right. The cashier uses the director's room, which is ceiled with glass, as a consulting room. The stenographers' room also is conveniently connected.

All this machinery, including the vault, is kept down to the height of the top of the screen, and the screen presents a solid front to the public. A door is left at either end—one for customers, cashier, and directors, and the other for clerks, all coming and going through the one doorway to the street.

Stairs are provided on either side of the entrance to supposed safety deposit vaults below, artificially lighted and ventilated. This provision for the deposit vaults presupposes a clerk below; in a village bank probably a luxury. The stairs could be moved within the control of the machinery, behind the screen if necessary.

This machinery is lighted overhead and ventilated from above, as shown in the section; the windows at the sides passing free behind the caps, as a screen of bronze frames, sash, and glass. The interior walls are lined with a mosaic of enameled ceramic work laid in broad panels marked by simple tines of gold mosaic, and the screen is to be constructed of terra-cotta and antique bronze, the terra-cotta being worked out in a soft Pompeiian red, and the bronze finished in verdigris. The building is constructed entirely of brick. The ornamental members throughout are of terra-cotta, except the windowsills and the caps, which are cast in bronze and, finished in antique verdegris. The floors in the public space are laid with a mosaic of unglazed ceramic. The design makes use of the structural feature of the piers carrying ceiling beams of the long span as the decorative element providing the enrichment of the façades, and this feature is merged with the gently sloping walls in eminently plastic fashion.

PROGRAM

The problem is to be treated primarily from a picturesque standpoint. The building is assumed to cost in the vicinity of twenty-five to thirty thousand dollars and be only one story in height, the interior arranged for a main banking room, a small consulting room, a director's room about 12 by 14 ft., a vault measuring outside of the brick walls 8 by 10 ft., and any other interior arrangements which may seem suitable. The main entrance is to be preceded by a small vestibule, and the building itself should be set back not less than 10 ft. from the street line and be isolated on all sides. The site is supposed to be a level one, and the bank will be in close proximity to the public library, the village church, the schoolhouse, and the courthouse, which together will form the center of a town of a few thousand inhabitants. The design is to be of such nature as is suitable for being carried out in burnt-clay products.—Editor's note in *The Brickbuilder*

A HOME IN A PRAIRIE TOWN

The Curtis Publishing Company, publishers of The Ladies' Home Journal, *four times commissioned Frank Lloyd Wright to design custom houses for publication in the magazine: in 1901, two designs were prepared, followed by a new design in 1907, and then another in 1945. The first two are included here, along with the texts the architect wrote to accompany them. "A Home in a Prairie Town" also included a proposal for a quadruple block plan with four houses, each placed in such a way as to take maximum advantage of the block site by using lawns and gardens to surround the houses and by positioning on each side of the house driveways leading to a central cluster of garages and carriage houses. This design was later adapted by Wright for his contribution to the publication* City Residential Land Development—Studies in Planning *by Alfred Yeomens (University of Chicago Press, 1916).*

The general features and particular details that were designed and published in February 1901 under the title "A Home in a Prairie Town" set forth the type of house that Wright was creating for the Midwest prairie. Windows are long bands of open swinging sash, set well in and under generous, protecting, overhanging roofs. The chimneys are broad and low, rather than the high, slender, precarious stacks common at the time. The roof line is likewise broad and low; combined with terrace walls, it accentuates the sense of the horizontal ground line that Wright found so pleasing on the prairie. [Published with five illustrations in The Ladies' Home Journal, *February 1901]*

A CITY MAN GOING TO THE COUNTRY PUTS TOO MUCH IN his house and too little in his ground. He drags after him the fifty-foot lot, soon the twenty-five foot lot, finally the party wall; and the homemaker who fully appreciates the advantages which he came to the country to secure feels himself impelled to move on.

It seems a waste of energy to plan a house haphazard, to hit or miss an already distorted condition, so this partial solution of a city man's country home on the prairie begins at the beginning and assumes four houses to the block of four hundred feet square as the minimum of ground for the basis of his prairie community.

"A Home in a Prairie Town" for *The Ladies' Home Journal* (Project). 1900. Perspective. Watercolor and watercolor wash on art paper, 25 x 15". FLLW Fdn#0007.001

The block plan to the left, at the top of the page, shows an arrangement of the four houses that secures breadth and prospect to the community as a whole and absolute privacy both as regards each to the community and each to each of the four.

The perspective view shows the handling of the groups at the center of the block, with its foil of simple lawn (omitting the foliage of curb parkways to better show the scheme and retaining the same house in the four locations merely to afford an idea of the unity of the various elevations). In practice, the houses would differ distinctly, though based upon a similar plan.

The ground plan, which is intended to explain itself, is arranged to offer the least resistance to a simple mode of living, in keeping with a high ideal of the family life together. It is arranged, too, with a certain well-established order that enables free use without the sense of confusion felt in five out of seven houses which people really use.

The exterior recognizes the influence of the prairie, is firmly and broadly associated with the site, and makes a feature of its quiet level. The low terraces and broad eaves are designed to accentuate that quiet level and complete the harmonious relationship. The curbs of the terraces and formal enclosures for extremely informal masses of foliage and bloom should be worked in cement with the walks and drives.

Cement on metal lath is suggested for the exterior covering throughout, because it is simple, and, as now understood, durable and cheap.

The cost of this house with interior as specified and cement construction would be seven thousand dollars:

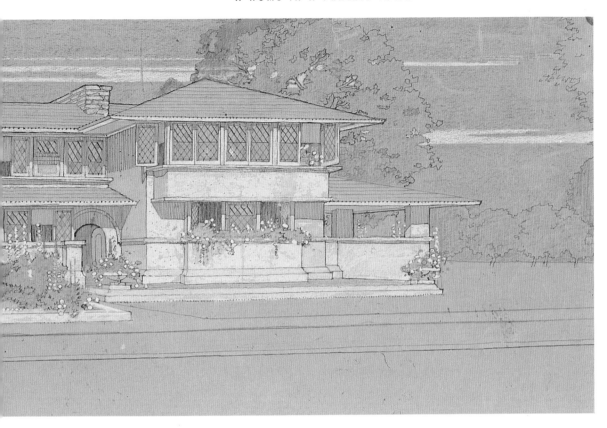

Masonry, Cement, and Plaster $2800.00
Carpentry 3100.00
Plumbing 400.00
Painting and Glass 325.00
Heating—combination (hot water .) . . . . . <u>345.00</u>
Total $6970.00

In a house of this character the upper reach and gallery of the central living room is decidedly a luxury. Two bedrooms may take its place, as suggested by the second-floor plan. The gallery feature is, nevertheless, a temptation because of the happy sense of variety and depth it lends to the composition of the interior and the sunlight it gains from above to relieve the shadow of the porch. The details are better grasped by a study of the drawings. The interior section in perspective shows the gallery as indicated by dotted lines on the floor plan of the living room.

The second-floor plan disregards this feature and is arranged for a larger family. Where three bedrooms would suffice, the gallery would be practicable, and two large and two small bedrooms with the gallery might be had by rearranging servants' rooms and baths.

The interior is plastered throughout with sand finish and trimmed all through with flat bands of Georgia pine, smaller back bands following the base and casings. This Georgia pine should be selected from straight grain for stiles, rails, and running members and from figured grain for panels and wide surfaces. All the wood should be shellacked once and waxed, and the plaster should be stained with thin, pure color in water and glue.

A SMALL HOUSE WITH "LOTS OF ROOM IN IT"

The house published in July 1901 under the title "A Small House with 'Lots of Room in It'" was very similar to the house Wright built the same year for Warren Hickox in Kankakee, Illinois. This house and neighboring, but larger, B. Harley Bradley house, can be considered the prototypes for many prairie homes that followed. They also represented the type of house Wright was designing for the moderately affluent in and around Chicago's suburbs. [Published with six illustrations in The Ladies' Home Journal, *July 1901]*

THE AVERAGE HOMEMAKER IS PARTIAL TO THE GABLE ROOF. This house has been designed with a thorough, somewhat new treatment of the gable with gently flaring eaves and pediments, slightly lifted at the peaks, accentuating the perspective, slightly modeling the roof surfaces, and making the outlines "crisp."

The plan disregards somewhat the economical limit in compact planning to take advantage of light, air, and prospect, the enjoyable things one goes to the suburbs to secure. With modern systems of heating, a distinct freedom in arrangement, denied to earlier builders, is made not only possible, but may be made comfortable with modest outlay. Two large rooms, with an entry performing the function of a little, formal social office, or a waiting-room, to relieve the living room of undesirable pressure, together with a simple arrangement of stairs and a working department, make up the scheme of the main floor.

In this case, the dining room is made the "feature," with a little indoor garden closing the perspective at its farther end. The dining table commands the outdoor garden at the rear, and the low windows on the gallery to the street front, the whole countering upon a simple fireplace of brick, which combines with the comfortable breadth of fireplace in the living room. The dining room is so coupled with the living room that one leads naturally into the other without destroying the privacy of either.

The living room is still the heart of the house and has access to both gallery and terrace and gives an interesting glimpse of entry and stair landing.

The working department is roomy and convenient. The range is set within a brick-lined, brick-floored alcove, formed by the two fireplaces, the space overhead ventilated into a chimney flue. The servants' stairway reaches the landing of the main stairway, and the servants' room and bath are situated over this landing, midway between the second and attic floors. The kitchen entry is from the side, and combines with the cellarway to avoid unsightly excrescences.

As the house is free in arrangement and the main rooms large, a simplicity of material and treatment is necessary. The exterior is plastered with cement plaster. The interior, trimmed with Georgia

"A Small House with 'Lots of Room in It'" for *The Ladies' Home Journal* (Project). 1900. Perspective. Ink on paper, 30 x 11".
FLLW Fdn#0008.001

pine, without moldings, put on over rough plaster, together with the Georgia pine floors, is to be stained one coat. The outside woodwork, except shingles, is also to be stained. Paint and varnish are not used.

A combination hot-water apparatus would serve to heat the house perfectly, hot air in the main body of the house and radiation in the dining room and entry.

The cost of the house proper, exclusive of grading and walks, would approximate:

Masonry and Stone Water-Table $1100.00
Plastering 600.00
Carpentry and Hardware. 2950.00
Heating 375.00
Plumbing, Sewer, and Gas Fitting 450.00
Staining and Glass 300.00
Electric Wiring 60.00
Total $5835.00

The block plans at the lower corners of the page show two schemes for placing the house upon an inside, one-hundred-foot lot. One, as shown in perspective view, broad side to the street; the other alongside the depth of the lot.

HIROSHIGE

京都名所
四條河原
夕涼

Ando Hiroshige (1797–1858), "The Cool of the Evening, Shijo Kawara," from *Famous Views of Kyōto*. 1835.
Woodblock print on Japanese paper: Oban, 15 x 10". FLLW Fdn Collection#3103.029

No one has yet been able to determine exactly when Wright's interest in Japan and Japanese prints began, but by 1906 he had amassed a sizable print collection.[1] There was a coterie of established print collectors in Chicago long before then, however; notably, Clarence Buckingham (1854–1913) and Frederick Gookin (1853–1936).[2] It seems likely, through connections with the Art Institute, that Wright and these men were known to each other.[3]

Wright probably began his own collecting soon after he opened his architectural practice in 1893.[4] He purchased more prints, kakemono, and folding screens on his first voyage to Japan in 1905. In March of the following year the Art Institute mounted an exhibition of his prints (later sold to Buckingham) by the artist Hiroshige, the accompanying catalog consisting of a list of the prints and the brief introduction republished here. This text constitutes the first of a series of articles Wright wrote concerning Japanese woodblock prints and the arts of Japan.

Ando Hiroshige (1797–1858), "Whirlpool at Awa" from *Famous Views of the Sixty Odd Provinces.* **1853.**
Woodblock print on Japanese paper: Oban, 10 x 15". FLLW Fdn Collection#3103.017

Two years later, in 1908, Wright collaborated with Gookin on the design of a much larger Japanese print exhibition at the Art Institute, for which he selected special wall colors, frames, and cords to complement the much broader spectrum of print artists included at that time.

Wright stated again and again that it was the simplicity of the prints—"the elimination of the insignificant"—and their underlying geometry that first attracted him. These same principles were critical to his architectural philosophy, and he would often use the prints to illustrate his arguments. [Published as a catalog without illustrations by The Art Institute of Chicago, 1906]

So obscure is the origin of the mass of work bearing the name of Hiroshige; so conflicting and useless is most so-called expert testimony concerning the chronology and proper assignation of the color prints here represented to a single artist or group of artists, that attributions of this nature can be little better than speculation. The real virtue of the work is none the less apparent and qualified to speak for itself; for properly considered it is the art not of a Hiroshige merely but of a people.

The appeal that it makes is a spiritual one unlikely to be heard by Western materialism with more than amused tolerance. It is too restrained, too chaste, for our immediate comprehension. It has little in common with the literal. It is far removed from literature. It is in kind a delicate musical instrument that has no need of lifted dampers nor loud pedals, nor does it need fleshly shade nor materialistic shadow. It is in itself a pure, loving sentiment, reserved and restrained as Shinto, serene as Buddhism.

The phase of art presented in this collection is that of the artisan class, the common people in the strict sense of the term, and attests the infinite delight, the inherent poetic grace not of the Japanese nobleman but of the hard-worked humble son of Nippon of seventy-five years ago. His face was deeply furrowed with pleasant lines and tanned the texture and color of brown leather; he wore out patiently and soon—yet this art, in which he found delight, shows that he was a MAN—not a slave!

This proof of spiritual quality so near to the heart of a people who have made a harmonious unit of their land and their life becomes daily more precious as our own pet commercial expedients sweep it forever into a past, fast becoming dim—never to be reclaimed. Entirely lost it will never be for already it is become a timely ferment in the artist mind of our own epoch. It is no longer the sequestered art of an isolated people but one of the most valuable contributions ever made to the art of the world.

1. Wright is known to have attended the 1893 Columbian Exposition, where the Japanese exhibit is said to have included a selection of prints. It has also been suggested that Joseph Lyman Silsbee, Wright's first Chicago employer, was a collector of "Orientalia" (Grant Manson, *Frank Lloyd Wright to 1910*, New York: Van Nostrand, 1958, p. 33), in which case Wright's introduction to prints could have been as early as the late 1880s.
2. Gookin is said to have begun collecting in the 1880s and Buckingham in the 1890s. Both men participated in the historic Japanese woodblock print exhibition at the Grolier Club in New York in 1896 (Julia Meech-Pekarik, "Frank Lloyd Wright's Other Passion," *The Nature of Frank Lloyd Wright*. Chicago: University of Chicago Press, 1988, p.130).
3. Wright first exhibited his work at the Art Institute, under the auspices of the Architectural Club, in 1894. Presumably, such preeminent collectors as Gookin and Buckingham would have had museum associations. Buckingham became, if he was not already at such an early date, a trustee of the Institute. Gookin was appointed the curator of the Buckingham collection, which was bequeathed to the Art Institute in 1913.
4. Several historic photographs of the late 1890s in the Frank Lloyd Wright Archives show prints displayed in Wright's home.

A FIREPROOF HOUSE FOR $5,000

Poured concrete as a mono-material in building was relatively new in 1906. Frank Lloyd Wright had used it splendidly in Unity Temple in Oak Park, Illinois, that year, and here he proposed its use for a residential design. Its particular advantage, he argued, was to render a building fireproof. The Curtis Publishing Company commissioned the design and this accompanying article. [Published with three illustrations in The Ladies' Home Journal, *April 1907]*

THE COST OF BUILDING HAS INCREASED NEARLY 40 PERCENT in the past six years. The thirty-five-hundred-dollar house of six years ago would cost nearly five thousand dollars now; so at the present time it would seem that five thousand dollars ought to represent a low enough cost standard, if the result be permanent and the cost of maintenance lessened.

Changing industrial conditions have brought reinforced concrete construction within the reach of the average homemaker. The maximum strength peculiar to the nature of both concrete and steel is in this system utilized with great economy. A structure of this type is more enduring than if carved intact from solid stone, for it is not only a masonry monolith but it is interlaced with steel fibers as well. Insulated with an impervious non-conducting inner coating it is damp-proof; it is, too, warmer than a wooden house in winter and cooler in summer.

The plan for a small house of this type, submitted here, is the result of a process of elimination due to much experience in planning the inexpensive house. What remains seems sufficiently complete and the ensemble an improvement over the usual cut-up, overtrimmed boxes doing duty in this class, wherein architecture is a matter of "millwork" and the "features" are apt to peel.

As an added grace in summer, foliage and flowers are arranged as a decorative feature of the design, the only ornamentation. In winter the building is well proportioned and complete without them.

No attic, no "butler's pantry," no back stairway have been planned; they would be unnecessarily cumbersome in this scheme, which is trimmed to the last ounce of the superfluous. A closet on the level of the stair landing takes care of trunks and suit-cases, and a dry, well-lighted basement storeroom cares for whatever doesn't classify in the various closets. The open kitchen, with pantry conveniences built into it, is more pleasant and as useful as the complement of kitchen, kitchen pantry, and "butler's pantry." Access to the stairs from the kitchen is sufficiently private at all times, and the

Fireproof House for *The Ladies' Home Journal* (Project). 1906. Perspective. Pencil on tracing paper, 33 x 15". FLLW Fdn#0614.004

front door may be easily reached from the kitchen without passing through the living room.

The walls, floors, and roof of this house are a monolithic casting, formed in the usual manner by means of wooden false work, the chimney at the center carrying, like a huge post, the central load of floor and roof construction. Floors and roof are reinforced concrete slabs approximately five inches thick if gravel concrete is used. The roof slab overhangs to protect the walls from sun, and the top is waterproofed with a tar and gravel roofing pitched to drain to a downspout located in the chimney flue, where it is not likely to freeze. To afford further protection to the second-story rooms from the heat of the sun, a false ceiling is provided of plastered metal lath hanging eight inches below the bottom of the roof slab, leaving a circulating air space above, exhausted to the large open space in the center of the chimney. In summer this air space is fed by the openings noted beneath the eaves outside. These openings may be closed in winter by a simple device reached from the second-story windows.

All the interior partitions are of metal lath plastered both sides or of three-inch tile set upon the floor slabs after the reinforced concrete construction is complete. After coating the inside surfaces of the outside concrete walls with a non-conducting paint, or lining them with a plaster-board, the whole is plastered two coats with a rough sand finish.

The floor surfaces are finished smooth with wooden strip inlaid for fastening floor coverings, or at additional cost noted they may be finished over a rough structural concrete with a half-inch thick dressing of magnesite mixed with sawdust, which renders them less hard and cold to the touch, and when waxed presents a very agreeable surface in any color.

The interior is trimmed with light wood strips nailed to small, porous terra-cotta blocks, which are set into the forms at the proper points before the forms are filled with the concrete.

In the composition of the concrete for the outside walls only finely screened bird's-eye gravel

is used, with cement enough added to fill the voids. This mixture is put into the boxes quite dry and tamped. When the forms are removed the outside is washed with a solution of hydrochloric acid, which cuts the cement from the outer face of the pebbles, and the whole surface glistens like a piece of gray granite. This treatment insures uniformity of color, and if the wooden forms have been properly made of narrow flooring smoothed on the side toward the concrete and oiled, the surface throughout should be smooth and even without unsightly seams.

The house has been designed four sides alike in order to simplify the making of these forms, and so that, if necessary, forms made for the one side may serve for all four.

The windows are casement type, swinging outward. The screens or storm sash are fitted within as a part of the window trim, swinging in when the windows need cleaning. All windows may be operated independently of screens by a mechanical device accessible from within at all times and closing beneath the windowsills. The outer sash might at no very great additional expense be made of metal.

The trellis over the entrance might give place to a concrete roof slab similar to the roof of the house, should a covered porch be a necessity.

The house may be placed with either the living-room front or the terrace front to the street, as indicated in the exterior perspectives.

Estimate of Cost:

Concrete construction, masonry and plastering	$3100.00
Carpentry, millwork, sash-doors and screens, labor and trimming	1100.00
Plumbing and furnace	460.00
Wiring	70.00
Painting and glazing	160.00
Hardware	90.00
	$4980.00
If magnesite floors are used add	320.00
	$5300.00

IN THE CAUSE
OF ARCHITECTURE

When the March 1908 issue of The Architectural Record was published, it featured the largest number of Wright's designs yet to appear in print. Accompanying this essay were eighty-seven illustrations—photographs of executed buildings and drawings for other projects. With its circulation extending not only to the American professionals but to their European counterparts as well, this early publication began to disseminate the ideas of Frank Lloyd Wright to a substantial audience. However, it was not so much in the United States that his architecture would be first recognized, but rather in Holland and Germany.

Kuno Francke, professor of the History of German Culture at Harvard, came to Oak Park to see Wright's work first-hand in 1908. He saw, also, that America was not ready for Wright. "Your life will be wasted here," he told Wright, "do come to Germany," which Wright did the following year.

The March 1908 essay, entitled "In the Cause of Architecture," was Wright's first developed statement about the cause to which he devoted his life. He opened the essay with the statement "Radical though it be, the work here illustrated is dedicated to a cause conservative in the best sense of the word." And near the close of the article, he wrote a broad and remarkable projection of the course his work would take: "As for the future—the work shall grow more truly simple; more expressive with fewer lines, fewer forms; more articulate with less labor; more plastic; more fluent, although more coherent; more organic."

When this article was published Wright was forty-one years old and at the apex of his career. Already realized were buildings that would exert tremendous influence on modern architecture, both in Europe and in the United States. Unity Temple, the Larkin Building, and the homes for Susan Lawrence Dana, Ward Willits, and Darwin D. Martin are but a few of the more than 110 of his designs Wright had seen built by this time.

But the so-called "prairie years" were coming to an end, and Wright was growing restless and dissatisfied with life and work in his Oak Park home and studio. As the year drew to a close, he wrote to his client and patron Darwin D. Martin: "In my own life there is much that is complex, at least. Life is not the simple thing it should be if within myself I could find the harmony that you have found. It is difficult for me to square my life with myself, and I cannot rest until it is done or I am dead."[2] [Published with 87 illustrations in The Architectural Record, March 1908]

Burton J. Westcott House. Springfield, Ohio. 1907. Plan and elevation. Pencil on tracing paper, 32 x 21". FLLW Fdn#0712.001

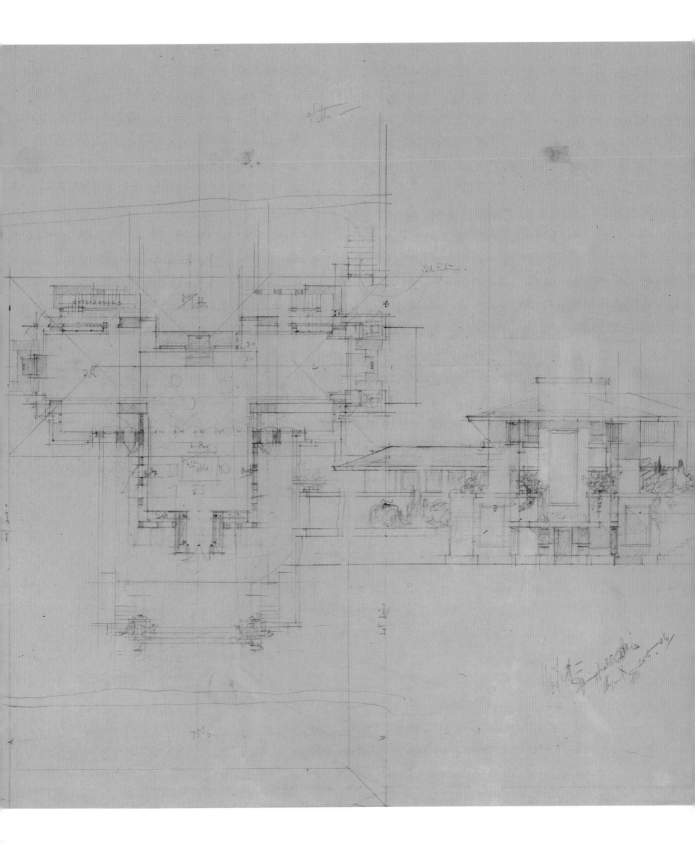

RADICAL THOUGH IT BE, THE WORK HERE ILLUSTRATED IS dedicated to a cause conservative in the best sense of the word. At no point does it involve denial of the elemental law and order inherent in all great architecture; rather it is a declaration of love for the spirit of that law and order and a reverential recognition of the elements that made its ancient letter in its time vital and beautiful.

Primarily, Nature furnished the materials for architectural motifs out of which the architectural forms as we know them today have been developed, and, although our practice for centuries has been for the most part to turn from her, seeking inspiration in books and adhering slavishly to dead formulae, her wealth of suggestion is inexhaustible; her riches greater than any man's desire. I know with what suspicion the man is regarded who refers matters of fine art back to Nature. I know that it is usually an ill-advised return that is attempted, for Nature in external, obvious aspect is the usually accepted sense of the term and the nature that is reached. But given inherent vision there is no source so fertile, so suggestive, so helpful aesthetically for the architect as a comprehension of natural law. As Nature is never right for a picture so is she never right for the architect—that is, not ready-made. Nevertheless, she has a practical school beneath her more obvious forms in which a sense of proportion may be cultivated, when Vignola and Vitruvius fail as they must always fail. It is there that he may develop that sense of reality that translated to his own field in terms of his own work will lift him far above the realistic in his art; there he will be inspired by sentiment that will never degenerate to sentimentality and he will learn to draw with a surer hand the every-perplexing line between the curious and the beautiful.

A sense of the organic is indispensable to an architect; where can he develop it so surely as in this school? A knowledge of the relations of form and function lies at the root of his practice; where else can he find the pertinent object lessons Nature so readily furnishes? Where can he study the differentiations of form that go to determine character as he can study them in the trees? Where can that sense of inevitableness characteristic of a work of art be quickened as it may be by intercourse with nature in this sense?

Japanese art knows this school more intimately than that of any people. In common use in their language there are many words like the word *eda-buri* which, translated as near as may be, means the formative arrangement of the branches of a tree. We have no such word in English, we are not yet sufficiently civilized to think in such terms, but the architect must not only learn to think in such terms but he must learn in this school to fashion his vocabulary for himself and furnish it in a comprehensive way with useful words as significant as this one.

For seven years it was my good fortune to be the understudy of a great teacher and a great architect, to my mind the greatest of his time—Mr. Louis H. Sullivan.

Principles are not invented, they are not evolved by one man or one age, but Mr. Sullivan's perception and practice of them amounted to a revelation at a time when they were commercially inexpedient and all but lost to sight in current practice. The fine-art sense of the profession was at that time practically dead; only glimmerings were perceptible in the work of Richardson and of Root.[3]

Adler and Sullivan had little time to design residences. The few that were unavoidable fell to my lot outside of office hours. So largely, it remained for me to carry into the field of domestic architecture the battle they had begun in commercial building. During the early years of my own practice I found this lonesome work. Sympathizers of any kind were then few, and they were not found among the architects. I well remember how "the message" burned within me, how I longed for comradeship until I began to know the younger men and how welcome was Robert Spencer, and then Myron Hunt, and Dwight Perkins, Arthur Heun, George Dean, and Hugh Garden. Inspiring days they were, I am sure, for us all. Of late we have been too busy to see one another often, but the "New School of the Middle West"[4] is beginning to be talked about and perhaps some day it is to be. For why not the same "Life" and blood in architecture that is the essence of all true art?

In 1894, with this text from Carlyle at the top of the page—"The Ideal is within thyself, thy condition is but the stuff thou art to shape that same Ideal out of"—I formulated the following "propositions." I set them down here much as they were written then, although in the light of experience they might be stated more completely and succinctly.

I—Simplicity and Repose are qualities that measure the true value of any work of art.

But simplicity is not in itself an end nor is it a matter of the side of a barn but rather an entity with a graceful beauty in its integrity from which discord, and all that is meaningless, has been eliminated. A wildflower is truly simple. Therefore:

1. A building should contain as few rooms as will meet the conditions which give it rise and under which we live and which the architect should strive continually to simplify; then the ensemble of the rooms should be carefully considered that comfort and utility may go hand in hand with beauty. Beside the entry and necessary work rooms there need be but three rooms on the ground floor of any house, living room, dining room, and kitchen, with the possible addition of a "social office"; really there need be but one room, the living room, with requirements otherwise sequestered from it or screened within it by means of architectural contrivances.

2. Openings should occur as integral features of the structure and form, if possible, its natural ornamentation.

3. An excessive love of detail has ruined more fine things from the standpoint of fine art or fine living than any one human shortcoming—it is hopelessly vulgar. Too many houses, when they are not little stage settings or scene paintings, are mere notion stores, bazaars, or junk shops. Decoration is dangerous unless you understand it thoroughly and are satisfied that it means something good in the scheme as a whole, for the present you are usually better off without it. Merely that it "looks rich" is no justification for the use of ornament.

4. Appliances or fixtures as such are undesirable. Assimilate them together with all appurtenances into the design of the structure.

5. Pictures deface walls oftener than they decorate them. Pictures should be decorative and incorporated in the general scheme as decoration.

6. The most truly satisfactory apartments are those in which most or all of the furniture is built in as a part of the original scheme considering the whole as an integral unit.

II—There should be as many kinds (styles) of houses as there are kinds (styles) of people and as many differentiations as there are different individuals. A man who has individuality (and what man lacks it?) has a right to its expression in his own environment.

III—A building should appear to grow easily from its site and be shaped to harmonize with its surroundings if Nature is manifest there, and if not try to make it as quiet, substantial and organic as She would have been were the opportunity Hers.*

We of the Middle West are living on the prairie. The prairie has a beauty of its own, and we should recognize and accentuate this natural beauty, its quiet level. Hence, gently sloping roofs, low proportions, quiet skylines, suppressed heavyset chimneys and sheltering overhangs, low terraces and outreaching walls sequestering private gardens.

IV—Colors require the same conventionalizing process to make them fit to live with that natural forms do; so go to the woods and fields for color schemes. Use the soft, warm, optimistic tones of earths and autumn leaves in preference to the pessimistic blues, purples, or cold greens and grays of the ribbon counter; they are more wholesome and better adapted in most cases to good decoration.

V—Bring out the nature of the materials, let their nature intimately into your scheme. Strip the wood of varnish and let it alone—stain it. Develop the natural texture of the plastering and stain it. Reveal the nature of the wood, plaster, brick, or stone in your designs, they are all by nature friendly and beautiful. No treatment can be really a matter of fine art when these natural characteristics are, or their nature is, outraged or neglected.

VI—A house that has character stands a good chance of growing more valuable as it grows older while a house in the prevailing mode, whatever

---

*In this I had in mind the barren town lots devoid of tree or natural incident, townhouses and board walks only in evidence.

Thomas P. Hardy House. Racine, Wisconsin. 1905. Perspective. Watercolor, gouache, and pencil on art paper, 17 x 9". FLLW Fdn#0506.002

that mode may be, is soon out of fashion, stale, and unprofitable.

Buildings like people must first be sincere, must be true, and then withal as gracious and lovable as may be.

Above all, integrity. The machine is the normal tool of our civilization, give it work that it can do well—nothing is of greater importance. To do this will be to formulate new industrial ideals, sadly needed.

These propositions are chiefly interesting because for some strange reason they were novel when formulated in the face of conditions hostile to them and because the ideals they phrase have been practically embodied in the buildings that were built to live up to them. The buildings of recent years have not only been true to them, but are in many cases a further development of the simple propositions so positively stated then.

Happily, these ideals are more commonplace now. Then the skylines of our domestic architecture were fantastic abortions, tortured by features that disrupted the distorted roof surfaces from which attenuated chimneys like lean fingers threatened the sky; the invariably tall interiors were cut up into box-like compartments, the more boxes the finer the house, and "Architecture" chiefly consisted in healing over the edges of the curious collection of holes that had to be cut in the walls for light and air and to permit the occupant to get in or out. These interiors were always slaughtered with the butt and slash of the old plinth and corner block trim, of dubious origin, and finally smothered with horrible millinery.

That individuality in a building was possible for each homemaker, or desirable, seemed at that

time to rise to the dignity of an idea. Even cultured men and women care so little for the spiritual integrity of their environment; except in rare cases they are not touched, they simply do not care for the matter so long as their dwellings are fashionable or as good as those of their neighbors and keep them dry and warm. A structure has no more meaning to them aesthetically than has the stable to the horse. And this came to me in the early years as a definite discouragement. There are exceptions, and I found them chiefly among American men of business with unspoiled instincts and untainted ideals. A man of this type usually has the faculty of judging for himself. He has rather liked the "idea" and much of the encouragement this work receives comes straight from him because the "common sense" of the thing appeals to him. While the "cultured" are still content with their small châteaux,

colonial wedding cakes, English affectations, or French millinery, he prefers a poor thing but his own. He errs on the side of character, at least, and when the test of time has tried his country's development architecturally, he will have contributed his quota, small enough in the final outcome though it be; he will be regarded as a true conservator.

In the hope that some day America may live her own life in her own buildings, in her own way, that is, that we may make the best of what we have for what it honestly is or may become, I have endeavored in this work to establish a harmonious relationship between ground plan and elevation of these buildings, considering the one as a solution and the other an expression of the conditions of a problem of which the whole is a project. I have tried to establish an organic integrity to begin with, forming the basis for the subsequent working out of a significant grammatical expression and making the whole, as nearly as I could, consistent.

What quality of style the buildings may possess is due to the artistry with which the conventionalization as a solution and an artistic expression of a specific problem within these limitations has been handled. The types are largely a matter of personal taste and may have much or little to do with the American architecture for which we hope.

From the beginning of my practice, the question uppermost in my mind has been not "what style?" but "what is style?" and it is my belief that the chief value of the work illustrated here will be found in the fact that if in the face of our present-day conditions any given type may be treated independently and imbued with the quality of style, then a truly noble architecture is a definite possibility, so soon as Americans really demand it of the architects of the rising generation.

I do not believe we will ever again have the uniformity of type which has characterized the so-called great "styles." Conditions have changed; our ideal is Democracy, the highest possible expression of the individual as a unit not inconsistent with a harmonious whole. The average of human intelligence rises steadily, and as the individual unit grows more and more to be trusted we will have an architecture with richer variety in unity than has ever arisen before; but the forms must be born out of our changed conditions, they must be *true* forms, otherwise the best that tradition has to offer is only an inglorious masquerade, devoid of vital significance or true spiritual value.

The trials of the early days were many and at this distance picturesque. Workmen seldom like to think, especially if there is financial risk entailed; at your peril do you disturb their established processes mental or technical. To do anything in an unusual, even if in a better and simpler way, is to complicate the situation at once. Simple things at that time in any industrial field were nowhere at hand. A piece of wood without a molding was an anomaly; a plain wooden slat instead of a turned baluster a joke, the omission of the merchantable "grille" a crime; plain

fabrics for hangings or floor covering were nowhere to be found in stock.

To become the recognized enemy of the established industrial order was no light matter, for soon whenever a set of my drawings was presented to a Chicago mill-man for figures he would willingly enough unroll it, read the architect's name, shake his head, and return it with the remark that he was "not hunting for trouble"; sagacious owners and general contractors tried cutting out the name, but in vain, his perspicacity was ratlike, he had come to know "the look of the thing." So, in addition to the special preparation in any case necessary for every little matter of construction and finishing, special detail drawings were necessary merely to allow the things to be left off or not done and not only studied designs for every part had to be made but quantity surveys and schedules of millwork furnished the contractors beside. This, in a year or two, brought the architect face to face with the fact that the fee for his service "established" by the American Institute of Architects was intended for something stock and shop, for it would not even pay for the bare drawings necessary for conscientious work.

The relation of the architect to the economic and industrial movement of his time, in any fine-art sense, is still an affair so sadly out of joint that no one may easily reconcile it. All agree that something has gone wrong and except the architect be a plain factory magnate, who has reduced his art to a philosophy of old clothes and sells misfit or made over-ready-to-wear garments with commercial aplomb and social distinction, he cannot succeed on the present basis established by common practice. So, in addition to a situation already complicated for them, a necessarily increased fee stared in the face the clients who dared. But some did dare, as the illustrations prove.

The struggle then was and still is to make "good architecture," "good business." It is perhaps significant that in the beginning it was very difficult to secure a building loan on any terms upon one of these houses, now it is easy to secure a better loan than ordinary; but how far success has attended this ambi-

Larkin Company Administration Building. Buffalo, New York. 1904. Interior. FLLW FA#0403.0046

Walter Gerts House (Project). Glencoe, Illinois. 1905. Perspective. Watercolor and ink on art paper, 25 x 18". FLLW Fdn#0615.004

tion the owners of these buildings alone can testify. Their trials have been many, but each, I think, feels that he has as much house for his money as any of his neighbors, with something in the home intrinsically valuable besides, which will not be out of fashion in one lifetime and which contributes steadily to his dignity and his pleasure as an individual.

It would not be useful to dwell further upon difficulties encountered, for it is the common story of simple progression everywhere in any field; I merely wish to trace here the "motif" behind the types. A study of the illustrations will show that the buildings presented fall readily into three groups having a family resemblance; the low-pitched hip roofs, heaped together in pyramidal fashion or presenting quiet, unbroken skylines; the low roofs with simple pediments countering on long ridges; and those topped with a simple slab. Of the first type, the Winslow, Henderson, Willits, Thomas, Heurtley, Heath, Cheney, Martin, Little, Gridley, Millard, Tomek, Coonley, and Westcott houses, the Hillside Home School and the Pettit Memorial Chapel are typical. Of the second type, the Bradley, Hickox, Davenport and Dana houses are typical. Of the third, atelier for Richard Bock, Unity Church[5],

the concrete house of *The Ladies' Home Journal,* and other designs in process of execution. The Larkin Building is a simple, dignified utterance of a plain, utilitarian type, with sheer brick walls and simple stone copings. The studio is merely an early experiment in "articulation."

Photographs do not adequately present these subjects. A building has a presence, as has a person, that defies the photographer, and the color so necessary to the complete expression of the form is necessarily lacking; but it will be noticed that all the structures stand upon their foundations to the eye as well as physically. There is good, substantial preparation at the ground for all the buildings and it is the first grammatical expression of all the types. This preparation, or water table, is to these buildings, what the stylobate was to the ancient Greek temple. To gain it, it was necessary to reverse the established practice of setting the supports of the building to the outside of the wall and to set them to the inside, so as to leave the necessary support for the outer base. This was natural enough and good enough construction but many an owner was disturbed by private information from the practical contractor to the effect that he would have his whole house in the

Larkin Company Administration Building. Buffalo, New York. 1904. Perspective. Sepia ink on art paper. 36 x 22".
FLLW Fdn#0403.002

cellar if he submitted to it. This was at the time a marked innovation though the most natural thing in the world and to me, to this day, indispensable.

With this innovation established, one horizontal stripe of raw material, the foundation wall above ground, was eliminated and the complete grammar of type one made possible. A simple, unbroken wall surface from foot to level of second story sill was thus secured, a change of material occuring at that point to form the simple frieze that characterizes the earlier buildings. Even this was frequently omitted, as in the Francis apartments⁶ and many other buildings, and the wall was let alone from base to cornice or eaves.

"Dress reform houses" they were called, I remember, by the charitably disposed. What others called them will hardly bear repetition.

As the wall surfaces were thus simplified and emphasized the matter of fenestration became exceedingly difficult and more than ever important, and often I used to gloat over the beautiful buildings I could build if only it were unnecessary to cut holes in them; but the holes were managed at first frankly as in the Winslow house and later as elementary constituents of the structure grouped in rhythmical fashion, so that all the light and air and prospect the most rabid client could wish would not be too much from an artistic standpoint; and of this achievement I am proud. The groups are managed, too, whenever required, so that overhanging eaves do not shade them, although the walls are still protected from the weather. Soon the poetry-crushing characteristics of the guillotine window, which was then firmly rooted, became apparent, and single-handed I waged a determined battle for casements swinging out, although it was necessary to have special hardware made for them as there was none to be had this side of England. Clients would come ready to accept any innovation but "those swinging windows," and when told that they were in the nature of the proposition and that they must take them or leave the rest, they frequently employed "the other fellow" to give them something "near," with the "practical" windows dear to their hearts.

With the grammar so far established, came an expression pure and simple, even classic in atmo-sphere, using that much-abused word in its best sense; implying, that is, a certain sweet reasonableness of form and outline naturally dignified.

I have observed that Nature usually perfects her forms; the individuality of the attribute is seldom sacrificed; that is, deformed or mutilated by cooperative parts. She rarely says a thing and tries to take it back at the same time. She would not sanction the "classic" proceeding of, say, establishing an "order," a colonnade, then building walls between the columns of the order reducing them to pilasters, thereafter cutting holes in the wall and pasting on cornices with more pilasters around them, with the result that every form is outraged, the whole an abominable mutilation, as is most of the architecture of the Renaissance wherein style corrodes style and all the forms are stultified.

In laying out the ground plans for even the more insignificant of these buildings, a simple axial law and order and the ordered spacing upon a system of certain structural units definitely established for each structure, in accord with its scheme of practical construction and aesthetic proportion, is practiced as an expedient to simplify the technical difficulties of execution, and, although the symmetry may not be obvious, always the balance is usually maintained. The plans are as a rule much more articulate than is the school product of the Beaux Arts. The individuality of the various functions of the various features is more highly developed; all the forms are complete in themselves and frequently do duty at the same time from within and without as decorative attributes of the whole. This tendency to greater individuality of the parts emphasized by more and more complete articulation will be seen in the plans for Unity Church, the cottage for Elizabeth Stone at Glencoe, and the Avery Coonley house in process of construction at Riverside, Illinois. Moreover, these ground plans are merely the actual projection of a carefully considered whole. The "architecture" is not "thrown up" as an artistic exercise, a matter of elevation from a preconceived ground plan. The schemes are conceived in three dimensions as organic entities, let the picturesque perspective fall how it will. While a sense of the incidental perspectives the design will develop is always present, I have great faith that if the thing is rightly put together in true organic sense with proportions actually right the picturesque will take care of itself. No man ever built a building worthy the name of architecture who fashioned it in perspective sketch to his taste and then fudged the plan to suit. Such methods produce mere scene-painting. A perspective may be a proof but it is no nurture.

As to the mass values of the buildings the aesthetic principles outlined in proposition III will account in a measure for their character.

In the matter of decoration the tendency has been to indulge it less and less, in many cases merely providing certain architectural preparation for natural foliage or flowers, as it is managed in, say, the entrance to the Lawrence house at Springfield. This use of natural foliage and flowers for decoration is carried to quite an extent in all the designs and, although the buildings are complete without this effloresence, they may be said to blossom with the season. What architectural decoration the buildings carry is not only conventionalized to the point where it is quiet and stays as a sure foil for the nature forms from which it is derived and with which it must intimately associate, but it is always *of* the surface, never *on* it.

The windows usually are provided with characteristic straight-line patterns absolutely in the flat and usually severe. The nature of the glass is taken into account in these designs as is also the metal bar used in their construction, and most of them are treated as metal "grilles" with glass inserted forming a simple rhythmic arrangement of straight lines and squares made as cunning as possible so long as the result is quiet. The aim is that the designs shall make the best of the technical contrivances that produce them.

In the main the ornamentation is wrought in the warp and woof of the structure. It is constitutional in the best sense and is felt in the conception of the ground plan. To elucidate this element in composition would mean a long story and perhaps a tedious one, though to me it is the most fascinating phase of the work, involving the true poetry of conception.

The differentiation of a single, certain simple form characterizes the expression of one building.

Quite a different form may serve for another, but from one basic idea all the formal elements of design are in each case derived and held well together in scale and character. The form chosen may flare outward, opening flower-like to the sky, as in the Thomas house; another, droop to accentuate artistically the weight of the masses; another be noncommittal or abruptly emphatic, or its grammar may be deduced from some plant form that has appealed to me, as certain properties in line and form of the sumach were used in the Lawrence house at Springfield; but in every case the motif is adhered to throughout so that it is not too much to say that each building aesthetically is cut from one piece of goods and consistently hangs together with an integrity impossible otherwise.

In a fine-art sense, these designs have grown as natural plants grow, the individuality of each is integral and as complete as skill, time, strength, and circumstances would permit.

The method in itself does not of necessity produce a beautiful building, but it does provide a framework as a basis which has an organic integrity, susceptible to the architect's imagination and at once opening to him Nature's wealth of artistic suggestion, ensuring him a guiding principle within which he can never be wholly false, out of tune, or lacking in rational motif. The subtleties, the shifting blending harmonies, the cadences, the nuances are a matter of his own nature, his own susceptibilities and faculties.

But self-denial is imposed upon the architect to a far greater extent than upon any other member of the fine art family. The temptation to sweeten work, to make each detail in itself lovable and expressive is always great, but that the whole may be truly eloquent of its ultimate function restraint is imperative. To let individual elements arise and shine at the expense of final repose is, for the architect, a betrayal of trust for buildings are the background or framework for the human life within their walls and a foil for the nature efflorescence without. So architecture is the most complete of conventionalizations and of all the arts the most subjective except music.

Music may be for the architect ever and always

Unity Temple. Oak Park, Illinois. 1904. Perspective. Watercolor on art paper, 26 x 12". FLLW Fdn#0611.003

a sympathetic friend whose counsels, precepts, and patterns even are available to him and from which he need not fear to draw. But the arts are today all cursed by literature; artists attempt to make literature even of music, usually of painting and sculpture and doubtless would of architecture also were the art not moribund; but whenever it is done the soul of the thing dies and we have not art but something far less for which the true artist can have neither affection nor respect.

Contrary to the usual supposition this manner of working out a theme is more flexible than any working out in a fixed, historic style can ever be, and the individuality of those concerned may receive more adequate treatment within legitimate limitations. This matter of individuality puzzles many; they suspect that the individuality of the owner and occupant of a building is sacrificed to that of the architect who imposes his own upon Jones, Brown, and Smith alike. An architect worthy of the name has an individuality, it is true; his work

will and should reflect it, and his buildings will all bear a family resemblance one to another. The individuality of an owner is first manifest in his choice of his architect, the individual to whom he entrusts his characterization. He sympathizes with his work; its expression suits him, and this furnishes the common ground upon which client and architect may come together. Then, if the architect is what he ought to be, with his ready technique he conscientiously works for the client, idealizes his client's character and his client's tastes, and makes him feel that the building is his as it really is to such an extent that he can truly say that he would rather have his own house than any other he has ever seen. Is a portrait, say by Sargent, any less a revelation of the character of the subject because it bears his stamp and is easily recognized by anyone as a Sargent? Does one lose his individuality when it is interpreted sympathetically by one of his own race and time who can know him and his needs intimately and idealize them, or does he gain it only by having

Isabel Roberts House. River Forest, Illinois. 1908. FLLW Fdn FA#0808.0004

adopted or adapted to his condition a ready-made historic style which is the fruit of a seedtime other than his, whatever that style may be?

The present industrial condition is constantly studied in the practical application of these architectural ideals and the treatment simplified and arranged to fit modern processes and to utilize to the best advantage the work of the machine. The furniture takes the clean-cut, straight-line forms that the machine can render far better than would be possible by hand. Certain facilities, too, of the machine, which it would be interesting to enlarge upon, are

taken advantage of and the nature of the materials is usually revealed in the process.

Nor is the atmosphere of the result in its completeness new and hard. In most of the interiors there will be found a quiet, a simple dignity that we imagine is only to be found in the "old" and it is due to the underlying organic harmony, to the each in all and the all in each throughout. This is the modern opportunity to make of a building, together with its equipment, appurtenances, and environment, an entity which shall constitute a complete work of art, and a work of art more valuable to society as a whole than has before existed because discordant conditions endured for centuries are smoothed away; everyday life here finds an expression germane to its daily existence; an idealization of the common need sure to be uplifting and helpful in the same sense that pure air to breathe is better than air poisoned with noxious gases.

An artist's limitations are his best friends. The machine is here to stay. It is the forerunner of the democracy that is our dearest hope. There is no more important work before the architect now than to use this normal tool of civilization to the best advantage instead of prostituting it as he has hitherto done in reproducing with murderous ubiquity forms born of other times and other conditions and which it can only serve to destroy.

The exteriors of these structures will receive less ready recognition perhaps than the interiors, and because they are the result of a radically different conception as to what should constitute a building. We have formed a habit of mind concerning architecture to which the expression of most of these exteriors must be a shock, at first more or less disagreeable, and the more so as the habit of mind is more narrowly fixed by so-called classic training. Simplicity is not in itself an end; it is a means to an end. Our aesthetics are dyspeptic from incontinent indulgence in "Frenchite" pastry. We crave ornament for the sake of ornament; cover up our faults of design with ornamental sensualities that were a long time ago sensuous ornament. We will do well to distrust this unwholesome and unholy craving and look to the simple line; to the clean though living form and quiet color for a time, until the true significance of these things has dawned for us once more. The old structural forms which up to the present time, have spelled "architecture" are decayed. Their life went from them long ago and new conditions industrially, steel and concrete and terra-cotta in particular, are prophesying a more plastic art wherein as the flesh is to our bones so will the covering be to the structure, but more truly and beautifully expressive than ever. But that is a long story. This reticence in the matter of ornamentation is characteristic of these structures and for at least two reasons: first,

they are the expression of an idea that the ornamentation of a building should be constitutional, a matter of the nature of the structure beginning with the ground plan. In the buildings themselves, in the sense of the whole there is lacking neither richness nor incident but their qualities are secured not by applied decoration, they are found in the fashioning of the whole, in which color, too, plays as significant a part as it does in an old, Japanese woodblock print. Second: because as before stated, buildings perform their highest function in relation to human life within and the natural efflorescence without; and to develop and maintain the harmony of a true chord between them making of the building in this sense a sure foil for life, broad, simple surfaces and highly conventionalized forms are inevitable. These ideals take the buildings out of school and marry them to the ground; make them intimate expressions or revelations of the exteriors, individualize them regardless of preconceived notions of style. I have tried to make their grammar perfect in its way and to give their forms and proportions an integrity that will bear study, although few of them can be intelligently studied apart from their environment. So, what might be termed the democratic character of the exteriors is their first undefined offence—the lack, wholly, of what the professional critic would deem architecture; in fact, most of the critic's architecture has been left out.

There is always a synthetic basis for the features of the various structures, and consequently a constantly accumulating residue of formulas, which becomes more and more useful; but I do not pretend to say that the perception or conception of them was not at first intuitive, or that those that lie yet beyond will not be grasped in the same intuitive way; but, after all, architecture is a scientific art, and the thinking basis will ever be for the architect his surety, the final court in which his imagination sifts his feelings.

The few draughtsmen so far associated with this work have been taken into the draughting room, in every case almost wholly unformed, many of them with no particular previous training and patiently nursed for years in the atmosphere of the work itself, until saturated by intimate association,

Avery Coonley House. Riverside, Illinois. 1908. FLLW Fdn FA#0803.0008

at an impressionable age, with its motifs and phases, they have become helpful. To develop the sympathetic grasp of detail that is necessary before this point is reached has proved usually a matter of years, with little advantage on the side of the college-trained understudy. These young people have found their way to me through natural sympathy with the work and have become loyal assistants. The members, so far, all told here and elsewhere, of our little university of fourteen years standing are: Marion Mahony, a capable assistant for eleven years; William Drummond, seven years; Francis Byrne, five years; Isabel Roberts, five years; George Willis, four years; Walter Griffin, four years; Andrew Willatzen, three years; Harry Robinson, two years; Charles E. White, Jr., one year; Erwin Barglebaugh and Robert Hardin, each one year; Albert McArthur, entering.

Others have been attracted by what seemed to them to be the novelty of the work, staying only long enough to acquire a smattering of form, then departing to sell a superficial proficiency elsewhere. Still others shortly develop a mastery of the subject, discovering that it is all just as they would have done it, anyway, and, chafing at the unkind fate that forestalled them in its practice, resolve to blaze a trail for themselves without further loss of time. It is urged against the more loyal that they are sacrificing their individuality to that which has dominated this work; but it is too soon to impeach a single understudy on this basis, for, although they will inevitably repeat for years the methods, forms, and habit of thought, even the mannerisms of the present work, if there is virtue in the principles behind it that virtue will stay with them through the preliminary stages of their own practice until their own individualities truly develop independently. I have noticed that those who have made the most fuss about their "individuality" in early stages, those who took themselves most seriously in that regard, were inevitably those who had least.

Many elements of Mr. Sullivan's personality in his art—what might be called his mannerisms—naturally enough clung to my work in the early years and may be readily traced by the casual observer; but for me one real proof of the virtue inherent in this work will lie in the fact that some of the young men and women who have given themselves up to me so faithfully these past years will some day contribute rounded individualities of their own and forms of their own devising to the new school.

This year, I assign to each a project that has been carefully conceived in my own mind, which he accepts as a specific work. He follows its subsequent development through all its phases in drawing room and field, meeting with the client himself on occasion, gaining an all-round development impossible otherwise, and insuring an enthusiasm and a grasp of detail decidedly to the best interest of the client. These privileges in the hands of selfishly ambitious or overconfident assistants would soon wreck such a system; but I can say that among my own boys it has already proved a moderate success, with every prospect of being continued as a settled policy in future.

Nevertheless, I believe that only when one individual forms the concept of the various projects and also determines the character of every detail in the sum total, even to the size and shape of the pieces of glass in the windows, the arrangement and profile of the most insignificant of the architectural members, will that unity be secured which is the soul of the individual work of art. This means that fewer buildings should be entrusted to one architect. His output will of necessity be relatively small—small, that is, as compared to the volume of work turned out in any one of fifty "successful offices" in America. I believe there is no middle course worth considering in the light of the best future of American architecture. With no more propriety can an architect leave the details touching the form of his concept to assistants, no matter how

sympathetic and capable they may be, than can a painter entrust the painting in of the details of his picture to a pupil; for an architect who would do individual work must have a technique well developed and peculiar to himself, which, if he is fertile, is still growing with his growth. To keep everything "in place" requires constant care and study in matters that the old-school practitioner would scorn to touch.

As for the future—the work shall grow more truly simple; more expressive with fewer lines, fewer forms; more articulate with less labor; more plastic; more fluent, although more coherent; more organic. It shall grow not only to fit more perfectly the methods and processes that are called upon to produce it, but shall further find whatever is lovely or of good repute in method or process, and idealize it with the cleanest, most virile stroke I can imagine. As understanding and appreciation of life matures and deepens, this work shall prophesy and idealize the character of the individual it is fashioned to serve more intimately, no matter how inexpensive the result must finally be. It shall become in its atmosphere as pure and elevating in its humble way as the trees and flowers are in their perfectly appointed way, for only so can architecture be worthy its high rank as a fine art, or the architect discharge the obligation he assumes to the public—imposed upon him by the nature of his own profession.

1. Frank Lloyd Wright, *A Testament* (New York: Horizon Press, 1957), p. 84.
2. Frank Lloyd Wright to Darwin D. Martin, December 2, 1908. The Frank Lloyd Wright Archives and University Archives, State University of New York at Buffalo.
3. Architects Henry Hobson Richardson (1838–1886) and John Wellborn Root (1850–1891). Richardson, architect of the 1885 Marshall Field Wholesale Store in Chicago, was primarily known for his very individualistic —"Romanesque-like"— rock-faced masonry buildings on the East Coast. Root, who moved to Chicago in 1872 following the great fire, is best known for the tall office buildings he designed in partnership with Daniel Burnham during the 1880s.
4. H. Allen Brooks identifies "New School of the Middle West" as Wright's phrase and states that it first appears here, at least in print, in this essay of 1908. Thomas T. Tallmadge about the same time coined the phrase "the Chicago School," which included at least some of the same people Wright mentions here. By 1912 the term "Prairie Style" had also appeared. The definition of these "schools" or "styles" of architecture shifted over time and continues to be confusing (H. Allen Brooks, *The Prairie School*. New York: W.W.Norton & Co., 1972. p. 10–11).
5. Actually Unity Temple in Oak Park, designed by Wright in 1904.
6. Francis Apartments. The Francis Apartments were built in Chicago in 1895 for the Terre Haute Trust Company of Indiana. They were demolished in 1971.

AUSGEFÜHRTE BAUTEN UND ENTWÜRFE VON FRANK LLOYD WRIGHT

While living in Florence, Italy, in the spring and summer of 1910, Wright worked on the illustrations and text for a monograph on his work to be published by the Berlin firm of Ernst Wasmuth. From the Oak Park studio were sent drawings and photographs of his buildings and projects that he, his son Lloyd, and his draftsman Taylor Woolley traced with quill pens and india ink. The final drawings were then sent to Berlin and transferred to lithographic stones.

Wright's introductory text to the monograph opens with extraordinarily lavish praise for the early Italian architects, painters, and sculptors whom he especially admired and whose work he was daily restudying and rediscovering in Florence. After reflecting on the great era of the early Italian Renaissance (which he refers to as the Gothic spirit), he considers his own work, which is of the twentieth century and on American soil: "I suggest that a revival, not of the Gothic style, but of the Gothic spirit, is needed in the Art and Architecture of the modern life of the world." This mission inspired some of Wright's most poetic and revealing writing about architecture and the fine arts.

According to Wright, the final edition of the monograph totaled 1,000 copies, 500 for sale in Europe and 500 for exportation and sale in the United States. The copies for the American market were lost in the 1914 fire at Taliesin; only 30, in badly smoked and charred condition, survived. However, the monograph was a great success in Europe, particularly in Germany and Holland. Together with the 1908 Architectural Record article and the Ausgeführte Bauten, a publication of photographs of his work released by Ernst Wasmuth in 1911, the monograph helped to introduce Wright's work to the contemporary architects of Europe. Lloyd Wright later recollected:

> Soon after the work was published in Germany, we found they were using the folio and drawings
> in schools and universities for textbooks. There men like Gropius and Mies van der Rohe were
> students of my age, i.e. 19 and 20 years old, and were greatly impressed and I heard later
> Gropius' mother gave him one of the collections, he claimed he made it his Bible.[1]

A modern movement in art and architecture was well underway in Germany and Austria. But that the Wasmuth monograph profoundly influenced contemporary European architects is evidenced by the work of those architects directly following its publication. Unity Temple in Oak Park, the Larkin Building in

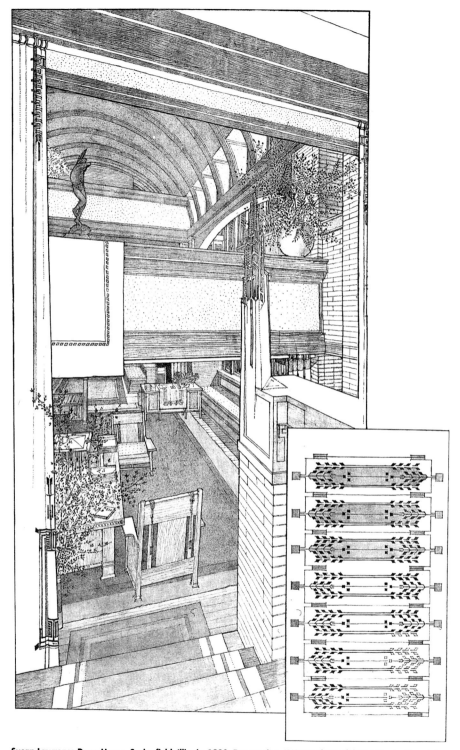

Susan Lawrence Dana House. Springfield, Illinois. 1900. Perspective, "Wasmuth Portfolio" Introduction plate.
FLLW Fdn#9905.041

Buffalo, and many of the great prairie houses influenced modern architecture, returning in form to the United States some years later, in a much misinterpreted adaptation, as the "International style."

Forty-one years later, in 1951, an exhibition of Wright's work, Sixty Years of Living Architecture, *had its European opening in the Palazzo Strozzi, in Florence. For this occasion Wright had planned to use "The Art and Craft of the Machine" as an introductory text; suddenly he discarded the 1901 manuscript and took up this one of 1910. With the opening scheduled for Florence, he no doubt associated the event with the meaningful time he had spent there with Mamah Cheney while working on the Wasmuth edition, a beautiful period in his life that ended in dreadful tragedy. [Published with 72 plates by Ernst Wasmuth, 1910]*

SINCE A PREVIOUS ARTICLE, WRITTEN IN AN ENDEAVOR TO state the nature of the faith and practice fashioning this work, I have had the privilege of studying the work of that splendid group of Florentine sculptors and painters and architects, and the sculptor-painters and painter-sculptors who were also architects: Giotto, Masaccio, Manna, Arnolfo, Pisano, Brunelleschi, Bramante, Sansovino, and Angelo.

No line was drawn between the arts in their epoch. Some of the sculpture is good painting; most of the painting is good sculpture; and in both lie the patterns of architecture. Where this confusion is not a blending of these arts, it is as amazing as it is unfortunate. To attempt to classify the works severely as pure painting, pure sculpture, or pure architecture would be quite impossible, if it were desirable for educational purposes. But be this as it may, what these men of Florence absorbed from their Greek, Byzantine, and Roman forebears, they bequeathed to Europe as the kernel of the Renaissance; and this, if we deduct the Gothic influence of the Middle Ages, has constituted the soul of the Academic fine arts on the Continent.

From these Italian flames were lighted myriads of French, German, and English lights that flourished, flickered feebly for a time, and soon smoldered in the sensuality and extravagance of later periods, until they were extinguished in banal architecture like the Rococo or in nondescript structures such as the Louvre.

This applies to those buildings which were more or less "professional" embodiments of a striving for the beautiful, those buildings which were "good school" performances, which sought consciously to be beautiful. Nevertheless, here as elsewhere, the true basis for any serious study of the art of architecture is in those indigenous structures, the more humble buildings everywhere, which are to architecture what folklore is to literature or folksongs are to music, and with which architects were seldom concerned. In the aggregate of these lie the traits that make them characteristically German, Italian, French, Dutch, English, or Spanish in nature, as the case may be. The traits of these structures are national, of the soil; and, though often slight, their virtue is intimately interrelated with environment and with the habits of life of the people. Their functions are truthfully conceived, and rendered directly with natural feeling. They are always instructive and often beautiful. So, underlying the ambitious and self-conscious blossoms of the human soul, the expressions of "Maryolatry," or adoration of divinity, or cringing to temporal power, there is the love of life which quietly and inevitably finds the right way, and in lovely color, gracious line, and harmonious arrangement imparts it untroubled by any burden—as little concerned with literature or indebted to it as the flower by the wayside that turns its petals upward to the sun is concerned with the farmer, who passes in the road, or is indebted to him for the geometry of its petals or the mathematics of its structure.

Of this joy in living, there is greater proof in Italy than elsewhere. Buildings, pictures, and sculpture seem to be born, like the flowers by the roadside, to sing themselves into being. Approached in the spirit of their conception, they inspire us with the very music of life.

No really Italian building seems ill at ease in Italy. All are happily content with what ornament and color they carry, as naturally as the rocks and trees and garden slopes which are one with them. Wherever the cypress rises, like the touch of a magician's wand, it resolves all into a composition harmonious and complete.

The secret of this ineffable charm would be sought in vain in the rarefied air of scholasticism or pedantic fine art. It lies close to the earth. Like a handful of the moist sweet earth itself, it is so simple that, to modern minds trained in intellectual gymnastics, it would seem unrelated to great purposes. It is so close that almost universally it is overlooked.

Along the wayside some blossom, with unusually glowing color or prettiness of form, attracts us: held by it, we accept gratefully its perfect loveliness; but, seeking to discover the secret of its charm, we find the blossom, whose more obvious claim first arrests our attention, intimately related to the texture and shape of its foliage; we discover a strange sympathy between the form of the flower and the system upon which the leaves are arranged about the stalk. From this we are led to observe a characteristic habit of growth, and resultant nature of structure, having its first direction and form in the roots hidden in the warm earth, kept moist by the conservative covering of leaf mold. This structure proceeds from the general to the particular in a most inevitable way, arriving at the blossom to proclaim in its lines and form the nature of the structure that bore it. It is an organic thing. Law and order are the basis of its finished grace and beauty: its beauty is the expression of fundamental conditions in line, form, and color, true to them, and existing to fulfill them according to design.

We can in no wise [sic] prove beauty to be the result of these harmonious internal conditions. That which through the ages appeals to us as beautiful does not ignore in its fiber the elements of law and order. Nor does it take long to establish the fact that no lasting beauty ignores these elements ever present as conditions of its existence. It will appear, from study of the forms or styles which mankind has considered beautiful, that those which live longest are those which in greatest measure fulfill these conditions. That a thing grows is no concern of ours, because the quality of life is beyond us and we are not necessarily concerned with it. Beauty, in its essence, is for us as mysterious as life. All attempts to say what it is are as foolish as cutting out the head of a drum to find whence comes the sound. But we may study with profit these truths of form and structure, facts of form as related to function, material traits of line determining character, laws of structure inherent in all natural growth. We ourselves are only a product of natural law. These truths, therefore, are in harmony with the essence of our own being, and are perceived by us to be good. We instinctively feel the good, true, and beautiful to be essentially one in the last analysis. Within us there is a divine principle of growth to some end; accordingly we select as good whatever is in harmony with this law.

We reach for the light spiritually, as the plant does physically, if we are sound of heart and not sophisticated by our education.

When we perceive a thing to be beautiful, it is because we instinctively recognize the rightness of the thing. This means that we have revealed to us a glimpse of something essentially of the fiber of our own nature. The artist makes this revelation to us through his deeper insight. His power to visualize his conceptions being greater than our own, a flash of truth stimulates us, and we have a vision of harmonies not understood today, though perhaps to be tomorrow.

This being so, whence came corrupt styles like the Renaissance? From false education, from confusion of the curious with the beautiful. Confounding the sensations awakened by the beautiful with those evoked by things merely curious is a fatal tendency, which increases as civilization moves away from nature and founds conventions in ignorance or defiance of natural law.

The appreciation of beauty on the part of primitive peoples, Mongolian, Indian, Arab, Egyptian, Greek, and Goth, was unerring. Because of this, their work is coming home to us today in another and truer Renaissance, to open our eyes that we may cut away the dead wood and brush aside the accumulated rubbish of centuries of false education. This Renaissance means a return to simple conventions in harmony with nature. Primarily it is a simplifying process. Then, having learned the spiritual lesson that the East has power to teach the West, we may build upon this basis the more highly developed forms our more highly developed life will need.

Nature sought in this way can alone save us from the hopeless confusion of ideas that has resulted in the view that beauty is a matter of caprice, that it is merely a freak of imagination—to one man divine, to another hideous, to another meaningless. We are familiar with the assertion, that, should a man put eleven stovepipe hats on top of the cornice of his building and find them beautiful, why then they are beautiful. Yes, perhaps to him; but the only possible conclusion is, that, like the eleven hats on the cornice, he is not beautiful, because beauty to him is utter violation of all the harmonies of any sequence or consequence of his own nature. To find inorganic things of no truth of relation beautiful is but to demonstrate the lack of beauty in oneself and one's unfitness for any office in administering the beautiful and to provide another example of the stultification that comes from the confusion of the curious with the beautiful.

Education seems to leave modern man less able than the savage to draw the line between these qualities.

A knowledge of cause and effect in line, color, and form, as found in organic nature, furnishes guidelines within which an artist may sift materials, test motives, and direct aims, thus roughly blocking out, at least, the rational basis of his ideas and ideals. Great artists do this by instinct. The thing is felt or divined, by inspiration perhaps, as synthetic analysis of their works will show. The poetry which is prophecy is not a matter to be demonstrated. But what is of great value to the artist in research of this nature is knowledge of those facts of relation, those qualities of line, form, and color which are themselves a language of sentiment and characterize the pine as a pine as distinguished from those determining the willow as a willow; those characteristic traits which the Japanese seize graphically and unerringly

reduce to simple geometry; the graphic soul of the thing, as seen in the geometrical analyses of Hokusai. Korin was the conscious master of the essential in whatever he rendered, and his work stands as a convincing revelation of the soul of the thing he portrayed. So it will be found with all great work— with the paintings of Velázquez and Frans Hals; with Gothic architecture—organic character in all.

By knowledge of nature in this sense alone are these guiding principles to be established. Ideals gained within these limitations are never lost, and an artist may defy his "education." If he is really for nature in this sense, he may be "a rebel against his time and its laws, but never lawless."

The debased periods of the world's art are far removed from any conception of these principles. The Renaissance, Baroque, Rococo, the styles of the Louises are not developed from within. There is little or nothing organic in their nature; they are put on from without. The freedom from the yoke of authority which the Renaissance gave to men was seemingly a great gain; but it served only to bind them senselessly to tradition and to mar the art of the Middle Ages past repair. One cannot go into the beautiful edifices of this great period without hatred of the Renaissance growing in the soul. It proves itself a most wantonly destructive thing in its hideous perversity. In every land where the Gothic or Byzantine, or the Romanesque, that was close to Byzantine, grew, it was a soulless blight, a warning, a veritable damnation of the beautiful. What lovely things remain, it left to us in spite of its nature or when it was least itself. It was not a development; it was a disease.

This is why buildings growing in response to actual needs, fitted into the environment by people who knew no better than to fit them to it with native feeling—buildings that grew as folklore and folksong grew—are better worth study than highly self-conscious academic attempts at the beautiful; academic attempts which the nations seem to possess in common as a gift from Italy, after acknowledging her source of inspiration.

All architecture worthy the name is a growth in accord with natural feeling and industrial means to serve actual needs. It cannot be put on from without. There is little beyond sympathy with the spirit creating it and an understanding of the ideals that shaped it that can legitimately be utilized. Any attempt to use forms borrowed from other times and conditions must end as the Renaissance ends, with total loss of inherent relation to the soul life of the people. It can give us only an extraneous thing in the hands of professors that means little more than a mask for circumstance or a mark of temporal power to those whose lives are burdened, not expressed, by it; the result is a terrible loss to life for which literature can never compensate. Buildings will always remain the most valuable asset in a people's environment, the one most capable of cultural reaction. But until the people have the joy again in architecture as a living art that one sees recorded in buildings of all the truly great periods, so long will architecture remain a dead thing. It will not live again until we break away entirely from adherence to the false ideals of the Renaissance. In that whole movement art was reduced to the level of an expedient. What future has a people content with that? Only that of parasites, feeding on past greatness, and on the road to extinction by some barbarian race with ideals and hungering for their realization in noble concrete form.

In America we are more betrayed by this condition than the people of older countries, for we have no traditional forms except the accumulated ones of all peoples that do not without sacrifice fit new conditions, and there is in consequence no true reverence for tradition. As some sort of architecture is a necessity, American architects take their pick from the world's stock of "ready-made" architecture and are most successful when transplanting form for form, line for line, enlarging details by means of lantern slides from photographs of the originals.

This works well. The people are architecturally clothed and sheltered. The modern comforts are smuggled in cleverly, we must admit. But is this architecture? Is it thus tradition molded great styles? In this polyglot tangle of borrowed forms, is there a great spirit that will bring order out of chaos? Vitality, unity, and greatness out of emptiness and discord?

The ideals of the Renaissance will not, for the Renaissance was inorganic.

A conception of what constitutes an organic architecture will lead to better things once it is planted in the hearts and minds of men whose resource and skill, whose real power, are unquestioned and who are not obsessed by expedients and forms, the nature and origin of which they have not studied in relation to the spirit that produced them. The nature of these forms is not taught in any vital sense in any of the schools in which architects are trained.

A revival of the Gothic spirit is needed in the art and architecture of modern life; an interpretation of the best traditions we have in the world made with our own methods, not a stupid attempt to fasten their forms upon a life that has outgrown them. Reviving the Gothic spirit does not mean using the forms of Gothic architecture handed down from the Middle Ages. It necessarily means something quite different. The conditions and ideals that fixed the forms of the twelfth are not the conditions and ideals that can truthfully fix the forms of the twentieth century. The spirit that fixed those forms is the spirit that will fix the new forms. Classicists and schools will deny the new forms and find no "Gothic" in them. It will not much matter. They will be living, doing their work quietly and effectively, until the borrowed garments, cut over to fit by the academies, are cast off, having served only to hide the nakedness of a moment when art became detached, academic, alien to the lives of the people.

America, more than any other nation, presents a new architectural proposition. Her ideal is democracy, and in democratic spirit her institutions are professedly conceived. This means that she places a life premium upon individuality—the highest possible development of the individual consistent with a harmonious whole—believing that a whole benefited by sacrifice of that quality in the individual rightly considered his "individuality" is undeveloped; believing that the whole, to be worthy as a whole, must consist of individual units, great and strong in themselves, not yoked from without in bondage, but united within, with the right to move in unity, each in its own sphere, yet preserving this right to the highest possible degree for all. This means greater individual life and more privacy in life—concerns which are peculiarly one's own. It means lives lived in greater independence and seclusion, with all toward which an English nobleman aspires, but with absolute unwillingness to pay the price in paternalism and patronage asked of him for the privilege. This dream of freedom, as voiced by the Declaration of Independence, is dear to the heart of every man who has caught the spirit of American institutions; therefore the ideal of every man American in feeling and spirit. Individuality is a national ideal. Where this degenerates into petty individualism, it is but a manifestation of weakness in the human nature, and not a fatal flaw in the ideal.

In America each man has a peculiar, inalienable right to live in his own house in his own way. He is a pioneer in every right sense of the word. His home environment may face forward, may portray his character, tastes, and ideas, if he has any, and every man here has some somewhere about him.

This is a condition at which Englishmen or Europeans, facing toward traditional forms which they are in duty bound to preserve, may well stand aghast. An American is in duty bound to establish traditions in harmony with his ideals, his still unspoiled sites, his industrial opportunities, and industrially he is more completely committed to the machine than any living man. It has given him the things which mean mastery over an uncivilized land—comfort and resources.

His machine, the tool in which his opportunity lies, can only murder the traditional forms of other peoples and earlier times. He must find new forms, new industrial ideals, or stultify both opportunity and forms. But underneath forms in all ages were certain conditions which determined them. In them all was a human spirit in accord with which they came to be; and where the forms were true forms, they will be found to be organic forms—an outgrowth, in other words, of conditions of life and work they arose to express. They are beautiful and significant, studied in this relation. They are dead to us, borrowed as they stand.

I have called this feeling for the organic character of form and treatment the Gothic spirit, for it was more completely realized in the forms of that architecture, perhaps, than any other. At least the infinitely varied forms of that architecture are more obviously and literally organic than any other, and the spirit in which they were conceived and wrought was one of absolute integrity of means to ends. In this spirit America will find the forms best suited to her opportunities, her aims, and her life.

All the great styles, approached from within, are spiritual treasure houses to architects. Transplanted as forms, they are tombs of a life that has been lived.

This ideal of individuality has already ruthlessly worked its way with the lifeless carcasses of the foreign forms it has hawked and flung about in reckless revel that in East, as well as West, amounts to positive riot.

Brown calls loudly for Renaissance, Smith for a French château, Jones for an English manor house, McCarthy for an Italian villa, Robinson for Hanseatic, and Hammerstein for Rococo, while the sedately conservative families cling to "old colonial" wedding cakes with demurely conscious superiority. In all this is found the last word of the *inorganic*. The Renaissance ended in this—a thing absolutely removed from time, place, or people; borrowed finery put on hastily, with no more conception of its meaning or character than Titania had of the donkey she caressed. "All a matter of taste," like the hats on the cornice.

A reaction was inevitable.

It is of this reaction that I feel qualified to speak; for the work illustrated in this volume, with the exception of the work of Louis Sullivan, is the first consistent protest in bricks and mortar against this pitiful waste. It is a serious attempt to formulate some industrial and aesthetic ideals that in a quiet, rational way will help to make a lovely thing of an American's home environment, produced without abuse by his own tools and dedicated in spirit and letter to him.

The ideals of Ruskin and Morris and the teaching of the Beaux Arts have hitherto prevailed in America, steadily confusing, as well as in some respects revealing to us our opportunities. The American, too, of some Old World culture, disgusted by this state of affairs and having the beautiful harmony in the architecture of an English village, European rural community, or the grandiloquent planning of Paris in view has been easily persuaded that the best thing we could do was to adopt some style least foreign to us, stick to it, and plant it continually; a parasitic proceeding, and in any case futile. New York is a tribute to the Beaux Arts, so far as surface decoration goes, and underneath a tribute to the American engineer.

Other cities have followed her lead.

Our better-class residences are chiefly tributes to English architecture, cut open inside and embellished to suit; porches and "conveniences" added: the result in most cases a pitiful mongrel. Painfully conscious of their lack of traditions, our get-rich-quick citizens attempt to buy tradition ready-made and are dragged forward, facing backwards, in attitudes most absurd to those they would emulate, characteristic examples of conspicuous waste.

The point in all this is the fact that revival of the ideals of an organic architecture will have to contend with this rapidly increasing sweep of imported folly. Even the American with some little culture, going contrary to his usual course in other matters, is becoming painfully aware of his inferiority in matters of dress and architecture and goes abroad for both, to be sure they are correct. Thus assured, he is no longer concerned and forgets both. That is more characteristic of the Eastern than the Western man. The real American spirit, capable of judging an issue for itself upon its merits, lies in the West and Middle West, where breadth of view, independent thought, and a tendency to take common sense into the realm of art, as in life, are more characteristic. It is alone in an atmosphere of this nature that the Gothic spirit in building can be revived. In this atmosphere, among clients of this type, I have lived and worked.

Taking common sense into the holy realm of art is a shocking thing and most unpopular in academic cir-cles. It is a species of vulgarity; but some of these questions have become so perplexed, so encrusted by the savants and academies, with layer upon layer of "good school," that their very nature is hidden; approached with common sense, they become childishly simple.

I believe that every matter of artistic import which concerns a building may be put to the common sense of a businessman on the right side every time, and thus given a chance at it, he rarely gives a wrong decision. The difficulty found by this man with the Renaissance, when he tries to get inside— that is, if he does more than merely give the order to "go ahead"—arises from the fact that the thing has no organic basis to give; there is no good reason for doing anything any particular way rather than another way which can be grasped by him or anybody else; it is all largely a matter of taste. In an organic scheme there are excellent reasons why the thing is as it is, what it is there for, and where it is going. If not, it ought not to go, and as a general thing it doesn't. The people themselves are part and parcel and helpful in producing the organic thing. They can comprehend it and make it theirs, and it is thus the only form of art expression to be considered for a democracy, and I will go so far as to say, the truest of all forms.

So I submit that the buildings here illustrated have for the greatest part been conceived and worked in their conclusion in the Gothic spirit in this respect as well as in respect to the tools that produced them, the methods of work behind them, and, finally, in their organic nature considered in themselves. These are limitations, unattractive limitations; but there is no project in the fine arts that is not a problem.

With this idea as a basis, comes another conception of what constitutes a building.

The question then arises as to what is style. The problem no longer remains a matter of working in a prescribed style with what variation it may bear without absurdity if the owner happens to be a restless individualist: so this question is not easily answered.

What is style? Every flower has it; every animal has it; every individual worthy the name has it in some

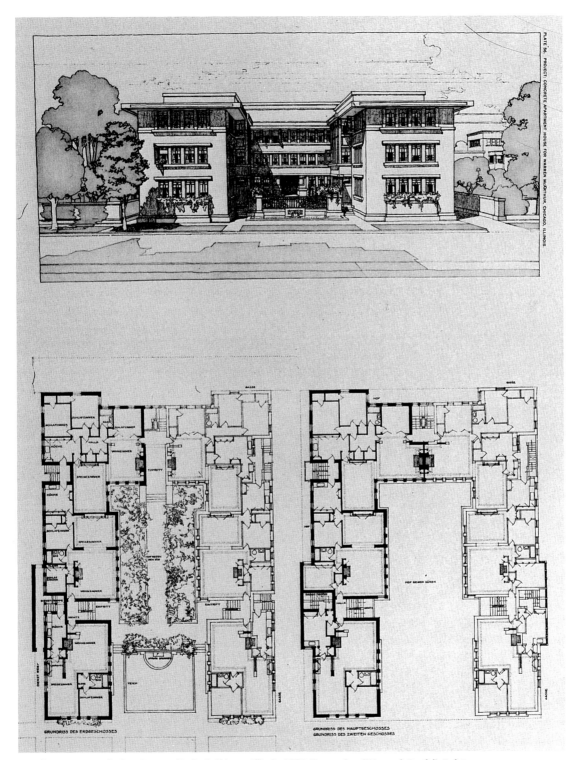

McArthur Apartments in Cast Concrete (Project). Chicago, Illinois. 1905. Perspective, "Wasmuth Portfolio" plate.
FLLW Fdn#0520.004

degree, no matter how much sandpaper may have done for him. It is a free product—a by-product, the result of an organic working out of a project in character and in one state of feeling.

A harmonious entity of whatever sort in its entirety cannot fail of style in the best sense.

In matters of art the individual feeling of the creative artist can but give the color of his own likes and dislikes, his own soul to the thing he shapes. He gives his individuality but will not prevent the building from being characteristic of those it was built to serve, because it necessarily is a solution of conditions they make, and it is made to serve their ends in their own way. In so far as these conditions are peculiar in themselves, or sympathy exists between the clients and the architect, the building will be their building. It will be theirs much more truly than though in ignorant selfhood they had stupidly sought to use means they had not conquered to an end imperfectly foreseen. The architect, then, is their means, their technique and interpreter; the building, an interpretation if he is a true architect in Gothic sense. If he is chiefly concerned in some marvelous result that shall stand as architecture in good form to his credit, the client be damned, why that is a misfortune which is only another species of the unwisdom of his client. This architect is a dangerous man, and there are lots of his kind outside, and some temptations to him inside, the ranks of the Gothic architects. But the man who loves the beautiful, with ideals of organic natures if all artist, is too keenly sensible of the nature of his client as a fundamental condition in his problem to cast him off, although he may give him something to grow to, something in which he may be a little ill at ease at the outset.

In this lies temptation to abuses. Where ignorance of the nature of the thing exists or where there is a particular character or preference, it is to a certain extent the duty of an architect to give his client something dated ahead; for he is entrusted by his client with his interests in matters in which, more frequently than not, the client is ignorant. A commission therefore becomes a trust to the architect. Any architect is bound to educate his client to the extent of his true skill and capacity in what he as a professional adviser believes to be fundamentally right. In this there is plenty of leeway for abuse of the client; temptations to sacrifice him in the interest of personal idiosyncrasies, to work along lines instinctively his preference and therefore easy to him. But in any trust there is chance of failure. This educational relationship between client and architect is more or less to be expected and of value artistically for the reason that, while the architect is educating the client, the client is educating him. And a certain determining factor in this quality of style is this matter growing out of this relation of architect and client to the work in hand, as well as the more definite elements of construction. This quality of style is a subtle thing, and should remain so, and not to be defined in itself so much as to be regarded as a result of *artistic integrity*.

Style, then, if the conditions are consistently and artistically cared for little by little will care for itself. As for working in a nominated style beyond a natural predilection for certain forms, it is unthinkable by the author of any true creative effort.

Given similar conditions, similar tools, similar people, I believe that architects will, with a proper regard for the organic nature of the thing produced, arrive at various results sufficiently harmonious with each other and with great individuality. One might swoop all the Gothic architecture of the world together in a single nation and mingle it with buildings treated horizontally as they were treated vertically or treated diagonally, buildings and towers with flat roofs, long, low buildings with square openings, mingled with tall buildings with pointed ones, in the bewildering variety of that marvelous architectural manifestation, and harmony in the general ensemble inevitably result: the common chord in all being sufficient to bring them unconsciously into harmonious relation.

It is this ideal of an organic working out with normal means to a consistent end that is the salvation of the architect entrusted with liberty. He is really more severely disciplined by this ideal than his brothers of the styles, and less likely to falsify his issue.

So to the schools looking askance at the mixed material entrusted to their charge, thinking to save the nation a terrible infliction of the wayward dreams of mere idiosyncrasies by teaching "the safe course of a good copy," we owe thanks for a conservative attitude, but censure for failure to give to material needed by the nation, constructive ideals that would from *within* discipline sufficiently, at the same time leaving a chance to work out a real thing in touch with reality with such souls as they have. In other words, they are to be blamed for not inculcating in students the conception of architecture as an organic expression of the nature of a problem, for not teaching them to look to this nature for the elements of its working out in accordance with principles found in natural organisms. Study of the great architecture of the world solely in regard to the spirit that found expression in the forms should go with this. But before all should come the study of the *nature* of materials, the *nature* of the tools and processes at command, and the *nature* of the thing they are to be called upon to do.

A training of this sort was accorded the great artists of Japan. Although it was not intellectually self-conscious, I have no doubt the apprenticeship of the Middle Ages wrought like results.

German and Austrian art schools are getting back to these ideas. Until the student is taught to approach the beautiful from within, there will be no great living buildings which in the aggregate show the spirit of true architecture.

An architect, then, in this revived sense, is a man disciplined from within by a conception of the organic nature of his task, knowing his tools and his opportunity, working out his problems with what sense of beauty the gods gave him.

He, disciplined by the very nature of his undertakings, is the only safe man.

To work with him is to find him master of means to a certain end. He acquires a technique in the use of his tools and materials which may be as complete and in every sense as remarkable as a musician's mastery of the resources of his instrument. In no other spirit is this to be acquired in any vital sense, and without it—well—a good copy is the safest thing. If one cannot live an independent life, one may at least become a modest parasite.

It is with the courage that a conviction of the truth of this point of view has given that the problems in this work have been attempted. In that spirit they have been worked out, with what degree of failure or success no one can know better than I. To be of value to the student they must be approached from within, and not from the viewpoint of the man looking largely at the matter from the depths of the Renaissance. Insofar as they are grasped as organic solutions of conditions they exist but to serve, with respect for the limitations imposed by our industrial conditions, and having in themselves a harmony of idea in form and treatment that makes something fairly beautiful of them in relation to life, they will be helpful. Approached from the point of view that seeks characteristic beauty of form and feature as great as that of the Greeks, the Goths, or the Japanese, they will be disappointing; and I can only add it is a little too soon yet to look for such attainment. But the quality of style, in the indefinable sense that it is possessed by any organic thing, that they have. Repose and quiet attitudes they have. Unity of idea, resourceful adaptation of means, will not be found wanting, nor that simplicity of rendering which the machine makes not only imperative but opportune. Although complete, highly developed in detail, they are not.

Self-imposed limitations are in part responsible for this lack of intricate enrichment and partly the imperfectly developed resources of our industrial system. I believe, too, that much ornament in the old sense is not for us yet: we have lost its significance, and I do not believe in adding enrichment merely for the sake of enrichment. Unless it adds clearness to the enunciation of the theme, it is undesirable, for it is very little understood.

I wish to say, also, what is more to the point, that, in a structure conceived in the organic sense, the ornamentation is conceived in the very ground plan, and is of the very constitution of the structure. What ornamentation may be found added purely as such in this structure is thus a makeshift or a confession of weakness or failure.

Where the warp and woof of the fabric do not yield sufficient incident or variety, it is seldom patched on. Tenderness has often to be sacrificed to integrity.

It is fair to explain the point, also, which seems to be missed in studies of the work, that in the conception of these structures they are regarded as severe conventions whose chief office is a background or frame for the life within them and about them. They are considered as foils for the foliage and bloom which they are arranged to carry, as well as a distinct chord or contrast, in their severely conventionalized nature, to the profusion of trees and foliage with which their sites abound.

So the forms and the supervisions and refinements of the forms are, perhaps, more elemental in character than has hitherto been the case in highly developed architecture. To be lived with, the ornamental forms of one's environment should be designed to wear well, which means they must have absolute repose and make no especial claim upon attention; to be removed as far from realistic tendencies as a sense of reality can take them. Good colors, soft textures, living materials, the beauty of the materials revealed and utilized in the scheme, these are the means of decoration considered purely as such.

And it is quite impossible to consider the building one thing and its furnishings another, its setting and environment still another. In the spirit in which these buildings are conceived, these are all one thing, to be foreseen and provided for in the nature of the structure. They are all mere structural details of its character and completeness. Heating apparatus, lighting fixtures, the very chairs and tables, cabinets and musical instruments, where practicable, are of the building itself. Nothing of appliances or fixtures is admitted purely as such where circumstances permit the full development of the building scheme.

Floor coverings and hangings are as much a part of the house as the plaster on the walls or the tiles on the roof. This feature of development has given most trouble, and so far is the least satisfactory to myself, because of difficulties inherent in the completeness of conception and execution necessary. To make these elements sufficiently light and graceful and flexible features of an informal use of an abode requires much more time and thought and money than are usually forthcoming. But it is approached by some later structures more nearly, and in time it will be accomplished. It is still in a comparatively primitive stage of development; yet radiators have disappeared, lighting fixtures are incorporated, floor coverings and hangings are easily made to conform. But chairs and tables and informal articles of use are still at large in most cases, although designed in feeling with the building.

There are no decorations, nor is there place for them as such. The easel picture has no place on the walls. It is regarded as music might be, suited to a mood, and provided for in a recess of the wall if desired, where a door like the cover of a portfolio might be dropped and the particular thing desired studied for a time; left exposed for days, perhaps, to give place to another, or entirely put away by simply closing the wooden portfolio. Great pictures should have their gallery. Oratorio is not performed in a drawing room. The piano, where possible, should and does disappear in the structure, its keyboard, or open work, or tracery necessary for sound its only visible feature. The dining table and chairs are easily managed in the architecture of the building. So far this development has progressed.

Alternate extremes of heat and cold, of sun and storm, have also to be considered. The frost goes four feet into the ground in winter; the sun beats fiercely on the roof with almost tropical heat in summer: an umbrageous architecture is almost a necessity, both to shade the building from the sun and protect the walls from freezing and thawing moisture, the most rapidly destructive to buildings of all natural causes. The overhanging eaves, however, leave the house in winter without necessary sun, and this is overcome by the way in which the window groups in certain rooms and exposures are pushed out to the gutter line. The gently sloping roofs grateful to the prairie do not leave large air spaces above the rooms; and so the chimney has grown in dimensions and importance, and in hot weather ventilates at the high parts the circulating-air spaces beneath the roofs, fresh air entering beneath the eaves through openings easily closed in winter.

Conductor pipes, disfiguring down-spouts, particularly where eaves overhang, in this climate freeze and become useless in winter, or burst with results disastrous to the walls; so concrete rain basins are built in the ground beneath the angles of the eaves, and the water drops through open spouts into their concave surfaces, to be conducted to the cistern by underground drain tiles.

Another modern opportunity is afforded by our effective system of hot-water heating. By this means, the forms of buildings may be more completely articulated, with light and air on several sides. By keeping the ceilings low, the walls may be opened with series of windows to the outer air, the flowers and trees, the prospects, and one may live as comfortably as formerly, less shut in. Many of the structures carry this principle of articulation of various arts to the point where each has its own individuality completely recognized in plan. The dining room and kitchen and sleeping rooms thus become in themselves small buildings and are grouped together as a whole, as in the Coonley house. It is also possible to spread the buildings, which once in our climate of extremes were a compact box cut into compartments, into a more organic expression, making a house in a garden or in the country the delightful thing in relation to either or both that imagination would have it.

The horizontal line is the line of domesticity.

The virtue of the horizontal line is respectfully invoked in these buildings. The inches in height gain tremendous force compared with any practicable spread upon the ground.

To Europeans these buildings on paper seem uninhabitable; but they derive height and air by quite other means and respect an ancient tradition, the only one here worthy of respect—the prairie.

In considering the forms and types of these structures, the fact that they are nearly buildings for the prairie should be borne in mind; the gently rolling or level prairies of the Middle West; the great levels where every detail of elevation becomes exaggerated; every tree a tower above the great calm plains of its flowered surfaces as they lie serene beneath a wonderful sweep of sky. The natural tendency of every ill-considered thing is to detach itself and stick out like a sore thumb in surroundings by nature perfectly quiet. All unnecessary heights have for that reason and for other reasons economic been eliminated, and more intimate relation with outdoor environment sought to compensate for loss of height.

The differentiation of a single, certain, simple form characterizes the expression of one building. Quite a different form may serve for another; but from one basic idea all the formal elements of design are in each case derived and held together in scale and character. The form chosen may flare outward, opening flower-like to the sky, as in the Thomas house; another, droop to accentuate artistically the weight of the masses; another be noncommittal or abruptly emphatic, or its grammar may be deduced from some plant form that has appealed to me, as certain properties in line and form of the sumach were used in the Lawrence house at Springfield; but in every case the motif is adhered to throughout.[2]

In the buildings themselves, in the sense of the whole, there is lacking neither richness nor incident; but these qualities are secured not by applied decoration, they are found in the fashioning of the whole, in which color, too, plays as significant a part as it does in an old Japanese woodblock print.

These ideals take the buildings out of school and marry them to the ground; make them intimate expressions or revelations of the interiors; individualize them, regardless of preconceived notions of style. I have tried to make their grammar perfect in its way and to give their forms and proportions an integrity that will bear study, although few of them can be intelligently studied apart from their environment.

A study of the drawings will show that the buildings presented fall readily into three groups having a family resemblance; the low-pitched hip roofs, heaped together in pyramidal fashion, or presenting quiet, unbroken skylines; the low roofs with simple pediments countering on long ridges; and those topped with a simple slab. Of the first type, the Winslow, Henderson, Willits, Thomas, Heurtley,

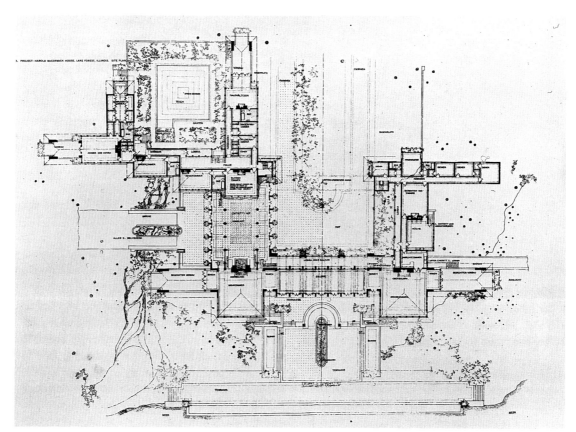

Harold McCormick House (Project). Oak Park, Illinois. 1907. Perspective and plan, "Wasmuth Portfolio" Introduction plate.
FLLW Fdn#0713.004/006

Heath, Cheney, Martin, Little, Gridley, Millard, Tomek, Coonley, and Westcott houses, the Hillside Home School, and the Pettit Memorial Chapel are typical. Of the second type, the Bradley, Hickox, Davenport, and Dana houses are typical. Of the third, atelier for Richard Bock, Unity Church, the concrete house of *The Ladies' Home Journal*, and other designs in process of execution. The Larkin Building is a simple, dignified utterance of a plain, utilitarian type, with sheer brick walls and simple stone copings. The studio is merely an early experiment in "articulation."

A type of structure especially suited to the prairie will be found in the Coonley, Thomas, Heurtley, Tomek, and Robie houses, which are virtually one-floor arrangements, raised at low-story height above the level of the ground. Sleeping rooms are added where necessary in another story.

There is no excavation for this type except for heating purposes. The ground floor provides all necessary room of this nature, and billiard rooms, or playrooms for the children. This plan raises the living rooms well off the ground, which is often damp, avoids the ordinary damp basement, which, if made a feature of the house, sets it so high above the surface, if it is to be made dry, that, in proportion to the ordinary building operation, it rises like a menace to the peace of the prairie.

It is of course necessary that mural decoration and sculpture in these structures should again take their places as architectural developments conceived to conform to their fabric.

To thus make of a dwelling place a complete work of art, in itself as expressive and beautiful and more intimately related to life than anything of detached sculpture or painting, lending itself freely and suitably to the individual needs of the dwellers, a harmonious entity, fitting in color, pattern, and nature the utilities, and in itself really an expression of them in character—this is the modern American opportunity. Once founded, this will become a tradition, a vast step in advance of the day when a dwelling was an arrangement of separate rooms, mere chambers to contain aggregations of furniture, the utility comforts not present. An organic entity this, as contrasted with that aggregation: surely a higher ideal of unity, a higher and more intimate working out of the expression of one's life in one's environment. One thing instead of many things; a great thing instead of a collection of smaller ones.

The drawings, by means of which these buildings are presented here, have been made expressly for this work from colored drawings, which were made from time to time as the projects were presented for solution. They merely aim to render the composition in outline and form and suggest the sentiment of the environment. They are in no sense attempts to treat the subject pictorially and in some cases fail to convey the idea of the actual building. A certain quality of familiar homelikeness is thus sacrificed in these presentments to a graceful decorative rendering of an idea of an arrangement suggesting, in the originals, a color scheme. Their debt to Japanese ideals, these renderings themselves sufficiently acknowledge.

1. Letter of February 3, 1966, from Lloyd Wright to Linn Ann Cowles, author of *An Index and Guide to An Autobiography* (New York: Greenwich Design Publications, 1976).
2. Much of this paragraph and the following paragraphs was only slightly reworded from "In the Cause of Architecture" (1908). This close repetition of ideas was not uncommon for Wright.

THE JAPANESE PRINT: AN INTERPRETATION

By 1912 Wright had been an avid and discriminating collector of Japanese prints for nearly twenty years. But he was more than a collector, he was a dedicated student of the print. All his life he would turn to Japanese prints and draw inspiration from them:

> I have never confided to you the extent to which the Japanese print as such has inspired me. I never got over my first experience with it and I shall never probably recover. I hope I shan't. It was the great gospel of simplification and that came over me, the elimination of all that was insignificant.[1]

Some four years before he wrote this treatise he had given a lecture on prints at the Art Institute, and he used that talk as the basis for this 1912 text, which was published as a book. His "interpretation" is really an in-depth study not just of the print but of the entire culture that it reflects and records.

He made a special point of introducing the study of Japanese prints to his apprentices at the Taliesin Fellowship. Each autumn he would host a "print party," opening with a Japanese dinner cooked on small hibachi stoves that he had brought from Japan. Four apprentices gathered around each stove on the terrace outside his studio. Dinner finished, they filed into the great studio at Taliesin, where he would emerge from the vault with armloads of prints by Hiroshige, Hokusai, Sharaku, and Utamaro—a great feast for the eyes. He explained them and pointed out their significance, how they were made, and what they portrayed. It was obvious that to him the prints were truly a feast not only for the eye, but for the soul, too. [Published without illustrations as a book by Ralph Fletcher Seymour, 1912]

THE UNPRETENTIOUS COLORED WOODCUT OF JAPAN, A thing of significant graven lines on delicate paper which has kissed the color from carved and variously tinted wooden blocks, is helpful in the practice of the fine arts and may be construed with profit in other life concerns as great.

It is a lesson especially valuable to the West, because, in order to comprehend it at all, we must take a viewpoint unfamiliar to us as a people, and in particular to our artists—the purely aesthetic viewpoint. It is a safe means of inspiration for our artists because, while the methods are true methods, the resultant forms are utterly alien to such artistic tradition as we acknowledge and endeavor to make effective.

So, I will neglect the smattering of information as to artists and periods easily obtained from any one* of several available works on the subject and try to tell what these colored engravings are in themselves, and more particularly of their cultural use to us in awakening the artistic conscience or at least in making us feel the disgrace of not realizing the fact that we have none.

Go deep enough into your experience to find that beauty is in itself the finest kind of morality—ethical, purely—the essential fact, I mean, of all morals and manners—and you may personally feel in these aesthetic abstractions of the Japanese mind the innocent and vivid joy which, by reason of obviously established sentiment, is yours in the flowers of field or garden.

A flower is beautiful, we say—but why? Because in its geometry and its sensuous qualities it is an embodiment and significant expression of that precious something in ourselves which we instinctively know to be Life, "An eye looking out upon us from the great inner sea of beauty," a proof of the eternal harmony in the nature of a universe too vast and intimate and real for mere intellect to seize. Intuitively we grasp something of it when we affirm that "the flower is beautiful." And when we say, "It is beautiful," we mean that the quality in us which is our very life recognizes itself there or at least what is its very own: so there vibrates in us a sympathetic chord struck mystically by the flower. Now, as it is with the flower, so is it with any work of art and to greater degree: because a work of fine art is a blossom of the human soul, and so more humanly intimate. In it we find the lineaments of man's thought and the exciting traces of man's feeling—so to say, the very human touch, offered to us in terms of the same qualities that make us exclaim that the flower is beautiful; and it is this quality of absolute and essential beauty in the result of the artist's creative efforts that is the Life of the work of art, more truly than any literal import or adventitious significance it may possess. But it is the quick, immediate perception of this subjective quality, or rather, perhaps, the ability to perceive it instinctively in the work of art, that is lacking in us—as a people. Failing in this perception we are untouched by the true vitalizing power of art and remain outside the precincts of the temple, in a realm, literal, objective, realistic, therefore unreal. In art that which is really essential escapes us for lack of a "disciplined power to see."

The most important fact to realize in a study of this subject is that, with all its informal grace, Japanese art is a thoroughly structural art; fundamentally so in any and every medium. It is always, whatever else it is or is not, structural. The realization of the primary importance of this element of "structure" is also at the very beginning of any real knowledge of design. And at the beginning of structure lies always and everywhere geometry. But, in this art, mathematics begins and ends here, as the mathematical begins and ends in music, however organically inherent here as there in the result.

But we have used the word structure, taking for granted that we agreed upon its meaning. The word structure is here used to designate an organic form, an organization in a very definite manner of parts or elements into a larger unity—a vital whole. So, in design, that element which we call its structure is primarily the pure form, an organization in a very definite manner of parts or elements into a larger unity—a vital whole. So, in design, that element which we call its structure is primarily the pure form, as arranged or fashioned and grouped to "build" the Idea; an idea which must always persuade us of its reasonableness. Geometry is the grammar, so to speak, of the form. It is its architectural principle. But there is a psychic correlation between the geometry of form and our associated ideas, which constitutes its symbolic value. There resides always a certain "spell-power" in any geometric form which seems more or less a mystery, and is, as we say, the soul of the thing. It would carry us far from our subject if we should endeavor to render an accurate, convincing account of the reason why certain geometric forms have come to symbolize for us and potently to suggest certain human ideas, moods, and sentiments—as for instance: the circle, infinity; the triangle, structural unity; the spire, aspiration; the spiral, organic progress; the square, integrity. It is nevertheless a fact that more or less clearly in the subtle differentiations of these

*Japanese Color Prints by Von Seidlit—the best book extant on the subject. The Masters of Ukiyoe, and History of the Ukiyoe, by Ernest Fenollosa. Japanese Illustrations, by Dr. William Anderson. Japanese Illustrations and Japanese Woodcuts, by E. S. Strange.

elemental geometric forms, we do sense a certain psychic quality which we may call the "spell-power" of the form, and with which the artist freely plays, as much at home with it as the musician at his keyboard with his notes. A Japanese artist grasps form always by reaching underneath for its geometry. No matter how informal, vague, evanescent, the subject he is treating may seem to be, he recognizes and acknowledges geometry as its aesthetic skeleton; that is to say—not its structural skeleton alone, but by virtue of what we have termed the symbolic "spell-power"—it is also the suggestive soul of his work. A Japanese artist's power of geometrical analysis seems little short of miraculous. An essential geometry he sees in everything, only, perhaps, to let it vanish in mystery for the beholder of his finished work. But even so, escaping as it does at first the critical eye, its influence is the more felt. By this grasp of geometric form and sense of its symbol-value, he has the secret of getting to the hidden core of reality. However fantastic his imaginative world may be, it competes with the actual and subdues it by superior loveliness and human meaning. The forms, for instance, in the pine tree (as of every natural object on earth), the geometry that underlies and constitutes the peculiar pine character of the tree—what Plato meant by the eternal idea—he knows familiarly. The unseen is to him visible. A circle and a straight line or two, rhythmically repeated, prescribe for him its essentials perfectly. He knows its textures and color qualities as thoroughly. Having these by heart, he is master of the pine and builds trees to suit his purpose and feeling, each as truly a pine and a pine only as the one from which he wrung the secret. So, from flying bird to breaking wave, from Fujiyama to a petal of the blossoming cherry afloat upon the stream, he is master, free to create at will. Nor are these forms to him mere specters or flimsy guesses—not fictitious semblances to which he can with impunity do violence. To him they are fundamental verities of structure, pre-existing and surviving particular embodiments in his material world.

What is true of the pine tree, for and by itself, is no less true in the relation of the tree to its environment. The Japanese artist studies pine-tree nature not only in its import and bearing but lovingly understands it in its habitat and natural element as well—which, if the geometry be called the grammar, may by equal privilege of figurative speech be termed the syntax. To acquire this knowledge, he devotes himself to the tree, observes analytically yet sympathetically, then leaves it, and with his brush begins to feel for its attitude and intimate relations as he remembers them. He proceeds from visualized generals to definite particulars in this contemplative study, and as soon as he has recognized really the first elements constituting the skeleton of the structure, which you may see laid bare in the analysis by Hokusai, his progress in its grammar and syntax is rapid. The Japanese artist, by virtue of the shades of his ancestors, is born a trained observer; but only after a long series of patient studies does he consider that he knows his subject. However, he has naturally the ready ability to seize upon essentials, which is the prime condition of the artist's creative insight. Were all pine trees, then, to vanish suddenly from the earth, he could, from this knowledge, furnish plan and specification for the varied portrayal of a true species—because what he has learned and mastered and made his own is the specific and distinguishing nature of the pine tree. Using this word "Nature" in the Japanese sense I do not of course mean that outward aspect which strikes the eye as a visual image of a scene or strikes the ground glass of a camera, but that inner harmony which penetrates the outward form or letter and is its determining character; that quality in the thing (to repeat what we have said before) that is its significance and its Life for us—what Plato called (with reason, we see, psychological if not metaphysical) the "eternal idea of the thing."

We may refer, then, to the nature of a "proposition" as we do to the nature of an animal, of a plant, of an atmosphere, or a building material. Nature, in this sense, is not to be studied much in books. They are little more than the by-product of other men's ideas of the thing, which in order to distill from it his own particular sense of its intrinsic poetry the artist must know at firsthand. This poetry he must find in the thing for himself, the poetry it holds in reserve for him and him alone, and find it by patient, sympathetic study. This brings us to the aesthetics of Japanese art.

Ideas exist for us alone by virtue of form. The form can never be detached from the idea; the means must be perfectly adapted to the end. So in this art the problem of form and style is an organic problem solved easily and finally. Always we find the one line, the one arrangement that will exactly serve. It is a facile art, incapable of adequate analysis, for it is the felicity of an intuitive state of mind and must, on the part of the student, be similarly recognized by intuition.

These simple colored engravings are a language whose purpose is absolute beauty, inspired by the Japanese need of that precise expression of the beautiful, which is to him reality immeasurably more than the natural objects from which he wrested the secret of their being. This expression of the beautiful is inevitable and there inheres in the result that inevitableness which we feel in all things lovely. This process of woodblock printing is but one modest medium by means of which he may express his sense of the universal nature of things, and which he justifies in his characteristic, highly expressive fashion.

So, these prints are designs, patterns, in themselves beautiful as such; and what other meanings they may have are merely incidental, interesting, or curious by-products.

Broadly stated then, the first and supreme principle of Japanese aesthetics consists in stringent simplification by elimination of the insignificant and a consequent emphasis of reality. The first prerequisite for the successful study of this strange art is to fix the fact in mind at the beginning that it is the sentiment of Nature alone which concerns the Japanese artist; the sentiment of Nature as beheld by him in those vital meanings which he alone seems to see and alone therefore endeavors to portray.

The Japanese, by means of this process—to him by this habit of study almost instinctive—casts a glamour over everything. He is a poet. Surely life in old Japan must have been a perpetual communion with the divine heart of Nature. For Nippon drew its racial inspiration from, and framed its civilization in accord with, a native perception of Nature-law.

Nippon made its body of morals and customs a strict conventionalization of her nature forms and processes; and therefore as a whole her civilization became a true work of Art. No more valuable object lesson was ever afforded civilization than this instance of a people who have made of their land and the buildings upon it, of their gardens, their manners and garb, their utensils, adornments, and their very gods, a single consistent whole, inspired by a living sympathy with Nature as spontaneous as it was inevitable. To the smallest fraction of Japanese lives what was divorced from Nature was reclaimed by Art and so redeemed. And what was the rule thus established progressively in individual and social life, making of it in itself an art—a thing of strange and poignant beauty—dominated all popular art production also and furnished the criterion.

This process of elimination and of the insignificant we find to be the first and most important consideration for artists, after establishing the fundamental mathematics of structure. A Japanese may tell you what he knows in a single drawing, but never will he attempt to tell you all he knows. He is quite content to lay stress upon a simple element, insignificant enough perhaps until he has handled it; then (as we find again and again in the works of Korin and his school) the very slight means employed touches the soul of the subject so surely and intimately that while less would have failed of the intended effect, more would have been profane. This process of simplification is in a sense a dramatization of the subject, just as all Japanese ceremonials are the common offices and functions of their daily life delicately dramatized in little. The tea ceremony is an instance. Nothing more than the most gracefully perfect way of making and serving a cup of tea! Yet, often a more elegant and impressive ceremonial than a modern religious service. To dramatize is always to conventionalize; to conventionalize is, in a sense, to simplify; and so these drawings are all conventional patterns subtly geometrical, imbued at the same time with symbolic value, this symbolism honestly built upon a mathematical basis, as the woof of the weave is built upon the warp. It has little in common with the literal. It is more akin to a delicate musical instrument that needs no dampers or loud pedals. Fleshly shade and material-istic shadow are unnecessary to it, for in itself it is no more than pure living sentiment.

Were we to contrast the spiritual grace of sim-ple wildflowers, with the material richness of dou-bled varieties under cultivation, we would institute a suggestive comparison of this unpretentious art of the East with the more pretentious art of the West. Where the art of Japan is a poetic symbol, much of ours is attempted realism, that succeeds only in being rather pitifully literal. Where the one is deli-cately sensuous, the other is only too apt to be stupidly sensual.

This intuition of the Japanese artist for drama-tizing his subject is no finer than his touch and tact are unerring. He knows materials and never falsifies them. He knows his tools and never abuses them. And this, too, just because he apprehends the secret of character at every chance contact with the actual. In the slight wash drawings of the kakemono, we find a more sheer and delicate manifestation of re-serve than in this more popular, and in a sense there-fore, more vulgar form of expression. Always latent, however, in the slightest and seemingly most infor-mal designs, in the least of these works as through the greatest, the geometric structure effects a potent spell. No composition can we find not affected by it and that does not bear this psychic spell meanwhile, as if unconscious of its precious burden, its efficient causes enwoven and subtly hid between the lines of its geometric forms. As the poor saint was believed to bear his mystic nimbus, so each humble master-piece asserts its magic of invisible perfection. Yet, this mystery is conclusively reduced by Japanese masters to its scientific elements, as exemplified by certain pages of textbooks by Hokusai, wherein the structural diagrams are clearly given and trans-formation to material objects shown progressively step by step.

This primitive graphic art, like all true art, has limitations firmly fixed; in this case more narrowly fixed than in any art we know. Strictly within these limitations, however, the fertility and resource of the Japanese mind produced a range of aesthetic inven-tions that runs the whole gamut of sentiment, besides reproducing with faithfulness the costumes, manners, and customs of a unique and remarkable civilization, constituting its most valuable real record—and with-out violating a single aesthetic tradition.

The faces in these drawings repel the novice and chill the student accustomed to less pure aes-thetic abstractions; and the use of the human form in unrealistic fashion has often been explained on the ground of religious scruples. Nothing more than the aesthetic consideration involved is necessary to justi-fy it. The faces in these drawings are "in place," har-monious with the rest, and one may actually satisfy himself on the subject by observing how the ten-dency toward realism in the faces portrayed by Kiyonaga[2] and Toyokuni[3] vulgarized results artisti-cally, introducing as they did, this element—no doubt, for the same reason that actors sometimes play to the applauding gallery. The faces as found in the prints of the great period were the Japanese countenance dramatized, to use the term once more. They were masks, conventions, the visual im-age of the ethnic character of a people varied by each artist for himself. A close student may identify the work of any particular artist by merely ascertain-ing his particular variation, the print being otherwise totally concealed. And although an actor was por-trayed in many different roles, the individuality of the countenance, its character, was held throughout in the mask.

You may never fail to recognize Danjuro[4] in all the various drawings by Shunsho[5] and other artists that he inspired, and you may recognize others when you have made their acquaintance. But the means by which this was accomplished are so slight that the convention is scarcely disturbed, and no re-alism taints the result. A countenance drawn to please us would vulgarize the whole, for its realism would violate the aesthetic law of the structure. You find something like this typical face in the work of the Pre-Raphaelites, Burne-Jones, and Rossetti. These are often inanities as distressing as the more legitimate conventions of the Japanese are satisfying, because they were made in a more or less literal set-ting; the whole being inorganic and inconsistent. You will find something of this conventionalizing tendency employed more consistently and artistical-ly in a Morris prose epic or verse tale, or in Spenser's

Faerie Queene, where raging knightly battles and frightful episodes move quietly remote and sedate across the enchanted reader's field of mental vision, affecting him simply by their picturesque outlines and charm of color, as might an old arras.

The use of color, always in the flat—that is, without chiaroscuro—plays a wonderful but natural part in the production of this art and is responsible largely for its charm. It is a means grasped and understood as perfectly as the rhythm of form and line, and it is made in its way as significant. It affords a means of emphasizing and differentiating the forms themselves, at the same time that it is itself an element of the pattern. The blacks are always placed flat in the pattern, as pattern for its own sake—a design within a design. Comments are often made on the wonderfully successful use of masses of deep black, but the other colors at their command are used as successfully, according to the same method, to an identical, if less emphatic effect.

As we see the prints today, it must be confessed that time has imbued the color with added charm. Old vegetable dyes, saturating and qualified by the soft texture of wonderful silken paper, soften and change with the sunlight of the moist climate, much as the colors in oriental rugs. Blues become beautiful yellows; purples soft browns; *beni,* or bright red, fades to luminous pink; while a certain cool green together with the translucent grays and the brilliant red lead are unchangeable. The tenderness of tone found in fine prints is indescribable. This is in great part due to the action of time on the nature of the dye stuffs or pigments employed. When first printed, they were comparatively crude, and much of the credit formerly given by connoisseurs to the printer should be accredited to age. When first printed, also, there was a certain conventionalized symbolism in the use of color, which time confuses. The sky was then usually gray or blue, sometimes yellow; the water blue; grass green; garments polychromatic; woodwork red lead, pink, or yellow. Owing to the manner in which the color was brushed upon the block, few prints are exactly alike, and sometimes great liberty was taken with the color by the printer, most interesting differentiations of color occurring in different prints

from the same block. In itself, the color element in the Japanese print is delight—an absolute felicity, unrivaled in charm by the larger means employed in more pretentious mediums. The prints afford a liberal education in color values, especially related to composition. A perfect color balance is rarely wanting in the final result, and although certain qualities in this result are in a sense adventitious, yet it should be strongly insisted, after all, that the foundation for the miracles of harmonious permutation was properly laid by the artist himself.

In this wedding of color and gracious form, we have finally what we call a good decoration. The ultimate value of a Japanese print will be measured by the extent to which it distills, or rather exhales, this precious quality called "decorative." We as a people do not quite understand what that means and are apt to use the term slightingly as compared with art, which has supposedly some other and greater mission. I—speaking for myself—do not know exactly what other mission it legitimately could have, but I am sure of this, at least—that the rhythmic play of parts, the poise and balance, the respect the forms pay to the surface treated, and the repose these qualities attain to and impart and which together constitute what we call good decoration, are really the very life of all true graphic art whatsoever. In the degree that the print possesses this quality, it is abidingly precious; this quality determines—constitutes, its intrinsic value.

As to the subject matter of the figure pieces, it is true that the stories they tell are mainly of the Yoshiwara,[6] or celebrate the lover and the geisha, but with an innocence incomprehensible to us; for Japan at that time—although the family was the unit of her civilization—had not made monopoly of the sex relation the shameless essence of this institution, and the Yoshiwara was the center of the literary and artistic life of the common people. Their fashions were set by the Yoshiwara. The geisha, whose place in Japanese society was the same as that of the Greek Hetaira, or her ancient Hindu equivalent, as for instance she appears in the Hindu comedy, the *"Little Clay Cart,"* was not less in her ideal perfection than Aspasia, beloved of Pericles. The geisha was perhaps the most exquisite product, scandalous as the fact may appear, of an exquisite civilization. She was in society the living Japanese work of art: thoroughly trained in music, literature, and the rarest and fairest amenities of life, she was herself the crowning amenity and poetic refinement of their life. This, all must recognize and comprehend; else we shall be tempted by false shames and Puritan prejudices to resent the theme of so many of the loveliest among the prints, and by a quite stupid dogmatism disallow our aesthetic delight in their charm. But we have very likely said enough of the print itself; let us pass on to consider what it has already done for us and what it may yet do. We have seen that this art exists—in itself a thing of beauty—inspired by need of expressing the common life in organic terms, having itself the same integrity, considered in its own nature, as the flower. Caught and bodied forth there by human touch is a measure of that inner harmony which we perceive as a proof of goodness and excellence.

It exists, a material means for us to a spiritual end, perhaps more essentially prophetic in function than it was to the people for whom it came into candid and gracious being. It has already spoken to us a message of aesthetic and ethical import. Indeed, its spirit has already entered and possessed the soul and craft of many men of our race and spoken again through them more intimately and convincingly than ever. That message we recognize in more familiar accents uttered by Whistler, Manet, Monet, the "Plein-air" school of France—Puvis de Chavannes, M. Boutet de Monvel—and through them it has further spread its civilizing, because its conventionalizing, simplifying, clarifying influence to the arts and crafts of the occident on both sides of the Atlantic. Every dead wall in the land bears witness to the direct or indirect influence of this humble Japanese art of the people; for it has given us what we some time ago called "poster art." Because of it, in England Aubrey Beardsley and his kith lived and wrought. Modern France, the first to discover its charm, has fallen under its spell completely; French art and Parisian fashions feel its influence more from year to year. The German and Austrian Secessionist movement owes it a large debt of gratitude. Yet the influence of this art is still young. The German mind has only recently awakened to its significance and proceeds now with characteristic thoroughness to ends only half discerned. It has spread abroad the gospel of simplification as no other modern agency has preached it and has taught that organic integrity within the work of art itself is the fundamental law of beauty. Without it, work may be a meretricious mask with literal suggestion or sensual effect, not true art. That quality in the work which is "real" escapes and the would-be artist remains where he belongs—outside the sanctuary. The print has shown us that no more than a sandbank and the sea, or a foreground, a telegraph pole, and a weed in proper arrangement, may yield a higher message of love and beauty, a surer proof of life than the sentimentality of Raphael or Angelo's magnificent pictorial sculpture. Chaste and delicate, it has taught that healthy and wholesome sentiment has nothing in common with sentimentality, nor sensuous feeling with banal sensuality; that integrity of means to ends is in art indispensable to the poetry of so-called inspired results; and that the inspiring life of the work of art consists and inheres, has its very breath and creative being within the work itself; an integrity, in fine, as organic as anything that grows in the great out-of-doors.

Owing to its marked ethnic eccentricity, this art is a particularly safe means of cultivation for us, because the individual initiative of the artist is not paralyzed by forms which he can use as he finds them, ready-made. It may become most useful on this very account, as a corrector of the fatal tendency to imitation—be the antidote to the very poison it might administer to the weak and unwary—to that corrupting, stultifying, mechanical parasitism that besets and betrays so often to his ruin, in these days of hustle and drive, the eager and ambitious artist. For the architect, particularly, it is a quickening inspiration, without attendant perils, owing to its essentially structural character and diverse materials and methods. To any and all artists it must offer great encouragement, because it is so striking a proof of the fact readily overlooked—that to the true artist his limitations are always, if but understood and rightly wooed, his most faithful and serviceable friends.

If, then, there is a culture we might acquire whereby the beautiful may be apprehended as such and help restore to us the fine instinctive perception of and worship for the beautiful, which should be our universal birthright instead of the distorted ideas, the materialistic perversions of which we are victims, we assuredly want to know what it is and just how it may be had. Nothing at this moment can be of greater importance to us educationally. For the laws of the beautiful are immutable as those of elementary physics. No work sifted by them and found wanting can be a work of art. The laws of the beautiful are like the laws of physics, not derived from external authority, nor have they regard to any ulterior utility. They preexist any perception of them; inhere, latent, and effective, in man's nature and his world. They are not made by any genius, they are perceived first by the great artist and then revealed to mankind in his works. All varieties of form, line, or color, all tendencies in any direction have, besides what value they may have acquired by virtue of the long cultural tradition recounting back to prehistoric man, a natural significance and inevitably express something. As these properties are combined, arranged, and harmonized, expression is gained and modified. Even a discord is in a sense an expression—an expression of the devil or of decay. But the expression we seek and need is that of harmony or of the good; known otherwise as the true, often spoken of as the beautiful, and personified as God. It is folly to say that if the ear can distinguish a harmonious combination of sounds, the eye cannot distinguish a harmonious combination of tones or shapes or lines. For in the degree that the ear is sensitive to sound—to the extent that it can appreciate the harmony of tones—in even a larger degree the eye will see and appreciate, if duly trained to attend them, the expression of harmonies in form, line, and color purely as such; and it is exactly harmonies of this kind, merely, which we find exemplified and exquisitely elucidated in Japanese prints.

Rhythmical and melodious combinations of tone otherwise only "noise" have portrayed the individualities of great souls to us—a Bach, Beethoven, or a Mozart; and while the practice of no musical rule of three could compass their art or sound the depths of their genius, there are definite laws of harmony and structure common to their art which are well known and systematically taught and imparted. So the mysterious impress of personality is revealed in certain qualities of this unpretentious art, as any even cursory observer must note, in the works of Harunobu[7], Shunsho, Kiyonaga, Hokusai, and Hiroshige.

The principles underlying and in a sense governing the expression of personal feeling and the feeling of personality as expressed in these prints, or for the matter of that in any veritable work of art, have now been clearly formulated anew for many of us by assiduous study of their works. Questions of aesthetics may no longer be so readily referred to with flippancy, as mere negligible "matters of taste." Aside from their ethnic character—the fact that the individuality of these expressions may be but the color, so to say, of some Japanese artist's soul—such expressions do convey an ideal of the conditions they seek to satisfy, for the simple reason that the expression was the sought and wrought response to spiritual need, which nothing less or else could satisfy. Just as Beethoven at his keyboard imposed upon tone the character of his soul, so by these simple colored drawings a similar revelation is achieved by the Japanese artist through the medium of dye stuffs and graven lines applied to sensitive paper, putting together its elements of expression in accord with brain and heart, attaining to beauty as a result insofar as the artist was true to the limitations imposed upon him by the nature of the means he employed. He might merely characterize his subject and possess little more than the eye of the great craftsman; or he might idealize it according to the realizing insight of the great artist; but in either case to the degree that the colors and lines were true to material and means delightfully significant of the idea, the result would be a creative work of art.

Now, all the while, just as in any musical composition, a conventionalizing process would be going on. To imitate that natural modeling of the subject in shade and shadow—to render realistically its appearance and position—would require certain dexterity of hand and a mechanic's eye certainly. But in the artist's mind there was a living conception at work—the idea: the revelation of the vision by means of the brush and dye stuffs and paper applied to engraved wooden blocks, with strict regard and devout respect for the limitations of materials, and active sympathy making all eloquent together; eloquent, however, in their own peculiar fashion as graven lines on sensitive paper, which has received color from the variously tinted blocks and wherein this process is frankly confessed—the confession itself becoming a delightful poetic circumstance. There results from all this a peculiar, exquisite language, not literature, telling a story regardless of the conditions of its structure. For a picture should be no imitation of anything, no pretended hole in the wall through which you glimpse a story about something or behold winter in summer or summer in winter. *Breaking Home Ties*, for instance, or any of its numerous kith and kin cannot be dignified as art. There are many degrees of kinship to *Breaking Home Ties* not so easy to detect, yet all of which bear the marks of vulgar pretense. The message of the Japanese print is to educate us spiritually for all time beyond such banality.

Not alone in the realm of the painter is the message being heeded, but also in that of the musician, the sculptor, and the architect.

In sculpture the antithesis of the lesson is found in the "Rogers Groups," literal replicas of incidents that as sculpture are only pitiful. Sculpture has three dimensions, possibilities of mass and silhouette, as well as definite limitations peculiar to itself. To disregard them is death to art. The Venus, the Victory[8], classics living in our hearts today, and a long list of noble peers, are true sculpture. But the slavish making of literature has cursed both painter and sculptor. They have been tempted to make their work accomplish what literary art may achieve so much better—forcing their medium beyond its limits to its utter degradation. And this is as true of decorative art and in a sense true of architecture. General principles deduced from this popular art of the Japanese apply readily to these problems of right aesthetic conventionalization of natural things, revealing the potential poetry of nature as it may be required to make them live in the arts. This culture of the East therefore brings to us of the West invaluable aid in the process of our civilization. We marvel, with a tinge of envy, at the simple inevitableness with which the life-principle in so slight a thing as a willow wand will find fullness of expression as a willow tree—a glorious sort of completeness—with that absolute repose which is as of a destiny fulfilled. Inevitably the secret of the acorn is the glory of the oak. The fretted cone arises as the stately pine, finding the fullness of a destined life in untrammeled expression of its life-principle simply, naturally, and beautifully. Then we go to Nature that we may learn her secret, to find out that there has been laid upon us an artificiality that often conceals and blights our very selves, and in mere course of time and the false education of our mistaken efforts, deforms past recognition the life-principle originally implanted in us for our personal growth as men and our expressive function as artists.

We find and feel always in Nature herself from zero to infinity, an accord of form and function with life-principle that seems to halt only with our attempted domestication of the infinite. Society seems to lose or at least set aside some rare and precious quality in domesticating or civilizing—no—that is, in this conventionalizing process of ours which we choose to call civilization. Striving for freedom we gain friction and discord for our pains. The wisest savants and noblest poets have therefore gone direct to Nature for the secret. There they hoped against hope to find the solution of this maddening, perplexing problem; the right ordering of human life. But however much we may love oak or pine in a state of Nature their freedom is not for us. It belongs to us no longer, however much the afterglow of barbarism within us may yearn for it. Real civilization means for us a right conventionalizing of our original state of Nature. Just such conventionalizing as the true artist imposes on natural forms. The lawgiver and reformer of social customs must have, however, the artist soul, the artist eye, in directing this process, if the light of the race is not to go out. So, art is not alone the expression, but in turn must be the great conservator and transmitter of the finer sensibilities of a people. More still: it is to show those who may understand just where and how we shall bring coercion to bear upon the material of human conduct. So the indigenous art of a people is their only prophecy and their true artists, their school of anointed prophets and kings. It is so now more than ever before because we are further removed from Nature as an original source of inspiration. Our own art is the only light by which this conventionalizing process we call "civilization" may eventually make its institutions harmonious with the fairest conditions of our individual and social life.

I wish I might use another word than "conventionalizing" to convey the notion of this magic of the artist mind, which is the constant haunting reference of this paper, because it is the perpetual insistent suggestion of this particular art we have discussed. Only an artist, or one with genuine artistic training, is likely, I fear, to realize precisely what the word means as it is used here. Let me illustrate once more. To know a thing, what we can really call knowing, a man must first love the thing, which means that he can sympathize vividly with it. Egypt thus knew the lotus and translated the flower to the dignified stone forms of her architecture. Such was the lotus conventionalized. Greece knew and idealized the acanthus in stone translations. Thus was the acanthus conventionalized. If Egypt or Greece had plucked the lotus as it grew and given us a mere imitation of it in stone, the stone forms would have died with the original. In translating, however, its very life-principle into terms of stone well adapted to grace a column capital, the Egyptian artist made it pass through a rarefying spiritual process, whereby its natural character was really intensified and revealed in terms of stone adapted to an architectural use. The lotus gained thus imperishable significance; for the life-principle in the flower is transmuted in terms of building stone to idealize a need. This is conventionalization. It is reality because it is poetry. As the Egyptian took the lotus, the Greek the acanthus, and the Japanese every natural thing on earth, and as we may adapt to our highest use in our own way a natural flower or thing—so civilization must take the natural man to fit him for his place in this great piece of architecture we call the

social state. Today, as centuries ago, it is the prophetic artist eye that must reveal this natural state thus idealized, conventionalized harmoniously with the life-principle of all men. How otherwise shall culture be discerned? All the wisdom of science, the cunning of politics, and the prayers of religion can but stand and wait for the revelation—awaiting at the hands of the artist "conventionalization," that free expression of life-principle which shall make our social living beautiful because organically true. Behind all institutions or dogmatic schemes, whatever their worth may be, or their venerable antiquity, behind them all is something produced and preserved for its aesthetic worth; the song of the poet, some artist vision, the pattern seen in the mount.

Now speaking a language all the clearer because not native to us, beggared as we are by material riches, the humble artist of old Japan has become greatly significant as interpreter of the one thing that can make the concerns, the forms, of his everyday life—whether laws, customs, manners, costumes, utensils, or ceremonials—harmonious with the life-principle of his race—and so living native forms, humanly significant, humanly joy giving—an art, a religion, as in ever varied moods, in evanescent loveliness he has made Fujiyama—that image of man in the vast—the God of Nippon.

1. Frank Lloyd Wright, address to the Taliesin Fellowship, June 20, 1954.
2. Torii Kiyonaga (1752–1815), prolific print designer perhaps best known for his tall, elegant women. Although the last major member of the Torii school, Kiyonaga was considered the great *ukiyo-e* master of the 1780s with tremendous influence through the end of the century, although he is believed to have given up printmaking about 1790.
3. Utagawa Toyokuni (1769–1825), an *ukiyo-e* painter and print designer whose most typical work depicted actors.
4. Ichikawa Danjuro, a famous Kabuki actor and the subject of numerous prints.
5. Katsukawa Shunsho (1726–1792) was one of the finest of the *ukiyo-e* actor print designers and a favorite of Wright's.
6. Pleasure was strictly controlled during the Tokugawa period (1603–1868), and the Yoshiwara was the licensed entertainment quarter of Edo, the "floating world" of the geisha and Kabuki theater.
7. Suzuki Harunobu (1724–1770) is known for his *nishiki-e,* brocade prints, of innocent youth. Although his prints were enormously popular until his death, the sweetness of his figures soon fell from favor and was replaced by the stately grace and elegance of Kiyonaga's courtesans.
8. The well-known *Winged Victory of Samothrace* was a favorite sculptural piece of Wright's. He had plaster casts of it made in reduced size and placed them in several of his early buildings.

IN THE CAUSE OF ARCHITECTURE: SECOND PAPER

When it was published in May 1914, this second paper in the series "In the Cause of Architecture" appeared without illustrations. In an introductory note, M. A. Mikkelsen, the editor of The Architectural Record, *mentioned that an "individual exhibit" of work Wright had completed since his return from Europe was to be held in conjunction with the Chicago Architectural Club's exhibition at the Art Institute.* [Published in The Architectural Record, May 1914]

—"Style, therefore, will be the man, it is his. Let his forms alone."

"NATURE HAS MADE CREATURES ONLY; ART HAS MADE men. Nevertheless, or perhaps for that very reason, every struggle for truth in the arts and for the freedom that should go with the truth has always had its own peculiar load of disciples, neophytes, and quacks. The young work in architecture here in the Middle West, owing to a measure of premature success, has for sometime past been daily rediscovered, heralded, and drowned in noise by this new characteristic feature of its struggle. The so-called movement threatens to explode soon in foolish exploitation of unripe performances or topple over in pretentious attempts to "speak the language." The broker, too, has made his appearance to deal in its slender stock in trade, not a wholly new form of artistic activity certainly, but one serving to indicate how profitable this intensive rush for a place in the "new school" has become.

Just at this time it may be well to remember that "every form of artistic activity is not Art."

Obviously this stage of development was to be expected and has its humorous side. It has also unexpected and dangerous effects, astonishingly in line with certain prophetic letters written by honest "conservatives" upon the publication of the former paper of 1908.

Although an utterance from me of a critical nature is painful, because it must be a personal matter, perhaps a seeming retraction on my part, still all that ever really happens is "personal matter" and the time has come when forbearance ceases to be either virtue or convenience. A promising garden seems to be rapidly overgrown with weeds, notwithstanding the fact that "all may raise the flowers now, for all have got the seed." But the seed has not been planted—transplanting is preferred, but it cannot raise the needed flowers.

To stultify or corrupt our architectural possibilities is to corrupt our aesthetic life at the fountainhead. Her Architecture is the most precious of the susceptibilities of a young, constructive country in this constructive stage of development; and maintaining its integrity in this respect, therefore, distinctly a cause.

When, twenty-one years ago, I took my stand, alone in my field, the cause was unprofitable, seemingly impossible, almost unknown, or, if known, was, as a rule, unhonored and ridiculed—Montgomery Schuyler[1] was the one notable exception to the rule. So swiftly do things "come on" in this vigorous and invigorating age that although the cause itself has had little or no recognition, the work has more than its share of attention and has attracted to itself abuses seldom described—never openly attacked—but which a perspective of the past six years will enable me to describe, as I feel they must render the finer values in this work abortive for the time being, if they do not wholly defeat its aim. Many a similar work in the past has gone prematurely to ruin owing to similar abuses— to rise again, it is true, but retarded generations in time.

I still believe that the ideal of an organic* architecture forms the origin and source, the strength, and, fundamentally, the significance of everything ever worthy the name of architecture.

And I know that the sense of an organic architecture, once grasped, carries with it in its very nature the discipline of an ideal at whatever cost to self-interest or the established order.

It is itself a standard and an ideal.

And I maintain that only earnest artist integrity, both of instinct and of intelligence, can make any forward movement of this nature in architecture of lasting value.

The ideal of an organic architecture for America is no mere license for doing the thing that you please to do as you please to do it in order to hold up the strange thing when done with the "see-what-I-have-made" of childish pride. Nor is it achieved by speaking the fancied language of "form and function"— cant terms learned by rote or prating foolishly of "progress before precedent"—that unthinking, unthinkable thing! In fact, it is precisely the total absence of any conception of this ideal standard that is made conspicuous by this folly and the practices that go with it. To reiterate the statement made in 1908:

This ideal of an organic architecture for America was touched by Richardson and Root, and perhaps other men, but was developing consciously twenty-eight years ago in the practice of Adler and Sullivan, when I went to work in their office. This ideal combination of Adler and Sullivan was then working to produce what no other combination of architects nor any individual architect at that time dared even preach—a sentient, rational building that would owe its style to the integrity with which it was individually fashioned to serve its particular purpose—a "thinking" as well as "feeling" process, requiring the independent work of true artist imagination—an ideal that is dynamite, cap and fuse, in selfish, insensible hands—personal ambition, the lighted match.

At the expiration of a six-year apprenticeship, during which time Louis Sullivan was my master and inspiration twenty-one years ago, I entered a field he had not, in any new spirit, touched—the field of domestic architecture, and began to break ground and make the forms I needed, alone—absolutely alone.

These forms were the result of a conscientious study of materials and of the machine, which is the real tool, whether we like it or not, that we must use to give shape to our ideals—a tool which at that time had received no such artistic consideration from artist or architect. And that my work now has individuality, the strength to stand by itself, honors Mr. Sullivan the more. The principles, however, underlying the fundamental ideal of an organic architecture common to his work and to mine are common to all work that ever rang true in the architecture of the world and free as air to any pair of honest young lungs that will breathe deeply enough. But I have occasion to refer here only to that element in this so-called new movement which I have characterized by my own work and which should and in a more advanced stage of culture would be responsible to me for use or abuse of the forms and privileges of that work. Specifically, I speak only to that element within this element,

---

*By organic architecture I mean an architecture that *develops* from within outward in harmony with the conditions of its being, as distinguished from one that is *applied* from without.

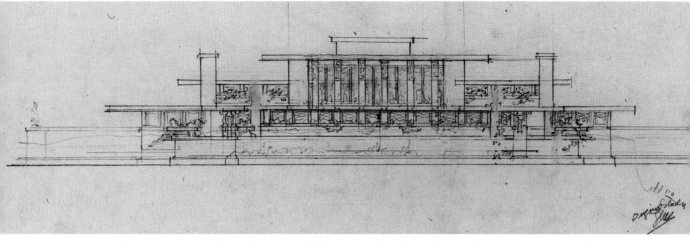

Kindergarten for Avery Coonley (Project). Riverside, Illinois. 1908. Elevation. Pencil on tracing paper, 21 x 12". FLLW Fdn#1108.005

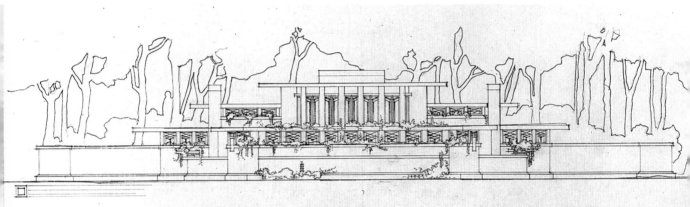

Elevation. Pencil on tracing paper, 28 x 30". FLLW Fdn#1108.007

Perspective. Pencil on tracing paper, 26 x 12". FLLW Fdn#1108.0019

now beyond private reach or control, ruthlessly characterizing and publicly exploiting the cause it does not comprehend or else that it cannot serve.

Someone for the sake of that cause must have some conscience in the matter and tell the truth. Since disciples, neophytes, and brokers will not, critics do not, and the public cannot—I will. I will be suspected of the unbecoming motives usually ascribed to any man who comes to the front on behalf of an ideal, or his own; nevertheless, somehow, this incipient movement, which it has been my life work to help outfit and launch, must be protected or directed in its course. An enlightened public opinion would take care of this, but there is no such opinion. In time there will be; meantime good work is being wasted, opportunities destroyed, or, worse, architectural mortgages on future generations forged wholesale: and in architecture they must be paid with usurious interest.

The sins of the Architect are permanent sins.

To promote good work it is necessary to characterize bad work as bad.

Half-baked, imitative designs—fictitious semblances—pretentiously put forward in the name of a movement or a cause, particularly while novelty is the chief popular standard, endanger the cause, weaken the efficiency of genuine work, for the time being at least; lower the standard of artistic integrity permanently; demoralize all values artistically until utter prostitution results. This prostitution has resulted in the new work partly, I have now to confess, as a by-product of an intimate, personal touch with the work, hitherto untried in the office of an American architect; and partly, too, perhaps, as one result of an ideal of individuality in architecture, administered in doses too strong, too soon, for architectural babes and sucklings; but chiefly, I believe, owing to almost total lack of any standard of artist integrity among architects, as a class, in this region at least. Of ethics we hear something occasionally, but only in regard to the relation of architects to each other when a client is in question—never in relation to sources of inspiration, the finer material the architect uses in shaping the thing he gives to his client. Ethics that promote integrity in this respect are as yet unformed and the young man in architec-

ture is adrift in the most vitally important of his experiences, he cannot know where he stands in the absence of any well-defined principles on the part of his confreres or his elders.

If I had a right to project myself in the direction of an organic architecture twenty-one years ago, it entailed the right to my work and, so far as I am able, a right to defend my aim. Also—yet not so clearly—I am bound to do what I can to save the public from untoward effects that follow in the wake of my own break with traditions. I deliberately chose to break with traditions in order to be more true to Tradition than current conventions and ideals in architecture would permit. The more vital course is usually the rougher one and lies through conventions oftentimes settled into laws that must be broken, with consequent liberation of other forces that cannot stand freedom. So a break of this nature is a thing dangerous, nevertheless indispensable, to society. Society recognizes the danger and makes the break usually fatal to the man who makes it. It should not be made without reckoning the danger and sacrifice, without ability to stand severe punishment, nor without sincere faith that the end will justify the means; nor do I believe it can be effectively made without all these. But who can reckon with the folly bred by temporal success in a country that has as yet no artistic standards, no other god so potent as that same Success? For every thousand men nature enables to stand adversity, she, perhaps, makes one man capable of surviving success. An unenlightened public is at its mercy always—the "success" of the one thousand as well as of the one in a thousand; were it not for the resistance of honest enmity, society, nature herself even, would soon cycle madly to disaster. So reaction is essential to progress, and enemies as valuable an asset in any forward movement as friends, provided only they be honest; if intelligent as well as honest, they are invaluable. Some time ago this work reached the stage where it sorely needed honest enemies if it was to survive. It has had some honest enemies whose honest fears were expressed in the prophetic letters I have mentioned.

But the enemies of this work, with an exception or two, have not served it well. They have been either unintelligent or careless of the gist of the whole matter. In fact, its avowed enemies have generally been of the same superficial, time-serving spirit as many of its present load of disciples and neophytes. Nowhere even now, save in Europe, with some few notable exceptions in this country, has the organic character of the work been fairly recognized and valued—the character that is perhaps the only feature of lasting vital consequence.

As for its peculiarities—if my own share in this work has a distinguished trait—it has individuality undefiled. It has gone forward unswerving from the beginning, unchanging, yet developing, in this quality of individuality and stands, as it has stood for nineteen years at least, an individual entity, clearly defined. Such as it is, its "individuality" is as irrevocably mine as the work of any painter, sculptor, or poet who ever lived was irrevocably his. The form of a work that has this quality of individuality is never the product of a composite. An artist knows this; but the general public, near-artist, and perhaps "critic," too, may have to be reminded or informed. To grant a work this quality is to absolve it without further argument from anything like composite origin, and to *fix its limitations.*

There are enough types and forms in my work to characterize the work of an architect, but certainly not enough to characterize an architecture. Nothing to my mind could be worse imposition than to have some individual, even temporarily, deliberately fix the outward forms of his concept of beauty upon the future of a free people or even of a growing city. A tentative, advantageous forecast of probable future utilitarian development goes far enough in this direction. Any individual willing to undertake more would thereby only prove his unfitness for the task, assuming the task possible or desirable. A socialist might shut out the sunlight from a free and developing people with his own shadow in this way. An artist is too true an individualist to suffer such an imposition much less perpetrate it; his problems are quite other. The manner of any work (and all work of any quality has its manner) may be for the time being a strength, but finally it is a weakness; and as the returns come in, it seems as though not only the manner of this work or its "clothes," but

also its strength in this very quality of individuality, which is a matter of its soul as well as of its forms, would soon prove its undoing to be worn to shreds and tatters by foolish, conscienceless imitation. As for the vital principle of the work—the quality of an organic architecture—that has been lost to sight, even by pupils. But I still believe as firmly as ever that without artist integrity and this consequent individuality manifesting itself in multifarious forms, there can be no great architecture, no great artists, no great civilization, no worthy life. Is, then, the very strength of such a work as this is its weakness? Is it so because of a false democratic system naturally inimical to art? or is it so because the commercialization of art leaves no noble standards? Is it because architects have less personal honor than sculptors, painters, or poets? Or is it because fine buildings are less important now than fine pictures and good books?

In any case, judging from what is exploited as such, most of what is beginning to be called the "New School of the Middle West" is not only far from the ideal of an organic architecture, but getting farther away from it every day.

A study of similar situations in the past will show that any departure from beaten paths must stand and grow in organic character or soon fall, leaving permanent waste and desolation in final ruin; *it dare not trade long on mere forms,* no matter how inevitable they seem. Trading in the letter has cursed art for centuries past, but in architecture it has usually been rather an impersonal letter of those decently cold in their graves for some time.

One may submit to the flattery of imitation or to caricature personally; every one who marches or strays from beaten paths must submit to one or to both, but never will one submit tamely to caricature of that which one loves. Personally, I, too, am heartily sick of being commercialized and traded in and upon; but most of all I dread to see the types I have worked with so long and patiently drifting toward speculative builders, cheapened or befouled by senseless changes, robbed of quality and distinction, dead forms, or grinning originalities for the sake of originality, an endless string of hacked carcasses, to encumber democratic front yards for five decades or

**Press Building for the *San Francisco Call* (Project). San Francisco, California. 1912.
Perspective. Ink and pencil on linen, 19 x 39".** FLLW Fdn#1207.001

more. This, however, is only the personal side of the matter and to be endured in silence were there any profit in it to come to the future architecture of the "melting pot."

The more serious side and the occasion for this second paper is the fact that emboldened or be-fooled by its measure of "Success," the new work has been showing weaknesses instead of the character it might have shown some years hence were it more enlightened and discreet, more sincere and modest, prepared to wait, to wait to prepare.

The average American man or woman who wants to build a house wants something different— "something different" is what they say they want, and most of them want it in a hurry. That this is the fertile soil upon which an undisciplined "language-speaking" neophyte may grow his crop to the top of his ambition is deplorable in one sense, but nonetheless hopeful in another and more vital sense. The average man of business in America has truer intuition, and so a more nearly just estimate of artistic values, when he has a chance to judge between good and bad, than a man of similar class in any other country. But he is prone to take that "something different" anyhow; if not good, then bad. He is rapidly outgrowing the provincialism that needs a foreign-made label upon "Art," and so, at the present moment, not only is he in danger of being swindled, but likely to find something peculiarly his own, in time, and valuable to him, if he can last. I hope and believe he can last. At any rate, there is no way of preventing him from getting either swindled or something merely "different"; nor do I believe it would be desirable if he could be, until the inorganic thing he usually gets in the form of this "something different" is put forward and publicly advertised as of that character of the young work for which I must feel myself responsible.

I do not admit that my disciples or pupils, be they artists, neophytes, or brokers, are responsible for worse buildings than nine-tenths of the work done by average architects who are "good school"—in fact, I think the worst of them do better—although they sometimes justify themselves in equivocal positions by reference to this fact. Were no more to come of my work than is evident at present, the

architecture of the country would have received an impetus that will finally resolve itself into good. But to me the exasperating fact is that it might aid vitally the great things we all desire, if it were treated on its merits, used and not abused. Selling even good versions of an original at second hand is in the circumstances not good enough. It is cheap and bad—demoralizing in every sense. But, unhappily, I have to confess that the situation seems worse where originality, as such, has thus far been attempted, because it seems to have been attempted chiefly *for its own sake,* and the results bear about the same resemblance to an organic architecture as might be shown were one to take a classic column and, breaking it, let the upper half lie carelessly at the foot of the lower, then setting the capital picturesquely askew against the half thus prostrate, one were to settle the whole arrangement as some structural feature of street or garden.

For worker or broker to exhibit such "designs" as efforts of creative architects, before the ink is yet dry on either work or worker, is easily done under present standards with "success," but the exploit finally reflects a poor sort of credit upon the exploited architect and the cause. As for the cause, any growth that comes to it in a "spread" of this kind is unwholesome. I insist that this sort of thing is not "new school," nor this the way to develop one. This is piracy, lunacy, plunder, imitation, adulation, or what you will; it is not a developing architecture when worked in this fashion, nor will it ever become one until purged of this spirit: least of all is it an organic architecture. Its practices belie any such character.

"Disciples" aside, some fifteen young people, all entirely inexperienced and unformed—but few have even college educations—attracted by the character of my work sought me as their employer. I am no teacher: I am a worker—but I gave to all, impartially, the freedom of my workroom, my work, and myself, to imbue them with the spirit of the performances for their own sakes and with the letter for my sake, so that they might become useful to me; because the nature of my endeavor was such that I have to train my own help and pay current wages while I trained them.

The nature of the profession these young people were to make when they assumed to practice architecture entails much more careful preparation than that of the "good school" architect; theirs is a far more difficult thing to do technically and artistically, if they would do something of their own. To my chagrin, too many are content to take it "ready-made" and with no further preparation hasten to compete for clients of their own. Now fifteen good, bad, and indifferent are practicing architecture in the Middle West, South, and Far West, and with considerable "success." In common with the work of numerous disciples (judging from such work as has been put forward publicly), there is a restless jockeying with members, one left off here, another added there, with varying intent—in some a vain endeavor to reindividualize the old types; in others an attempt to conceal their origin, but always—*ad nauseam*—the inevitable reiteration of the features that gave the original work its style and individuality. To find fault with this were unfair. It is not unexpected nor unpromising except in those unbearable cases where badly modified *inorganic* results seem to satisfy their authors' conception of originality; and banalities of form and proportion are accordingly advertised in haste as work of creative architects of a *"new school."* That some uniformity in performance should have obtained for some years is natural; it could not be otherwise, unless unaware I had harbored marked geniuses. But when the genius arrives nobody will take his work for mine—least of all will he mistake my work for his.

"The letter killeth." In this young work at this time, still it is the letter that killeth, and emulation of the "letter" that gives the illusion or delusion of "movement." There is no doubt, however, but that the sentiment is awakened which will mean progressive movement in time. And there are many working quietly who, I am sure, will give a good account of themselves.

Meanwhile, the spirit in which this use of the letter has its rise is important to any noble future still left to the cause. If the practices that disgrace and demoralize the soul of the young man in architecture could be made plain to him; if he could be shown that inevitably equivocation dwarfs and eventually destroys what creative faculty he may possess—that designing lies, in design to deceive himself or others, shuts him out absolutely from realizing upon his own gifts—no matter how flattering his opportunities may be—if he could realize that the artist heart is one uncompromising core of truth in seeking, in giving or in taking—a precious service could be rendered him. The young architect who is artist enough to know where he stands and man enough to use honestly his parent forms as such, conservatively, until he feels his own strength within him, is only exercising an artistic birthright in the interest of a good cause—he has the character at least from which great things may come. But the boy who steals his forms—"steals" them because he sells them as his own for the moment of superficial distinction he gains by trading on the results—is no artist, has not the sense of the first principles of the ideal that he poses and the forms that he abuses. He denies his birthright, an act characteristic and unimportant; but for a mess of pottage, he endangers the chances of a genuine forward movement, insults both cause and precedent with an astounding insolence quite peculiar to these matters in the United States, ruthlessly sucks what blood may be left in the tortured and abused forms he caricatures and exploits—like the parasite he is.

Another condition as far removed from creative work is the state of mind of those who, having in the course of their day's labor put some stitches into the "clothes" of the work, assume, therefore, that style and pattern are rightfully theirs and wear them defiantly unregenerate. The gist of the whole matter artistically has entirely eluded them. This may be the so-called democratic point of view; at any rate it is the immemorial error of the rabble. No great artist nor work of art ever proceeded from that conception, nor ever will.

Then there is the soiled and soiling fringe of all creative effort, a type common to all work everywhere that meets with any degree of success, although it may be more virulent here because of low standards, those who benefit by the use of another's work and to justify themselves depreciate both the work and worker they took it from—the type that will declare, "In the first place, I never had your

Midway Gardens. Chicago, Illinois. 1913. Perspective. Watercolor and color pencils on tracing paper, 41 x 17".
FLLW Fdn#1401.004

shovel; in the second place, I never broke your shovel; and in the third place, it was broken when I got it, anyway"—the type that with more crafty intelligence develops into the "coffin worm." One of Whistler's "coffin worms" has just wriggled in and out[2].

But underneath all, I am constrained to believe, lies the feverish ambition to get fame or fortune "quick," characteristic of the rush of commercial standards that rule in place of artist standards, and consequent unwillingness to wait to prepare thoroughly.

"Art to one is high as a heavenly goddess; to another only the thrifty cow that gives him his butter," said Schiller; and who will deny that our profession is prostitute to the cow, meager in ideals, cheap in performance, commercial in spirit: demoralized by ignoble ambition? A foolish optimism regarding this only serves to perpetuate it. Foolish optimism and the vanity of fear of ridicule or "failure" are both friends of ignorance.

In no country in the world do disciples, neophytes, or brokers pass artist counterfeit so easily as in these United States. Art is commercialized here rather more than anything else, although the arts should be as free from this taint as religion. But has religion escaped?

So the standard of criticism is not only low—it is often dishonest or faked somewhere between the

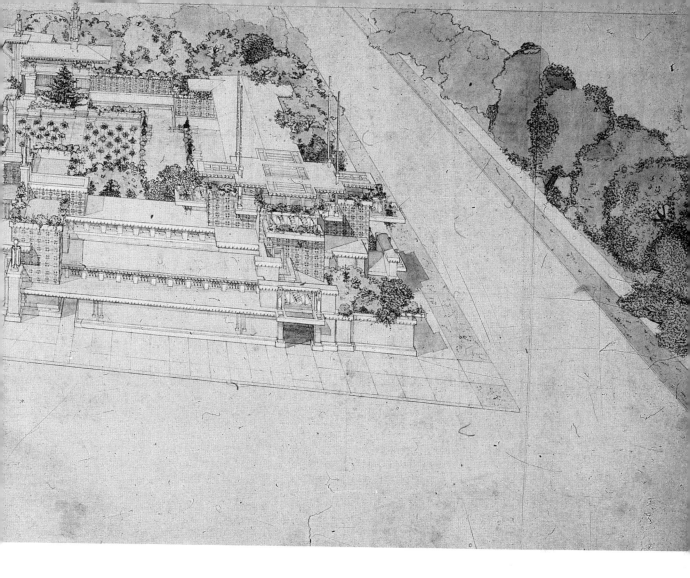

two, largely manufactured to order for profit or bias. Criticism is worked as an advertising game- traders' instincts subject to the prevailing commercial taint. Therein lies a radically evil imposition that harms the public, that also further distorts, confuses, and injures values and promotes bad work; that tends to render the integrity of artist and commerce alike a stale and unprofitable joke, and to make honest enemies even harder to find than honest friends. The spirit of fair play, the endeavor to preserve the integrity of values, intelligently, on a high plane in order to help in raising the level of the standard of achievement in the country and to refrain from throwing the senseless weight of the mediocre and

bad upon it—all this is unhappily too rare among editors. The average editor has a "constituency," not a standard. This constituency is largely the average architect who has bought the "artistic" in his architecture as one of its dubious and minor aspects, or the sophisticated neophyte, the broker, and the quack, to whom printers' ink is ego-balm and fortune.

So until the standard is raised any plea for artist integrity is like a cry for water in the Painted Desert. As for competent criticism, the honest word of illuminating insight, where is it? Nothing is more precious or essential to progress. Where is the editor or critic not narrow or provincial? Or loose and ignorant? Or cleverly or superficially or cowardly commercial? Let him raise this standard! Friend or foe, there is still a demand for him even here; but if he did, he would fail—gloriously fail—of "success."

Is architecture, then, no longer to be practiced as an art? Has its practice permanently descended to a form of mere "artistic activity?"

The art of architecture has fallen from a high estate—lower steadily since the Men of Florence patched together fragments of the art of Greece and Rome and in vain endeavor to reestablish its eminence manufactured the Renaissance. It has fallen—from the heavenly Goddess of Antiquity and the Middle Ages to the thrifty cow of the present day. To touch upon these matters in this country is doubly unkind, for it is to touch upon the question of "bread and butter" chiefly. Aside from the conscienceless ambition of the near-artist—more sordid than any greed of gold—and beneath this thin pretense of the ideal that veneers the curious compound of broker and neophyte there lurks, I know, for any young architect an ever-present dread of the kind of "failure" that is the obverse of the kind of "success" that commercialized standards demand of him if he is to survive. Whosoever would worship his heavenly goddess has small choice—he must keep his eye on the thrifty cow or give up his dream of "success"; and the power of discrimination possessed by the cow promises ill for the future integrity of an organic architecture. The net result of present standards is likely to be a poor wretch, a coward who aspires pretentiously or theoretically, advertises cleverly and milks surreptitiously. There is no real connection between aspiration and practice except a tissue of lies and deceit; there never can be. The young architect before he ventures to practice architecture with an ideal, today, should first be sure of his goddess and then, somehow, be connected with a base of supplies from which he cannot be cut off, or else fall in with the rank and file of the "good school" of the hour. Anyone who has tried it knows this; that is, if he is honest and is going to use his own material as soon as he is able. So the ever-present economic question underlies this question of artist integrity, at this stage of our development, like quicksand beneath the footing of a needed foundation, and the structure itself seems doomed to

shreds and cracks and shores and patches, the deadening compromises and pitiful makeshifts of the struggle to "*succeed!*" Even the cry for this integrity will bind the legion together, as one man, against the crier and the cry.

This is Art, then, in a sentimental Democracy, which seems to be only another form of self-same hypocrisy? Show me a man who prates of such "Democracy" as a basis for artist endeavor, and I will show you an inordinately foolish egotist or a quack. The "Democracy" of the man in the American street is no more than the Gospel of Mediocrity. When it is understood that a great Democracy is the highest form of Aristocracy conceivable, not of birth or place or wealth, but of those qualities that give distinction to the man as a man, and that as a social state it must be characterized by the honesty and responsibility of the absolute individualist as the unit of its structure, then only can we have an art worthy the name. The rule of mankind by mankind is one thing; but false "Democracy"— the hypocritical sentimentality politically practiced and preached here, usually the sheep's clothing of the proverbial wolf, or the egotistic dream of self-constituted patron saints—is quite another thing. "The letter killeth"; yes, but more deadly still is the undertow of false Democracy that poses the man as a creative artist and starves him to death unless he fakes his goddess or persuades himself, with "language," that the cow is really she. Is the lack of an artist-conscience, then, simply the helpless surrender of the would-be artist to this wherewithal Democracy with which a nation soothes itself into subjection? Is the integrity for which I plead here no part of this time and place? And is no young aspirant or hardened sinner to blame for lacking it? It may be so. If it is, we can at least be honest about that, too. But what aspiring artist could knowingly face such a condition? He would choose to dig in the ditch and trace his dreams by lamplight, on scrap paper, for the good of his own soul—a sweet and honorable, if commercially futile, occupation.

It has been my hope to have inspired among my pupils a personality or two to contribute to this work, some day, forms of their own devising, with an artistic integrity that will help to establish upon a firmer basis the efforts that have gone before them and enable them in more propitious times to carry on their practice with a personal gentleness, wisdom, and reverence denied to the pioneers who broke rough ground for them, with a wistful eye to better conditions for their future.

And I believe that, cleared of the superficial pose and push that is the inevitable abuse of its opportunity and its nature, and against which I ungraciously urge myself here, there will be found good work in a cause that deserves honest friends and honest enemies among the better architects of the country. Let us have done with "language" and unfair use of borrowed forms; understand that such practices or products are not of the character of this young work. This work is a sincere endeavor to establish the ideal of an organic architecture in a new country; a type of endeavor that alone can give lasting value to any architecture and that is in line with the spirit of every great and noble precedent in the world of forms that has come to us as the heritage of the great life that has been lived, and in the spirit of which all great life to be will still be lived.

And this thing that eludes the disciple remains in hiding from the neophyte, and in the name of which the broker seduces his client—what is it? This mystery requiring the catch phrases of a new language to abate the agonies of the convert and in the name of which ubiquitous atrocities have been and will continue to be committed, with the deadly enthusiasm of the egomania that is its plague? First, a study of the nature of materials you elect to use and the tools you must use with them, searching to find the characteristic qualities in both that are suited to your purpose. Second, with an ideal of organic nature as a guide, so to unite these qualities to serve that purpose, that the fashion of what you do has integrity or is *natively fit,* regardless of preconceived notions of style. *Style is* a by-product of the process and comes of the man or the mind in the process. The style of the thing, therefore, will be the man—it is his. *Let his forms alone.*

To adopt a "style" as a motive is to put the cart before the horse and get nowhere beyond the "Styles"—never to reach *Style.*

It is obvious that this is neither ideal nor work for fakirs or tyros, for unless this process is finally so imbued, informed, with a feeling for the beautiful that grace and proportion are inevitable, the result cannot get beyond good engineering.

A light matter this, altogether? And yet an organic architecture must take this course and belie nothing, shirk nothing. Discipline! The architect who undertakes his work seriously on these lines is emancipated and imprisoned at the same time. His work may be severe; it cannot be foolish. It may lack grace; it cannot lack fitness altogether. It may seem ugly; it will not be false. No wonder, however, that the practice of architecture in this sense is the height of ambition and the depth of poverty!

Nothing is more difficult to achieve than the integral simplicity of organic nature amid the tangled confusions of the innumerable relics of form that encumber life for us. To achieve it in any degree means a serious devotion to the "underneath" in an attempt to grasp the *nature* of building a beautiful building beautifully, as organically true in itself, to itself and to its purpose, as any tree or flower.

That is the need, and the need is demoralized, not served, by the same superficial emulation of the letter in the new work that has heretofore characterized the performances of those who start out to practice architecture by selecting and electing to work in a ready-made "style."

1. Montgomery Schuyler (1843–1914) was a journalist for *The New York Times,* a critic and historian of American architecture, and one of the founders of *The Architectural Record.*
2. Another reference to Whistler's "Ten O' Clock" lecture, although Whistler's text reads: "There are those also, sombre of mien, and wise with the wisdom of books, who frequent museums and burrow in crypts; collecting—comparing—compiling—classifying—contradicting."

ON MARRIAGE

This brief statement was found among Wright's papers after his death. Although not included with his other manuscripts, which his secretary, Eugene Masselink, prudently labeled and boxed, Wright had carefully saved it along with personal papers. Written in 1915, after the murder of Mamah Borthwick Cheney, it is Wright's response to the criticism unleashed upon him by neighbors, friends, and clients when he left Catherine for Mamah. This is but one of the several writings in which he justified his actions. At the time Wright wrote this, Catherine was still refusing him a divorce and he was living with Maud Miriam Noel. [Unpublished]

NO PROSTITUTE ON THE STREET AS SUCH IS A SOCIAL menace. She is a symptom—it is the wife with the soul of a harlot "protected" by marriage in practices that evade all responsibility who is the "menace." It is the man whose desires must be gratified at whatever cost to others so it be no bar to his "respectability"—no "stain" upon his "name." Not what he is, but what he passes for that contents him—He is a menace. My open life for six years has hung helplessly in this welter of insult, slander, murder, and character assassination because the life grew out of a form which the law had fastened upon it, because the form ceased to express the *spirit* of that life. But it seems the form alone was sacred, the *form* was an institution in itself and it really mattered—matters very little about the *life*: that could make-shift for itself as best it might—it was of minor importance. Still it must live and have its being and yet for all it undertook "provide" whatever humanly is needed or can be provided materially or spiritually. The "form" must stand—it is sacred, and this has always been so to as great or a lesser degree since time was. But is it fair to impose an obsolete form upon life that has outgrown it in order to punish that life by

turning loose upon it all the destructive agencies at the command of society and, at the same time, demand that all the obligations created by it be met and satisfied by it?

Well they have been met by me and so far as a privilege; the work I was expressly fitted to do has gone on stronger, better, and more purposeful than ever. But there is a limit to human abilities and human endurance.

I know no solution can be offered by "society" that is decent or tolerable because society is more "form" than substance. Manhood and womanhood may suggest something however for both are strong as ever. Instead of breaking down faith in the human nature behind all this fear of misunderstanding and unrest—I have found it staunch and true where I least expected it; if it was the reverse, where I most expected it.

So I know by the gift that is in me in the light of my bitter experience that manhood and womanhood are as sound and strong-hearted as ever, and the struggle for the highest life one knows is the only life there is—for anyone.

PLAN BY FRANK LLOYD WRIGHT

The publication of this article and its accompanying drawings put on record Wright's first serious promotion of decentralization. This theme, the relief of urban and suburban congestion by means of more spacious, parklike planning, continued to interest him. He offered solutions, both in text and design, intermittently throughout his life. His first serious, in-depth publication on the subject was The Disappearing City, *published in 1932, revised and expanded in 1945 as* When Democracy Builds, *and further rewritten and expanded in 1958 as* The Living City. *The model and plans for Broadacre City, Wright's city of the future, find their roots in this article. [Published with four illustrations in* City Residential Land Development, *May 1916]*

"Fool! The Ideal is within thyself.
Thy condition is but the stuff thou shalt use to shape that same Ideal out of."—Carlyle

ACCEPTING THE CHARACTERISTIC AGGREGATION OF business buildings, flats, apartments, and formal and informal dwellings for well-to-do and poor, natural now to every semi-urban section about Chicago, this design introduces only minor modifications in harmony with the nature of this aggregation.

The proposed site locates the given tract upon the prairie within eight miles of the city's center, and so makes it an integral feature of Chicago. The established gridiron of Chicago's streets therefore has been held as the basis of this subdivision. The desired improvements have been effected by occasional widening or narrowing of streets, shifts in the relation of walks to curbs, the provision of an outer border or parkway planted with shrubbery to withdraw the residences somewhat from the noisy, dusty city streets (shelters in which to await cars are features of this parkway at street crossings), the arrangement of a small decorative park system planned to diversify the section in the simplest and most generally effective manner possible, and, finally, the creation of a new system of resubdivision of the already established blocks of the gridiron.

Grouped within the small park system are recreation features such as groves, open playgrounds, tennis courts, pools, music pavilion, athletic field, and sheltered walks. The groups are so planned that adults and young people are attracted to the less quiet portion of the park near the public buildings, the children and more quietly inclined adults to the small park in the opposite direction.

The inevitable drift of the population toward the business center of the city is recognized in the grouping of the business buildings, more formal dwellings, and apartment buildings, large and small, on the streets next to the railway going to the city's center. A branch bank, post office, temple of worship and secular clubhouses, branch library and exhibition galleries, cinematograph and branch of civic theater are also grouped with the business buildings; but all these are grouped as features of the small park system. To the rear of the theater and also located on the street railway to town is the central heating plant and garbage reduction plant, with smokestacks made into sightly towers. Here also there is a public garage, and near the center of this side of the block a public produce market is designed in the form of a large open court, the court paved and screened from the park by a simple pergola.

These various buildings are all utilized as "background" buildings and so are continuously banked against the noisy city thoroughfare, and the upper stories are carried overhead across intervening streets to give further protection from dust and noise and to provide, in a picturesque way, economically roofed space for the combination business and dwelling establishments that cling naturally to the main arteries of traffic.

By thus drawing to one side all the buildings of this nature into the location they would naturally prefer, the greater mass of the subdivision is left quiet and clean for residence purposes. No attempt is made to change the nature of these things as they naturally come. The commercial buildings, however, are arranged with a system of interior courts which care for all the necessities that are unsightly. Space is thus provided, quietly and in order, adapted to all commercial requirements, with great economy of expenditure necessary for exterior effect, and without the exposure of unsightly conditions. The market has been treated as a desirable picturesque feature of the whole arrangement. The bank and post office are located where they will be passed morning and evening to and from the city, as are the various shops. There is but one temple for worship, but there are sectarian clubrooms opening on courts at the sides and rear and in connection with it.

The library has top-lighted galleries for loan collections and a cinematograph hall. With this library are grouped separately a boys' club, a branch of Y.M.C.A., and apartments for men. The school buildings, kindergarten, teachers' departments, and

Y.W.C.A. building are grouped on the opposite side of the quarter-section on the axis of the children's recreation grounds. A shallow boating and swimming pool and a zoological loan collection from, say, Lincoln Park are features of the park system on this side. All building groups have internal green courts for privacy as well as their relation to public playground, greensward, and shrubbery. The space between this park portion of the quarter-section and the outside city street to the south is devoted to an inexpensive type of detached dwelling, with closed interior courts. Facing the outside city street are modest, grouped cottages for working men and women.

The division of the small park systems into two groups draws the children going and coming from school, kindergarten, and playground in the direction opposite to the business quarter.

The remainder, the larger proportion of the quarter-section, has been left intact as a residence park, developed according to the principle of the "quadruple block plan." This remaining area has been kept as large and unbroken as possible, as it is from the sale of this property that the profit would come that would make the park system possible.

In this real body of the subdivision an entirely new arrangement of the resubdivision of property is shown, dispensing with alleys, and wherein the simple expedient of an established building line protects every individual householder from every other one and insures maximum community benefits for all.

At the same time it is possible to put as many houses in all necessary variety upon the ground (several schemes of arrangement are shown) and still maintain these benefits, as is possible now under the wasteful, absurd, and demoralizing practice which universally obtains, wherein the unsightly conditions of city life are all exposed to the street, and either a dirty alley is open to the sides of the blocks or useless rear courts are left with all outhouses abutting upon them, rendering the prospect of the entire neighborhood unsightly to everyone and making impossible any real privacy for any one. Under the present system of subdivision, all attempts at beautifying the premises may prove futilities, as any man turned loose upon his own lot may render himself obnoxious to his neighbors.

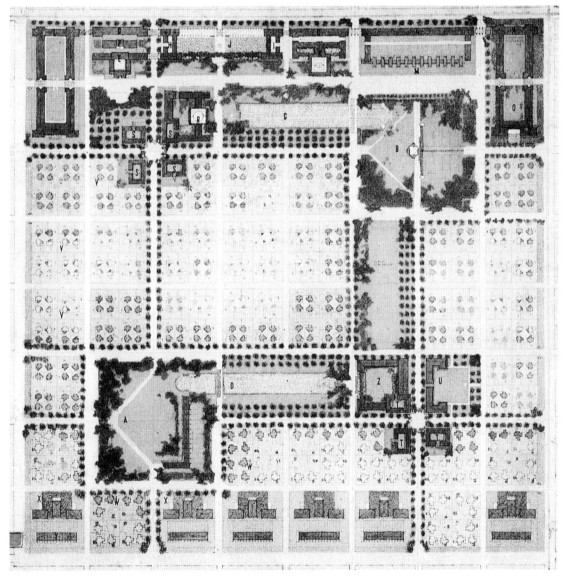

Model Quarter Section for City Residential Land Development (Project). Chicago, Illinois. 1915. Plan. FLLW Fdn#1508.002

The "quadruple block plan" will prove immune from the possibilities of such abuse. Each householder is automatically protected from every other householder. He is the only individual upon the entire side of his block. His utilities are grouped to the rear with his neighbors' utilities, and his yard, front or rear, is privately his own. His windows all look upon open vistas and upon no one's unsightly necessities. His building is in unconscious but necessary grouping with three of his neighbors', looking out upon harmonious groups of other neighbors, no two of which would present to him the same elevation even were they all cast in one mold. A succession of buildings of any given length by this arrangement presents the aspect of well-grouped buildings in a park, of *greater picturesque variety than is possible where façade follows façade.*

Architectural features of the various buildings in the general public group recognize and emphasize in an interesting way the street vistas, and nowhere is symmetry obvious or monotonous. The aim has been to make all vistas equally picturesque and attractive and the whole quietly harmonious.

The virtue of this plan lies in the principle of subdivision underlying its features—the practical, economic, and artistic creation of an intelligent system of subdivision, insuring greater privacy together with all the advantages of cooperation realized in central heating, shorter sewers, well-ordered recreation areas, the abolition of all alleys, fewer and shorter cement walks and driveways, and airiness of arrangement in general with attractive open vistas everywhere. Always there is the maximum of buildings upon a given ground area, dignity and privacy for all.

There is an idea in this plan of subdivision which I believe to be valuable to the city and immediately available wherever several blocks remain without substantial improvement, because it may be put into practice without concession to the cupidity of the average real-estate man, since he gets as many lots to sell under this system as he does in the one now in use. Moreover, the quadruple arrangement insures to the purchaser greater freedom and privacy with no decrease of any privileges he now enjoys. It is as valuable for low-cost cottages as for luxurious dwellings.

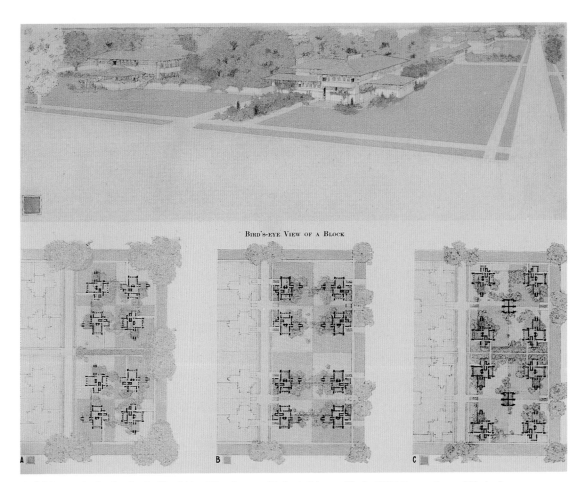

BIRD'S-EYE VIEW OF A BLOCK

Model Quarter Section for City Residential Land Development (Project). Chicago, Illinois. 1915. Perspective and block plan.
FLLW Fdn#1508.001

BIRD'S-EYE VIEW OF THE QUARTER-SECTION

Model Quarter Section for City Residential Land Development (Project). Chicago, Illinois. 1915. Perspective. FLLW Fdn#1508.003

Artistically this principle is susceptible of infinite variety of treatment without sacrificing the economic advantages which the householder gains through commercial repetition and to which he is entitled. The individual unit may vary harmoniously and effectively with its neighbors without showing as under present conditions veritable monotony in the attempt to be different.

In skilled hands these various treatments could rise to great beauty, but, even if neglected, the nature of the plan would discipline the average impulse of the ordinary builder in a manner to insure more harmonious results.

Other rhythms in grouping than those suggested here are easily imagined, so that all the charm of variety found in the Gothic colleges of Oxford could easily find its way into the various workings of the underlying scheme.

Much has been written, said, and done recently in relation to civic planning all over the world. For the most part, what has happened with us in this connection is what has happened to us in individual building: we are obsessed by the Old World thing in the Old World way with the result that, in this grim workshop, our finer possibilities are usually handed over to fashion and sham. Confusing art with manners and aristocracy, we ape the academic Gaston or steal from "My Lord" his admirable traditions when our own problems need not fashioning from *without,* but development from *within.*

ANTIQUE COLOR PRINTS FROM THE COLLECTION OF FRANK LLOYD WRIGHT

*O*f all the Westerners who have been attracted to Japanese fine art, praised it, understood it, and appreciated it, Frank Lloyd Wright was among the most prominent.

To be sure, his love—really a passion—for the Japanese print was constantly expressed by the poetic and always insightful way in which he wrote about it.

On October 12, 1917, he prepared this text for an exhibition of his growing collection. The exhibition was sponsored by the Arts Club of Chicago from November 12 to December 5, 1917. The Fine Arts Building, where the exhibition was held, had a long association with Frank Lloyd Wright. In 1908 he had designed a bookstore, Browne's, located in the building; the following year he built another gallery, the Thurber Art Gallery, and in 1914 he designed the Mori Oriental Art Shop, both also located in the building. It is interesting to note that it was in this building that Aline Barnsdall established a community theater and first met Wright there in 1914–1915. Later she would move to southern California and formally secure Wright as her architect for both residential and theatrical commissions. [Published without illustrations as a catalog by the Chicago Arts Club, 1917]

SHIBARAKU [1]

IT IS THE JAPANESE WORD FOR "WAIT A MOMENT"— a dramatic moment made famous by the great actor Danjuro, in the role of that name, as he came forward in the splendid red flowing robes patterned with the gigantic white crests that were the *mon* of his distinguished house.[2] To all who would "look," this is the "wait and listen" moment to let it be said that in ancient Tokyo an art was born nearer "democratic" than any ever seen. The people loved and possessed it. It was made for them, except as the humble artists made it for themselves with that joy in the making that alone lives in art.

You are to see a few rare, perishable leaves from a prolific, wondrous volume, and richly voluminous and beautifully embroidered it was in that time. Since then what has escaped destruction has been scattered by the winds of chance to the far corners of Earth. For Tokyo civilization was as frail as it was exquisite. Its framework and utensils were of beautifully treated wood and silken paper. Its sword was keen and of steel.

Were it not for reverential Japanese care for things beautiful, all these scattered leaves, these exciting traces of the image-seeking mind, would have perished because they were then regarded no more seriously than we now regard printed souvenirs of our holidays and seasons or photographs of favorite actors and actresses. And since the time of Harunobu, all Tokyo has been shaken or burned to the ground at least five times.

Country people returning from visits to the new capital—Tokyo—stowed the *nishikiye*[3] (brocade prints) away in the devices of their domesticity and forgot them, or pasted them on screens, or hung them upon pillars of their houses as decoration, and so were the unwitting means of saving most of "our" collections.

From remote country districts, from Ise to Sendai, little by little as prices have soared prints have come fluttering back to Tokyo to be seized and gloated over by the Epicurean collector with his strange combination of love and self-interest—love for the beautiful and sordid calculation.

But thanks to his acquisitive instinct!

He, too, has been the means of handing over to us in great variety the precious record of a glory that was Old Japan; a civilization wherein art was not divorced from nature, when Eternity was Now.

It is a record rich with the motifs that made that civilization what it was to the eye.

And it was primarily a festival for eyes.

The figure pieces of this great period from 1740 to 1820 reveal the incomparable instinct for harmonious elegance that characterized the time and its traditions. The range of discovered subjects is already wide—as wide as it is likely to be, although a few still come to light each year.

The work ranges from the monumental simplicity of the primitives of the Kwaigetsudo[4], printed in black, and the painted *urushiye*[5], to the fully developed color prints in the sweet refinement of Harunobu and the bewildering gamut of Shunsho. Then on by way of masterly Kiyonaga with his regal compositions and swinging, calligraphic stroke to the dissolute, sentient grace of the consummate Utamaro, the idol of the "artist absolute." Then downward to the decline and confusion of all noble qualities in Yeisen, Yeizan, and Kunisada.[6]

The landscapes (a later development) are the most complete and poetic interpretations of a natural domain ever recorded by native sons.

Fascinating as each subject is in itself, it is in the aggregate that the salient native charm and full integrity of means to ends of this art and craft becomes so convincing and entrancing. Then it lives as a vivified revelation of that unity in variety that is the soul of the whole visible world of form—and that does not pass. It is of the inward sea, treasure of the profound depths of the soul.

These garnered leaves from a perished volume are stamped with an intrinsic art. So long as art lives, they will remain the basis of a worldwide clearing away of the rubbish vain "realism" has unloaded upon a too human world. Imbued with a point of view inevitable to them, our vision too, seeks essentials of form, line, color, and the rhythms peculiar to each. Scenes familiar enough to us all about us live again with significance renewed and refreshed, not only as landscape or as Japanese prints, but a simplifying light, spiritual in quality, has come through them to unburden the Western mind sagging with its sordid load.

Our land is richer in every sense than their land.

They were richer in what life is than we are.

These Iridian sheets of tender, lustrous fiber, stamped with colored carvings, teach us lessons we have good reason to receive with gratitude.

The slender stock the whole world holds of these perishable documents ought to be cherished and guarded by custodians not too selfish—and yet sensible, too, of the priceless character of the record held in trust as an original force, a light in all future culture.

The Japanese were awakened too late to the precious character of this inheritance peculiar to them.

The aristocracy despised it as vulgar. The old type of aristocracy despised anything held in common. The new aristocracy had not yet arisen. It is still slow in coming.

The subject matter of the figure pieces is still offensive to Japanese polite society. Not so with the landscapes of Hiroshige and Hokusai; and as the art and institutions of Old Japan give way to uglier

Western models the Japanese gentleman of leisure now sees the most valuable poetic record of a beauty fast passing away forever from him and from his land, filched from his children before his eyes—and for a sum paltry enough. With characteristic prodigality where works of art are concerned, he now vies with others in paying "the highest price." But the value of works of art in Japan seems, along with the other modern improvements, to be augmented by the importance of him who once owned it or the size of the sum paid for it. No Japanese cares to make and hold a collection if foredoomed to remain inferior in it, and our Western collections have gained much in recent years by this trait of his.

Hiroshiges—"outcasts" of a few years ago—are now bought by the Japanese themselves at prices that make the hardened avidity of even the American collector hesitate.

Hiroshige is the latest arrival in the sacred places of upper printdom. His fertility of resource and his industry are alike amazing. Yet, among the thousand or more subjects signed by him none lacks true artistic distinction seen properly printed. For it must be born in mind, that this product was stamped in a mutable medium, upon a mutable substance, by a means that could never be twice alike except by strange coincidence. After it was stamped, the fabric of the whole underwent transmutation by time and was modified, as light had its way with colors that etherealize as they wane. So the fabric as a whole is one of delightful differences and heartbreaking or ravishing surprises. Frequently I have got together five or six—all prints of the same subject designed by Hiroshige, so differently printed that they were in effect many different designs.

No subject of a composition, which there is good reason to believe is by Hiroshige, is negligible in art. But art and craftsmanship are inseparable in the print. The bane of any attempt to form an idea of the splendid flight and range of his genius is found when the craftsmanship failed in the disreputable remnant of cheap, badly printed editions carelessly struck from worn-out blocks, to be had for a dollar or two in curio shops. These inferior prints have cursed and confused their superiors which are alone representative, and especially so, since Hiroshige prints of superior editions are as rare as primitives.

Hiroshige is coming into his own, largely through the conservation in the past ten years of really fine examples of his work in the great collections by the discerning amateur. The Spaulding collection of Boston[7] is an astonishing revelation of Hiroshige's extent and the grasp and sweep of his genius. It is almost unbelievable that so much good work could be done within the lifetime of a single artist. But Hiroshige loved much, so was tireless and doubtless inspired many to take his designs and work with him upon them "in character" and in details that might safely be entrusted to them by the master. But why attempt to explain?

It is certain that the mass of work signed by his name is all of a piece and in the same feeling, except certain instances in later work.

While the style swings easily from the delicate, expressive tenderness and grace of the early horizontal compositions to the sure strength and splendid breadth of the uprights in the *Hundred Views,* it is the same character, the same hand, the same soul in all.

As always about artistic phenomena, literature has gathered about the print since the initial brochures of the Goncourts. Primarly it was French. France, the discoverer, discovered the print. In English we have been treated to much perfunctory misinformation. Germany later took up the subject with more weight than light. Japan at last is contributing with authority.

America, meantime, has taken to prints as she takes to everything, reckless of cost and determined to win—whatever that may mean. But we have genuine amateurs among us who understand, and in the hands of several such are the greatest collections in the world, save, possibly one, and that one is French. Minor collections of great importance are many and in good hands. America, too, has the best of the literature, for not only can she say it; she can sing it better than anyone ever said it. There is no dearth of writing, nor ever will be.

There are not enough exhibitions.

So a fascinating world within a world has grown rapidly among us these past twenty years, increasing steadily in extent and significance as collections have grown richer and as appreciation deepens, and the collections become shrines for the artist pilgrims in need of worship or in search of light.

But still the precious original is all too sacred to the few who, chosen by it, are enslaved by it; because it is no secret that the prints choose whom they love and there is then no salvation but surrender.

1. *Shibaraku* is considered one of the "eighteen favorite Kabuki plays" and was the showpiece of Ichikawa Danjuro I, one of the greatest Kabuki actors. The word *shibaraku* refers to an interlude in this play when the actor introduces himself. In Danjuro's case he was allowed to write his own text.
2. *Mon* are family crests. The Ichikawa crest of three concentric white squares, which appears in all the woodblock prints of Danjuro, is sometimes mentioned as the possible inspiration for one of Wright's own logos designed in 1939.
3. *Nishikiye,* "brocade prints," were fully developed color prints that first appeared in the 1760s. The term refers to their resemblance to fine fabrics.
4. It is difficult to know which Kaigetsudo Wright is referring to here. The works of this school so closely resemble each other that for many years scholars thought that they were all done by Ando Kaigetsudo. Current scholarship now identifies five followers of Ando. Ando himself did not design prints, so Wright could be referring to Anchi, Dohan, Doshin, Doshu, or Doshū. All flourished in the early eighteenth century and were known for their portrayal of tall, elegant courtesans in beautiful kimono. See Lawrence P. Roberts. *A Dictionary of Japanese Artists* (New York: Weatherhill, 1976).
5. *Urushiye,* literally "lacquer prints," are hand-colored prints. The color was thickened and made glossy with glue resembling a lacquer surface.
6. Keisai Eisen (1790–1848), Kikugawa Eizan (1787–1867), and Tsunoda Kunisada (1786–1864). All three of these woodblock artists are considered part of the "decadent" group, which was active during the first half of the nineteenth century. Unlike their contemporaries Hokusai and Hiroshige, who brought the landscape print to prominence during this time, these designers of actor and beautiful woman prints were unable to achieve the standards of their predecessors.
7. Wright purchased thousands of prints for William Spaulding and his wife, beginning with his 1913 trip to Japan. Considered one of the finest collections of Japanese prints in the world, the Spauldings bequeathed their collection to the Museum of Fine Arts, Boston.

THE PRINT AND
THE RENAISSANCE

That Wright was attracted to Japan and Japanese art was probably inevitable given his quest for an "organic architecture." He had discovered in the Japanese print collateral evidence for his own process of simplification and "the elimination of the insignificant." His increasing knowledge of Japan only strengthened his belief that Japanese art and life "really did have organic character, was nearer to the earth, and a more indigenous product of native conditions of life and work; therefore, more nearly 'modern' as I saw it, than any European civilization alive or dead," as he wrote in his autobiography.

This essay, written in 1917 but never published, was probably prepared in conjunction with his exhibition of Japanese prints in the same year in the Fine Arts Building in Chicago. Rather than extolling the Japanese print, however, Wright emphasizes that Western civilization has been corrupted as a direct result of the Renaissance. He criticizes Western architecture:

We ought to be tired of patching things together for effect. . . sick and ashamed of getting things somewhere and sticking them . . .upon the outside—instead of developing the thing done from within, making it intelligently stand forth as the nature of the thing.

He champions the native architecture of Japan:

Their buildings, like the rocks and trees, grew in their places. Their gardens were idealized patterns of their landscapes. They were native shrines, in themselves a form of worship for their native land.

While elegance was commonplace—there was no commonplace elegance.

But Wright seemed unable to escape the spell the Japanese print had cast over him, and he returned to it again and again, as though it was an object lesson in what the current era could still learn:

Truth and Beauty blossom only from integrity of means to ends—and integrity that is a fountain of youth in Art. It is light too, a love light, that seemed to die away with the birth of the Renaissance. It glows for us today in the countenance of that modest messenger of light from the Far East—from the "morning-land"—the humble Japanese print.

[Unpublished manuscript]

THE JAPANESE PRINT COMES, A HUMBLE MESSENger FROM the Far East, to emphasize the futility of the Renaissance—that setting sun of Art all Europe mistook for dawn. A Renaissance that our "democracy" has reduced to mere scene painting in "period" interiors of an exterior masquerade not of style, but of styles.

In the print, we have something integral to look to. Something sound in principle. Something upon which a whole philosophy of art might be constructed if a philosophy of Art could precede Art and so do us any good. I don't suppose it could or would.

When the artistic thing is done, the Artist does it as naturally as Kiyonaga or Hiroshige did it, and we then deduce and explain and expound.

Philosophies and theorems follow performance in Art.

But while philosophies and theories of Art multiply, principles are shamefully neglected.

We will develop no culture worth having while fashion, predilection, and prejudice answer for principles.

It is the principle of the print that interests me now.

When I first saw a fine print about twenty-five years ago, it was an intoxicating thing. At that time Ernest Fenollosa[1] was doing his best to persuade the Japanese people not to wantonly destroy their works of art. In their craze for European civilization they had made bonfires of priceless treasures. In a fury of shame and contempt for what they were—they glorified in ruthlessly sacrificing them in honour of what they imagined our culture to be. For a strip of European cloth you might have owned a gold screen by Okyo or Korin[2] or a miracle in gold lacquer some great artist's lifetime had perfected. Fenollosa, the American, did more than anyone else to stem the tide of this folly. On one of his journeys

home, he brought many beautiful prints. Those I made mine were the narrow tall decorative forms—*hashirakake*[3]—that I appreciate today even more than I did then.

These first prints had a large share, I am sure, in vulgarizing the Renaissance even then for me. Already Victor Hugo's prophecy—that the Renaissance was the setting sun of Art all Europe mistook for dawn—had opened my eyes. Nothing less than radical, the simplifying, clarifying light they wore like a nimbus then, has been shining for me ever since.

They are saints of sincerity and simplicity. Their mission, the elimination of the insignificant.

The first principle of the print as a print (the only one we may consider) is integrity of means to ends.

It is not trying to be something it is not, and cannot be.

It is a print charmingly conscious of the fact and satisfied that it is no more or else.

This is a greater virtue than appears in statement and rare in our day.

WHAT IS THE NATURE OF THE PRINT?

Physically it is a silken piece of paper stamped and stained with a pattern of lines and colors. It has kissed color and patterns from raised lines and surfaces carved in various blocks of cherry wood, the lines and surfaces left raised by cutting or wasting away parts of the block not needed for the lines or color surfaces of the pattern.

First there is the design or pattern. Next woodcutting or carving. Then the brushing of flat color on the raised lines or surfaces of the carving. Then the accurate placing of the paper on the colored carving and deft pressure that stamps the paper evenly against the raised lines and surfaces and stains them with the color. A different block and another impression are needed for each color. So the paper is stamped and stained with different colors by pressing it in turn against variously carved and tinted blocks. *Estampes*—or stamps—the French call them.

Rather narrow limits for a work of Art, and in that there is a valuable lesson.

The print began as a crude thing. But the imagination of the artist seized it. Lines clearly beautiful as lines flowed over it. Subtle rhythms thus entered into the spacing and shaping of the surfaces of flat color—color used for its own sake. Mind asserts itself in traceries upon it—scenes and interesting forms take shape, and with no attempt at realism it conveys ideas and emotions and gives delight. Harmonies above and beyond the thing—but true to it, live spiritually for us in the flat, slight thing we call the print.

Yet, as a medium of expression, it has nowhere been forced beyond its limits. On the contrary, every circumstance of its making is delightfully confessed in the result.

The pressure on the raised lines and surfaces is delightful as *gaufrage*.[4]

The inevitable gradation of the brush stroke, is lovely as *notan*.[5] The grain of the woodblock itself is a beautiful qualification of the color. The texture of the paper gives sheen to the color as it stains its fiber. The very constitution of paper and color are such that they harmonize and develop softer richer harmonies with age. In a word, the craft of the print is integral with its Art.

It is, therefore, a legitimate means to the artist's desired end. And the Artist was artist enough not to try to make it do something it couldn't do naturally. How simple it all is. Nevertheless, it is an organic thing. A spiritual treasure!

THE JAPANESE PRINT IS AN ORGANIC THING

That is the fundamental characteristic I want to show you. Art and Craft are a unit made one. Astonishingly insignificant as the whole thing seems, it is for just the lack of such simple significance, that modern art is dying.

Integrity of means to ends is absolutely necessary to a work of art that will live forever. And after

all is said and done, what is it but the same integrity that is the fundamental principle of Life itself!

The Art in anything is this insight, the Love in it, the Life in it, the God in it! Simple as may be the natural means used to produce a work of Art the means may never be falsified. If they are, the love that was the art in the thing, failed in that insight, which is virtue failed—in understanding, and so, must go down! This first principle of the print could save this great "democracy" from the degradation of imitation or the folly of originality, for its own sake. But a guiding principle is like a sword in the hand: God help us all, bystanders that we are, when a man wields one without understanding, "spurred to acts of unseemliness and indiscretion by an undue sense of right."

The Japanese print has already spoken to us a message of aesthetic and ethical import. Its spirit has already entered into and possessed many of the artist souls of our race and has spoken through them more convincingly than ever.

Every dead wall in the land bears witness to its influence, direct or indirect. Beardsley, Whistler, Manet, Monet, Puvis de Chavannes, de Monvel, Matisse, and Picasso all have sensibly "seen" the print.

We are familiar now with Cubist and Futurist and other ists and isms. We recognize them as symptoms of the unrest that sometimes begets progress. Symptoms I think that the world is getting rather tired of, its "human" qualities, its corpse worship. I've noticed that when we use the word "human" we use it usually to explain or condone some weakness or some "cussedness" in man or woman, or to apologize for them in some way.

It is time we turned from "realism," with its appeal to human sentimentality and selfishness, to a reality with more God in it. The photographer and the Machine are doing realism very well now. The photographer and the Machine have taken a huge and senseless burden from the artist's shoulders. He is ungrateful and unemployed. Ungrateful because he regards the photographer and Machine as competitors, or ought to. The artist is unemployed because "democracy" has not yet learned, or maybe has forgotten, what he is for. Democracy is hardly to blame, because only in rare instances does the artist know now himself. The conditions of his existence have all changed. He has lost his grip on reality. Realism was his confession of impotence. He is willingly seduced into shining by the reflected light of past achievement by special pleading like Mr. Whistler's dangerous "Ten O'Clock"[6] perhaps and blissfully imagines all he is. Often he is a spectacular egoist coveting the spotlight so easy to gain in "Art," where personality plus is eagerly mistaken for capacity or genius, but I know that often too he is still a candidate for truth.

Call him Cubist or call him Futurist or more favorite and simple names if you will. He is forced now to see that line has a language of its own regardless of a sheep or a hearse or any picture of anything. He is forced to see that color has qualities all its own akin to music and that color like sound has notes precious for their own sake. He finally sees too that form is significant only when it follows function and that otherwise it is matter out of place. But now he sees that it has feeling as it resolves itself into surfaces and nuances, independently of the human figure.

More exciting still, he is discovering that these qualities may be harmonized, arranged, and composed with wonderful expression of spiritual moods and qualities with no story at all—just when perversely enough, music is beginning to feel that it needs a story. He has been having "a parrot and monkey" time with the Beautiful meanwhile. Like a mischievous small boy, he has tied his tin can to the tail of truth and caused an awful commotion. But that is not all. He is less objective now—more subjective, prophetic—more in place.

The print began to do this work twenty-five years ago, and although the debt of gratitude we already owe it has been hastily obscured—brazenly denied—or genuinely forgotten—it is at the basis of this awakening.

Originally it let the light in on the plodding, painstaking, picture-making, academic Western Artists' glum world. Already it has slain Turner and Bougereau. Why name the growing list already marked for slaughter? But more valuable than all it is a virile threat to our Renaissance of the Renaissance.

We ought to be tired of patching things together for effect. We ought to be sick and ashamed of getting things somewhere and sticking them on to anything nowhere except upon the *outside*—instead of developing the thing done from *within*, making it intelligently stand forth as the nature of the thing. A new country is a new opportunity.

Why blindly repeat the empty forms and institutions of a civilization frantically confessing itself a failure? The spirit of a true art form never dies. The forms themselves as forms when taken from their time and place usually do.

Never yet has Art been successfully transplanted, and our country is conclusive proof that it never will be. It is the ideal founded upon the principle of organic integrity that was lacking in the Renaissance so far as Architecture and the allied arts and crafts were concerned. But it is now the ideal vitally necessary to any upbuilding of culture for America if we are going to have one worth having.

We have lost touch with the simplicity and force of origins and clamber as we imagine, all around above them, pretending but finding nothing.

As Goethe sang in his "Hymn to Nature"— "the wellsprings of human activity are few"— quickly exhausted—as quickly renewed.

These several eternal wellsprings are always the artists' motifs. So it is never so much what the artist does as the way in which he does it. If he does it his way with the insight that is love—Art and Individuality are born. Individuality is the most precious of qualities as it is the supreme entertainment of life.

As we see it around about us, it is the work— the artistry of the Supreme Artist, evidence of his love in his work, his joy in it. We find it in the trees and rocks and animals—sometimes even in people. And wherever we find it there life really is.

Wherever *life* is there is *soul*, for what else is Life? For one, I am happy to believe that soul is not confined to the human race. I can only regard the visible world as supreme artistry, eternally developing, in which inheres this principle of organic integrity and the laws of inherent unity.

We must comprehend and obey if we would create soul with soul. We may create, then, in the image of the Creator, and our work will be at one with the work of the Supreme Artist.

Meredith[7] said we might be rebels against laws but that if we were for nature we were never lawless. Nature in integral sense, that is.

The Kingdom of Art, as the fountain of youth, is within, and both abide in principle.

Harunobu and Hiroshige, perhaps, did not bother much about principle. It was not necessary. There was much conscious knowledge in what they did, and we have records of a very scientific attitude on their part toward their art. But for them the time was ripe. There was nothing in their way. What unity there was in the life of the Yedo[8] of their day: how every detail of life had harmonious character and thrilling individuality.

From the black-hooded samurai and the gorgeous *oiran*[9] to the doorsteps and paper lanterns of the poor, nothing seemed out of feeling or out of place.

Their buildings, like the rocks and trees, grew in their places. Their gardens were idealized patterns of their landscapes. They were native shrines, in themselves a form of worship for their native land.

While elegance was commonplace—there was no commonplace elegance.

This Democracy of ours is rapidly being buried beneath a rubbish heap. The best and worst of all the world torn from its roots and dumped in upon us by precept and education and wealth. Mongrel taste and wasted sentimentality flung into a melting pot of ambition to issue into a morgue of dead styles. We are left to work our way out to homogeneous character and individuality if we can. We can never do it without principle for a center line—or a leading string if you prefer. Sophisticated thinking, backward to fundamentals, is more essential to our enterprise than ever before in Art if we are going to prove or hold fast anything like culture that is not a fashionable sham.

Europe on the eve of wretched, inglorious catastrophe had begun to turn to the East for more light—to turn for inspiration to the "morning-land," the land where art dawned for our civilization. Oriental origins were begging to be eagerly sought.

I believe we are going to school for these genuine origins, again. They will give us real help in the work of establishing the significance of form as form once more upon the Earth and teach us how to satisfy our needs with organic quality in the expressions of Life we call Art.

This time we will know enough to avoid an Oriental or a Mohammedan "Renaissance" because the strong ethnic character of our sources of inspiration will forbid its use ready-made and also because the light in it is of the quality obscured if not wholly lost in the "period" we call the European Renaissance. It is outraged and insulted by the buffoonery of our Renaissance of the Renaissance.

The Japanese print is a creation in the sense that I have tried to predicate as the sense of all true fine art. It is intrinsic as such and will not pass away. It will work on in our imaginations until we too look to the significance of fundamentals once more, to the poetry of sincerity. We of today are too easily satisfied: too content to applaud the singer and "throw in" the song. Continually we mistake the interpretive for the creative artist. We like to make that mistake. It makes life so much easier and more agreeable for most of us.

We need superficial enthusiasms to go on with our mode of life and to keep our institutions going.

But there is a great difference between interpretation and creation, a difference vitally significant to us just at this critical stage of our development. We must learn to know what that difference is.

Victor Hugo was not a very great artist, perhaps, but he was a great man, with prophetic vision. His warning in *Nôtre-Dame* to the culture of his time that "the book will kill the edifice" (that great critical synthesis of the European Renaissance) has come true. The book has killed the edifice and all that the edifice means in Art and Craft.

The Renaissance and the book have despiritualized and literalized the thought of the world and, commercialized in the name of Christianity, have dragged a blight of the Beautiful over the whole Earth. See the depths of depravity the Renaissance reached in the soulless altars it has placed in the precious Gothic churches of the Middle Ages; the atrocious mutilations of their façades—with its heartless, cruel pediments—its senseless forms. Never have I been able to contemplate them or the prostitution of my own country's opportunities by its school without rage and a resolve—not for revenge—but for achievement that would let the light in on such degradation so clearly that even the "first-class passengers" of M. Andrews's hymn might "read the meaning plain."[10] This soulless thing has had the upper hand of Art and has betrayed the Artist, and he in turn has betrayed his people long enough! This cowardly intruder would strangle the hope of integral beauty, of Life, of a native in its infancy, in its cradle, protected by academic authority!

So long as we have "period" interiors and their equivalent in Art, installed by professional decorators in this exterior masquerade of "styles," we are doomed to no culture fundamentally significant of Truth and Beauty. Truth and Beauty blossom only from integrity of means to ends—and integrity that is a fountain of youth in Art. It is a light too, a love light, that seemed to die away with the birth of the Renaissance. It glows for us today in the countenance of that modest messenger of light

from the Far East—from the "morning-land"—the humble Japanese print.

1. Ernest F. Fenollosa (1853–1908) was one of the earliest American enthusiasts of Japanese art. While teaching in Japan he became active in the preservation of the traditional arts, which were seriously threatened when "Westernization" was embraced by the nation after the Meiji Restoration of 1868. He was also the first curator of the Japanese department of the Museum of Fine Arts, Boston, and wrote extensively on Ukiyo-e.
2. Maruyama Okyo (1733–1795) and Ogata Korin (1658-1716) were important figures in the history of Japanese painting. Korin, as the artist from whom the *Rimpa* school took its name, is probably the better known in the West.
3. *Hashirakake* (literally "pillar hangings") are prints designed to be hung on interior columns. Long and narrow, they measure approximately 26" × 4½".
4. *Gaufrage,* in woodblock printing, refers to the embossing achieved by printing from uncolored blocks.
5. *Notan* refers to contrasting areas of light and dark masses, or light and shade.
6. Whistler's 1885 "Ten O'Clock" lecture was an attack on contemporary art theory. Wright's reference here is confusing because he actually agreed with Whistler's beliefs about what art should be.
7. Possibly George Meredith (1828–1909), English novelist and poet.
8. Yedo (Edo) was the shogunal seat until the Meiji Restoration of 1868. When the Emperor Meiji officially moved his residence from Kyoto, the imperial capital since 794, to Edo the name was changed to Tokyo (Eastern Capital).
9. *Oiran* were high-class courtesans celebrated for their beauty and elegance. They were a favorite subject of the print artists.
10. See "The Architect," p. 45.

CHICAGO CULTURE

The love-hate relationship that flourished between Wright and Chicago is nowhere more apparent than in this article of 1918, which was read to the Women's Aid Organization. Although it is a scathing criticism of the cheapness of the "nouveau riche" and such tastes that thrived in the city at that time, it also praises the many fine people Chicago produced, from Jane Addams to Carl Sandburg. Wright extends special praise to his former employers, Louis Sullivan and Dankmar Adler, and at the same time praises the architects John Root and Daniel Burnham. It is interesting to reflect on the fact that the writing of this article in 1918 coincided with the reunion of Sullivan and Wright after a twenty-five year schism. Sullivan had fired Wright in 1893; in 1918 he telephoned Wright in Wisconsin and set the stage for a reconciliation. [Speech, published in On Architecture, *1940]*

TEN YEARS AGO, AT A DINNER GIVEN BY A VISITING ARTIST (Ashbee of London,[1] who had criticized us rather freely), one of our magnates got up and boasted that "Chicago wasn't much on culture now, maybe, but when she did get after culture she'd make culture hum." Chicago brag, but true! Chicago got after culture. Chicago has made culture hum. The kind of culture Chicago "got after" likes it and hums loud. No one interested in the subject can ignore it. But I want to say more about the men and the culture that are getting after the culture that Chicago "got after."

No one thinks of this city as the art center of the Western world. It is famous for so much else and otherwise. And yet the broad free spirit of Chicago has given great things in art to the light here, that if conceived elsewhere would have died stillborn. This is due to Chicago's superior discernment. I do not pretend that it is due simply to the nature of the thing.

Chicago is the national capital of the essentially American spirit. Chicago, in spite of the culture she "got after," is a very real place. To know Chicago is an experience in first principles: a despair and a great hope. A despair, not so much because Chicago is cruel and crude as because "culture" has been stuck upon its surface as a businessman's expedient or thoughtlessly bought by the rich as luxury. Bought in blissful ignorance of the more vital, less fashionable contribution Chicago has to make to life.

Is anything uglier than just dirt, unless it is noise? We have both in abundance. Someone defines dirt as matter out of place, and in this sense Chicago's culture is dirt; matter out of place in all its ugliness. Hundreds of thousands of houses that are little stage settings in various periods where "Pa" and "Ma" don't belong, and where it would be immoral, shocking, or absurd for them to be and seen in which they seldom fail to be ridiculous. See the assortment on the drive or any favored section of the city! See our "beastly rich" in their store clothes at the opera; our badly overdressed business women in their tall white shoes or their equivalent in our offices. A type of little girl badly overdone has made her appearance on our streets, pseudo-Parisian probably. Our hotels, one and all, parade an air of magnificence and expense as a substitute for privacy, modesty, and comfort, offering the outward show of the continental hotel without real service, without politeness, without individuality.

Yes, life is on too easy or too hard terms here in Chicago if without money, and with it, still empty of the warmth, cordiality, and individuality that make life in Europe enjoyable almost everywhere.

The pernicious papier-mâché elegance of our theaters is, in architectural spirit, level with the morals of the Folies-Bergère. The city's public buildings are foolish lies. The Art Institute itself is a stupid building with no countenance and elaborate flanks; the Public Library, two buildings one on top of the other in disgraceful quarrel; the Post Office, a boyish atelier project regardless of its purpose; the City Hall, a big bluff in vain "classic" costing the city many thousands a month for huge columns, themselves a troublesome and expensive load instead of carrying the load as columns used to do. A certain careless prosperous dishonesty characterizes the cultural fabric of the city of Chicago as it does of America.

One of Chicago's influential, admirable architects, and one who has built some good houses and fine industrial buildings, told me not long ago of a wealthy widow from some town down in the Middle West who came to ask him to build a monument to her husband, a local politician some months dead. She wanted to buy an exact replica of the Greek monument to Lysicrates to be set up on their lot in the hometown cemetery. To her, a beautiful thought for her dead husband.

Hoping to dissuade her, Mr. Shaw[2] told her of the great cost of such an undertaking. But happening to go East about that time he met some of the influential architects of New York, Boston, and Philadelphia. At dinner he told the story and to his surprise they said, "By all means go back and build it for her; a beautiful thing like that couldn't fail to be educational." There it is. The costly fallacy behind all this stark, staring, naked. The shameless

irrelevant use of a beautiful thing; its abuse, therefore, justified as educational! With such advocates on top, what chance has the eternal fitness of things underneath?

Abuse, you see, is "academic" now.

Another traveled rich woman adored the Petit Trianon. She must have it for a house, only it was a story too low. So Mr. Shaw put another story on the Trianon for her. If he had not done it someone else would have and probably would have done it worse. Mr. Shaw said so.

I sneered, and he turned and showed me a Gothic building he had just finished as a home for some Chicago businessman and asked if I liked it any better. It was chaste, severe, very well done, like a little stage setting of a twelfth-century play, of course, with modern improvements. I utterly failed to imagine anyone entering it otherwise than in costume. And yet this hard-headed Chicago businessman elected to buy Gothic. That was his cultural expedient. Really, are we too, in Chicago, plundering the Old World of all its finery and dressing ourselves up in it regardless, as a kind of masquerade? I can see it as great fun (very expensive fun), but how can it be seen as culture when the essence of all true culture is a *development* of self-expression?

No, not *culture*. It is a cheap *substitute* for culture hired and paid for by the hour. Accumulation, not realization. Purchase, not production.

A despair.

Nevertheless, set against this fashionable folly with its fatuous inelegance there is something vital, indigenous to Chicago, the seeds of a genuine culture, the great hope of America quietly working here eventually to come up through this imposition, to show it for what it is and refute it.

Even our pretended culture is not yet vicious. It is thoughtless always; boorish, often; sometimes low; always wasteful; usually absurd; but Chicago takes this sham culture as "the thing" with no real thought about it at all nor any real taste for it. Therefore, it is potential vulgarity when not inane. Only when we do accept it with "that little knowledge which is a dangerous thing" does it become hopeless.

The big impulse of great unspoiled power has its oversoul in Chicago in significant movements in architecture, music, literature, the theater, education, and recreation; culture that means a true new life worthy of a great new nation. These movements and the men who made them are at home in Chicago. And they ought not to be wasted.

Time was when, if Chicago had a boy who shied at business, seemed good-for-nothing, therefore, she would send him down to the Art Institute to have an "artist" made of him. She thought maybe *that* was what was the matter with him. Even now it is a popular superstition that aesthetic people have long, slim hands, a graceful habit in beatitudes, jar easily from them, and shudder slightly when jarred.

Perhaps the aesthetic "consumer" is like that.

The aesthetic "producer" certainly is not.

Homer, Michelangelo, Bramante, Rodin, Carlyle, Goethe, Shelley, William Blake, and Beethoven were more like the ideal of the creative artist reared by Romain Rolland in *Jean-Christophe*.

The artist's needs are as other men's, intensified. He is broad, strong, resourceful, typified by a love of life that survives great trials and comes through with a song in his heart, resilient, however his spirit be outraged or his body broken.

Zarathustra's prayer is his, "This do I ask of Thee, O Lord; speak and make me to know the truth."

It is where life is fundamental and free that men develop the vision needed to reveal the human soul in the blossoms it puts forth; blossoms we choose to call "works of art," and we sometimes neglect to call the worker artist, but subsequent generations never do. In a great workshop like Chicago this creative power germinates, even though the brutality and selfish preoccupation of the place drive it elsewhere for bread.

Men of this type have loved Chicago, have worked for her, and believed in her. The hardest thing they have to bear is her shame. These men could live and work here, when to live and work in New York would stifle their genius and fill their purse. As a New York preacher put it, "New York is a good place in which to sell fish, but there are no trout in her streams." The art of the talented men who have gone to New York has gradually succumbed to the fashionable squalor and ceaseless gyration of the place, as their bodies might to a mortal sickness. New York still believes that art should be imported; brought over in ships; and is a quite contented marketplace.

So while New York has reproduced much and produced nothing, Chicago's achievements in architecture have gained worldwide recognition as a distinctively American architecture.

Louis Sullivan gave America the skyscraper as an organic modern work of art. While America's architects were stumbling at its height, piling one thing on top of another, foolishly denying it, Louis Sullivan seized its height as its characteristic feature and made it sing; a new thing under the sun!

One of the world's greatest architects, he gave us again the ideal of a great architecture that informed all the great architectures of the world.

Chicago's Auditorium[3], an early work of his and his great-souled executive partner Dankmar Adler, is one of the city's first civic triumphs famous throughout the world as an architect's masterpiece. Some of its delicate golden traceries have been obliterated and the quiet balance of the big beautiful room destroyed by a petticoat of red paint below its waistline, applied by a Chicago society amateur. Perhaps Chicago is the only city in the world that would permit an affront of the kind to one of its greatest men to pass unrebuked. It is because this "culture" we have on top is necessarily pseudo-Venetian or pseudo-something; it can be nothing else. But the Auditorium still stands, a noble achievement.

Men who give great impulse to the city's character, men who are the life of its ideas, are never official or a part of its social machinery.

In John Root, too, Chicago had a man of genius. He outlined the Columbian Fair that astonished and delighted the world. Daniel Burnham, his partner, seized it in his powerful executive grasp and it was realized. The same grasp has left the city a plan for a greater Chicago, essentially good. It will be realized, too, but in its execution, entrusted as it is to Beaux-Arts graduates, it will finally resemble anything but an individual expression of the great Chicago smokestack that is more truly a work of art than the gray ghosts of a dubious past now haunting the lakefront part at the foot of Monroe Street.

Looking north you may see them, smoke-stacks and pylons together. It is the pretentious pylons that suffer by contrast.

In domestic architecture we have what some are calling the "New School of the Middle West." This great Chicago prairie has a quiet beauty all its own. But these dwellings referred to recognize circumstance and fact with quiet masses, fashioned in new spirit with sure, sweeping lines. They are rational, individual, and organic. The world outside America—France, Germany, Austria, England, Holland, and Japan—have found these buildings beautiful.

Chicago industrial buildings, too, have set a new standard of excellence for the whole world. Many of them are works of art, perhaps, because that is where we really live.

The queen of Holland's architect, Berlage,[4] said, after coming here in quest of American culture, that the two things that impressed him most were Niagara Falls and the Larkin Building.

All this is a Chicago contribution to an art academically declared to be moribund!

In Jens Jensen[5], the landscape architect, Chicago has a native nature poet who has made the West Park system a delight to the country. He is a true interpreter of the peculiar charm of our prairie landscape. Jens Jensen should be interpreter-in-chief for Chicago for our wonderful park system; a system that together with our small playgrounds is one of the finest civic-urban features of the world; a recreation ground beyond compare. No small-hearted city, no city except Chicago, could have established it or would have made the sacrifices necessary to maintain it. It is not least among the things to this city's everlasting credit.

After these fundamental aspects of the city's individual growth comes music.

Chicago has established good music in its midst. Theodore Thomas stayed here and found support. Chicago built a permanent home for his orchestra; a home that broke Theodore Thomas's heart because it was unfit for its purpose. The only place in it where music can be heard to advantage is just beneath the ceiling. But Chicago is not to

blame for that. This love of music was an early sign that Chicago had a soul. Now a music-loving Chicago public understands and insists upon good music. Soon we will require chamber music, and quartets like the Kneisels and Flonzaleys will belong to us. We have a composer or two attracting the attention of the music-loving world, less exotic than most, John Carpenter and Felix Borowsky. Harriet Monroe founded here the only American magazine of poetry, and it is a well-deserved success with its Vachel Lindsay, Carl Sandburg, and a host of young writers whose mark is made on the literary life of their country.

Margaret Anderson's *Little Review*[6] made its passionate, young bow here in the cause of literary freedom. It has fled to New York, no place for a freedom-loving thing in the arts; it will return or die.

Chicago, too, is the "big town" of those distinctively American forces in letters. Booth Tarkington, John McCutcheon, and George Ade, lively interpreters of the American thing; Booth Tarkington's work is a delight.

The literary list is, of course, a long one and likely to make my catalog tedious, but Chicago is the home of Gene Field, Hamlin Garland, Will Moody, Ernest Poole, Henry Webster, Robert Merrick, the Browns of *The Dial*, I. E. Friedman, Chatfield-Taylor, our own B.L.T.[7], Ring Lardner, and Jack Lait. And there is Edgar Lee Masters and Thorstein Veblen, with his theory of the leisure class, George Foster, and Clarence Darrow, all a very moving and characteristic world in itself. Literature is the ubiquitous art of this age. Everybody writes something. Everywhere literature flourishes like the dragon's teeth sown ages ago. They must have been "type." Even the newspaper editorial is becoming a factor in modern life, thanks to the initiative (giving the devil his due) of the publisher, William Randolph Hearst.

We can escape literature nowhere, and its entire fabric is drenched with sex. Newspapers recklessly smear sex everywhere. Every magazine everywhere has its nauseating ritual of the "girl" cover. The "he-and-she" novel is omnipresent, and the play is not more than a play of sex, while the concoctions for the tired businessman grow faster and more furious year by year. We are emerging from the darkness, in which sex's fundamental characteristics have been kept, to exposure gratuitous to say the least.

The very extravagance in all this is the hopeful sign of impending reaction.

Chicago's sky pilots rank with any, anywhere. David Swing, Jenkin Lloyd Jones[8], Bishop Cheney, Rabbi Hirsch, and Doctor Gunsaulus.

Jane Addams is a Chicago institution all by herself of worldwide fame and influence. What a fine possession she has been for Chicago.

In education, John Dewey and Francis Parker are to our credit.

The "Little Theater," growing out of the new theater movement and Donald Robertson, took root here first in Maurice Brown's unostentatious "Little Theater" in the Fine Arts Building. It is a "movement" now and scattered over the country with headquarters in New York. New York doesn't believe anything really is until she has seized it and it "arrives" in New York. That is the way she seems to have of originating things. But she frankly prefers to import European models. They are more in keeping.

We have painters and sculptors, too—too many of them. Winners of salon prizes; men and women of undoubted talent like Lawton Parker, Jerome Blum, Pauline Palmer, William Henderson, Zukalsky, McNeil, and Lorado Taft.

But unfortunately we have less than nothing for them to paint or carve except the likenesses of well-to-do society folk. The fundamental condition of the painter's and sculptor's existence has been neglected by the very institution that devoted itself to forwarding them. But they seem to go right on trying to make an art of painting and sculpture for its own sake, and the easel picture has become our favorite vice, comparable to pie, porches, and ice water.

Existing, really, for the painter and sculptor we have the Art Institute of Chicago, the best-located, largest, and most successful in point of attendance of any institution of art in America. Happily, Chicago people are beginning to love it. Like the cathedral of the Middle Ages, it is the one place in the city that should never be closed to the people at any time, even if it took three shifts to keep it open. A "gift" that would make that possible would have real democratic style and would need no bronze tablet to impress it upon the gratitude of the people or the character of our future.

The Arts Club of Chicago has extended the work of the Art Institute by profiting by "Institute" mistakes. The Arts Club may prove valuable to Chicago.

One of the most valuable assets of "the Institute," Emma Church, broke away from it some time ago and has established and maintained a school of her own, doing work that has won significant recognition. Until recently the Art Institute had a monopoly on the professed "artistic" side of our culture.

For twenty-five years past the destiny of this important organ of our coming culture has been in the hands of a small group of public-spirited men who have loved works of art with more heat than light and have collected much and given it all to Chicago. These men, together with Lorado Taft, Ralph Clarkson, and Charles Francis Browne (sculptor and painters), have served the Art Institute of Chicago faithfully and well. Is it ungrateful to say that they, collectors, sculptor, and painters, are all that is the matter with it now?

The Art Institute has the greatest opportunity to aid and comfort the real culture that is getting after Chicago and to correct and mold or mitigate the horror of the culture she got after, were the Institute free; at least free to reject what passes for conservative when it is only stupid, or passes for right-mindedness when it is only prejudice. Free, that is, to get down beneath traditions of sculpture and painting to the real fundamentals of *culture*. It probably will become more free and vital. But academic centers have never been the life of art in any creative individual, city, or a nation. Original impulses live outside, hostile to established orders. Institutions are in their very nature hostile to these impulses. That hostility is the only way they have of remaining "institutions."

Academic recognition of good work is safe only when it may honor the *institution*, not the individual who has won what they covet and consent to honor themselves by accepting.

Centers like the Art Institute of Chicago should be reservoirs, conserving the sap of these "hostile" activities, making it available to young, inquiring, or rebellious minds.

Never should these forces be so edited and emasculated as to be useless to the future.

Abuse of *institutional* privileges in a democracy must cease or we will always take the name for the thing. This is especially true in art. If democracy means anything at all in a fine-art sense it means easier, surer recognition of the qualities of the individual; greater respect for the *nature* of individuality, not the usual premium put upon mediocrity in the interest of so-called public safety just because there are pretenders and shame in the world. Every noble forward movement will have its sordid, soiled fringe. It is better for democracy that any number of talents be given opportunity to prove unworthy than that one possible genius be denied.

Democracy can live by genius only. Its very soul is individuality.

An art institute should be no editor of genius in the spirit of connoisseur or collector. It should be an opportunity, a staff in the hand, a cloak for genius in the bitter wind that assails genius and criminal alike.

Were you to see the exhibition of the work of pupils covering the period of the life of this institution given here last month, you would find painting worthy of high praise. Sculpture, much of it, but only a little worthy of a second look.

In architecture and allied arts and crafts, nothing. Oh! So much less than nothing!

This as culture is like an overhanging cornice, topside down upon the ground where the foundation ought to be. A wasteful pitiful perversion!

A sense of the altogether, that is, the eternal fitness of each to each and the each in all to the all in all, is the fundamental essential to culture, in individuals, citizens, or a country. And the crying need of this time and this place. The "altogether" in this sense always has been as it will always be more important than thrilling paintings or marble statues but without in the least lessening their desirability.

They will take their places as the heightened expressions, perhaps, of its qualities, after these qualities have been established. Connoisseurs, critics, collectors increase, yet commonplace elegance is here, there, and everywhere.

Harmonious elegance is desperately rare.

Fashion exists for commercial purposes only.

The fashionable thing is valueless to culture.

In art, democracy means that some thought of your own, some feeling you have about the thing yourself, should enter into everything you have or do, so that everything you have may be your own and everything you do be sincerely yourself. Democracy in this true sense is really the highest form of aristocracy the world has ever known. The aristocracy of qualities, not of birth or circumstances. Now, this should be as true of the art institute as it is of art. Slaves of fashion, human sheep, are the curse of this ideal; relics of an aristocracy that was an imposition and now is passing in anguish.

But civilization with us is simmering down to a case of too much "Marshall Field" to be culture. One is tempted to remark upon the amount of "Marshall Field" each fashionable woman carries about upon her person or drags after her by the hand, if she has children. It is alone an occupation; a feverish, unhappy, competitive quest; a blight; an undemocratic folly.

One beautiful dress, really individual and becoming, one hat that suits the face and both together sympathetic to the wearer, are worth all the fashionable changes in the shops; even if one had to wear just that hat and just that dress for life because they cost so much. Of course, such things would cost more in time and study on your part and on the part of the artists who will be employed then and who will deserve to be well paid.

The same thing applies to your house and your furnishings and to your works of art.

If only we could get the significant outlines of democracy fixed within our vision we would have arrived, at least, at the beginning.

This is the spirit that must characterize Chicago.

Out of it, in time, will come something better worth living for than the senseless jam of ill-considered things that clutter the persons, the homes, and the thought of our Chicago women, rob their men of anything worthwhile to show for their ceaseless, grinding efforts and of their children, their finest hope for the future.

Nevertheless, Chicago is the only great city that is America-conscious, that has a sense of destiny; American. The case for American originality is at stake here. Chicago must find culture from *within* or all America is reduced to a colony of Europe; we of Chicago are her only hope.

When I think of the vast growth that is Chicago, realize that it all happened within the past fifty years, it seems one of the marvels of history that it is no worse than it is.

But we can now see what may easily be, if instead of the expedients of the businessmen drugged by commercialism we would cling to the practical and to principle for a time.

Chicago would establish then the great hope; democracy in its great fine-art sense. Chicago's location is little more than an accident. It was virtually born in a swamp. It has been the chief butcher shop of the world.

No wonder Chicago bought and borrowed her culture ready-made, and wears it as a cook wears her "picture hat," very much on one side, or well down over her eyes, stuck it on anyhow as best she can. She had to have the picture hat, along with the best of them, and have it quick. Any thinking about it had to be done afterward. If only Chicago would devote herself to thinking about it now and would discard the damned thing.

Not so much mischief has yet been done as has already been done to Tokyo by borrowed garments, exotic "culture." Tokyo is the most awful of modern instances, although within fifty years New York's cultured expression, her "picture hat," will seem as odious and old-fashioned as General Grant Gothic does now. It will seem as enlightened as the brownstone fronts on Dearborn Avenue, as beautiful as the sacred old Pullman Building, our first skyscraper. The same thing as this in principle is what New York has done. It is better done, that is all, and so, more dangerous.

The practices behind even our best efforts are foreign. They belong to "the Renaissance"; the setting sun of art all Europe mistook for dawn. The more enlightened artists of Europe know it. But we proceed with our expedient renascence of the Renaissance.

This supposed pretended democracy of ours is being rapidly buried beneath a rubbish heap, best and worst of all the world torn from its moorings, dumped in upon us by precept, by education, by "business is business," and by capricious, irresponsible wealth.

Mongrel taste with its derelict sentimentality is flinging it all into this welter of dangerous ambitions whence it emerges fit only for the morgue, a mangled style.

This soulless thing, the Renaissance, has had the upper hand of art, has betrayed the artist; and he in turn has betrayed his people long enough. Let us have done with it forever.

Protected by academic authority is this cowardly imitation of an imitation in the hands of men themselves no less an imitation, yet who, somehow, are accepted as artists on their own or each other's say-so. They would strangle the hope of integral beauty in a growing people, in a great nation, in its infancy; yes, and in Chicago in its cradle. Because, for commercial and society reasons, we have had to have the semblance of culture for our great sudden city, put up quick, like a painted signboard above a shop; it has all been too easy for such men as advised Howard Shaw to go back and build the Choragic Monument[9] to Lysicrates for the Illinois politician's widow; men who would sell us anything we would take, sell our birthright, or mortgage our future to the past beyond redemption, barter it for a mess of pottage or for public recognition for an hour.

Our so-called culture, today, is a costly imposition upon our life in Chicago. No skill can make it right. Only revolt can save the city for culture that is for all time and develop the integrity of means to ends that is the fountain of youth in art.

A great artist looking from the windows of this building toward those gray ghosts, the pylons haunting the lakefront opposite Monroe Street, was asked by a friend who saw him thus regarding them, what he thought about them. He said, "If that is what the American people stand for now, from this time dates the downfall of the republic."

Some symbol, some proof of real culture, is needed of the city's genius in one preeminent, self-expression. One thing Chicago must do as a symbol of her life: she must take her great heritage, the lakefront, and shape it to her own liking. She must do something with it the like of which the world has not yet seen and that belongs in spirit to her.

The independence of Chicago, her integrity, her destiny as the capital of the American spirit is at stake.

The life of the soul of Chicago depends upon the rescue of this treasure of our people from fashionable degradation.

The artist is of his people and his time, and for them, whether accepted by them or not. He is uncoverer; discoverer of truth in new guise.

The creative artist is engaged in unwrapping the winding sheet that holds the world in bondage. He alone can set the world free.

He is no damnable excrescence on the face of things. He is never the parasite nor the traitor.

But, he must state his inspiration in terms of the character and need of his own time, of his own people; and his work is no less universal on that account.

Egyptian art was stated in terms of Egypt.

Just as a human being has his race stamped upon his features, great art will have the conditions of its existence indelibly fixed in its expression or as one of the fundamental laws of its very being. The art in a thing is the *understanding* in it, the *life* in it, the *love* in it. There is no substitute for art in this business of culture. Culture comes through being, not buying. Culture has never been bought. In all the life of all the ages opulence has eventually destroyed it. Culture is not something that you "take on" like polish. It is "the nature of the thing" developed to its highest qualities of usefulness and beauty.

Chicago has *everything* but culture!

1. Charles Robert Ashbee (1863–1942), a London architect deeply involved with the English Arts and Crafts movement, was one of the first European enthusiasts of Wright's work.
2. Howard Van Doren Shaw (1869–1926) was a Chicago architect whose style was "establishment," if eclectic. Apparently on friendly terms with Wright, he demonstrated no interest in an American architecture for the twentieth century, and "English" is most commonly associated with his work.
3. Chicago Auditorium, built 1887–1889.
4. Hendrik Petrus Berlage (1856–1934) was the most important pioneer of modern architecture in the Netherlands and was instrumental in introducing Wright's work into that country.
5. Jens Jensen (1859-1951) designed Garfield, Columbus, and Humboldt parks while chief landscape architect of the West Park District.
6. The *Little Review* was a periodical published in Chicago from March 1914 to December 1916.
7. Bert Leston Taylor (1866–1921), a columnist best known for "A Line o' Type or Two" he wrote for *The Chicago Tribune* under the signature B.L.T. The column was highly regarded, widely read, and set a standard many found difficult to emulate.
8. The Rev. Dr. Jenkin Lloyd Jones (1843–1918), a man of great physical stamina and intellectual power, was Frank Lloyd Wright's uncle. Jones was a prominent Unitarian minister and reform leader in Chicago from the 1880s on.
9. A reference to the monument to Lysicrates built in Athens in 334 B.C. to commemorate the victory of a choric group, whose patron was Lysicrates, in a contest of song honoring Dionysus. "Choragic" is the adjectival form of *choragus,* the leader of the chorus in an ancient Greek play.

THE NEW IMPERIAL HOTEL

In this, Wright's first published article about the new Imperial Hotel[1], he was writing for a Japanese audience and interested foreigners. Published in early 1922, the essay is a defense of his design, which had come under attack from a number of directions[2], and a critique of the contemporary Japanese architectural vision, or lack thereof. When asked why he did not make the building more "modern," he replied, "There was a tradition there worthy of respect, and I felt it my duty as well as my privilege to make a building belong to them so far as I might."[3]

Wright's building was still under construction at the time of this article's publication, with a date for completion yet to be established. A fire in the main building of the first Imperial Hotel, still in operation at the time, made it imperative that the pace of construction be accelerated. Accordingly, the north wing of guest rooms and the central dining hall were completed in time for a visit from the United States' Secretary of the Navy and his entourage in July, just prior to Wright's final return to the United States.

Wright often wrote in depth about his experiences building the Imperial Hotel. That he loved the culture and art of Japan is obvious in the long chapter he devoted to that country in his autobiography. In addition to the articles that appear here, Wright also submitted an article to Liberty Magazine *that was published in the December 3, 1927 issue, for which he was paid $1,350, a substantial sum at the time. That article, somewhat amplified, was incorporated into his autobiography five years later. More writings on the Imperial Hotel were published in* Architecture and Modern Life *in 1937 and in* The Natural House *in 1954. [Published without illustrations in* Kagaku Chishiki, *April 1922]*

ART IS UNIVERSAL WHEN IT IS ART IN THE TRUE SENSE. ALL artists are brothers, living or dead. I happen to be an American architect, that is all, just as my brothers happen to be Japanese or French or Indian or English architects.

I came to Japan to show how an organic expression of the ancient spirit of architecture was possible in new terms in modern times—not only possible but more alive and warmly related to life than the cold, dead forms Japanese architects go abroad to copy. In this spirit I have made a building that looks and feels at home in Japan and is no mongrel: any study of its parts in relation to the whole will prove it thoroughbred.

This building—the new Imperial Hotel of Tokyo—is not designed to be a Japanese building: it is an artist's tribute to Japan, modern and universal in character.

The Imperial Hotel. Tokyo, Japan. 1916. FLLW Fdn FA#1509.0098

The Imperial Hotel. Tokyo, Japan. 1916. FLLW Fdn FA#1509.0095

While there is something Japanese, Chinese, and of other ancient forms living in this structure as all may see, there is neither form, idea, nor pattern copied from any, ancient or modern. It is reverent to old Japan, that is all.

In it, the most modern conscious ideal of architecture is living—and that is the idea of a work of art as beauty organic or integral—and therefore working from within outward as contrasted with the idea of art as something applied or put on from the outside or merely something for its own sake. There is, therefore, a fine integrity of means to ends visible throughout the structure and a development of parts in relation to the whole similar to any consistent expression of nature, like the trees or a flower. Practical necessities whole.

Simple materials have been used in rather easy fashion because character of the form or idea seemed more important than the quality of texture.

In a building of this size under the circumstances both together could not be had. Japanese workmen are yet unfamiliar with masonry and so workmanship is necessarily crude. Therefore, the texture of the building is perhaps coarse for Japanese taste—more like a woolen tapestry than a silk brocade; more like hand-woven linen than satin. It is really a gigantic masonry brocade of brick and stone and copper fused together with concrete inlaid with steel fiber.

When I agreed to undertake a work so difficult, so entirely removed from industrial conditions or methods I know, I felt that the Japanese people needed help because they were throwing away the forms of their old life and borrowing new ones they could not understand: forms already in the scrap heaps of the civilizations that produced them.

In all Tokyo there was not a single building by a native or "foreigner" who really understood the

The Imperial Hotel. Tokyo, Japan. 1916. FLLW Fdn FA#1509.0058

meaning either of architecture or of what he did in the name of architecture, nor one that showed a real love for Japan.

These buildings were bad copies, in bad technique, of bad originals. The buildings that were most strange, most different from old native buildings, were the models of these ugly empty shells, where no spirit of the beautiful could dwell for a moment.

Japan, whose origins reach back into and are lost in the primitive Chinese, certainly had richer sources of inspiration within herself than any other nation. Chinese architecture is the most vivid and noble of all forms of architecture, and this architecture was Japan's inheritance.

Japanese architects have betrayed their country.

During the time I have been engaged upon this work I have not changed my mind regarding the needs of Japan but have abandoned any idea that Japanese architects realize those needs. They are

learning to do the "foreign thing" a little better—yes—sometimes doing it well, as in the new Mitsubishi Bank—a sarcophagus—perfect in propriety in some land far from Japan. It has, however, nothing to do with Japan's case except as a servile obsession, a mockery. It serves to indicate how wide of any mark that is her own her perceptions are at the present time.

And I have seen little on the part of the Japanese people themselves to indicate that they were convinced of the empty folly of imitation. They seem passionately to prefer it.

In all effort resulting in real progress there is a center line of principle: this principle is all that is worth study, and once grasped and mastered the more excellent result comes as a matter of course.

In this grasp of principle, Japanese efforts in architecture are lacking. Lacking that element, Japanese modern life will remain confused, become mongrel and utterly superficial, and the Japanese will be at the mercy of whims and caprices that have made evil things fashionable since civilization began—which was probably when fig leaves became desirable in the Garden of Eden. Fashion and sham will rule the East as they have ruled the West.

It seems to me it is in architecture the derby hat, kimono, and gaiters all over again—that period of absurd confusion followed in civil matters by silk-hatted, frock-coated "correctness" and in military matters the gorgeous harness borrowed from three nations in exchange for samurai elegance and simplicity. The mongrel period depicted so faithfully in color prints by Kiyochika.[4]

In architecture, the parallel of the "derby-kimono-gaiter" period is found in the Ginza monstrosities. The correct Mitsubishi Bank corresponds to the civil "silk-hatted, frock-coated element"—and ambitious public buildings borrowed from three nations are the parallel of borrowed militaristic glory. I suppose that in the excitement of changes so sudden significance is lost and not missed, or perhaps temperamentally the Japanese prefer the mystery of the curious to the clarity of the beautiful, which becomes more and more evident as the good, as the true.

Therefore the new ideal entering consciously by way of art into the modern life of the world of which the new Imperial Hotel is an instance may have small chance of recognition.

This new ideal consciously entering by way of art in modern life is the concept of beauty as organic unity—as integral in the thing made, or work done, as we say, by man, in the same sense as in things made or work done, as we say, by God.

The works of the soul of man are no less fruits of the tree that is man than plums are true to the plum tree or the grapes true to the vine. And unless these works as fruit are integral, organic—indigenous in the same sense, they will decay, become poisonous, and fall.

It is by culture only that the tree or vine is brought into bearing, and in the same manner only will the soul of man be brought to bear "good fruit" or works—that is to say, produce that unity in his work which is beauty.

There are various trees bearing various fruits and you can tie pears on plum trees and harvest neither pears nor good plums. The Japanese can tie foreign fruit on their human tree and admire them for a time, thinking themselves clever, but the fruits will rot, become poisonous, and drop off, the tree remaining unfruitful.

Only as the tree itself is cultured by true understanding of the principle common to all trees and is developed in the spirit of its own peculiar expression will the Japanese human tree ever bear fruit again. Art is universal, knowing no limits of time or place and every great work of art is for all the world, but nevertheless, time and place are conditions, are the limitations within which—yes, by means of which—individuality is born: that is to say wherein the fruit becomes a grape, an apple, or a plum. That principle does not change. In order not to violate immutable principle we refrain from tying grapes on fig trees, although the principle producing both is the same—one principle. It would seem therefore that we instinctively recognize individuality as supreme need or entertainment in the scheme of man, to be ignored or trifled with only at risk of decay. We dispose of it by attributing it to a "Law of Nature."

We perceive it intellectually when we speak of fitness to purpose or of form following function or of function following form.

There is a principle of unity to be observed, of which individuality is proof to the spirit, and to be preserved by us in what we do in life—if we would really live. If we trifle with it or ignore it, life gets beyond us: we are sterile.

It is useless to say that eventually all this disappears in atonement with God, where neither individuality, which is a proof of unity, nor mere differences, which are signs of ignorance, will exist. If that atonement is ever reached, it will be through the highest human vision of the life of a man as expressed in terms of work and individuality, although the one may be called joy and the other be called worship. We shall rise through these "limitations" to what is above them by observing obedience while perceiving the principle.

The Imperial Hotel. Tokyo, Japan. 1916. FLLW Fdn FA#1509.0101

We live by truth alone—by integrity: by whatever is integral or indigenous in so far as we really live at all.

The spirit of truth alone is integral, whatever is truly indigenous expresses it in some degree: it is symbolized by whatever is truly organic. By establishing this integrity in our lives, our work will be good fruit.

There is no begging we can do. There is no compromise to be made by borrowing, there is no shortcut that has ever led anywhere, although mankind has continually grafted to make the one and transplanted to find the other. Nation after nation in quest of civilization has gone down in fruitless attempts to beg, borrow, or steal what is only to be had from within.

This is something of the thought at the center of the new ideal of art entering modern life, of which the new Imperial Hotel is an instance—and why it ought to be worth studying. The world is deathly sick of artists as superficial ornaments, sick of art as an expedient.

Japanese civilization had a fine instinct for the kind of integrity in works outlined here as the new conscious ideal. It was not conscious unfortunately, or it would not now be lost or under a cloud. If it is ever won back again it will be won consciously through sophistication following intensely bitter experience and deep inner struggle.

Japan is tragic at this time—although there is, I should say, no sense of this on her part.

Japanese art is sick with sentimentality, because it has lost integral character.

And what I see passing for tragedy upon the Japanese stage is not tragedy at all—it is gruesome murder. All attempts at the tragic end in that, where a sense of the divine is absent. In other words, where an inherent sense of true human proportion is not illuminated by the glory of sacrifice of lesser to greater with principle either at stake or as judge. Call the principle God if you are in the habit of doing so.

Japan is tragic at this time because her own aesthetic abstractions in the past with a fine instinct for integrity were perfect and beautiful, and now the abyss no nation has ever yet crossed fascinates her as it yawns at her feet.

If Japan arises from the abyss or crosses it, it will be because what was true in old Japan finds itself, developing in strength and character, reaching true expression in what is peculiar to the Japanese, although broadened and deepened in a universal sense. Then unity will be integral in her life once more; this time conscious, sure in spiritual strength.

Will Japan make the necessary sacrifices or persist in egotistic illusion, sentimental, insignificant tears, lazily imitative, militaristic, and meaningless except as ignorant waste or wasteful ignorance of life—life regarded as principle?

In a sympathetic spirit, the architecture of the new Imperial Hotel is an offering to Japan in this her time of trial by an artist who owes much to her ancient spirit, one who would contribute his might to repay the debt, hoping to awaken and inspire his Japanese brothers in architecture to independent efforts of their own.

There is little to mark sunrise from sunset except progress. In a nation's lifetime a century is but a day. Change may be rapid, progress slow. So when the emblem of the rising sun is seen upon Japan's flag floating over the land, who can say that the symbol is a rising and not a setting sun?

1. The first Imperial Hotel to open at the present location was built in 1890. By the middle of the next decade, following the end of the Russo-Japanese War, foreign visitors to Japan had greatly increased and hotels in Tokyo and Yokohama could not meet the demand for rooms. By 1909 a clear directive to build a new Imperial Hotel capable of meeting increased demand had been issued. A number of years passed, however, before an architect was hired. Wright appears to have secured the commission by 1913, but was not officially hired until 1916.
2. Paul Mueller, the Chicago builder, whom Wright asked to come to Japan to work with him, had come armed with the conviction, held by other architects and engineers, that Wright's foundation plan would not work.
3. Frank Lloyd Wright, *A Testament* (New York: Horizon Press, 1952), p. 123.
4. Kobayashi Kiyochika (1847–1915) studied oil painting and photography, developing a new style of expression in woodblock prints. Although not the first Japanese artist to use the principles of perspective, his use of scientific principles of light and shade make his work radically different from that of earlier *Ukiyoe* artists.

EXPERIMENTING WITH HUMAN LIVES

"**E**xperimenting with Human Lives" was published in 1923 by Ralph Fletcher Seymour of Chicago. Seymour had also published The Japanese Print in 1912. Wright wrote the article while his studio was temporarily located at Olive Hill, the complex he had designed for Aline Barnsdall in Hollywood. He had returned to the United States in 1922 following work on the Imperial Hotel in Tokyo and had been living in California a little over one year when the Kanto earthquake leveled most of Tokyo and Yokohama on September 1, 1923. The enormous scope of the disaster prompted him more than one month later to write these observations on building construction in earthquake-prone areas. His own theories of construction, as evidenced in the Imperial Hotel, had been put to the ultimate test during the earthquake: the structure's survival had proved Wright correct. [Published without illustrations in an undated pamphlet]

THE RIM OF THE PACIFIC BASIN IS NO PLACE TO EXPERIMENT with human lives in the interest of an architectural expedient. Los Angeles, San Francisco, Tokio, all on the rim of this great basin, are infested by that expedient. That expedient is the tall steel-frame building we call the skyscraper, and it has no better scientific, aesthetic, or moral basis for existence as a bid for human sacrifice than the greed of the speculative landlord, the unworthy ambition of commercialized architects, or false civic pride that encourages and protects both. This great basin of the Pacific is overloaded—overloaded with gigantic waters. Occasionally, as faults and fissures occur in its floor owing to the strains of this overload, water rushes down with enormous pressure to internal fires—creating steam and gases of incalculable power—seeking escape through other internal crevices leading to the upper air and convulsing and altering the conformation of the earth-crust in doing so. If this, as a theory

of seismic convulsion, is too simple to be scientific, there are many more complex to choose from—but the fact remains that the red line of seismic convulsion clings to the rim of the basin. The region ought to be considered in the light of its record.

Tokio and Yokohama again raise the question, WHY THE SKYSCRAPER?—a question from time to time successfully evaded by landlord and commercialized architect—and by false civic pride.

Chicago and New York owing to naturally congested areas had a real problem to meet and met it—perhaps wisely at that time by the invention of the skyscraper. If confined to similar areas and circumstances it might be justified.

But with changed conditions, the skyscraper, never more than a commercial expedient, is become a threat, a menace to the welfare of human beings. It is dangerous to construct, dangerous to maintain, dangerous to operate, and inevitably, as buildings ought to live, short-lived, destined to end finally in horrible disaster, even if not attacked from beneath. In any case the skyscraper has become an immoral expedient, one that demoralizes its neighbors, when it does not rob them, compelling them to compete in kind or perish.

No adjustment of the equities it destroys has yet been made. There is now no escape from it and no redress.

Its whole case is economic—but economic only as a pet temporary expedient of American get-rich-quick enterprise. Sooner or later all steel framing will perish even where conditions are most favorable to its existence.

In Tokio, conditions were naturally unfavorable. All steel perishes there with fearful rapidity owing to extraordinary humidity and a salt-sea atmosphere, machinery under Tokio sheds becoming useless from rust within the year. Steel pipe in Tokio buildings goes out of commission in from five to fifteen years.

In the light of advices now coming from Japan, all steel-frame buildings were death traps to some serious degree, their "architecture" shaken from the skeletons in the upper stories and, in some cases, even the lower stories shattered and fell in the street. The Nagai building collapsed completely, burying hundreds in its ruin. The Kaijo building likewise.

In seismic disturbance, the perpetual wrenching or jolting of the semi-rigid frame weakens, cracks, or breaks off its concrete shell, exposing the steel to flames which always accompany heavy temblors, and steel, exposed to flame, soon bends its riveted knees and comes to the ground. Even when the skeletons themselves stand they are practically useless for rebuilding. What foolhardy courage to reclothe inappropriate, hazardous, skeletons that human souls may come again in droves to inhabit them just because the day of reckoning is out of sight, though surely lurking ahead or perhaps just around the corner. Shocks come suddenly. Elevators jam when frames are twisted. It is impossible to empty the buildings quickly. Fright and panic take their toll, though the building may stand.

The compensations offered by the skyscraper are all to the realty owners and to the sort of pride typified by the canyons of lower New York. The congestion induced by the exaggerated repetition of floor area creates great real-estate values but tends eventually to destroy those values, as may now be seen in Los Angeles. In that city, this congestion turns to the disadvantage of the city proper by raising various contiguous business centers at the very gates of the city itself, creating a competitive confusion having some benefits but far greater waste.

In Chicago and New York, the tax upon the service of the streets demanded by the multiplication of skyscrapers is so great in congestion and cost that it is now seriously proposed to assess the land value in multiples for each six stories imposed upon the land and tax it accordingly. This is proposed in justice to the city which pays the cost of the service and in justice to the adjoining owners of lower buildings who are deprived of the use of the streets. Mrs. Hetty Green foresaw this and leased her land subject to taxes to be paid by the tenants. She refused to build skyscrapers.

When the principle underlying scheme or method is wrong—as it is wrong in the steel-frame structure (considered as anything more than a commercial or temporary expedient)—nature is invited to bring about the destruction of that scheme or method. Nature invariably accepts that invitation.

The law of gravitation and what we call the elements have shown and will continue to show how frail is the best effort of man when chance or time combine them in a cataclysm such as has swept through the heart of Japan. And what reason beyond a fatuous hope have we that such disturbances will cease or even diminish?

Yankee skyscrapers are outrageous in Tokio from any practical standpoint. From any cultural standpoint, they were merely another version of the derby hat, Boston gaiters, frock coat, or the "hard straw" which preceded them—which in fact introduced them.

All these negations—products of Western culture—were harbingers of this new era of commercial conquest, this abnegation of Japan in the course of foreign "civilization."

Tokio, already congested on its natural basis of two stories, must be pushed by our favorite Yankee expedient in building and our salesmanship, to a further congestion based upon eight or ten stories, at whatever cost to human lives or outrage to aesthetic character.

I have lately read of some of the difficulties overcome in planting these modern commercial engines in Tokio, of how the transportation of the gigantic steel posts on manpower pushcarts over muddy roads was accomplished, nevertheless and notwithstanding. It seems not to occur to the writer that his proofs of superior progress are against him on his own showing; his difficulties, those of forcing upon a situation an unsuited, unsuitable product at enormous sacrifice and waste to all but the company operating the disadvantages at cost, plus ten percent. He sentimentalizes over the labors of women coolies but glories in the inhuman sacrifices exacted from the whole nation in the name of what he ignorantly assumes to be and arrogantly calls Progress. Further and apropos of the recent disaster the head of a skyscraper company says—(*The Los Angeles Times* quotes him)—that these Tokio steel frames were made rigid so as to move all in one piece, this being accomplished by extraordinary bracing—introduced for that purpose.

Rigidity, it seems, was considered desirable by the skyscraper builders. A necessity it would be, in fact, to prevent the "architecture" from cracking and scaling from the skeletons. Yet tenuous flexibility is the chance for life of any sound construction in an earthquake—flexibility of foundation, flexibility of superstructure secured by continuous, lateral binding instruments from side to side in the floor planes of the structure, and the balancing of all loads well over vertical supporting members by means of the cantilever.

Were one of these steel death traps to be reduced to a scale model, say six feet high, the thickness and strength of the steel accurately reduced in true proportion, the folly of any attempt to make rigid a steel frame, say 200×200 feet on the ground ten stories high, would immediately become apparent. The scale model would not bear an eccentric wrench without cracking or displacing whatever were placed in contact with it or around it to "protect" it. A blast from a blow torch, were the steel exposed, would crumple it completely.

The more nearly rigidity were approximated, the worse the result would be as it could never be fully achieved.

A very tall and narrow structure would more easily be rendered invincible to quake, if properly set into the soil.

And in the matter of the Oregon fir piles reaching to hard-pan—so laughably simple a solution of all Tokio's building troubles as it was said in this same article to be—they would wreck the structure quicker than any other expedient that could be imagined, as the jar on the hard material, the impact of solids upon a solid surface, would prove a most destructive agency. The proof may be seen today in Tokio.

Tokio should be reconstructed upon a more permanent and rational plan—her wires underground, her streets widened and shaded, the principal residence and business areas restricted to two or three stories.

The first story—and, if three stories, the second—should be hollow or double walls made of reinforced concrete blocks—interlaced by one-quarter-inch steel rods every sixteen inches, vertically and horizontally. These walls should extend to the windowsills of the top story or be used as a railing for balconies or for the top-story windows. Upon these walls, resting well within them, the continuous concrete floor slabs should be placed at proper levels, the horizontal reinforcing bars interlocking with the vertical bars of the walls.

Within the outer walls and resting upon the upper floor slab should be set and securely doweled the lightest possible scientific timber framing of walls and roof of top story, wired laterally together with telegraph or other rustless wire.

The roof should be plastered and covered with light copper tiles, the outside and inside of the upper story walls covered with plaster or other plastic fireproof material, the ceilings covered with a combination of wood and sheet copper ornamented in infinite variety.

Masonry tiles should be abandoned. They have already murdered uncounted thousands.

Certain restricted and specified areas of each building might be extended in tower forms to five or even seven stories provided the walls of each story were set within the walls of the story below, telescope-wise, and the walls of each story diagonally braced with light rods or heavy wire within each surface. These upper wall surfaces should be framed with wood and be covered with plastic fireproof surfacing or with copper tiles.

Restrictions of this nature would yield great variety of opportunity for design and treatment, the skyline of the city becoming as picturesque as could be desired. Trees would thrive along the curb and people as well—there would be safety and sunshine for all with no unduly congested areas.

Where the necessary extra precautions could be afforded, certain commercial or public structures by paying a tax to adjoining property owners could be allowed five stories, the same rules being observed. The top stories should be light wooden construction, the outside walls covered with plastic or light metallic material in all possible various picturesque combinations of form and color. Upon certain sites—individual and complete in themselves, as such, probably set back from the street—a seven-story privilege might be given, similarly taxed, but such sites naturally would be few and far between.

The foundations should be flexible; that is, concrete piles poured into holes made in the mud or ground and a reinforced linear slab built on the mud as on a cushion. The softer the ground upon which they rested, the safer the buildings would be, if the proper proportions were observed in the construction. Concrete blocks with steel interlaced two ways and joints poured are advocated because a really flexible wall thus secured is less liable to damage from flexure or torsion and one that would show no cracks. The light continuous concrete floor slabs for all floor areas below the roof would insure practical safety from devastation by fire.

Such an aggregation of buildings would be practically earthquake-proof and fireproof on any large scale, and as human habitations could be made very beautiful in the aggregate or individually. And such construction is the cheapest possible, at the same time that it would be warm in winter and cool in summer and dry in both.

But, with equal force, what is set out here applies not only to Los Angeles and San Francisco, but great cities throughout the world.

The activities of the speculative "realtors" create deliberately the congestion that raises ground values and rates to fabulous figures, and there we have the landlord. In the day of steam, this congestion or concentration, as it might justly then be called, was a convenience, if not a necessity. In these days of electrical transmission, the automobile, and telephone, this concentration becomes needless congestion—it is a curse.

To curb the "landlord," actual or potential, whose name in America is legion, is essential before the man who really creates these values will have or favor the sort of city or the kind of building that is sane, beautiful, and safe.

That man is now crowded into skyscrapers, bungalow courts, and ten-story apartments or twenty-story hotels, and he drives through vast, practically empty spaces held at high figures to get from one group of congested buildings to another group equally congested, and all around both lies vast acreage, withheld, untouched. In New York (Manhattan) every lot having not more than a four-story building on it is considered vacant by realtors.

Modern transportation may scatter the city, open breathing spaces in it, green it, and beautify it, making it fit for a superior order of human beings—but many first-class funerals among the ground-speculators must be held or called for before that can happen, at least so long as the people are—well—what they are. They are land-tied, skyscraper-tied, themselves helplessly if not hopelessly involved in the petty interests that exploit or mortgage their future.

The solution of all great problems is simple—that is to say, an organic matter of putting the right thing in the right way in the right place.

And because it is simple it is difficult and because it is difficult, it is rare.

Imperial Hotel. Tokyo, Japan. 1916. FLLW Fdn FA#1509.0018

Custom is a kind of gravitation in itself, all but fatal to radical progress, just as the gravitation formulated by Newton is fatal to all not physically able to withstand it.

The Yankee skyscraper is false work. It meets and overcomes the difficulties it creates gratuitously itself, solely by *tour de force*. It challenges the vengeance of Time and Nature.

Mr. Woolworth built an outstanding monument to the landlord in the Woolworth Building and incidentally his architect made of it a more or less conscious reminder of the greatness of the Middle Ages. He seemed to approximate that grandeur in his building, but his stake was lost before he began to build. Except as a bit of scene-painting raised to heaven in false pride for a day, it has small meaning. And this is pitifully, tragically true, just because with us a day seems as a century. Our aim in these matters should be to make a century but as a day.

In a single century—but why speculate? To look so far ahead is to be out of joint with the times. To build for all time is no intention or ambition of our people at present, it seems—and to look even that century in the face in examining our chain of cause and effect in the search for its weakest link is a thankless, unpopular clamor. We have a here-today-and-gone-tomorrow mentality—

an out-of-sight, out-of-mind conscience in aesthetics. Advocates of a square-deal we are, commercially and morally, but we excel only in matters of two dimensions.

In all matters pertaining to the third dimension when we consider that dimension as "depth" we are deficient.

Or taking the third dimension as that quality in the thing that makes it integral—taking the matter into that realm of quality that makes efforts or effects of the thing not on it considering the sort of intelligence that makes whatever is achieved a development from within and not something merely applied from without—this quality, in this sense, we have barely yet begun to comprehend. How then shall we insist upon it? It is this matter in this sense that applies here to the abolition of the skyscraper and what it stands for in our life today.

The herding instinct is stronger in these United States than ever before, perhaps. "Democracy" encourages or inflames it. The skyscraper is an imposition upon that instinct. Any imposition once fixed upon "the herd" is ripe for exploitation. Here this source of supply for the profiteer is ripe and just where the profiteer would have it.

The skyscraper is now an institution—an American Institution of which we are proud. Entire groups of industrial establishments depend upon it for a living. We are proud of it as a distinctively American achievement, a proof of our superior abilities, our superior civilization. Paris, London, and Berlin resisted it as a thing fraught with horrible consequences—physical, moral, and aesthetic, unwholesome in all these.

Those consequences mean little to us, it seems—even where great injury or quick doom is certain.

Our cities grow more and more a concession to the herd instinct and less and less places for the development and emphasis of the quality of individuality—and they become more and more unfit places for human beings, who value that quality of individuality as the most precious asset of human kind, as the supreme entertainment of life. Who sleeps, who lives in New York and Chicago's canyons if he can get away?

Imposition once fixed, thought ceases in the herd as it has ceased in the case of the skyscraper—and even such horrible proofs of unsoundness and unfitness as come from Tokio—even the possible obliteration of those human rights and advantages which are normal to the best in humanity and therefore moral—are soon forgotten or make a momentary diversion, and folly rides hard once more unchecked.

Architecture—the great proof of quality of any race or nation has Tradition and Time as essentials of its nature—essentials which in the skyscraper are 0reduced to a mere expedient. And we furnish this shining example of false pride and stupid ambition, this creator and creation of, not the feudal, but the ubiquitous American landlord, handsomely served by his commercialized architect, as proof of the greatness of our era, our civilization, our country. Both landlord and architect are aided and abetted by civic pride, which reflects and protects the enterprise of both—conceiving it as virtue in them and a virtue in itself to encourage them.

Despair may wait upon it, human agony pay tribute, all that is precious in the soul of man be insulted by it—but it is one of our "cherished institutions" fixed therefore upon the herd consciousness as normal. As well try to move the moon or stars until its appointed curse has been wrought. There seems no way to check it except by radical legislation based upon a radically different conception of what constitutes a modern habitable city than any we are giving to the world.

THE NEW IMPERIAL HOTEL, TOKIO

Between April 1923 and February 1924 The Western Architect published three articles in which Wright explained his designs for the new Imperial Hotel in Tokyo. The first of these articles is a general description of the building, including the reasons for erecting such a hotel in the first place. In writing about the type of plan he elected to use, Wright points out that it was not an "office building hotel" along American lines, but "a system of gardens and sunken gardens and terraced gardens—of balconies that are gardens and loggias that are also gardens—and roofs that are gardens—until the whole arrangement becomes an interpenetration of gardens. Japan is Garden-land. This is not realized in the photographs as they were made before the building was entirely finished, and before this part of the work was fairly begun."

The second and third articles are a two-part essay entitled "In the Wake of the Quake," in reference to the disastrous Kanto earthquake of September 1923.[1] When the quake struck, leveling most of Tokyo and Yokohama and killing more than 100,000 persons, Wright was living in Los Angeles. At first, reports came to him that the new Imperial Hotel was destroyed along with most other major buildings. But a few days later there came a telegram from Baron Okura, head of the board of directors of the hotel and staunch supporter of Wright's work on the project:

HOTEL STANDS UNDAMAGED AS MONUMENT OF YOUR GENIUS/ HUNDREDS OF HOMELESS PROVIDED BY PERFECTLY MAINTAINED SERVICE/ CONGRATULATIONS/OKURA IMPEHO.

Wright's articles are not about the description of the tragedy, but rather about the methods of construction that rendered the building capable of riding through the worst earthquake in Japan's recorded history. [Published with 11 illustrations in The Western Architect, April 1923]

THE IMPERIAL IS THE FIRST IMPORTANT PROTEST AGAINST the Gargantuan waste adopted by Japan from old German precedents when there were no worse ones. It is a conservation of space, energy, and time by concentration and the invention of practical ways and means to that end. Just such conservation as this existed in Old Japan and is at work in this building to help establish in the new life, now inevitable to them, that same wonderful unity.

Every utilitarian need is insisted upon as an ordered thing in a harmonious whole; that is what the old Japanese life insisted upon with telling and beautiful effect.

The Imperial has no quarrel with life as lived upon any civilized basis now, but at the present time it does belong in point of character and purpose to the more advanced stage of culture, because it insists upon utilitarian needs as ordered features of a sentient whole and finds its "effects" in making them so.

The Imperial Hotel has, therefore, in most essential respects, been fixed ahead of the abuse and waste of the hour—to be, in the meantime, attacked as a challenge to that old waste and abuse. This would be true of any building, doing in its own way the thing that has always been done in a more familiar way.

I. THE PURPOSE OF THE BUILDING

The Imperial Hotel is not a hotel at all in the accepted sense of that term. It is a delightful place of sojourn for travelers and a place of varied entertainment for the social functions of the life of Tokio, the Japanese Capital.

The "Hotel," however, is less than one-half the substance of the whole, or its function or its cost. It is—as it has always been—a concession to the foreign invasion, rather than an investment.

There is also a center of entertainment which is more important and profitable, and an investment rather than a concession. This center is a clearinghouse for Japan's social obligations to "the foreigner" and the Japanese social life of the Capital. This central group contains a masonry promenade, or central paved court, 300 feet long by 20 feet wide, 16 various private supper rooms, and various parlors

being appropriately grouped about it; a masonry theater seating 1,000 people, opening directly from it. The theater has a revolving stage. There is, below the theater, also opening directly from the promenade, a terraced cabaret seating at tables 300 people, with dancing space and stage. Above the theater, reached directly from the promenade, is a spacious foyer opening to the main roof garden—above this is a banquet hall with capacity to seat a thousand at table. A splay and cantilever gallery is continued all around this room, springing upward to a pendentive roof. Like the theater this room too—is done in imperishable materials—a great building in itself.

These various rooms for important public functions have adequate toilet accommodations, service rooms, and galleries, or avenues of intercommunication, and are all associated directly with enclosed gardens, terraces, and balconies. The Imperial Hotel, therefore, is not designed as a profitable undertaking in the ordinary commercial sense, but it is so as a distinguished center of social entertainment for the life of the capital, in a sense that is unique.

II. THE NATURE OF THE IMPERIAL AND ITS PROBLEM

In a pool of conflicting ideas and competitive races like Tokio, there is always much that is obscure, lurking behind walls that are unknown languages. But the thing that stands out to me most sharply in this experience is the incapacity for any sacrifice of habitual "use and wont" on the part of the average human being. Not only that, but the bitterness with which any suggestion of the sort is resented as a personal affront. Instead of being intrigued and interested by an attempt to inculcate a finer and better "use and wont," one more in keeping with true civilization, civilization seems to have been abandoned by the average guest in an oriental hotel at yen twenty per day.

A hotel primarily is a place for human creatures—certainly. And a hotel is a dangerous place in which to put a premium upon human intelligence, human aesthetic needs, or human appreciation of a beautiful environment.

In the confusion consequent upon the English, German, French, Chinese, or Russian idea of "the right thing" there does seem to be a consensus of opinion regarding "the right thing" in a hotel. It is a guest room that is a vast compound, the vaster the better, in which to spread around a freight-carload of luggage; a big tub in another nearby room; plenty of big windows on at least two sides of the compound, three preferred, an enormous upholstered platform, 72 feet square, 3 feet above the floor—to sleep on; another big room with an outside window in which to throw things or hang them; no sense of a ceiling at all; an aggregation of over-sized, over-stuffed furniture that can be dragged about regardless or pushed aside entirely; food and water always handy; Boy San just outside the door day and night; a cuspidor.

As for light and heat, plenty of both, with doors and windows wide open.

But the Imperial has aimed higher than to stall and feed and groom and bed that captious animal with quite all the license which would be popular. The Imperial therefore is not a hotel. The creature comforts are all there but also an aspiration to something better although not so big and less barbarous; something more on the order of what might be found in a gentleman's home in a modern country house.

In the Imperial, therefore, the Art of Architecture comes to grips with reality for the sake of a better order—a popular mission—but one that will not immediately be popular. A management imbued with this idea is as essential to its success as are the features of the building itself, and more so. The old management, by whom the building was initiated, changed during the course of construction. Aisaku Hayashi was the managing director. Another manager, H. S. K. Yamaguchi, personally popular and successful in the conduct of a resort hotel, was appointed, and while undertaking an enterprise shaped in detail to suit the ideas of another manager, he has attacked the problem with spirit and a desire to succeed in every feature of his responsibility. What Mr. Yamaguchi in his difficult position will achieve, remains to be seen.

The enterprise, although initiated many years ago by the Imperial Household as a social necessity in connection with Japanese social life in contact with the foreigner, has proved profitable. As the social life of the Capital grew in foreign style, it became desirable to expand and date the enterprise somewhat ahead in order to keep it, as it always has been, the social center of the life of the Japanese Capital. So, while it has been and will be profitable under good management, it is, as was stated above, not a commercial venture, not an investment in an ordinary sense.

That is why it was laid out as a group of buildings in a system of gardens and terraces and not as an "office building hotel" along American lines. That is why the attributes of culture have been sought in its design and appointments; that is why a love for beauty must characterize the guest who really belongs to the Imperial.

The world moves with incredible rapidity. Concentration of space by means of concentrated conveniences has already gone far. The ship began it, the Pullman car took it up, the ocean liner went further, and now the high-class hotel on costly ground is at work upon it all over the world.

In the new Imperial the quality of beauty and integrity of the whole is established by making each unit (albeit a smaller unit) an integral part of a great and harmonious whole. That broader relationship affords a richer experience, a fuller life for each individual than could possibly be where more license in more space would turn that individual loose at the expense of the whole. In all this there is the economic limit—that is, the degree to which the human animal will submit to the larger and the finer interest. Who can say just where that limit lies—or should lie—except that, in an effort to establish a superior thing, that limit should be fixed ahead of the abuse and waste of the hour?

III. THE AESTHETIC MOTIF

The Imperial Hotel is designed as a system of gardens and sunken gardens and terraced gardens—of balconies that are gardens and loggias that are also gardens—and roofs that are gardens—until the whole arrangement becomes an interpenetration of gardens. Japan is Garden-land.

This is not realized in the photographs as they were made before the building was entirely finished, and before this part of the work was fairly begun. Until the intended foliage develops in relation to enclosures and preparations made for it in the structural scheme, the Imperial is something like a sycamore without its leaves. Its structure asserts itself so boldly as to pain the sensitive beholder committed by use and wont to the modifying member. Having devoted my life to getting rid of that expedient in Architecture, or in Society, or in Life, it is with difficulty that I realize the shock to sensitive Renaissance nerves the utter neglect of this member causes, and the sense of outrage the frustrated sensibilities of the school-bred architect receives from such bold assertions and contrasts as confront him and bear him down in this building.

The Imperial is perhaps the most "shameless offense against the modifying member" that has ever been committed. There is a strength of purpose behind the thrust of slab and spread of the cantilever in this structure that is without a parallel. So much so that modified and modifying architects gravely decide that it were better had it never been built at all. What a small world is the world of the "modifying member!" In any serious analysis, how lacking in any fundamental character. It is the world of yesterday in a futile endeavor to foreclose upon today, in order that tomorrow may be as yesterday.

Therefore, this modifying member, graceless and stultifying hypocrite that it is, is here rejected, and the structure appeals directly to nature for modification. In course of time the building will receive it richly and wear it nobly, as an appropriate raiment, the one enhancing the other.

I am not of those who conceive a building as a carved and sculptured block of building material. That is two-dimension thinking. A room or group of rooms expressed in an arrangement and grouping of wall enclosures, together with the surmounting slabs or planes: fenestration, not embrasures merely, but knitting all together in one fabric as a harmonious whole; that is a building.

This sense of building is the three-dimension conception of Architecture. In this conception, integral effects in both materials and methods are the only effects.

The question I would ask concerning any architect or his building would be, is the architect's mind or is his work in two or in three dimensions? Is his work extraneous—applied from without, or an integral development from within?

This is not the standard of the schools. This is a far more subtle and difficult standard. This criterion must be found *inside* and not picked up outside.

It is the Imagination that is challenged, and not the Memory.

Whatever, in an aesthetic sense, the faults of the Imperial may be, I can truly say that it is all of one piece in honest materials, honestly made; that it is a virile study in coherent scale and that scale broadly adapted and adjusted to the human figure; a strong and purposeful foil for natural foliage and verdure—enhanced by it and enhancing it; it belies nothing intentionally, copies nothing, but reveres the spirit of Oriental art, without losing its own individuality; a missionary with a sense of beauty, believing in the importance of preserving the individuality of the soul to whom it would minister. It has consistent style as a whole, although owing nothing to styles.

Faults or no faults, sincere work of this type ought to be valuable at this stage of Japan's culture, and to the thoughtful it will be so.

It would be equally valuable to us if we would look at it, for what it has to give, because our own architectural situation is not so different from Japan's as we like to think it is. We are under the same necessity to develop an indigenous architecture. The Japanese once had such an architecture and now must create it again for a changed life condition. We have never had it and have only mixed traditions of many races almost as unsuited to our present use as are the old Japanese traditions to their use. We too, must create an architecture for our own changed life conditions.

A western editor of an Architectural Journal laments that the export of "American Architecture" to Japan is likely to be damaged by this "experiment." Japanese architects, "American trained," are insulted by it—he thinks, and he says they have a right to feel cheated. If the Western editor is right I am not sorry.

The Imperial is a protest in every sense against the commercialism that would standardize a world to make a market even for "American Architecture." If only the United States might look that architecture squarely in the face with the eyes of the Beaux Arts or the European architects who despise it for the servile thing it really is, and if they would deprive the commercial sheep who commend and sell it—of their "franchise"—but what vain hope! Architecture "ready-made" like our manners or our institutions is a necessity to us, as to Japan, for but slightly different reasons. There is no remedy except one to come afterward that will tear down what the fashion-monger builded upon the labor of the hard-pressed and hard-working pioneer, or none that will not eventually have to throw away the product of the fashionable accidents or social indiscretions that have "Art" in charge—shall I say in trust—for the moment.

And what a sacrilege it is, to see Japan taking this performance or betrayal from us second hand, upon faith!

In several of the photographs of the Imperial Hotel, the environment of Japanese modern civilization in Tokio may be glimpsed. Japanese culture has met with Occidental architecture as a beautiful work of art might meet with a terrible "accident." It is trampled and obliterated by the waste of senseless German precedents or literally ironed flat by sordid facts brought over from America in ships.

American commercial buildings ten stories tall, or more, steel frames, inserted walls, are ravaging Tokio's architectural possibilities just as the "derby hat" and "Boston gaiters," or the "hard straw" have already insulted the kimono and *geta*.

The present plight of Japan in this matter of "civilization" is pathetic. To participate in this masked form of commercial subjugation, would be to participate in a crime Japan is deliberately invited by Western "interests" to commit.

Therefore, the new Imperial Hotel is not an American building in Tokio any more than was inevitable in the circumstances. It is not a Japanese building, however, nor intended to be an Oriental building. It is an architect's sincere tribute to a unique nation, a building that respects Oriental tradition, at the same time that it keeps its own individuality as a sympathetic friend on Japanese soil.

I have been astonished to find such bitterness and such confusion of opinion concerning this attempt to assist Japan to her own architectural feet, to help find an equivalent for her ancient supremacy in Art.

The Imperial does not profess to be that new form, but it does break away in that direction, a revolt and a suggestion. This simple statement of motive taken in connection with the photographs may serve to enlighten some, but will probably only deepen the chiaroscuro into which the whole seems to be thrown for the time being, by and for others: so helpless are authorities and "professions" when deprived of their accepted "standards."

The animosity of Morality has often shocked and revolted me, but the citizen's "sneer" directed in a democracy toward an idea or an individual suspected of the idea that he has an idea, is always at every turn a disagreeable surprise. Democracy has benefits, but liberality toward ideals not one's own is not one of them. At least among those "professing" anything.

Tastes or methods may well differ, but when principles are at cross-purposes, or when Principle encounters Sham, or Sham to preserve itself, obscures Principle, there can be no peace.

Man is mocked by events in his struggle to express his little vision of great Truths. Out of every great endeavor perhaps some little good here or significance there will eventually be gathered into the "common good," just as thoughts great hearts once broke for, we now breathe cheaply as the common air. What virtue lies in any effort will survive although the whole result be turned down as outrageous by senseless "authority," or be aborted of its aims by officious interference.

This is faith—and essential to all good work for human progress.

Naturally I believe the Imperial right and square on the center line of human progress, and I know very well why I believe it.

IV. THE BUILDING OF THE BUILDING

The difficulties overcome to acquire the proper materials, many of them made for the first time in Japan, and to instruct and control the industrial and commercial elements in the doing of a new thing in unfamiliar materials and by many methods necessarily new in a strange country, where I could not speak the language and only a few assistants could speak mine, may be imagined.

Masonry building is still in its infancy in Japan.

The scheme of construction as fabricated upon a 4'-0" unit was simple, so far as possible suited to hand-labor conditions as they still exist in that country. There was a stone and brick outer and inner shell, the outer shell the finished surface of the building, both outer and inner shells laid up to certain practicable heights and then concrete poured between them after laying in the necessary steel work for reinforcement. The outside brick shell was laid of bricks, especially made, that formed a 2" wall with 4" spurs within the wall 4'-0" on centers. The inside face of the walls was laid up with 4" × 12" tile blocks with dovetailed grooves which, made by ourselves, were used for the first time in Japan. Intensive hand methods were necessary to avoid wrecking the fragile shells in pouring the concrete.

The third material, which was the plastic material used to articulate and decorate the structure, was a lava which I found was used as the ordinary "stone" of the region. We located a superior quarry and quarried it ourselves. This light lava, weighing 96 pounds per cubic foot, is easily worked when fresh from the quarry. It is an admirable material that has stood the test of centuries—similar to Travertine in character but with a more picturesque quality. Objection was made to using so common a material for a fine building, but the objection was overcome and a great part of the forms that articulate the structure and into which it is actually cast are of this material, or itself cast into the structure like the bricks and the reinforcement tied in to it from behind. The edges of the projecting reinforced concrete slabs were all faced with this lava. The cornices or eaves are all projecting floor or roof slabs, perforated, faced with lava, and interlaced with copper. The lava was easily cut or carved, and the Japanese

were especially skillful in this work, so this cut lava became, naturally, the characteristic ornamentation of the structure. Wherever it was felt necessary to relieve it, copper turned turquoise blue, blue by surface treatment—an anticipation of the work of time—was cast in with it, and gold mosaic was inlaid in the pattern of the carving.

The "fusing" together of these materials perfectly was under the constant supervision of Paul Mueller, whose devotion to the work for nearly four years is the best guarantee of thorough stability any work could have. To build this building we took a central organization accustomed to building docks and warehouses for the navy department and augmented it by such labor as could be picked up in Tokio or the provinces. This provincial labor made it necessary to quarter about three hundred workmen and their families on the building site in addition to those who resided in Tokio.

For four years the site was a swarming hive of human activity and the work made more than usually difficult by this congestion, but a congestion natural enough, nearly everywhere in Tokio.

In planting this building upon soft ground in an earthquake country, the mud cushion 60'-0" in depth was good insurance if the strength of a sufficient depth of it could be made available at the surface. I intended to do this by boring 9" holes 2'-0" on centers, 9'-0", and filling them with concrete, or the holes to go to a proper depth to be ascertained by tests. These holes were to be bored over the area required to give sufficient strength to carry the loads with a certain squeeze that could be allowed with safety to the structure; pins of sufficient number, in a pin cushion.

The tests were made, but in executing the foundation along these lines the ground was found to be full of boulders and old piles, and so Mr. Mueller punched the holes with a tapered wooden pile instead of boring them as intended. The friction was less and the ground shaken, but the result was sufficiently good.

As a proof of the method of construction and the faithfulness with which it was executed there came the earthquake of April 1922, the most severe Tokio had experienced in more than fifty years—

three years after the foundation had been put in. Levels taken along the base line of the building afterwards showed no deviation whatever due to seismic disturbance. Except where movement was allowed for, at the expansion joints, not a check or a crack or fallen piece of stone could be found as a result of this terrific distortion which caused every workman in the building to throw aside his tools and rush outside to the street. I myself, caught in the upper story of the wing where the architect's office was located, walked out onto the roofs with Endo San[2], who had remained with me, and looked down at the excited crowd—gesticulating and badly frightened—in the street below. I was dripping with perspiration myself, knees none too steady. But I knew now by actual test the building was safe, several terrific crashes that had occurred during the quake being the falling of chimneys of the old Imperial at the rear, chimneys that had been left standing seventy feet high after the burning of the hotel a short time before.

It is useless to attempt to describe the troubles that beset the great enterprise from beginning to end. They were the troubles that beset any unusual thorough work that is an invention and innovation, anywhere, but complicated by the difficulty of communicating freely and directly with the forces actually at work. This was offset by the unfailing politeness and willingness of the workmen, the faithfulness too, of all those concerned in the work, except those entrusted with contracts who were no better and no worse than their equivalent in our own country.

V. A LABOR OF MIND AND BODY

Whatever the faults of their building may be, in building it the Japanese have shown a capacity for devotion to an ideal rare in any country. As a people they are sensitive to criticism. Hitherto they were protected by a completely established custom and code in which they had refuge or could take refuge at any time. Now they are easily bewildered or confused by the conflicting ideas or the contradictory testimony of the "new civilization."

They are prone to regard every matter as "personal," and the Oriental sense of "fate" and love of

luxury is at work always in them. Their endurance at long, drawn-out, hard labor, mental or physical, is less than that of Western races. Their efficiency, in our sense of the term, is therefore less.

In their language there is no word to translate our word "Integrity"; none for "Love"; none for "Art" except *bijitsu*, another form of the wrestling *ji-ujitzu*— clever tricks. "Beauty" is a word they seldom use and never as we use it. With them the word refers to something like a painted lady, cheap and on the surface.

But probably this is because a Japanese never speaks of that most sacred to him. To show deep feeling or to bare his inmost thoughts is to wear his heart upon his sleeve, a vulgarity impossible to him. They have many words in their language which show a deep sense of all the things signified to us by the words quoted above, but in a more subtle sense than conveyed by our own words.

The Japanese people are a pleasure-loving, emotional people deeply inhibited by centuries of discipline so severe as to be unthinkable to us. They have been fused or welded into a homogeneous mass in which the friendliness and forbearance practiced toward one another is very beautiful.

The Japanese workman has a higher sense of his own worth and his own way than our workmen, and his position in Japan is more independent in most essential respects than that of the members of our unions. He seems to have, naturally, with no "unions," a community of interest and a solidarity of purpose which "unions" were necessary to effect in Western countries.

The Japanese craftsman, when personally interested, is the finest craftsman in the world; but he likes to be an independent worker in his own behalf. To him piecework is a far more satisfactory basis than a day's work and also for his employer. The old system of labor brokerage is still in force, a certain broker controlling and selling the labor of many men who are still his henchmen. This broker delivers them to the work, but there his responsibility ceases. They are then free to work as they please to produce the desired results.

As the countenance of the building began to emerge, the workmen became intensely interested and with an intelligence of appreciation unrivaled anywhere in my experience. I shall never forget their touching farewells nor the sense of kindly co-operation in what all believed to be great work for the future of Japan.

Among the Japanese workmen there is a true gentleness and fineness to be found here only among truly cultured people. The Imperial—shall I say "Hotel?"—means to me the labor of this sympathetic group of freemen in concrete form, a thing wrought as I imagine the great buildings of the Middle Ages were wrought, to stand for centuries as a supreme achievement of human imagination and human cooperation; massed effort directed toward a certain achievement in which all shared.

The very bricks and lava, steel and concrete, stay but to record the passing of the fingers and brains that laid and left them in place. A tremendous vital, voluntary force swept through great piles of inert matter and gave form and life for all time to a great building—belonging first to that voluntary force. Whoever may "own" the result is merely a custodian, who, on trial, takes on trust the labor of mind and body recorded in the thing now called the new Imperial.

1. Wright himself was in the Imperial Hotel annex in April 1922 when a "significant" earthquake occurred. This should not be confused with the great Kanto quake of September 1923.
2. Arata Endo (d. 1951) was Wright's chief Japanese assistant on the Imperial Hotel. Endo supervised the hotel's completion after Wright's return to the United States in 1922.

IN THE CAUSE OF ARCHITECTURE: IN THE WAKE OF THE QUAKE— CONCERNING THE IMPERIAL HOTEL, TOKIO

[Published with 2 illustrations in The Western Architect, *November 1923]*

IN THE VIRTUE OF INTEGRAL CHARACTER, LIES THE VIRTUE of the building of the Imperial, as shown conclusively in the contrasts revealed at such terrific cost by the cataclysm which has recently wrung the heart of Japan. And in this triumph of integral character over destructive forces lies the only reason for public explanation of those methods which were peculiar to myself in this work, the faithful execution of which protected it from destruction or damage. No one person occupying the building at the time of the terrible distortion was injured in the slightest degree, nor did the building go out of commission for a moment.

In conception, the Imperial was radical and thorough. It was conceived as a building in Japan, Japan honored and loved as a great treasure house of art—art growing from nature and use. It was conceived for Japan to be built by Japanese and that it was so built was due largely to the initiative, vision, and persistence of Aisaku Hayashi—then managing director of the Imperial Hotel Company. Japanese tradition and Japanese building methods were not unfamiliar to me when I went to Tokio seven years ago to gather data for preliminary drawings. I could not build a Japanese building, nor did I want to do so—nor was it necessary or desirable. But I could build a building addressed to the Japanese people as an epic of their race and inspire them to efforts of their own in making the new fireproof buildings,

necessary to their changed life, more appropriate to that life.

Such foreign forms as they had already adopted, mostly German, were hung, like the "American architecture," as a screen in front of their real lives—a screen as false and ugly as anything in this world.

I knew then, as I know now, that all this commonplace of foreign "culture" thus paraded was, like their "democratic" institutions, a temporary expedient. The Nation lived, had its being and was ruled from within its past—with patriarchal wisdom and profound oriental feeling.

So one may sense in the forms of the building I designed for them something of this—in the simply determined masses, enclosing garden courts, in the sculptured lava, the perforated projections of masonry floor slabs sifting patterned sunlight on sturdy walls—the spirit of that ancient Tradition informs all, pervades the whole, copying nothing. And in doing this, I am accused of having ruined the export to Japan of "American Architecture," whatever that is. I suppose commercial architecture is meant.

I. STATEMENT OF THE PROBLEM

How to construct this edifice, how to state this feeling in concrete and steel was my problem. The extent to which modern machinery and methods could be utilized was problematical. The structure, as I could see, would have to be largely "handmade." And the structure was to take its place with safety upon sixty feet of soft mud where earthquakes continually threatened every standing thing with destruction soon or later.

And the idea of building a super-dreadnought, flexible as a ship is flexible, floating it on the mud as a battleship floats on saltwater, gradually unfolded itself to me.

Already I had made economical foundations for some of my buildings in the Middle West with a posthole augur, the holes filled with concrete. It occurred to me that if I treated the site of the Imperial as a cushion into which I would stick masonry pins of sufficient number and depth to utilize, by friction, the depth of the comparatively stiff mud at the surface, and find out to what extent I could safely squeeze the whole area under the building in addition to that, with no serious damage to the building in settling to place, I would have the best possible insurance against violence from below. I would have a foundation that would be resilient and shallow enough probably to offer no grasp to ground undulation. The ground in a serious quake, I had observed, undulates like waves at sea. Imagine what that movement does to a stiff construction reaching deep into the ground or resting on solid surfaces and rising to considerable height.

Before I left Tokio, at that time, I got some Japanese well drillers to bring their primitive apparatus and bore holes in the proposed site some 8' 0" and 16' 0" in depth, some 8" and others 9" in diameter, throwing in the concrete quickly after pumping out the water. These test holes were about 2' 0" apart. I found that one of my 8' 0" × 8" diameter piles set in soil that would barely support 1,000 pounds to the square foot, would carry 3,500 to 4,500 pounds on about 3½ cubic feet of concrete; it would then begin to drive. The piles, 2' 0" apart, sustained the same load. And, in addition to this, I had the superficial squeeze of the 2' 0" × 2' 0" area at 1,000 pounds per square foot, still at my disposal and with no appreciable effect upon the pile.

This was with the ragged, bored hole and no shaking up of the ground. With these facts, I re-

turned to my Wisconsin home to work on the plans, after leaving with Hayashi San the drawings for the bricks for the thin brick shell of the outside wall faces; and of a hollow brick for the inside wall faces, intending to lay up both shells to a height of a foot or two, laying in reinforcement where needed, and then filling between the shells in layers of that depth all around the structure at one time. I had long before conceived the idea of a self-formed building, deposited in strata, gradually rising uniformly over the whole area to avoid unequal settlement of the floating foundations.

Concrete is unsatisfactory as a facing material in Japan because of continual wet. So, as some other facing material had to be found, brick used as a mosaic, cast solidly in with the concrete core, seemed to offer the element of color and warmth desirable in a place of human residence. The outer and the inner brick shells, bonded as I contrived them, became one with the concrete when the spaces between them were poured. The structure was, therefore, practically a monolith, as is evidenced by the fact that in no place has a single brick scaled from its core during the recent destructive trembler.

We found the fire-clay that would burn a dull orange color down the peninsula near Shizuoka and near some old pottery kilns. We bought the kilns and built others. These fire bricks were new in Japan and the hollow bricks were made there for the first time. Later we turned out a very fine perforated pattern brick, "the Fujiwara" which was used for ventilation screens and as screens for lights in the building; and other pattern bricks, the "Genroku" and the "Genji," used as string-courses, all new in Japan. Hayashi San undertook this manufacture himself as no one could be found to make them. The pardonable pride with which he would exhibit samples of his work to visitors at his office may have been equaled, but I think it has never been, unless on his part, since September 1, 1923.

But, I had not at this time become familiar with the lava called Oya stone nor possibilities in working it, or I would have adopted it instead of brick. This is my chief regret—that the Imperial Hotel is not all Oya stone, hollowed out behind and used as forms for the concrete core. The cost would have been less, the effect more a harmonious unit, a sculptural whole, less domestic certainly, but domestic enough and thoroughly noble.

To recapitulate, I had in mind the floating slab on the concrete pins, carrying a self-formed building, so far as walls and piers were concerned. All walls having outer and inner shells of brick and stone and poured in layers with wet concrete, the piers constructed on similar principles reinforced, where necessary, with commercial steel rods laid in as required. I intended to have no steel beams, no shop work of any kind, not a rivet in the structure. It was so designed and so built. I was also determined to avoid the murderous roof tiles by the use of a hand-worked, copper roof, and I got this by grace of the low price of copper in Japan at the time we arrived at this stage of the work. As a principle in design I kept the center of gravity always as low as possible; hence, the heavy "battered" (sloping) walls.

II. WORKING OUT THE PLANS

In working out the concrete laterals, slabs, and beams with my engineers at my workshop at Taliesin, I found the structure getting beyond control in weight. From the very beginning of this work, the size and weight of the members, forced by the accepted standards and "legal factors of safety" were a threat to the stability of the structure in violent movement, instead of safe insurance as intended. It was then I brought the cantilever principle into service. It had always appealed to me as a scientific means with new architectural possibilities, used purely as such, and also as a working principle in the slab, continuous over supports, extended beyond the walls into balconies, canopies, cornices, etc.

By this simple means, I centralized and balanced the loads over interior supports, supports I purposely exaggerated in size in my designs. In any disturbance from below, these loads would be carried as a waiter's tray is carried, balanced on his upraised arm and fingers.

By the use of this principle, a good example of which is at work in the central banquet hall mass of the building, all laterals were not only lightened by cantilever reactions; but all laterals became continuous binding integuments from side to side of the structure, at each floor or roof level throughout the building balanced by exterior overhangs where possible. Under the central roof of this portion, these slabs became a continuous ring as well. At intersections of laterals and verticals, the reinforcement was interlocked on the principle of flexibility—in view of crisis.

But still the concrete in the laterals "to be carried by itself" seemed to me excessive, and not until I got Mueller into action in our draughting room on the work itself, did I get the results I wanted in lightening these dead loads. As will appear later, I made a concession at that time in this connection, which is a source of regret, in abandoning the flush slab for a coffered construction.

As a further concession to the principle of flexibility and the natural expansion and contraction of concrete, the building was cut into sections at plan intersections and also in the length of the wings. The original drawings showed these sections 40 feet in length. In execution, in the wings, they were made nearly twice that length, with the result that more separation occurred than was desirable. Always under seismic influence these sections would grind, chipping the edges somewhat, but the natural contraction and expansion was more than desirable or necessary. I am inclined to believe that in monolithic, concrete construction, no matter what the nature of the reinforcement may be, 60 feet without relief is the desirable mass limit in that climate. Where the thermometer reaches greater extremes, 40 feet would be enough.

Out of this principle of the cantilever came the forms of the buildings, forms which offended and frightened an architect or two, but which proved not only safe and sane but to be especially sound in the ordeal through which the construction finally passed unharmed.

Inherent in this cantilever principle, with its useful reactions, is the means of a new expression in architecture. We have been confined hitherto, to an expression based upon human experience with post and lintel and all of our sense of architectural form is based upon that concept—upon that and the modifying member aesthetic architects devised to slide one gracefully over the other to conceal the slab.

We may now have release from time-honored plat-itudes and try our wings with the "flying slab."

This insolent blasphemy has been met by the standard cries of "freak" and "bizarre." Both words, since time immemorial, have been the cry of medi-ocrity at bay. I believe only the provincial mind finds it necessary to use the words and then strictly in self-defense or fear.

III. THE EXECUTION OF THE WORK

These ideas were all simple enough, but in execu-tion, they required direct, unremitting, personal de-votion of the best talent obtainable.

They had it. Not only was I personally on the structure or next door within hailing distance for fifty-one months, short intervals each year being spent in America, but I persuaded the directors to al-low me one high-class assistant, familiar with my ways and work—the best procurable at any price. We were to go through with our own organization and it seemed to me then there was no other way to go. Finally, through Hayashi's efforts I got permis-sion to send for Paul F. P. Mueller, the Chicago builder, old comrade-in-arms, who unselfishly came and for more than four years scarcely a rod was laid or bucket of concrete poured, that the eye of this master builder was not upon the work.

When he arrived at Yokohama, I met him and also, a distinct disappointment. He came charged with a message from Chicago engineers to the effect that my foundation scheme was unsound and to urge me to abandon it. Also he came with the fixed idea that concrete posts and beams, with screen walls set in, was the best construction scheme for the building because the poured shells I had laid out would be sure to topple over.

I well recall my sensations at that moment. He will remember that I told him he had made a long journey for the pleasure of viewing an unique coun-try; that he was too late to help me and might as well go back when he had seen it, as the ideas upon which the building would be built were already es-tablished, the materials in hand and the ground cleared for action.

Like the man he is, he stood by—a tower of strength to me from then on, pitching in to perfect the methods I had undertaken.

We made more tests with the short pile, poured trial walls, and went ahead with our own orga-nization, Aisaku Hayashi, as captain and purchasing agent, representing the owners; Nakahama, with Na-gao as chief, the contracting agents (formerly navy contractors); the architect's office, already constructed on the ground, the head of the whole operation.

Another devoted figure, without whose un-remitting faithfulness the services of Mr. Mueller and myself would have landed against a blank wall, was Arata Endo, a graduate in architecture at the Imperial University of Japan, who recruited our of-ficial ranks with some twenty young students from that institution or from Kyoto or Waseda. And but for his old Samurai spirit of devotion to his leader at any personal sacrifice whatsoever and his far superi-or intelligence not to be surpassed for character and ability, the Imperial Hotel would have been an im-possibility in Japan.

Yet, throughout the group of young men he gathered together in the office, young architects and engineers, some twenty of them, there was rare de-votion. And while the oriental spirit was there to puzzle and vex us, we of the West—there were but three of us—called upon to explain previous expla-nations again and again and to correct corrections without end with patience—we, I say, wore out of-ten and cursed. But that unfailing politeness of theirs held, and I never expect to see again such forbear-ance on the part of anyone so abused as these boys and their Japanese workmen displayed, nor such universal gentility of conduct, with a rare exception or two.

It became necessary, however, for Hayashi San to explain that rages were characteristically "West-ern" and meant nothing. They were "foreign style." So the victims would heave to and watch with qui-et amusement or a fine indifference such bursts of outraged humanity as never were dramatized on the stages of the world.

[continued on page 187]

IN THE CAUSE OF ARCHITECTURE: IN THE WAKE OF THE QUAKE— CONCERNING THE IMPERIAL HOTEL, TOKIO

[Published without illustrations in The Western Architect, *February 1924; continued from page 186]*

IV. CHANGES AS THE WORK PROCEEDED

SOME CHANGES IN PROGRAM HAD TO BE MADE. I HAD intended to cast the concrete piles in a bored hole inserting them with no disturbance of the old layer of topsoil, bringing over boring machines for this purpose. Mr. Mueller found it is impracticable owing to the presence of old piles and boulders in the soil and much of the mud too soft, so the holes were punched by driving in a slightly tapered wooden pile, 9" diameter and 8' 0" long, pulling it out and throwing in concrete smartly before the water could rise. A readjustment of the pile diagram was made necessary by this method, a method eminently practicable as Japanese contractors were readily found with apparatus to do the work.

Another change in method to which I have alluded, in the interest of lightening the construction, was from the flush slab I had worked out to a joist and girder system following the same general principles. I had fallen down on the steel deliveries I had contracted for in America and found that the American Trading Company had a large stock of Kahn bars in Tokio.

The lightening of the roof slabs by the use of this system appealed to me, but the furring of the ceiling entailed did not. But I consented to the redesigning of the floors on this basis, expecting to save greatly in weight and cost. This is the second regret I have to record, because, by the time the expensive coffering was done in the wood forms and the furring securely fitted to the ceiling and the precast plaster slabs safely fastened up, the saving in weight was not more than 10 percent and the cost was greatly increased. In similar circumstances, I will cover the flush floor centering with shallow precast, patterned concrete blocks with wire netting laid in them turned out and upward at the outer edges, and upon these blocks rest the flush slab, leaving a beautiful finished ceiling no more than 10 percent heavier than the joist and beam furred ceiling, and a far more integral affair in every sense, a method more in keeping with the principles I am advocating here.

The lava or Oya stone, weighing about 96 pounds to the cubic foot, proved so cheap and workable a material that I used it far more than I originally intended not regretting, as I have said before, that the brick was used at all. This material made good forms for concrete hollowed out by hammer-axes from behind, the reinforcing steel worked under it or between the joints or to dowels set into the stone at the joints. This material cost—

set in place, carved, and plain together—about $2.90 per cubic foot. What terra-cotta would have cost with ocean freight and duty may be imagined.

This lava and the way in which we used it in Tokio attracted the slant of terra-cotta interests hanging architecture to the Tokio steel frames, and an architect or two, sympathetic to that much-abused, fine material, cut sticks and dusted my coat-tails for me, for using a building material resembling "cheese" in appearance. That was how Oya looked to them. They said so. And as a matter of fact, I had trouble convincing the directors that a common material, underfoot in Tokio streets everywhere, was good enough for the finest building in Japan. But I had carefully investigated its properties and we used it. We bought a quarry of especially fine material at Oya, worked it ourselves, and taught the quarrymen to quarry it so that we could lay it on its natural bed exposing the edges of the strata to the weather. The way Oya lava overflowed that site and was carried up into the building was astonishing, something like 360,000 cubic feet having disappeared with some holes still to fill, and outside pavements yet to be laid.

In certain features I added to the building heights after the footings were in and also added much lava to the interiors, which necessitated the employment of the "reserve" as I called it. This was a system of adding to our footings without extra cost, except what it would have cost had it been done before the building was under construction.

In this connection I may as well mention that this means of acquiring additional footings on occasion originally intended to be employed when faults appeared in the subsoil, which were not revealed by trial borings, had to be employed where what seemed to be a subterranean stream took its way diagonally across the lot. Owing to this and to the fact that I was unable to carry the building up uniformly as intended, some settlement cracks had to be dealt with with this "reserve" wherever we crossed this hidden groove. Strangely enough, the quake closed this fault and some cracks caused by it, the whole structure taking its place more solidly as on a more even keel in the muck, probably shaken completely to level bearings for all time. It would not be too

much to say that instead of being damaged by the quake, the building was actually benefited by it.

V. THE APPURTENANCE SYSTEMS

Early, before the preliminary sketches were completed, I consulted H. F. Durr, of Chicago, as to the advisability of electrifying everything, heating, lighting, cooking, elevators, and water heating. At that time his report was distinctly unfavorable. We then worked it out for fuel oil and a power house. But several years later as we approached the point when a real solution was imperative, as Hayashi San was still for electrification and a compromise I proposed did not appeal to him, we did electrify the building.

On my own account I had some experiments made with the Cutler-Hammer heating unit that seemed to put a feasible face on the matter of heating; cooking apparatus was already coming more generally into use: so we electrified the whole building as the cost of current in Tokio was cheaper than anywhere else in the world, except in Sweden.

In this connection I laid out trenches for the piping system in the ground under the building, free of construction, the lead sewer and water pipes and the conduit pipes sweeping by bends from their distributing trenches to vertical pipe shafts rising between bathrooms, the pipes again sweeping from the vertical shaft to the bathroom fittings. I had originally intended to use wrought-iron pipe in this work, but after investigating the fate of iron pipe in Tokio buildings, finding it going out of commission in five to fifteen years, I tore out what had already got in and allowed only lead with wiped joints to go into the building anywhere except in the nickel fittings of bathrooms and kitchen. A look into a pipe shaft at the Imperial is like looking into an animal abdomen—a smooth mass of winding intestines. All pipes were accessible, hung free of construction.

As a reserve and resource in case of catastrophe I had insisted upon a large pool of water, or reservoir, which I used as an architectural feature at the entrance to the grounds. And this provided the water not only for the emergency hotel service, but to give additional protection from fire across the street, when otherwise none would have been obtainable. This pool the directors were determined to "cut out" as an extravagance. I saved it only by "rough" tactics at the crucial moment.

The details of these general propositions were, of course, infinite, oftentimes vexatious, and sometimes seemingly impossible. But the fact that the building never went out of service during the quake is the answer to any doubt as to their efficiency or desirability. These details of lighting, heating, and mechanical equipment were all in the hands of Mr. Durr, who, at my request, sent Harry F. Mills to Tokio to superintend the installation, which was entirely done by Japanese workmen. The only materials not found in Japan were the hardware, machinery, bathroom and kitchen fixtures, and the steel bars. Japanese machinery and hardware is of uniformly low-grade, owing to poor steel and defective alloys, but this is improving. And before the building was finished we could have had steel bars in Japan, 10 percent less efficient. The only machinery we could make stick were the concrete mixers (the workers would avoid them sometimes), the electrical hoist (for concrete only). The other materials, including the lava, all went up the typical incline on coolie shoulders.

I had instructed Mueller to bring a stone planer and pneumatic chisels, thinking to save labor in working the straight, long, lava courses. But the thing was soon buried in the stone chips that flew from hammer-axes in the clever hands of a hundred or more stonecutters, and we sold it for old iron to somebody who may have been connected with some American building concern. I am just wondering, as I write, what became of the pneumatic chisels. Both Mr. Mueller and myself held classes to teach the use of the "darby," the flote, and the rod in plastering. It could not be done. I got the workmen upon a hanging scaffold to clean down the building by a personal appeal to their chief, Nagao, and a personal appeal to personal pride many times repeated. I did this in a spirit of fun to discountenance Mueller, who wagered it couldn't be done.

Both Mueller and myself were caught in a glacial drift of six or seven hundred workmen and their bosses and their padrone labor system—laborers who couldn't speak a word of English; and we were often carried with it, helpless and protesting.

Mueller ultimately learned three words of Japanese coupled with English unfit for publication. They were *mizu* (water) *massugu* (meaning straight) and— but I forget what the other was. But his lieutenants, Fujita, Ito, and Yamamura soon learned what certain agonies on his part signified and he got results, though sometimes he would have to pick up a recreant workman like a cat, by the scruff of the neck and drop him off the building.

Especially did we struggle against the "layout": the batter boards fixed at proper levels horizontally and the cross wires overhead, from which depended the strings stretched down and fastened at each and every corner in the whole structure. The time and lumber necessary to erect these guides may be imagined, sometimes veritable towers being necessary to give this overhead wire line from which the maze of strings depended. Perhaps 15 percent of labor costs went into this system. But without it there was no movement whatever, do what we would. It was impossible for Japanese workmen to lay brick or set stone without these preliminaries, without these sacred rites exercised by the masonry foremen. As well try to dethrone the Buddha himself.

As to labor costs, neither Mueller nor myself knew much at first, except in a vague general way by hearsay, and, latterly, facts worth mentioning. I tried to introduce modern checking and time-keeping system by brass check, while finally after months of coaxing and bullying, it did go into effect.

I remember looking at one of the temporary matting shelters and the pole scaffolding of the inclines running around other buildings as used in Tokio and thinking, "At any rate, we'll show them how to avoid all that," not knowing that it was a wise concession to the wretched climate. If we had erected such a shelter as a concession to Tokio's continual rainy days, the *nubai* (rainy season) of which we knew nothing, and to shield the oriental workmen from fierce sunlight and combined wind we could have saved nine months time, at least, in completing the work and could have worked in comfort the rest of the time. We had the inclined plane anyway. It would have been better to have had it their own way all around the building.

I mention these things to show how wasteful and unreasonable it is to expect an ancient, established craft system, undoubtedly in its own way the cleverest and most efficient in the world, to come to book along the lines of the modern machine. It is wisdom to go with them as far as the general direction of the work will allow. And if the work is well undertaken, that direction will go far in order to keep their efficiency and keep their "face." This matter of face is a very interesting oriental institution, well worth considering too, in any plan of action in Japan.

I do not know that a formal permit for the new Imperial Hotel was ever fully issued by the Metropolitan Police of Tokio. The department realized it was beyond its depth and stood by. The officers visited us and we visited them occasionally. They insisted upon certain details in the matter of septic sewage disposal, but otherwise mostly maintained a discreet silence. Nor could a permit to build the building, as built, be obtained in any of our American cities: permits to build most of those buildings that came shaking down around it, could be got.

The "factor of ignorance," i.e. the "factor of safety," owing to the personal devotion of ourselves, could be and was very largely eliminated and new facts concerning the performances of cantilever slabs and beams, posts and walls are available to Tokio. In consequence, data which will enable fireproof concrete buildings to compete more favorably in the future with other forms of construction not so desirable.

VI. THE FACT THAT IS WORTHWHILE

The fact that is worthwhile, in considering the construction of the Imperial Hotel, it seems to me, is the fact that here a simple system of construction, sound in itself, became a piece of architecture naturally and forcefully expressing that system and the conditions it was built to serve. What features the Imperial has are evolved from use and necessity and the nature of this construction, like the elevator housings at the stairways, like the perforated roof slabs becoming decorative cornices, other floor slabs becoming balconies, canopies, flying bridges, etc. And as to lighting, heating, furnishing even, all were made a part of and one with the structure in effect.

As stated in the beginning, the building is an appropriate organic whole from which the element of construction cannot be subtracted or separated even in quality of style. This is the architectural gospel the Imperial preaches to Tokio and to the world, standing upon the threshold of great change in Japanese institutions. It teaches the value of the third dimension: of that element in thought or effort that makes whatever is done an integral affair.

The Imperial Hotel at Tokio is an architect's building, not an engineer's building—just as a skyscraper in Tokio is an engineer's and not an architect's building.

The difference is all the difference between a thing organic, complete in itself, and a patched composite, made and made regardless.

There is technical engineering in the construction of the Imperial Hotel in master hands at all points, but such engineering is an architect's expression of an architectural idea. There is no architecture in the construction of a Tokio skyscraper, except the camouflage now shattered or in the street.

VII. THE ENEMY TO ARCHITECTURE

What is the ethical gospel carried by tall steel frames in Tokio? A doctrine of expediency—a negation of human rights, save the right of the landlord to repeat his property area *ad libitum, ad nauseam*: repeat it regardless of congestion, regardless of the welfare of the man who really *is* the city, and that man is the citizen; repeat it, too, regardless of the rights of the neighbor, who, unable to build so high, loses the right to the streets, his light, his safety, unless he does compete. And to whom goes the profits from this tyranny of the skyscraper?

From an engineering standpoint, it has failed, with its basic theory of "rigidity" and its fatal stilts to "hardpan," its appliqué of "architecture." It is now shown unsound, unsafe, with no basis other than that of commercial greed. And in all cities built on the rim of the Pacific basin, where the red line of seismic convulsion runs, these frames have proved to be deathtraps for human beings, a commercial trifling with human lives that has ended in disaster.

From the standpoint of the art of architecture, the steel-frame skyscraper does not exist, except where some great artist has seized it and frankly clothed its temporary bones with a mastic covering frankly plastic as such—and such cases are rare—as they ought to be. There is no place even for these in Tokio. In Tokio, the skyscraper was economically, aesthetically, morally, an outrage, forced by Yankee salesmanship upon an already frightfully congested city. It was a merciless forcing of the fearful disadvantages of a native industrial situation at cost plus 10 percent, plus machinery, plus overhead to the salesmen. Yet such buildings were not called "freaks," not "bizarre": no, but symbols of commercial enterprise and the extension of American civilization. These Yankee expedients have done more to ruin Tokio, to drag it to the dead level of a commercialized American city unfit for human beings, and to outrage the traditions and sensibilities of a great nation and a loving, lovable people than anything that has happened to them since Perry opened the port or since the Germans got through with them. The derby hat, "hardstraw," frock coat, and Boston gaiters introduced the steel frame skyscraper to Tokio. It took this terrible catastrophe to human beings and property to root them out. In Tokio this particular Yankee excrescence was short-lived.

VIII. IN EXTENUATION

In this reference to "THE ENEMY," I refer to no individuals, but to an "institution": an institution entrenched unfairly in the herd instinct, an instinct which American abuse of democracy inflames: an enemy not subject to noblesse oblige: an enemy giving no quarter, no matter what may be the quality of its adversary, seeking always to defend its own profits by arrogating to itself the sanctions of that authority conferred by custom and at any cost whatsoever to culture. That enemy is the architectural parasite—a commercial pirate gradually doing to death the possibilities of true greatness in the civilization of these United States. To attack the popular giant openly is to go like David—sling and stone in hand. The stone in my sling is the Imperial Hotel. I, too, know my aim.

The source of the deepest gratitude the human heart can know is found in the fact that *Principle* does not fail.

My curtain speech is finished. The leading figures in the drama have met the audience. I turn to go away, before those powerful silent men, whose reservoir of capital and credit provided the beau-tiful site upon which to build the building and that kept the throng of busy workmen fed with pay envelopes as they passed out through the gates—before the part played by these men occurred to me.

Certainly the responsibility they assumed was splendidly carried out in the face of many doubts and trials—trials augmented by many natural enemies.

First, always, there was Baron Okura, whose magnificent art museum, a gift to Tokio, now lies in ruins: an active, successful, youthful veteran of eighty-four, head of the board, whose faith may have wavered, but whose support never did. When our funds gave out, the building half-finished, it was he who placed me at his right hand at the troublous meeting, and, reaching across the table, shook my hand cordially and told me that if I would go through the building would be finished as he would personally assume the responsibility and find the necessary funds. He did find them.

Baron Shibusawa, known in diplomatic circles as the "grand old man of Japan," often present representing the interests of the Imperial Household, but whose manifold interests left most of the policy of the enterprise to Baron Okura.

Then there was Asano San, senior head of the great Asano cement and shipping interests, who was always present at board meetings, a great financial power in Japanese industry. His massive head and keen gaze from under his enormous, shaggy, white eyebrows, alarming but for the kindly twinkle in his eyes.

There was Murai San, whose tobacco interests the government took over, a merchant prince with wonderful homes in Tokio and Kyoto and elsewhere—a kindly friend and genial influence on the board.

There was Wakao San, the banker, who, in the interest of a small flock of small stockholders, made meticulous inquiry into details, and others whose faith was placed in the powerful interests I have mentioned, and who took little active official part in the program.

The financial resources of these men—or the interests they represented—gave to us to build the building I have been describing. The building, for what it may be worth as property, they receive in return for their "investment."

But, together with ourselves, they have given to the world whatever, above property, the building has to give—artistic, scientific, or moral. The great issues involved have become theirs also, and while this older generation, upon whose shoulders the burden of financial management rested have shifted, now, the burden to the younger, stronger, but also more slender shoulders of their sons, may that older generation long find quiet joy and refuge in their super-dreadnought, knowing it has weathered the storm.

LOUIS HENRY SULLIVAN: BELOVED MASTER

Wright first arrived in Chicago early in the spring of 1887. He was twenty years old when he ran away from his family and his studies at the University of Wisconsin in Madison to pursue a life in architecture. Chicago, it seemed to him, was the place to start. It was rebuilding after the fire of 1871, and he wanted to be a part of the vitality pulsing throughout the newly constructed city. He took various jobs, with the architect Joseph Lyman Silsbee—a friend of Wright's uncle Jenkin Lloyd Jones—then with Beers, Clay and Dutton. But hearing of the work of the firm of Adler and Sullivan, he soon applied for a job with Louis Sullivan and was accepted.

He first worked on the interior decorative schemes for the Chicago Auditorium. That Wright was a skilled draftsman Sullivan saw in the sketches Wright presented to him when applying for the job. Soon he was elevated to the position of chief of design and given an office of his own, with thirty draftsmen working under him. He quickly absorbed lessons from Sullivan, called him "Lieber Meister," and became, as he said, "the pencil in his [Sullivan's] hand." But a conflict arose when Sullivan discovered Wright was accepting outside commissions for various residences in Oak Park. To Sullivan that seemed to be a breach of contract. The two had a violent argument, and when the clash of tempers reached its peak, Sullivan abruptly fired Wright. This was early in the spring of 1893, after an association of nearly seven years.

Following the Panic of 1893, the great building boom came to an end in Chicago. The firm of Adler and Sullivan broke up, and Sullivan went his own way. He was never to recover the distinguished style or the significance of building that he and Dankmar Adler had achieved. With Adler's superb knowledge of engineering and Sullivan's insightful and poetic designing skills, they had created the first truly American skyscraper—an aesthetic expression as well as a structural one.

Twenty-five years later, in 1918, Wright was called by Sullivan to meet him in Chicago. Sullivan was close to poverty, his office closed, his possessions stored, his health poor and his conditions even poorer. Over the next six years Wright helped him whenever he could, bringing him money, clothing, buying meals for him, and paying the hotel bills. Always referring to him as "Wright" in the early years, Sullivan now called him "Frank," but the letters between them are a heartbreaking account of Sullivan's decline. Finally, on April 11, 1924, Wright visited him for the last time. Sullivan presented him with the first copy of his autobiography, The Autobiography of an Idea. Inscribing it to him, he remarked, "Frank, it is you who has created the new architecture in America, but I do not believe you could have done it without me." Sullivan died three days later. When Wright made the design for the National Life Insurance Company skyscraper, published in The Architectural Record four years later, he dedicated the design to Louis Sullivan. [Published with 2 illustrations in The Western Architect, June 1924]

THE BELOVED MASTER WHO KNEW HOW TO BE A GREAT friend is dead. My young mind turned to him in hope and affection at eighteen, and now, at middle age, I am to miss him and look back upon a long and loving association to which no new days, no new experiences may be added.

He needs no eulogy from me, this man of men, this high-minded workman—who would not sell out! He would take no less than his price—and his price was too high for his time! His price for Louis Sullivan, the Architect, was as high as principle is high; for Louis Sullivan, the sentient human being, his price was not high enough. He was prodigal with his bodily heritage. Recklessly he flung it into the crucible that was his soul, or carelessly he wasted it in physical reactions to dispel loneliness, the loneliness that is the result of disillusionment— the loneliness that every great, uncompromising mind knows well and dreads and inherits, together with those who have gone the lonely road before him where only one at a time may tread. His lesser-self was his, to do with as he pleased. He spent it with that extravagance that goes with the opulent nature, rich in resources, and we had him for a shorter time in consequence. The loss was ours— perhaps it was not his.

To know him well was to love him well. I never liked the name Frank until I would hear him say it, and the quiet breath he gave it made it beautiful in my ears and I would remember it was the name of freemen—meant free. The deep quiet of his temper had great charm for me. The rich humor that was lurking in the deeps within him and that sat in his eyes whatever his mouth might be saying, however earnest the moment might be, was rich and rare in human quality. He had remarkable and beautiful eyes—true windows for the soul of him. Meredith's portrait of Beethoven—"The hand of the Wind was in his hair—he seemed to hear with his eyes," is a portrait I have never forgotten. If someone could give the warmer, different line, that would give the Master's quality! I feel it and I have tried—but I cannot write it.

I left him just after the Transportation Building brought him fame—to "make my own," and did not find him again until he was in trouble—some nine years ago, and needed me. Since that time the relation between us, established so early and lasting at that early period seven years, seemed, although the interruption was seventeen years long, to be resumed with little or no lapse of time. We understood each other as we had done always.

Somehow I am in no mood to talk about his work. I know well its vital significance, its great value, the beautiful quality of its strain. I know too, now, what was the matter with it, but where it fell short, it fell short of his own ideal. He could not build so well as he knew nor so true to his thought as he could think, sometimes, but sometimes he did better than either.

Genius he had as surely as there is Genius in the great work called Man. The quality of that Genius his country needed as the parched leaf or the drying fields need dew or rain. A fine depth was in him and he was broad enough, without reducing the scale of it, or showing up the quiet strength of it. And yet his country did not know him!

He loved appreciation. He was pleased as a child is pleased with praise. No measure of it was too much for him, because he well knew that no such measure could reach his powers, much less go beyond them. And any achievement visible as praiseworthy he knew was as nothing compared to what already was achieved in the consciousness that was his.

He was a fine workman. He could draw with consummate skillfulness. He could draw as beautifully as he could think and he was one of the few architects of the age who could really think. I used to fear his graphic facility—this virtuosity of his, as an enemy to him in the higher reaches of his genius. It was not so. The very extravagance of his gift was a quality of its beauty in an age when all in similar effort is niggardly or cowardly or stale.

I feel the emptiness where he was wont to work. The sterility of my time closes in upon his place. Machine-made life in a Machine-age that steadily automatizes, standardizes, amortizes the living beauty of the Life he knew and loved and served so well—seems desolation, damnation! Without him the battle seems suddenly to have gone wrong—the victory in doubt!

Here, in our country, where individual distinction of the highest order must be distorted or swamped in the cloying surge of "good taste!"

Here, where free initiative is treated as dangerous or regarded as absurd!

Here, where the Gift is suspected, feared, or hated unless entertainment can be got out of it!

Here, where the plain man has, in a bogus Democracy, license to sneer at all above him or sit on all below him!

Here, where thought is ankle-deep, activity noncreative, but both, in motion and quantity, over all heads!

Here, in a country so nobly dedicated, root and branch, to Truth and Freedom as no more than Justice, yet where the government itself officially encourages the mental grip of "the middle," the sacred average that all but paralyzes head and heart and hand!

Here where a stupendous, mechanized industry is fast becoming reflected in mechanized mentality, sterilizing Life, Love, Hope—standardization, without light from within is stagnation!

Here where there are religions but no Religion!

Here where there are arts but no Art!

Here where religion and art are utterly divorced from life and automatic substitutes everywhere are in the shop windows, in the streets, in the seats of the mighty, in the retreats of the humble, in the sanctuaries of the Soul!

Here where Institutes turn out droves of illustrators and egotists—manikins, instead of interpreters and givers!

Here where tainted minor arts make shift in profusion and disorder upon the ruins of the great Arts!

Here, in this blind aggregation of wealth and power, a great Master was, in despair, forced to relinquish his chosen work in *Architecture*, the great Art of Civilization needed now as of time immemorial, the Art of all arts most needed by his country—and was compelled to win recognition in a medium that is the all-devouring monster of the age—the literal art that has sapped the life and strength of all the other great Arts and to no good purpose: no, to the everlasting harm of culture and good life, to the eventual impoverishment of the human establishment! Inasmuch as there are five senses, five avenues open to man's communion with Life—four-fifths of human sensibility is lost when one Art usurps the place of the other four. Human beings are fast becoming human documents, Humanity, a litany!

Here, in free America, this prophetic mind with trained and gifted capacity for the regeneration of this now ugly, awkward work of this world, in living forms of Beauty, was little used and passed by, that the process, inexorable as Fate, might not be interrupted—nor little hoards of little men be unduly squandered above the animal plane of economic satisfaction!

That a country in such need, his country—any country—at such a time—a crisis—should have failed to use one of her great men—in many respects, her greatest man—to do the work he loved and in which he was not only competent but prophetic—is terrible proof of how much more disastrous is half-knowledge, than either Ignorance or Folly could ever be. This I call Tragedy!

And now this book, *The Autobiography of an Idea*—his book—has come to convince an unwilling world, tainted with that hatred for superiority that characterizes a false Democracy, of what it missed in leaving a man of such quality to turn from the rare work he could do, to give, in a book, proof of that quality in a medium his kindred had learned to understand—proof of his quality—too late.

It is a characteristic triumph of Genius such as his that he should lay this book upon the library table of the nation he loved, as he died! His fertility was great enough to scatter seed no matter what the disability—no matter what the obstruction. If the eye of his country was uneducated, inept, objective, illiterate or merely *literal*; if its sense of Beauty of Form as Idea or Beauty of Idea as Form was unawakened, he took literature, the literal medium by which the literal may most easily be reached and, perhaps, literally made to understand—grasped it and made himself known—the Master still.

But he was most needed where the workmen wait for the Plan—where the directing Imagination must get the work of the world done in such master-fashion that mankind may see and forever more believe that Spirit and Matter are one—when both are real. Realize that Form and Idea are one and inseparable—as he showed them to be in that master-key to the Skyscraper as Architecture—the Wainwright Building. To this high task he came as an anointed prophet—to turn disillusioned to the cloister as so many have turned before him and will so turn still—although his cloister was the printed page—the book, that, opened now, all may read.

Any appreciation of the Master must be an arraignment of the time, the place, the people that needed and hungered for what he had to give, but all but wasted him when he was fit and ready. Yes, in the neglect of this great man's genius and his power to get many more noble buildings built for his country than he was allowed to build—we see the hideous cruelty of America's blind infatuation with the Expedient—this deadly, grinding, spoilation of the Beautiful.

Louis Sullivan was a sacrifice to the God of Temporal Things by a hardworking, pioneering people, too vain of the culture of lies in their heads, over empty, hungry hearts, a heedless people living a hectic life no full hands may ever make worth while—and who either could not or would not know him. The regret and shame those feel who knew his quality—who knew what his hand held ready to give to truly enrich his kind, the impotent rage that all but chokes utterance that this treasure of a greatly rich and powerful nation was neglected, was comparatively unknown—when the opportunism

of the inferior, the fashionable, the imitative were in favor, is hard to bear.

What is left to us is the least of him—but it will serve.

Out of the fragments of his dreams that were his buildings—out of the sense of Architecture as entering a new phase as a *plastic* Art—great things will yet be born. Everything he did has some fine quality, was some solution of a difficult problem—some sorely needed light on practical affairs. Practical? Truly here was a practical man in a radical sense, rooted in Principle, and as richly gifted as he was impressionable—as deep-sighted as he was far-seeing.

The work the Master did may die with him—no great matter. What he represented has lived in spite of all drift—all friction, all waste, all slip—since time began for man. In this sense was Louis Sullivan true to tradition—in this sense will the divine spark, given to him from the deep center of the universe and to which he held true, be handed on the fresher, more vital, more potent, enriched a little, perhaps much, by the individuality that was his. There is no occasion for deep despair—although chagrin, frustrated hopes, broken lives, and broken promises strew the way with gruesome wreckage. The light that was in him lives—and will go on—forever.

Later when I have him more in perspective, I intend to write about and illustrate his work. It is too soon, now. I hope to make clear in unmistakable concrete terms, what is now necessarily abstract. A privilege I feel as mine and one I know from him that he would be pleased that I should take, as I have assured him I sometime would do.

24

LOUIS HENRY SULLIVAN: HIS WORK

[Published without illustrations in The Architectural Record, *July 1924]*

LOUIS SULLIVAN'S GREAT VALUE AS AN ARTIST-ARCHITECT —alive or dead—lies in his firm grasp of principle. He knew the truths of Architecture as I believe no one before him knew them. And profoundly he realized them.

This illumination of his was the more remarkable a vision when all around him cultural mists hung low to obscure or blight every dawning hope of a finer beauty in the matter of this world.

As "the name of God has fenced about all crime with holiness," so in the name of Architecture the "Classic" perpetually inserts skillful lies to hide ignorance or impotence and belie creation.

But the Master's was true creative activity—not deceived nor deceiving. He was a radical and so one knew, always, where to find him. His sense and thought and spirit were deep-rooted in that high quality of old and new which make them one and thereby he was apprised of the falsity of outward shows that duped his fellows and that dupe them still.

The names, attributes, and passions of earth's creatures change, but—that creation changes never; his sane and passionate vision leaves testimony here on earth in fragments of his dreams—his work.

His work! Who may gauge the worth of the work of such a man? Who shall say what his influence was, or is, or will be? Not I.

That his work was done at all was marvelous. That it could *be*, under the circumstances we call Democracy and that so mock his own fine sense of that much abused idea, was prophetic and for his country the greatest and most potent suggestion.

Here in this aspiring land of the impertinent, impermanent, and of commercial importunity, he never struck his colors. The buildings he has left us are the least of him—in the heart of him.

He was of infinite value to the country that wasted him, because it could not know him.

Work must be studied in relation to the time in which it presented its contrasts, insisted upon its virtues, and got itself into human view. Remember if you can the contemporaries of Louis Sullivan's first great work, the Chicago Auditorium. Those contemporaries were a lot of unregenerate sinners in the grammar of the insensate period of General Grant Gothic.

Imagine this noble calm of the auditorium exterior and the beautiful free room within, so beautifully conceived as a unit with its *plastic* ornamentation, the quiet of its deep cream and soft gold scheme of color, the imaginative *plastic* richness of this interior and compare both with the cut, butt, and slash of that period—the meaningless stiffness that sterilized the Chicago buildings for all their ambitious attitudes and grand gestures. They belonged to a world to which the sense of the word "*plastic*" had not been born. That the word itself could get itself understood in relation to architecture is doubtful—and then see what Louis Sullivan's creative activity from that time on meant to Architecture as an Art.

Back of that first great performance of his was a deepening knowledge, a tightening grasp on essentials. Much in the great effort got away from him; it wore him out; it was all at tremendous pressure, against fearful odds—but the Chicago Auditorium is good enough yet to be the most successful room for opera in the world. I think I have seen them all. His genius burst into full bloom with the impetus of the success and fame that great enterprise brought to him and to Adler. Dankmar Adler, his partner, was a fine critic. A master of the plan and of men. His influence over Louis Sullivan at that time was great and good.

The Getty Tomb was a work that soon followed the Auditorium, as did the Wainwright Building[1] in St. Louis to greater purpose. The Getty Tomb in Graceland Cemetery was a piece of sculpture, a statue, an elegiac poem addressed to the sensibilities as such. It was Architecture in a detached and romantic phase, a beautiful burial casket, "in memoriam," but—a memorial to the architect whose work it was. His "type," the "form that was peculiarly his was never better expressed."

When he brought in the board with the motive of the Wainwright Building outlined in profile and in scheme upon it and threw it down on my table, I was perfectly aware of what had happened. This was Louis Sullivan's greatest moment—his greatest effort. The "skyscraper," as a new thing beneath the sun, an entity with virtue, individuality and beauty all its own, was born.

Until Louis Sullivan showed the way, the masses of the tall buildings were never a complete whole in themselves. They were ugly, harsh aggregates with no sense of unity, fighting tallness instead of accepting it. What unity those masses now have, that pile up toward New York and Chicago skies, is due to the Master-mind that first perceived one as a harmonious unit—its height triumphant.

The Wainwright Building cleared the way, and to this day remains the master key to the skyscraper as a matter of Architecture in the work of the world. The Wainwright and its group were Architecture living again as such in a new age—the Steel Age—*living in the work of the world!* The Practical therein achieving expression as Beauty. A true

service rendered humanity in that here was proof of the oneness of Spirit and Matter, *when both are real*—a synthesis the world awaits as the service of the artist and a benediction it will receive when false ideas as to the nature and limitation of art and the functions of the artist disappear.

The Transportation Building[2] at the Columbian Exposition cost him most trouble of anything he ever did. He got the great doorway "straight away," but the rest hung fire. I had never seen him anxious before, but anxious he then was. How eventually successful this beautiful contribution to that fine collection of picture-buildings was, itself shows. But the Transportation Building was no solution to the work of the world as was the Wainwright Building. It was a "picture-building"—but one with rhyme and reason and, above all, individuality; a real picture, not a mere pose of the picturesque. It was not architecture in its highest sense, except as a great theme suggested, an idea of violent changes in scale exemplified, noble contrasts effected—meanwhile its excuse for existence being the enclosure of exhibition space devoted to transportation. It was no masterful solution of a practical problem. It was a holiday circumstance and superb entertainment, which is what it was intended to be. It was original, the fresh individual note of vitality at the Fair—inspiring, a thing created but—something in itself, for itself alone. Except that if here—where a mischief was done to architectural America from which it has never recovered, by the introduction of "the classic," so called, in the Fair buildings, as the "Ideal"—had that note of individual vitality as expressed in the Transportation Building been heeded for what it was worth, that mischief might largely have been averted. Only the Chicago Auditorium, the Transportation Building, the Getty Tomb, and the Wainwright Building are necessary to show the great reach of the creative activity that was Louis Sullivan's genius. The other buildings he did are blossoms more or less individual upon these stems. Some were grafted from one to the other of them, some were grown from them, but all are relatively inferior in point of that quality, which we finally associate with the primitive strength of the thing that got itself done regardless and "stark" to the Idea: sheer, significant, vital.

As to materials, the grasp of the Master's imagination gripped them all pretty much alike. As to relying upon them for beauties of their own, he had no need—no patience. They were stuff to bear the stamp of his imagination and bear it they did: cast iron, wrought iron, marble, plaster, concrete, wood. In this respect he did not live up to his principle. He was too rich in fancy to allow anything to come for its own sake between him and the goal of his desire. It would have been to him like naturalistic noises in the orchestra.

Where his work fell short, it fell short of his ideal. He could not build so well as he knew, nor so true to his thought as he was able to think—often. But sometimes he did better than either.

I see his individual quality in that feature of his work that was his sensuous ornament—as I see the wondrous smile upon his face—a charm, a personal appealing charm. So very like and so very much his own. It will be cherished long, because no one has had the quality to produce out of himself such a gracious, beautiful response; so lovely a smile evoked by love of beauty. The capacity for love, ardent, true, poetic, was great in him as this alone would prove. His world in this was interior, esoteric, peculiar to himself. It is none the less precious for that. Do you prefer the Greek? Why not? Do you admire the Chinese? Why not, as a matter of course? Do you prefer the Romanesque? It is your privilege. Perhaps you respond to old Baroque? Your reactions to Gothic you find more satisfying? Doubtless. But do you realize that here is no body of culture evolving through centuries of time a "style," but an *individual* in the poetry-crushing environment of a cruel materialism, who in this, invoked the goddess that hitherto whole civilizations strove for centuries to win, and won her with this charming smile—the fruit of his own spirit.

Ah, that supreme, erotic, high adventure of the mind that was his ornament! Often I would see him, his back bent over his drawing board, intent upon what? I knew his symbolism—I caught his feelings as he worked. A Casanova on his rounds? Beside this sensuous master of adventure with tenuous, vibrant, plastic form, Casanova was a duffer; Gil Blas a torn chapeau; Bocaccio's imagination no higher than a stable boy's. Compared to this high quest, the Don's

was as Sancho Panza's ass. The soul of Rabelais alone could have understood and would have called him brother. How often have I held his cloak and sword while he adventured in the realm within, to win his mistress; and while he wooed the mistress, I would woo the maid! Those days! And now, I say, this caress that was his own, should be his own, forever sacred to him and treasured high for its own sake—this rhythmic pulse of the wings of America's creative genius. Whoso has the temerity to undertake to imitate it will fail. Take his principle who will, none may do better—and try the wings that nature gave to you. Do not try to soar with his. Has the time come when every man may have that precious quality called style for his very own? Then where, I ask you, are the others? Eros is a fickle god and hard to please. Musing with blinded eyes, he has heard from earth the music of an immortal strain; henceforth, will take no less.

Genius the Master had—or rather it had him. It possessed him, he reveled in it, squandered it, and the lesser part of him was squandered by it. He lived! And compared to what came to him in life from his effort, the effort itself being a quality of it, the greatly successful careers were, I imagine, relatively lifeless.

Yes, genius he had in the most unequivocal sense—true genius—there is no other kind—the effect of which is not seen in his own time, nor can it ever be seen. Human affairs are of themselves plastic in spite of names and man's ill-advised endeavors to make them static to his will. As a pebble cast into the ocean sets up reactions lost in distance and time, so one man's genius goes on infinitely forever, because it is always an expression of *principle*. And therefore, in no way does it ever run counter to another's genius. The Master's genius is perhaps itself a reaction, the initial force of which we can not—need not—see.

Of one thing we may be sure—the intuitions of such a nature, the work to which he put his hand, no less than the suggestion he himself was to kindred or aspiring natures, is worth more to the future in all conservative or progressive sense than all the work of all the schools, just as example is more valuable than precept.

Is it not true that *individuality* is the supreme entertainment of life? Surely it is the quality most precious in it and most worthy of conservation; veritably the visible hand of the Creator! Here, in Louis Sullivan was an example as clear and convincing as any, anywhere at any time, under conditions as unpromising to fulfillment as ever existed.

Is it not probable that the social solidarity that produced the great "styles" exists no longer in the same sense and that never more will such a manifestation appear, especially in a nation composed of nationalities like ours? But, as free opportunity offers, when America awakens spiritually or is awakened by spirit, individuality will come to flower in almost as many styles as there are individuals capable of style. And there will arise more and more men who are capable of it. Until we have a wealth of vital expression. We will then only need order in the aggregate—an "order" which will be established eventually by the nature of the individual intelligence capable of style—*itself* perceiving the necessity for it and making it therefore a veritable condition of every such individual expression. The nature capable of style is more capable than any other of the appropriate conduct of that power, when and wherever need be.

Is not that a more desirable and logical conclusion to draw from the principle upon which this country was founded than that of the dead level of a mongrelized version of the "Classic," a renaissance of Renaissance should be allowed to characterize the mongrel as mongrel—and nothing more?

H. H. Richardson, great emotionalist in architecture that he was, elected to work in the "style" Romanesque. The Master dug deeper and made style for himself out of the same stuff the Romanesque was made from and the Gothic too. With all these examples before us of "styles," surely man may penetrate to the heart of *Style* and unveiling its secret be master of his own. And as a master of this type was Louis Sullivan—esoteric though his synthetic style may be. The leadership of Stanford White was esoteric, his mind that of a connoisseur. His gift was selective, and we owe, to him and his kind the architectural army of "good taste" that smothers the practical in applied expedients—an army whose beauty-worship is content with the beauty of the painted lady, the henna, paste, and rouge, or the more earnest kind, the avid antiquarian, or the far too credulous historian. What does it matter if Tradition's followers fail to see that Louis Sullivan's loyalty to tradition was wholly complete and utterly profound? His loyalty was greater than theirs, as the Spirit transcends the Letter. What lives in New York architecture is little enough and in spite of its grammar and far beyond the style-mongering it receives in the atelier. It is the force of circumstance piling itself inexorably by mere mass into the sky—the darkening canyons that are paths leading into darkness, or to Death! It seems incredible now, but such unity as those tall masses may have is due to the mastermind, that first conceived and contributed one as a unit. The Wainwright Building cleared the way for them—and to this day remains the master key to the skyscraper as Architecture the world over. Why is it so difficult for standardization to receive to a greater degree the illumination from within that would mean Life instead of Death? Why is the vision of such a mastermind lost in the competitive confusion of so-called ideas and jostling ambitions? Why is the matter, except for him, still all from the outside—culture nowhere sane nor safe except as the imitation or the innocuous is safe—which it never is or was. Look backward toward Rome!

Yes the great Master's contribution as to form may die with him. No great matter. This Way-shower needs no piles of perishable granite, no sightly shapes to secure his immortality or make good his fame. It is his fortune that in the hearts of his fellows his gift was real. The boon to us of his journey on this earth in the span of life allotted to him, is beyond all question, all calculation. His work was the work of a man for men—for sincere humanity. The look of the thing he did may or may not appeal to the imagination trained to regard certain rhythms, spacings, forms, and figures as architecture. Many faults may be laid to him but they are the rough hewn edges of the real thing. And what he did even more than the way he did it will always repay painstaking study if it is free study. It can only vex and puzzle the pedantic mind and end in its hostility—the hostility that never more than entertained and amused him although eventually it did destroy his usefulness. That hostility of the provincial mind is found on the farm, in the small town on Main Street, on Fifth Avenue, in the Seats of the Mighty, in the Church, in New York, and in Hollywood. Wherever that type of mind is found it will accept no radical, because anything radical is the death of the provincial. Instinctively the provincial mentality feels this, and fears it, and therefore hates. And Louis Sullivan was a radical in the same sense that the Ideal Man was the consummate radical of human history.

Not long ago—weary—he said to me in a despondent moment that it would be far more difficult now to do the radical work he did—more difficult to get accepted than when he worked. The dead level of mediocrity had risen to the point where herd-psychology had accepted as normal the "good form" of the school and stopped thinking. The inevitable drift had set in. But no, it is not so! The torch flung to the Master hand from the depths of antiquity, from the heart of the world, and held faithfully and firmly alight and aloft for thirty years at least by him, shall not go out. It has never yet since time began for man, gone out. Willing hands have already caught the divine sparks and little running fires are lighted on the hills and glimmer in the dark; some flickering and feeble; some with more smoke than fire; some guttering in candle grease; but some—clear, candescent flame—that shall rise high and higher until the darkness the tired, wayworn Master saw—that specter looming as the horror of his country's shade—will fade in true illumination. Hope too long deferred will make the strongest hearts foreboding. For the consummate radical, the Kingdom on Earth was "at hand" nineteen hundred years ago. It is a little nearer now. This laborer in the same vineyard with a similar hope to the same purpose has gone, his hope still high. The sire of an immortal strain has gone unterrified into the gulf, which we call Death. A great chief among men's spirits, he has been made one with Nature—and now he is a presence to be felt and known in darkness and in light, spreading a vital and benign influence wherever quick dreams spring from youthful minds or careworn, toil-stained comrades to his thought may need—"that Light whose smile kindles the universe: That Beauty in which all things work and move."

"He lives, he wakes, 'tis Death is dead—not he." Not he, who in a world that chains and fetters humankind was Life's green tree. A benediction, he that will outlive the Curse—live down the Lie.

1. The Getty Tomb was built in 1890; the Wainwright Building in 1890–1891.
2. The Transportation Building was built in 1891–1893.

25

FACTS REGARDING
THE IMPERIAL HOTEL

Wright wrote three articles in 1925 for the Dutch publication Wendingen. One of them was a description of the construction of the Imperial Hotel, in which he describes the building techniques in more depth than in his other writings on the hotel. Obviously, this article was written prior to the Kanto earthquake of September 1923. But as it first appeared in print in Wendingen, it is included here along with the two other articles he wrote for that magazine: "In the Cause of Architecture: The Third Dimension"; and a special concluding message, "To My European Co-Workers."

Wendingen was a Dutch periodical to which the architect H. Th. Wijdeveld contributed many articles which directed the development of contemporary architecture in Holland. The format of the magazine greatly appealed to Wright, and he was pleased that Wijdeveld selected his work for publication. All the drawings and photographs that appeared were sent over from his studio at Taliesin. These essays first appeared as three essays in seven separate issues of Wendingen. They later were assembled into book form, the double pages hand bound in a large, square format. A special copy, bound in white calfskin, was sent to Wright, and inside the various architects of Holland had inscribed messages of congratulations to him. He treasured this book above all others of his work. [Published with 6 illustrations in Wendingen, 1925]

FACTS REGARDING THE IMPERIAL HOTEL FIRST. THE NEW Imperial is a hotel of solid masonry construction containing commodious public rooms and two hundred and eighty-five bedrooms together with two hundred and twenty-five outside bathrooms. This much however is less than one-half its substance or its function or its cost.

It is also a center of entertainment—a clearinghouse for Japan's social obligations to "the foreigner" and this group contains the 300-foot masonry promenade with sixteen private supper rooms—a masonry theater with revolving stage. In the theater there are one thousand seats. There is below the theater a terraced cabaret seating at tables three hundred people with dancing space and stage. Above the theater is the banquet hall with capacity to seat a thousand at table. A gallery is continued all around it. Like the theater, it too is done in imperishable materials—a great

Imperial Hotel. Tokyo, Japan. 1916. Construction, 1921. FLLW Fdn#1509.0076

building in itself. Group I, the hotel, would cost anywhere in America at least two million dollars, probably much more—furnished.

Group II, the entertainment group would cost two and a half million dollars at least, anywhere in the U.S.A. The Imperial Hotel, furnished, cost 20 percent less per *tsubo* than any building in Tokyo erected under foreign influence during the past five years has cost, unfurnished. There are 10,400 *tsubo* of actual free floor-space in this building, excluding terraces and gardens. A *tsubo* is 36 square feet.

SECOND. The ceiling heights, of typical bedrooms average 9' 4", they vary slightly in the different stories. The typical small guest-room is 15' × 18' with a 6' × 10' bathroom included in the outside forecorner. The typical large room is 15' × 22' with a 6' × 10' bathroom included in the outside forecorner.

There are many larger rooms en suite. Some of them 36' wide. Each room has ample glass surface as any truthful occupant will testify—summer or winter. The rooms and bathrooms are all outside rooms opening on gardens or streets.

If we study the building method of Italy or other semitropical nations we find thick walls—small openings and rather high ceilings—high ceilings because there was no forced draught used in former times. High ceilings in Japan, which has a climate of extremes work both ways—for comfort in summer—dead against it in winter, because heating is very expensive in Japan. The cool chambers protected by the masses of the masonry itself are the best protection against heat of the sun. And provided the air is kept circulating from the coolest places from which it can be taken and delivered from beneath the roof surfaces to the outside air, the best has been done that could be done for comfort in humid hot weather.

This is the design of the Imperial and the means taken to work it out have gone more thoroughly into the matter and the system and is more complete than in any other modern building known.

THIRD. The "stone" is a lava called "Oya." It is the "stone ordinaire" of Japan. It is indestructible by water or fire. It will not disintegrate—it is not to be penetrated by moisture. When first quarried it is soft

and easily workable. It hardens on exposure to the weather and turns yellow. I found buildings with arrises still sharp and clean that had been standing thirty-five years; saw it where it has been underground for seventy years. It weighs 96 pounds per cubic foot—about the weight of green oak.

It is cupped by pockets of burned wood left as the lava flowed down over the forests. It is an ideal building stone similar to Travertine or Caen but with finer character than either. I would be content to have it and no other for the rest of my life as a medium with which to build. Because it was so easily worked I could hollow it out and use it for forms into which the concrete slabs of cantilevers or walls were cast and the steel reinforcement be tied into the joints as well as hooked into the material from beneath and all cast solidly together with the concrete. Wherever there was a chance for a flaked off piece, copper was used in connection with it to insure it.

No terra-cotta—no stones—could furnish the same security as this lava for the features of the building in an earthquake country.

The proof of this came with the earthquake in April 1922. This was the most severe earthquake in Japan for fifty-two years and there was no check nor crack nor fallen piece in the finished construction anywhere. Next day the building was visited by architects, societies, insurance companies, and others and the facts here stated may easily be verified. This work was done under the constant personal supervision of Mr. Mueller.

Exceptions taken to this free use of lava as a plastic material were silenced by the earthquake.

FOURTH. In the erection of the new Imperial Parliament buildings, the scheme of foundation originally designed for the Imperial Hotel has been adopted.

In the original design I had intended to bore the holes for the concrete piles but owing to the fact that old piles and stones abounded in the soil Mr. Mueller found it more advantageous to punch the holes with a wooden tapered pile. This system of foundation saved my clients hundreds of thousands of dollars over the usual system; but more important than that, I believe it to be the logical system for any earthquake country, or a soft ground locality like

Chicago or Tokyo. This foundation was undertaken in the interest of my clients, carefully, after many preliminary tests extending over a period of a year or more—with full knowledge of all that the matter entailed. Apparently an old subterranean water course took its way diagonally across the building lot in a streak about 20' wide and made itself felt in the building as it went up—but the natural means of reinforcement which was part of the original design known as "the reserve" was employed. And I was enabled to increase heights or weights after the foundations were in by employing the same means with no greater expense than had it been put in in the first place.

The scientific basis, tests, and figures upon which this foundation was put in will sometime be put on record by myself.

Levels taken with an instrument a day or two after the terrible quake of April 1922 showed no deviation whatever of the footings by seismic disturbance anywhere throughout the vast length and breadth of the great structure.

Only a tyro in building would spend his clients' money to avoid the natural squeeze to the extent of several inches on ground like that on which the Imperial stands. The entire foundation was intended to settle to this extent; and such settlement was provided for.

FIFTH. The swimming pool is tile-lined and purified by violet rays.

As a temporary engineering expedient—I retained the water in the tank; construction completed, the tank may be pumped out or in at will.

All gravel walks or drives are temporary only. Oya pavements are everywhere where people tread on the ground outside the building.

SIXTH. The masonry theater has seats for one thousand people. It has four 5'-6" pairs of doors opening to two stairway halls directly accessible and reaching as directly the garden at the rear.

It has also four pairs of doors 5'-6" wide on the main floor and a balcony opening to the 300' masonry promenade. Two more exits 80" wide are provided in the balcony opening to the promenade

balcony or adjoining terraces. At the rear of all of these balconies, swinging windows open to adjacent fireproof rooms or terraces. The theater is a "grotto" sculpted out of stone cast into the structure as an integral part of it. There is nothing to burn except the backs of the seats, and there is nothing "suspended" in it. It is safer than any stucco interior could possibly be.

And here a word concerning the splay and cantilever construction which I have adopted in this building throughout. The cantilever in reinforced concrete construction, when it is an extension of a continuous slab, affords a reaction that makes wide spans economically possible, balances weights over centers instead of leaving them to grasp at the sides of walls, and affords scientifically the overhanging projections which here make the novice nervous. In this building the cantilever is a principle of construction as free and romantic in fact as is the conception of the whole in form.

For an earthquake country it is an ideal system because the tremor of superimposed loads is centered squarely and fairly on supports. In a change I desired to make, the resistance to destruction of one of the larger overhangs was almost incredible.

As used in this structure it is worthy of study for its own sake. It is a new element that means a new form of Architecture.

Reality is no more to be set aside in Architecture than in other expressions of human thought and feeling. Great Art is an inner experience, coming to few, but what constitutes Truth in Art is one with Truth in Life. A seemingly insane world fights cruel battles to defend the foolish "rituals" that continually confuse it. By egotism Man is pushed further and further from origins, from inner "experience" until the voice of Principle sounds far away to him if heard at all. Truth is costly, it too, is an inner "experience." It cannot be labeled, pigeonholed, or made into rituals and live. The modern Renaissance is a ritual and doomed.

Throughout its length and breadth the new Imperial is a thoroughbred—a great building grown great in rugged native materials, built for and by and in the land in which it stands and is tied in with its Traditions. No light matter! What could one of

Belshazzar's slaves know about a thing like that? Let him call Daniel.

It is an architect's tribute to a unique nation he has loved. Nor is one single utilitarian feature deserted in this Imperial Guest House—they are the very features of the whole. One may at first not like them—but if one has studied Architecture as a scientific Art and not merely accepted it as a salesman's formula or a recipe for cooking—then the harmonious organic nature of the whole will, in time, please, edify—thrill, I say, and one may conscientiously and consistently endorse it as truly and splendidly sane. Light and shade play lovingly with the patterned, fretted, overhanging cornices, sifting patterned sunsplashes on sturdy walls, tempering but not obstructing the light. A true and simple gaiety. No other building seems to have this charming grace caught from foliage overhead in a wood or from pine branches overhanging a road.

Yet with all its grace and modernity, the Imperial has the strength of the primitive—it harks back to origins. The quality of the Imperial, as the Japanese say, is *shibui*—meaning a thing at first disliked, coming back again—interested, back again—beginning to see, and ten times revisited—loved. We have no such word. It refers to a quality in a thing that asserts itself as beauty only when one has grown to it.

There is the strength of Joy in the forms of the Imperial—the joy of strength—standing square and sturdy on their mud cushion against impending earthquakes. One may not like them—at first, but go again and see and then go again and again.

Shibui! A mysterious, quiet—deep in the oriental Soul beneath the oriental surface—fruit of an experience ages older than any culture the occident yet knows. These United States could crawl on suppliant knees to breathe its spirit and be ennobled by it. Nothing in our gift can equal this in theirs—this treasure of the humble seeking reality.

The Imperial stands true to the spirit of old Japan, it speaks a truth slumbering in those ancient depths; it is true in itself to the work it was meant to do: to shelter, give aid, comfort and entertainment to Japan's guests. It is refreshing to seekers after Truth because it has been ennobled by the strength of the primitive. The Imperial is a building not for apologists—but for enquirers, not for fakirs busy with superficial taste and morality, but for seekers of evidence of the vital creative power of Man. In the Imperial the Art of Architecture comes to grips with reality for the sake of a better order. It has no quarrel with life as lived now, but belongs at the present time to the more advanced stage of culture because it insists on every utilitarian need as an ordered thing in a harmonious whole. It is a conservation of space, energy, and time by concentration and the invention of practical ways and means to this end. This is just such conservation as existed in old Japan. That selfsame principle is here at work and should help the Japanese to reestablish that wonderful thing in the new life that appears inevitable to them. The Imperial is the first great protest against the gargantuan waste adopted by Japan from the old German precedents when there were no better ones. Since then the world has moved with incredible rapidity. Conservation of space by concentrated conveniences has gone far. The ship began it, the Pullman car took it up, the Ocean Liner went further, and now the modern Hotel, on costly ground, is at work upon it. The element that enjoyed the license of the old never-to-be-heated waste space—the element that obliterated everything with a freight-carload of luggage— put its feet up on the table and spit on the floor as regardless of environment as a horse in a stable, just so the bedding was there and the feed and water handy— won't like the Imperial at first—some of them never will.

TO MY EUROPEAN CO-WORKERS

[Published without illustrations in Wendingen, *1925]*

HEER WIJDEVELD ASKS ME FOR A MESSAGE TO MY co-workers of the "old world," I who am of this alleged "new world" that is America, see this new world among you, as I see your alleged old world in this one—and we all seem to desire much the same thing. Although we may phrase our sense of it differently or seek it in different ways, it is true that some Principle is working in us to get something—or maybe itself only—born, and we are the happy or anguished victims of its purpose as the case may be.

This seems material enough for infinite miracles.

The tree lives and fulfills its destiny, its "design" inevitably. The life-principle of the tree seems fixed and simple. Ours is really as simple though perhaps more flowing, and it is a song in our hearts, the Symphony of Nature. The song is seldom heard clearly even by those who yearn most sincerely and take most pains to hear it. It is like beautiful music in another room heard faintly and more distinctly as the door, for some reason unknown to us, opens or again closes as we listen. Nevertheless, this Principle that makes the music and that we sometimes, according to habit, call Man or Truth or Love, will have its way with us, all of us, new in old or old in new, and we serve. We become as that Man-principle wills and we are all one in effect as we are infinite in variety. Nothing we make as creative artists is ever wholly lost, if when we made it we have listened well enough to hear the music in what we do. This thing we call Happiness is our sense of action when we are touched or moved by Truth, nothing more or less, indefinite or ephemeral though it may appear. Every work of art is a great deed—and the

"thought" in it, the highest form of Action. In this Action we truly live and—are compelled to seek. So we artists live many lives and die as many deaths, eternally perhaps.

We become greater in service to the general effect, more harmonious a part of the whole—the "Universal" as we call it, as we coincide with the nature of Principle and the Principles of what we call Nature.

Meantime we communicate by means of signs, Symbols—and we too are in a sense ourselves no more than faulty Symbols as we do so; unwilling Symbols of Reality; feeble signs of the Principle, the Song of which we, by our intent listening, are learning to sing.

Any letter or numeral is a sign. A word is a symbol. Paintings, sculpture, poems, or buildings are all Symbols. Institutions, Manners, Customs, Traditions, good or bad, all are but the residuum of "Living"—to become debris left stranded upon the shores of time as life recedes or goes from them entirely, further on, perhaps.

Sun, Moon, and Stars are Symbols—Matter, no more than a symbol of what is living Spirit within. So it is natural we should regard Life as the one thing of value, and keep the life in our Symbols as expressions of Spirit—throwing them aside when they become useless or insignificant—burying them respectfully if there is need and time.

The "General effect," or "universe" or "organic whole" of life is too vast for us to seize in our imaginations—nor is it necessary to so grasp it. To fret concerning Cause or Purpose is as wise as was the boy who cut out the head of his drum to see where the sound came from. No creative artist ever does fret much about it—unless he falls sick and ceases to create and so loses direction.

We sense enough of the character of the "organic altogether" by five primitive senses made into a superior sixth, or as we evolve, perhaps infinitely more, and we gain some healthy knowledge by rightly feeling our relationship to it: that feeling we call Love. When it takes form we call it Beauty. When the feeling is in action as creative-artist we call it intuitive-inspiration. When it is at work in this Love we call it Art. We grow to ever greater perception as we faithfully and gratefully cultivate life in this sense. Our civilization depends for its value upon that cultivation, as we say, "culture." In every faithful expression of this love of life in the work of making paintings, statues, books, or buildings, or in other great deeds as expressions of Man, we grow in power to make greater likenesses—to greater comprehension.

As seed in the earth responds to light in expanding to realization of life-principle, so we respond to this life-light which is within us and gives birth to "Forms."

The growth of the Seed is a primitive symbol of our own growth, if we say Truth is Light or Love. Man makes a symbol for this light and calls it God. We cannot despise the Symbol just because reactionaries abuse it by using it as a thing of value in itself. When we try to discard it and soar in what seems a superior realm, we are probably sick with longing or weary of pretense and stupidity, tired of waiting for something to happen; a nostalgia of the soul, it may be. But we are then unfruitful to humanity because we are untrue to the reality of ourselves and so uncreative in a form of living death. Death was given us not to use to arrest or destroy beauty—but, as the greatest German has said, that we might have more life. When we ourselves become abstractions we are lost—because then we are using the symbol as a thing in itself—abusing its privilege. We are "on" Life, not "of" it—and betray our birthright inevitably. We ought to be "unhappy" and are, because we are inhuman, not fulfilling therefore, our "design," our destiny. We are drying in the ground if we are "Seeds"; the Sap is not running, we are not putting forth leaves if we are "trees"; we are not according to design, uncreative, if human beings.

Humanity has no "duty" toward the artist. The Artist none toward Humanity. It is all a matter of privilege on either side as a matter of course. It is a sense of privilege both need, rather than the sense of duty. Humanity is a quality, an element in all the artist does.

He is that element incarnate.

Life itself is the supreme impulse as Artist and Living is the supreme work of art. And human beings? Faulty "Symbols" made to communicate meanwhile in a process of Love, Birth, Growth, and Decay: a procession privileged to play in and upon and to reflect the idea that is Life. The artist is in no trance. His dream finds its work and finds its mark in the Eternity that is Now. Life is concrete—each in each, and all in all although our horizon may drift into mystery. In harmony with Principles of Nature and reaching toward Life-light, only so are we creative. By that Light we live, to become likewise. And all that need ever be painted or carved or built—are significant, colorful shadows of that Light.

IN THE CAUSE OF ARCHITECTURE: THE THIRD DIMENSION

[Published with 13 illustrations in Wendingen, *1925]*

TWENTY-SEVEN YEARS AGO A SOCIETY OF ARTS AND CRAFTS was projected at Hull House in Chicago. The usual artist disciples of Morris and Ruskin, devoted to making things by hand, and a professorial element from the university were assembled. Jane Addams, the founder of Hull House, had invited me to be present and toward the end of the enthusiastic meeting asked me to contribute to the discussion. I had then been practicing Architecture for some years and I knew what I had to say would be unwelcome—so begged leave to present my project in writing at the next meeting. I prepared the "Art and Craft of the Machine," which I then delivered, advocating the patient study of the Machine at work as the first duty of the modern artist. I had invited to be present at the meeting sheet-metal workers, terracotta manufactures, tile and marble workers, iron workers, wood workers, who were actually turning out the work that was architectural Chicago, therefore the architectural heart of America. The thesis I presented, simply stated, was—that the old ideals that had well served the handicraft of old were now prostituted to the machine—which could only abuse and wreck them, that the world needed a new ideal recognizing the nature and capability of the machine as a tool and one that would give it work to do that it could do well—before any integrity could characterize our Art. I named many things which I had found the machines then in use in the trades could already do better than it had ever been possible to do them by hand—instancing the emancipation from the old structural necessities that the machine, as an artist's tool, had already brought about. Finally, I proposed that the society be formed to intimately study the Machine's possibilities as a tool in the hand of the artist, to bring it into the service of the Beautiful—instead of serving as then and now—to destroy it.

Several brilliant disciples of Ruskin and Morris from the University of Chicago swept my propositions aside in a mood of sentimental eloquence—I was voted down and out by the enthusiastic disciples of Ruskin and Morris (whose sacred memory, it seems, I had profaned) and the Society was formed upon the same old basis of pounding one's fingers making useless things, that had been the basis of countless other "Art Societies" that had come to nothing in the end. So, together with my small band of modern industrials, I withdrew.

The Society as it was formed was a two-dimension affair that might foster Art as a pleasant amateur accomplishment, a superficial matter. It had rejected the third dimension—the integral element—on suspicion.

The Machine as an artist's tool—as a means to a great end in Art—did not exist for Ruskin and Morris, nor for the academic thought of that day.

Nor did the disciples of Ruskin and Morris, nor the architects and artists present at that much later date, see it then. They do not see it yet and that is, very largely, what is the matter with Artist[s] and with the Art, that is also craft, today.

The old structural necessity in Architecture is dead. The Machine has taken it upon itself and the *"raison d'être"* of the forms that were Architecture has therefore been taken away from them.

As the skeleton of the human figure is clothed with tissue in plastic sense to give us the human form, so the Machine has made possible expressive effects as plastic in the whole—as is the human figure as an idea of form.

In all the crafts, the nature of materials is emancipated by the Machine and the artist is freed from bondage to the old post-and-lintel form, the pilaster and architrave are senseless, and Architecture in superimposed layers is now an "imposition" in every sense.

A modern building may reasonably be a plastic whole—an integral matter of three dimensions: a child of the imagination more free than of yore, owing nothing to "orders" or "styles."

Long ago both "orders" and "styles" became empty rituals—they were never Architecture—they were merely forms cast upon the shores of time by the Spirit of Architecture in passing. Architecture is the living spirit of building truly and beautifully.

So the ground for a new life of Architecture of the third dimension—an integral Architecture—is furrowed thus by the Machine and still fallow awaits the seed of common sense to germinate and grow in it, great true forms—a vital living Architecture.

But like all simple things—too common to be interesting, too hard work to be attractive, the mastery of the Machine is still to come; and a harsh ugliness, in relentless cruelty, obscures the common good.

The principle of the Machine is the very principle of Civilization itself now focused in mechanical forms. Servants of brass and steel and mechanical systems construct Civilization's very form today!

We have, whether we like it or not, here introduced an element into human life that is mastering the drudgery of the world, widening the margin of human leisure. If dominated by human greed it is an engine of enslavement—if mastered by the artist it is an emancipator of human possibilities in creating the Beautiful.

Yet the Machine is forced to mutilate and destroy old ideals instead of serving new ones suited to its nature—and because artists are become mere fashionable accidents or social indiscretions instead of masters, civilization is forced to masquerade in forms of "Art" false a century ago; the architectural "Renaissance" a sun still setting—mistaken still for sunrise.

To face simple truth seems too fearful a thing for those now claiming the title and place of the "artist." The simpletons hug their fond prejudices and predilections in foolish attempts to make them by book or hook or crook into queer little fashionable lies or gorgeous shams, so satisfied with results that any sane and sensible treatment of a project according to its nature is laughed at by and large; dubbed a freak and shown the door. Architecture in the hands of "Architects" has become a meaningless imitation of the less important aspect of the real thing: a mean form of bad surface decoration. It is Engineering that now builds.

Until the spirit of this modern Engineering finds expression as integral decoration, which is the third dimension coming into play, Architecture does not live at all.

The tools that produce work—(and by tools industrial systems and elements are also meant)—are now asked to do work to which they are wholly unsuited—"Styles" of work that were originated by hand when stone was piled on stone, and ornament was skillfully wrought upon it with clever human fingers: forms that were produced by a sensate power. Much as we may love the qualities of beauty then natural to such use and wont—we must go forward to the larger unity, the plastic sense of the "altogether" that must now be knowledge where then it was but instinct. The haphazard and picturesque must give way to ordered beauty emancipated from human fingers; living solely by human imagination controlling, directing great coordinations of insensate power into a sentient whole. Standardization and repetition realized and beautified as a service rendered by the Machine and not as a curse upon the civilization that is irretrievably committed to it.

I am not sure that the artist in this modern sense will be much like the picturesque personality of yore—in love with himself. Perhaps the quality in this modern will take off the curls and flapping hat of that love and show himself as sterner stuff in a most unpopular guise. Nor will he be a "business man." The reward of exploitation he will not have. His task will be otherwise and elsewhere—in the shops—in the factories, with the industrial elements of his age—as William Morris tried to be with them and for them; hot with face turned backward to the Medieval world, as his was, but forward to a new one—yet unseen.

In that new world, all the resources that have accumulated to Man's credit as the Beautiful will only be useful in the Spirit in which they were created and as they stood when they were original and true forms. The Renaissance in Architecture was always false except that the admixture of ideals and races necessarily confused origins and so stultified them. And finally there is seen in America the logical conclusion of the ideal of "re-hash" underlying the European Renaissance, a mongrel admixture of all the styles of all the world. Here in the United States may be seen the final Usonian degradation[1] of that ideal—ripening by means of the Machine for destruction by the Machine. The very facility with which the "old orders of Beauty" are now become ubiquitous hastens the end. Academic thought and educational practices in America, seemingly, do not realize that the greatest of modern opportunities is being laid waste for the lack of that inner experience which is revelation in the Soul of the Artist-mind; that sense of the third dimension as an essential factor to direct and shape the vital energy of these vast resources with integral forms if they are ever to have any spiritual significance at all—if America is ever to really live.

And I know that America is a state of mind not confined to this continent—but awakening over the whole civilized world.

America by virtue of her youth and opportunity is logical leader—were she not swamped by European backwash—sunk in the "get culture quick" endeavor of a thoughtless, too-well-to-do new country like this—buying its culture ready-made, wearing it like so much fashionable clothing, never troubled by incongruity or ever seeking inner significance.

A questionable bargain in the Antique, this culture—knocked down to the highest bidder, for cash.

Through this self-satisfied, upstart masquerade—with its smart attitude and smug sensibilities—this facetious parasite, skeptical of all save Fashion, this custom-monger whose very "life," as it sees it, would be taken by Truth—the new ideal must little by little work its way upward.

Among every hundred thousand opportunities, in the commercial sense, sacrificed to Fashion and Sham—we may hope for one, sincerely groping for reality, one willing to run the gauntlet of ridicule in a great cause; one to risk the next "job" in single-minded devotion to the one in hand—or for that matter all that might come after—for the precious sense of devotion to the freedom of Truth in creative work.

All that the new order signifies will not yet be found perfectly demonstrated in any one building. Each of the more sentient efforts will have a suggestion of it—a rare one may prophecy certain qualities to come in attributes already manifest—the seed time is now but the harvest shall not be yet.

First, we shall see a process of simplification—a rejection of the old meaningless forms—an erasure of the laborious mess of detail now striving, sweating for "effect." We will have a clean line, a flat surface, a simply defined mass—to begin with. What a rubbish heap will be behind this effort when it is got well under way!

Again to life will be called a sense of materials used for their own sake: their properties of line, form, and color revealed in treatments that aim to bring them out in designs that employ their beauty as a fair means, truthful in a consistent whole. Columns, lintels, voussoirs, pilaster, architrave, capital, and cornices—the whole grammar of the Art of building fashioned when the handicraft that imposed layer on layer in the old structural sense made it a fine thing—now false—inutile: the spirit of the old gone forward—made free.

Form, in the new plastic sense, is now infinitely more elastic. The third dimension enters with the "plastic" ideal as the very condition of its existence. Realism, as the outside aspect, is inutile. The abstraction that is the "within" is now reached.

Steel framing contributes a skeleton to be clothed with living flesh; reinforced concrete contributes the splay and cantilever and the continuous slab. These are several of the new elements in building which afford boundless new expressions in Architecture, as free, compared with post and lintel, as a winged bird compared to a tortoise, or an aeroplane compared with a truck.

The plastic order brings a sense of a larger unity in the whole—and fewer parts—monoliths where once we were content with patched and petty aggregates; soaring heights and sweeping breadths of line and mass uninterrupted by niggling handicraft units, as the laboriously made aggregation in two dimensions gives way to the unity born of conditions—plastic now—the third dimension essential to its reality.

The Larkin Building, like all the work I have done, is an essay in the third dimension, a conservative recognition of the element of the Machine in modern life. In it the old order has been rejected that the Principle of Architecture may live anew. The building expresses the interior as a single great form.

Unity Temple asserts again the quality and value of the third dimension in asserting the form within to be the essential to find expression. The reinforced concrete slab as a new architectural expression, is here used for its own sake as "Architecture." This building is a cast monolith. A transition building it is, wherein the character of the wooden forms or boxes, necessary at this time in casting concrete construction, are made a virtue of the whole in "style": that process of construction made a conscious aesthetic feature of the whole. Its "style" is due to the way it was "made." A sense of the third dimension in the use of the "box" and the "slab"—and a sense of the room within as the thing to be expressed in arranging them are what made Unity Temple; instead of the two-dimension-sense of the traditional block mass sculptured into architectural form from without.

The Coonley house at Riverside is of a type employing simple individual units, adapted each to its separate purpose, finally grouped together in a harmonious whole—simple materials revealed in its construction. The style of the Coonley home is due to this simple use of materials with a sense of the human figure in scale, the prairie as an influence and a sense of the horizontal line as the line of domesticity: this home and all its relatives grows as a part of its site. It grows from it and is incorporated with it, not planted on it. And this sense of the indigenous thing, a matter of the third dimension, is a first condition of any successful treatment, of any problem, in the modern sense—as it was the secret of success in all great old work wherever it may be found, subconscious then. But it must be used consciously now as a well-defined principle. Any building should arise from its site as an expressive feature of that site and not appear to have descended upon it—or seem to be a "deciduous" feature of it. This "third dimension" element in architecture made more concrete when the work of Art is regarded as a plastic thing modeled as a fluid flowing whole, as contrasted with the idea of superimposition or aggregation or composition in the old structural sense, which was largely a two-dimension affair. No longer may we speak of "composition."

Plastic treatments are always out of the thing, never something put on it. The quality of the third dimension is found in this sense of depth that enters into the thing to develop it into an expression of its nature.

In this architecture of the third dimension "plastic" effects are usually produced from this sense of the within. The process of expression is development proceeding from generals to particulars. The process never begins with a particular preconceived detail or silhouette to secure which the whole is subsequently built up. In such two-dimensional mental processes the sense of third dimension is wholly absent, and not a natural thing but an applied thing is the inevitable result.

All the buildings I have built—large and small—are fabricated upon a unit system—as the pile of a rug is stitched into the warp. Thus each structure is an ordered fabric; rhythm and consistent scale of parts and economy of construction are greatly facilitated by this simple expedient: a mechanical one, absorbed in a final result to which it has given more consistent texture, a more tenuous quality as a whole.

I have wanted to build industrial buildings in America but unfortunately, though trained as an engineer and in commercial building, I have become known as an artist-Architect, the term "artist" being one of reproach in my country and therefore, for the moment shunned in the commercial field.

While I should have preferred to be employed in this field at home, I have been, for five years, constructing in a foreign country a romantic epic building, an architect's tribute to a unique nation he has much loved. This structure is not a Japanese building—nor an American building in Tokio. It is simply a free interpretation of the oriental spirit, once more employing the old handicraft system and materials to create a rugged, vital, monolithic building that would help Japan to create the necessary new forms for the new life that is her choice and inevitable to her now. I felt it desirable to do this without outraging all the noble Traditions which made that civilization a remarkable and precious thing in its own time.

But as a concession to the new spirit, the lava in this building and the brick are not used as structural materials. They are used as plastic covering "forms" cast in with the whole structure in decorative masses for their own sake. Where post and lintel construction is resembled it is a mere coincidence of not importance enough to be avoided.

The Olive Hill work in Los Angeles is a new type in California, a land of romance—a land that, as yet has no characteristic building material and no type of building except one carried there by Spanish missionaries in early days, a version of the Italian church and convent—now foolishly regarded as an architectural "Tradition." I feel in the silhouette of the Olive Hill house a sense of the romance of the region when seen associated with its background and in the type as a whole a thing adaptable to California conditions. This type may be made from the gravel of decayed granite of the hills easily obtained there and mixed with cement and cast in molds or forms to make a fairly solid mass either used as

blocks to compose a "unit-slab" system or monolithic in construction. This is the beginning of a constructive effort to produce a type that would fully utilize standardization and the repetition of easily manhandled units. One of the essential values of the service rendered by the Machine, as elements in an architecture modeled by the "third dimension" is this standardizing of a convenient unit for structural purposes: I am still engaged in this effort.

It is a mistaken notion that the legitimate use of the Machine precludes ornamentation. The contrary is the case. Pattern—the impress of the imagination, is more vital than it ever was in the use of any other system or "tool" in any other age. But before we can find the significant expressions that give poetry and endless variety to this new architecture in any integral sense, we shall first have protested the old "ornamentation" by reverting to clean forms expressive as such in themselves. Little by little, the use of significant virile pattern will creep in to differentiate, explain, and qualify as a property of the third dimension as poetry. And the materials and structural enclosures will ever be increasing thereby in significance and what we call beauty. Imagination will vivify the background and expression of modern life, as truly and more universally and richly than was ever before seen in the world—even in the aesthetic background of the Moors or the Chinese.

The sneer of "factory aesthetics" goes by its mark.

It is the Imagination that is now challenged, not the Memory.

When the industrial buildings of a country are natural buildings and vital expressions of the conditions underlying their existence—the domestic architecture of that country will be likewise true; a natural, indigenous expression of modern life in its broader aspects and finer opportunities. This natural expression must be conditioned upon service rendered by the Machine—the Machine bringing man the fruits, that in olden times belonged only to the mastering few—to belong now to the many. In this we see the Machine as the forerunner of Democracy.

But then the Machine will not be, as now, engaged in impartially distributing meretricious finery of a bygone age, senselessly, from avenue to alley, but as that "finery" was once really fine, so again fullness and richness of life fitted to purpose in infinite poetic variety shall come to us.

Beauty may come abide with us in more intimate spirit than ever graced and enriched the lives of the masterful-few in the ancient "Glory that was Greece" or the "Grandeur that was Rome," if we master the Machine in this integral sense. It is time we realized that Grecian buildings have been universally overrated as Architecture: they are full of lies, pretence, and stupidity. And Roman architecture, but for the nobility of the structural arch, a thing now dead—was a wholly debased version of the better Greek elements that preceded it. Both civilizations have been saddled upon us as the very ideal so long that our capacity to think for ourselves is atrophied. Yet, we may now, from the vision opened by the ideal of a plastic architecture, look down upon the limitations of this antique world with less respect and no regret. We have wings where they had only feet, usually in leaden shoes. We may soar in individual freedom of expression where they were wont to crawl—and we are the many where they were the few. A superior breath and beauty in unity and variety is a universal possibility to us—if we master the Machine and are not, as now, mastered by it.

In the modern Machine we have built up a monster image of ourselves that will eventually destroy us unless we conquer it—and turn it from its work of enslavement to its proper and ordained work of emancipation. Then, in its proper place—the margin of human leisure immeasurably widened—the plastic in Art become a free-flowing channel for imaginative creative effort, we will have a background for life that is integral—a setting incomparably more organic and expressively beautiful as a whole than has ever been known before in the world—and more than that, an expression in itself of the best ideals, the purest sentiment for the beauty of Truth in all forms of life—ever yet realized by Man.

---

1. The first known written reference by Wright to the term *Usonia*. The term, meaning the United States and its culture, is further defined in "In the Cause of Architecture: The Architect and the Machine," p. 227.

THE PICTURES WE MAKE

During the spring of 1927 Wright and Olgivanna were living in New York at the apartment of his sister Maginel Wright Barney. It was a time when he had no architectural work, and his principle earnings came from The Architectural Record, *whose editor had commissioned him to write the series "In the Cause of Architecture." Furthermore, he had accrued terrible debts due to the rebuilding of Taliesin and various legal entanglements prompted by suits brought against him by his ex-wife, Miriam Noel. Olgivanna was in jeopardy of being deported because of problems with her visa. When the courts threatened to expel her from the country, several of Wright's influential friends, led by Senator Henry J. Allen, former governor of Kansas, were able to secure her safe refuge in the United States.*

If his article of 1918 in which he attacked certain aspects of Chicago's culture (p. 154), seems a strong and vitriolic attack, its bitterness in no way compares with this even more amplified criticism of the urban life of New York City. Indeed, Wright's four-month forced residence in Manhattan provoked, some years later, the idea for Broadacre City, his solution, or antidote, to urban living. [Unpublished essay]

FOR FOUR MONTHS I'VE BEEN MARKING TIME IN NEW YORK, dying a hundred deaths a day on the New York gridiron in the stop-and-go of the urban criss-cross.

Hanging above this spasmodic to-and-fro, in-and-out, up-and-down, is agonizing uproar. Any human being caught in it finds himself to be all out of drawing with the universal mechanical-aspect of everything about him. Anything human, articulate in him, is drowned in noise just as his movements are frustrated by adverse motion. The more efficient man's machines become the more insignificant he becomes himself, it seems.

I have waited to cross from street to street; waited to get suspended on elevators in the vertical streets up-ended on interior streets; waited to get out again and get on to the busy gridiron again; waited for red lights to go on or white lights to come off or both to go off or go on again: waited indoors and waited outdoors.

Outside are you in the red? You are wrong. In the white, you are right. Inside you are in the red: you are going down. You are in the white: you are going up.

I have waited, carefully, and watched my step that I might live to wait again and continue, again, to wait. Miraculously I have preserved life and identity in common with six million others more or less as I am.

I have seen the Deluge. It is the printed matter that inundates the city, piled on street corners, stacked in every lobby, waiting at the gates of every train, waiting on the floor outside the hotel bedroom door. Everywhere something on which to sit may be found or an occasion be found to sit, crowds may be seen with faces properly dim and dreary over papers, semi-books, or demi-magazines, mostly pages of pictures—what brains the vast gregarious multitude has, blotting up "news" in the form of sensational pictures of recent murder or scandal or sport, scientific misinformation or smooth politics. The Deluge is supposed to turn these concerns inside out for significance, but, mostly, only contributes another picture of the pictures to the picture and adds to the general confusion a fresh falsity.

The throng seems to see nothing—they are the blind, hurrying by.

And at night the wilderness of electric signs, a crush of cabs, and crowds afloat or afoot to get into the crowds of photo pictures or crowds of plays.

Small gray action photographs, all but lost are its meager offerings in the midst of exaggerated palace-splendors of a vulgar sort.

Many plays are on the stages of a curious assortment of new and old playhouses—plays of sex appeal, sex intrigue: sex satisfaction. Plays on sex triumphant, sex foiled, or sex despoiled—until the one passionate interest evident as the living nerve in pictures and "shows" is "sex." The leg is the living symbol, the never-failing "motif" in this civilization of ours. The leg is the real significance that is known in it. Legs make the truest picture we have most artistically done. Whether we know it or not, it is true that customs and manners are fashioned upon "the leg." Silken legs rising from shapely shoes to flexing knees moving along the streets in masses everywhere make one believe society, by way of the short skirt, turned centipede or millipede coming and at the same time going: on the sidewalks an interweaving of myriad legs.

A glance above at the close-sheathed heads is more reassuring. There is still the look of happy intelligence in the eyes that peer from beneath the edges of the hoods. Evidently this is the era of triumph for the millipede.

Men? A drab characterless crowd with no style. Drab hats carefully bent with studied carelessness over what countenances circumstances may have left to them—carelessness curiously ineffective and unconvincing.

The men have been blotted out by the fashions allotted to them as they have themselves, perhaps, been blotted up by the opposite sex?

Between times I have searched luxurious shops and gigantic stores for beautiful things: things that might be worn or looked at for themselves for the sake of their significance, or that I should want to live with for the same reason. I have seen an enormous glut of everything—and seen nothing of intrinsic value as culture.

In styles, luxuries, buildings, motor cars; in whatever is bought and sold or may be had for love or money, I have looked for significance of form: some integrity to justify these pictures we are so busy making—but to find only that legs are truly significant. "Things" of art or craft or of architecture are only in all this scene a pictorial irrelevance. Even such thinking as passes in the popular current for thought is merely pictorial, too. The fiction is sometimes true. Truth has become fiction.

Looking for interior significance in all this bewildering quantity certainly ends in nothing true to itself. Looking for an exterior of anything anywhere, except bare machinery, that might have been allowed to live for the sake of the inner-life of the thing itself—leads to the conclusion that the "picture" is here in everything, for its own sake only.

We, then, must admit this age to be the age of the picture-minded; and that means in art at best, childlike and at worst, childish.

The pictorial age! So far as the expression of our own life goes in the "things" we make, that life goes by default. The pictures we make for ourselves of ourselves, to each other, or of what is honestly ours, or of what we really are, all are something else. Few, if any, of them know how to be honest.

So greater New York seems, in a singularly significant sense, the Triumph of the Insignificant.

The insignificance is, however, significant.

But aside from this search for significant expression in art and craft, what driving force is in it all! It burrows and builds, tears down and rebuilds, and thunders along as though thunder it must. It goes and grows more go-full in the going. This motor-car culture! It comes furiously upon itself to bound and rebound with the furious energy in it.

There is in it the exaltation of the "joy ride," and a joy ride needs no objective for there is pleasure enough in just "going."

Who cares where this is all going? The important thing is the stimulus—or is it the relief—in this act of "going."

Why, then, should the pictures we make or break as we come and go mean more than entertainment? If they entertain or flatter us and delude us into a belief in our own virtue in this motion which is our notion just now, and, too, our emotion—why bother about significance?

At any rate we go faster, further, and more comfortably than man ever did before. We can stay most anywhere, live safer and more softly in regard to any or all of the five senses than ever before.

Should we, then, so newly arrived at that, find fault? It is to remember that we are a lot of erstwhile Europeans turned loose in liberty, all seemingly jealous of each other in it—a proverbial hungry orphan turned loose in the bakeshop—what might be expected of him is what may be expected of us until hunger, of the sort, is satisfied.

What hunger? Well I should say the universal hunger for the picture.

We enjoy nothing so much as the pictures we ourselves imagine we make. To make them—that instinct of the child—is, in us, at large in liberty and we revel in the pictorial!

But this hunger to gratify life by "making the picture" is not good enough. It is as physical a hunger as that of the orphan in the bakeshop, if we fairly take the simile from the stomach to the mind.

Imagination functions in all this on a rather low plane.

A deeper sense of reality will some day make the hunger for the picture a demand for significance, or refuse the picture.

I have always sympathized with the mortal who neatly blew out his brains and left a note behind to explain that "he was tired of all this eternal buttoning and unbuttoning."

We erect a tedious, flimsy pictorial screen, mostly buttons, between reality and ourselves. And we assemble a similar one out of our "things"! A cult of "things" is what this "culture" is now that we call civilization—really is it only an imperative need on the part of the society to seem, rather than to be, competently backed up by the policeman and the college, all encouraged and consoled by the "picture."

It is easy to be bitter and say bitter things about it all when you commence hunting "significance" as well as physical responsibility for "buttons."

Perhaps we are improving upon famous hypocrisies of the past in this heterogeneous mix of Goldsteins, O'Tooles, Smiths, Jones, Wanamachers, Petroviskis, Petersons, Carrambas, Ledoux, and Teufelmachers, all broiling together on the New York gridiron and groping for a common denominator.

But meanwhile it is astonishing to see all these erstwhile aliens now wearing similar buttons in the same places, all making the same gestures on the same occasions and, in the multiplicity of their concerns religious, political, familiar, all as snugly alike as peas in a pod—or growing so! Growing so because the country aims to standardize all as soon as possible to a type that does seem to be slowly emerging from the melting pot and that we may begin to speak of, and speak to, as "American."

Beneath all these gratuitous human inhibitions whatsoever, there lives something that holds the struggling human mass firmly together. Its mechanism is automatically working to some common end.

There seems to be the same organic quality in the human life that is struggling here toward "recognition" that we have seen at work in trees and plants and the ordered cycle of the seasons. It seems to cohere and persevere in spite of waste and slip and perhaps will until the man evolves who will demand significance and refuse to be interested in "picturizing" except as the pictures are a by-product of a reality he understands.

Some day in America a man will not be content to shamelessly borrow the antique to make false pictures to characterize his own fresh-life. The machine that enables the efficiency of his desire for pictures to now outrun his understanding to the contrary, notwithstanding.

But I am an artist interested in significance only where it may be a beautiful expression of this life of our own, in our buildings, costumes, theater, decoration, the art and craft of the age, those "things," therefore, that are the use and proof of culture in any age.

So, in this enormous pig-piling I look for that, tired, yet the more hungry for significance. Frustrated, but clinging to hope—as you may see.

Some great essential in this whirling vortex must be falsely covered up.

Something essential to realization is missed from sight—hushed up.

It is as though this ideal of democracy, to which we imagine we hold fast, depended upon forcing a half-truth or a bold untruth upon the truth of ourselves and others, until the hypocrisy that is "the picture" is common and necessary in order to enable us to live at all. Become second-nature.

It is, therefore, impossible for society to see itself, and, except in rare individuals, it is unlikely that men or women will ever see themselves face to face. In this moral cowardice we may see all the justification there is for recourse to such "picture making" as ours.

False shames always forbid salutary acknowledgements. To successfully deny the animal we falsify, we have invented various kinds of "spirituality" and turn from the fundamental earth-element in us to beyond the skies. We even pass laws and arrest the man to get him into the picture we imagine we are making.

To be "unspiritual" is to be dreaded because it is to be unpictorial. To be a materialist is to be damn'd for the same reason.

The platform, therefore, from which we are to climb by a slender cord to greater heights is officially kicked from under our feet before we are ready to leave it by our own strength—and we are hanged by the rope we would climb by. Thanks to the shallow idealists who are responsible for the present picture!

Just as truly as it is a mere picture "they" are making with all their pictures, so is the significance of the final picture known to none.

The astounding thing in it all is the deadly animosity bred by the sameness, the unanimity, the conformity of it.

The fame and the shame of it all comes to the same thing. Mostly mechanical, it is a thing of stuffs and buttons, of empty symbols and half-forgotten rites, carpenter work, engines, and wheels; a framework of steel and an "outside" upon which every resource of money and brains is lavished to make it—regardless—a picture that will please the mentors: themselves no less pictorial.

A thirsting desert of congregated humanity on hard pavements, pathetically clinging, for all its cocksureness, to memories of natural beauty. Human beings still looking forward or backward to grass and trees, hills, fields, and streams; longing, secretly, for the sea spaces or the desert spaces. Human beings, meanwhile keeping alive little mementos of all that, like fireplaces that burn wood, sometimes in shop windows. And for that reason human beings, to salvage what humanity they have left, cling to the works of great art into which antique cultures stored up proof of their love and understanding of nature qualities—fortunately thus stored up as proof of quality now seen as their pottery, painting, and sculpture. These things are become now precious relics, embodiments of qualities in form and idea that were loved and that lived in that far-off time? Well, cling then. Cling with instinctive feeling to those things of ancient culture and cling desperately. In this terrible drift toward monotony, cling to those sentient ties that are relic still to the original birthright of the races. But you cling mostly in vain as may be seen beneath the surface because it is evident there, even now, that we shall fail to make them ours, that way.

But we do cling to "relics" here in this rendezvous-with-riches of all the races, and try to see the taste relics as a cherished or copied reflection of "virtue."

Vaulted "modernity" is everywhere clinging, by instinct, and attempting by attitudinizing or by "picturizing," pitiful enough, to vicariously re-create the joys of those great periods and makeshift to live in the imitation, neglectful, however, of the proper gestures. But "imitation," too, will soon be trampled down and out by the human herd—stampeding itself as a herd, because of the machine.

The artifex alone can give us the significance we lack, and help us to arrive at such expression that the art of the inevitably artificial will be to the human spirit what clear springs of water, blue sky, green grass, and noble trees are to parched human senses. For where the artificial is a necessity, there the artist must be creatively at work on "significance," as a higher form of life, or the life of the human spirit will perish in its endeavor.

The "artificiality" laid upon us by the desire to be civilized is not a matter only of appearances. The artificial is not merely superficial if there is necessity for it. And there is that necessity in our era. That necessity carries within itself the secret of the beauty it must have to keep it fit to live with or to live in or to live on. That beauty may even be something to live for. The picture, when that interpretation of necessity arrives, will take care of itself. The picture will be a natural result, a consequence, not a cause.

Eventually are we going to have to live for the necessarily artificial whether we want to or not and be compelled to allow necessity its own honest beauty?

Unless what we now miscall culture is made natively fit and not allowed to remain "artificially artificial," this picture we are now so extravagantly making can only hasten the end. The buttons, stuffs, dictums, wheels, and "things" we are now making will smother the essential life they were made to conceal and this experiment in civilization we fondly call democracy will find its way to the scrap heap, one into which no subsequent race will paw for proofs of our quality, with much success.

Suppose some catastrophe should wipe out Usonia at this moment.

Suppose, in ten centuries, historians or antiquarians should seek significance of what we were in the veins of us—in the ruins that remained, what would they find? What is the nature of this pictorial contribution to the life and wisdom or the beauty of the ages? Going forward to look back upon

it—what could we see, were our tentative attempt to be suddenly interrupted and finished as it stands?

Would the future find that we were a jackdaw people with a monkey psychology given over to the vice of devices looking to devices for salvation?

Just the same, they would find bits of every civilization that ever took place in the sun hoarded in all sorts of irrelevant places in ours.

They would dig up traces of Greek sarcophagi for banking-house, twelfth-century cathedrals for meeting houses—relics of dwellings in twenty-seven varieties, none genuine in character, all absurdly mixed. They would find toilet appurtenances of former ages preserved as parlor ornaments in ours. They would find a wilderness of wiring, wheels, and complex devices of curious ingenuity—and buttons. They might get traces of devices that enabled men to take to the air like birds, or go into the water as fishes, or both together and they could get relics of our competent schemes of transportation and remarkable voice transmission. But I think [the] most characteristic relic of all would be our plumbing: our baths, water closets, and wash bowls, white tiles and piping. Next would be the vast confusion of riveted steel work in various states of disintegration where it was imbedded in concrete. Where the steel was not so buried all would be gone except here and there where whole machines might be entombed in concrete chambers and so preserved to arouse speculation and curiosity. Or cause amusement as they might be taken as relics of a faith in devices—a faith that failed! Of the cherished "picture" nothing would remain.

Our books might, some of them, be preserved to assist discovery, although chemicalized paper would probably have destroyed them utterly. Such glass and pottery as we make could tell little but falsehoods. Certain fragments of stone building would remain to puzzle the savant, for they would be Greek or Roman or medieval—Gothic, Egyptian, or Byzantine, or a pseudo-"Renaissance" that was something that never told anyone anything at all. Only our industrial buildings could tell anything worth knowing about us. But few of them would survive that long—only those where steel was buried in concrete. The glass would be found but the frames and all else gone. They would have no skyscraper to gauge us by. Not one would be there.

How and where, then, were it suddenly interrupted, would our great progressive democratizing based upon picturizing take its place in the procession of civilizations that rose and fell in appointed times and places?

And yet—in this attempt behind the picture, we may see culture becoming more plastic? Are not our modern ideas less a constructed thing and more constructive where we are beginning to emerge from the first intoxication of liberty? The eventual consequence of freedom surely is the elimination of the insignificant. Imprisoning forms and abstractions grow weaker as character grows stronger according to nature and this it can only do in freedom such as we profess—if only we will practice it. And in spite of our hypocrisy and adventitious reactions we really do yearn to practice that freedom to a greater extent, inhibition and prohibition, notwithstanding.

Yes, there is a new sense of truer freedom growing up in all this cruel waste. A freedom, already impatient of pseudo-classic picturizing, that will sweep our borrowed finery, and the pictures we make in it, to the museums and live.

THE FRANK LLOYD WRIGHT COLLECTION OF JAPANESE ANTIQUE PRINTS

On January 6 and 7, 1927, a portion of Wright's collection of Japanese prints was sent to the Anderson Galleries in New York for exhibition and auction. Wright then wrote this substantive introduction to the sales catalog. The sale was ordered by the Bank of Wisconsin so that the mortgage it held on Taliesin could be paid. The debt incurred at this point was largely due to the expense of rebuilding Taliesin after the fire of April 1925. This would not be the first time that Wright turned to his vast collection of woodblock prints and culled certain ones for sale in order to offset his debts. [Published as a catalog by Anderson Galleries, 1927]

THIS COLLECTION OF JAPANESE ANTIQUE PRINTS HAS BEEN made by one who, beginning twenty-four years ago to cultivate the print and profit by the revelations it brought to Western minds about that time, has never since ceased to learn from it and be refreshed by it as a thing of intrinsic spiritual value. This ought to mean of genuine fine-art value. And it does.

As compared with other objets d'art, the Japanese print is still undiscovered except by the chosen few who initiate "movements" or as "highbrows" batten upon them and endanger the true cultural values by presenting their fad as a hallmark of the aesthetic elect. The fact remains that the message brought to the Western art world by the print is fundamental to our present cultural structure, so far as it may be considered to have any new aesthetic life at all. But the lesson has been learned superficially only. We may go to school more deeply in earnest than before to the purity and wisdom and gospel of elimination that it preaches.

Most of the "shop talk" of the modern artist is a filtering through the turgid realism of the occidental brain of the thing that supremely and calmly these prints in themselves *are*: Beauty abstract in immaculate form; so concise in expression, so true to the means by which it exists as imagery of graven lines stamped on silken paper and patterned with color stamped on it likewise, that as inoculated tissue they hold their visions with a native grace supreme in the history of art.

But to have these supreme values it is essential that the print be a perfect specimen of its kind. It was a most sensitive craft that produced it, probably high-water mark in the craftsmanship of the world; and for every "perfect" specimen there were many not quite flawless. Never were two alike. Especially was there great waste in the engravings of landscapes designed by Hiroshige. Prints of Hokusai's designs, for some reason, are more uniformly good, except the late editions. Of every subject of the early periods, of every print seen there may be only a few copies in existence, and often but one. Of the glorious middle period from 1700 to 1800 the same thing applies, because while carefully kept when they were kept at all, Tokyo, their original home, has been shaken or burned to the ground four or five times—and now a sixth—since they originated. It is evident that we see today but a small section of the horizon as it originally existed. The prints were never much treasured by the Japanese aristocracy. This fact, with the fragile nature of their hold on life, unless treasured, accounts for their rarity.

America, since the sales of European collections in the past few years, owing to old world conditions, has been concentrating the world's stock in her museums and the private collections of a few wealthy men whose connoisseurship is an avocation affording them much joy, but the public not much profit, until, as in the case of the Spaulding Collection of Boston, they become the property of fine-art museums, as most of them seem destined to do in course of time. But were the world's stock to be distributed among the museums and schools where students might come into contact with them, not more than a dozen such institutions could hope to have representative collections, and all the other thousands of them merely a suggestive piece or two.

Compared with their intrinsic value as valid works of great art and with the market measure of other art objects, the prices paid for them are relatively insignificant. The examples brought together here are extraordinarily fine, most of them the very finest obtainable by a search lasting more than twenty years; and without exception they have all been proved so, through the process of selection and elimination by one who has been more intimately in touch with the Japanese print collections of the world during those years than almost anyone else. This is also true of the Hiroshige landscapes as found in this collection. They show to what heights this art of colored wood engraving rose in the hands of craftsmen inspired by those greatest of landscape artists—Hokusai and Hiroshige. This may be seen only when the *notan* is perfect, the blacks transparent, and the register flawless, as in these examples.

The first solo exhibition of Hiroshige landscapes was made by the present writer and collector at the Art Institute of Chicago upon his first return from Japan in 1907[1]. The appreciation of the landscape has been slower than that of the figure pieces owing to the fleshy nature of oriental realism, and to the fact that so many carelessly printed specimens are always found in sales and in curio shops. But the fine specimen of the choice subject is more rare and more important to us, and, as may be seen in these selected and proved pieces, of supreme artistic value.

While the pursuit of the finer specimens of the Japanese print has been largely limited to a few connoisseurs of wealth and influence in Europe, Japan, and America, the increasing number of people with artistic judgement who are now attracted to them as rare and beautiful things, buying them for the joy of owning a specimen or two of undoubted distinction, are perhaps the best friends of this art—an art that America, by virtue of her wealth and foresight, seems destined to hold in trust for posterity. In Japan there remain but two collections of any note; in Europe not more than three or four. In America there are perhaps sixteen major collections, and several of them—larger than any two abroad—are already promised to art museums. The collection of one museum—The Metropolitan Museum of Art, New York—is even now a distinguished and representative one.

As a marketable product in shops in Japan or America or Europe, the fine specimens of this art and craft are practically extinct; so that "market values" so-called, if ever they existed, have ceased to exist, and the supreme thing of its kind is priceless. The portfolio is an increasingly valuable institution in our aesthetic life. And it may have no content so significant, so valid intrinsically, and so vital to America's future artistic development, as fine specimens of the creations of that group of artists working in happy seclusion during the era of Japanese art that blossomed in the print, from the year 1700 to 1840. Compared with their nearest equivalents, engravings and etchings by great European masters, they may still be had at a lesser price. Yet they are more important to our future as a safe means of inspiration, are far greater as aesthetic treasures.

The specimens gathered together here may be subdivided into several groups:

1. Rare primitives, including Harunobu.
2. Figure pieces from Harunobu to Sharaku.
3. Actor prints (*hosoye*)[2]

The actor prints included here are all valuable human documents, recording as they do in painstaking detail the costumes and customs of old Japan. The record is authentic, as these drawings portray actual characters in Japanese life and legend as costumed and presented on the stage of Yedo in this period.

The leader in the designing of these actual characterizations was Shunsho, whose work was really *nishikiye* "brocade pictures"—the name the populace knew them by. His designs were "brocade," while those of Shunyei—a great contemporary devoting himself to the same type—were "mosaics," as to color treatment. The "line" of the two masters is as radically different as in Harunobu and Kiyonaga.

Shunko, usually excellent, was similar to Shunsho, as were a number of others designing prints of this type in that period.

Shunyei is undoubtedly one of the virile figures of the entire school, equaling Sharaku in characterization and as a delineator of general effects, far his superior.

It is in these actor prints that the full charm and force of the art are shown most surely and that it achieves its most felicitous results. The record so made is the most valuable commentary on a civilization which was unique, and aesthetic beyond any other of which we possess memorials or traditions. We have here a truly indigenous art, rendered by the most perfect craftsmanship ever seen. But for this documentary evidence coming down to us in this slender form, all authentic traces of it would have disappeared forever.

The so-called actor prints in *hosoye* form are great possessions from this standpoint, as well as from that of the complete triumph of art over the severe limitations set by the nature of the print itself—as a print. They run the whole gamut of varied emotion-al expression, never failing to achieve the precise effect intended. And the variety is extraordinary.

Another special type within the main group is the *hashirakake* or slender *kakemono* for the wooden posts or pillars of the Japanese house— decorative forms in which all the Ukiyoe artists seemed to take delight. It is one of the most characteristically Japanese and most useful to us from a decorative standpoint as it undoubtedly was to them.

4. The Landscapes of Hokusai and Hiroshige. Hokusai was the greatest *interpreter* of the spirit of Japanese life in Japanese landscape; Hiroshige the most truthfully simple *presenter* of its lineaments and people as he saw and loved them—and laughed with them, for he was an incorrigible humorist. The one was a great artist in his handling of "nature"; the other a simple poet satisfied to present it as he felt it. Both were valuable cultural assets beyond anything of a similar nature elsewhere in the world. Both were native sons preserving a record of a vanishing world within this world which they loved and understood, and which by the narrow margin of their work alone has appeared before us to teach us our own way forward—at what seems a period of chaos, of mere photographic ideas of form leading nowhere.

5. *Kwacho*—Birds and Flowers. The *kwacho* group embraces a special phase of expression in Japanese art. The ideal here seemed to be to create charming graphic poems accompanied frequently by a literal one, the one enhancing the other—the Japanese script seeming in no way to mar the effect, even when written on the sky spaces of the print. And often it was so managed as to add to rather than detract from the composition as a whole.

6. Upright Views. Red sealed.*
The Hundred Views of Yedo.
For some reason, or many, the fashion at this period turned the horizontal landscape block upright and a

*The red seals which have sometimes hurt the sensibilities of the connoisseur are really an essential factor in the effect of the whole. They are invaluable in producing that "atmosphere" which is so clearly "out-of-doors" in this series. They are a characteristic Japanese subtlety—bold as they seem.

new thing under the sun came with it, through Hiroshige—a breadth and bigness of treatment that insist upon a sense of the whole scene of which the view shown is but a glimpse in detail. The large objects crossing the view, between which you peer at the scene beyond, or just coming in or going out or passing beneath, caught by a mere fraction in some cases, but always giving atmosphere and a sense of reality, are peculiar to this work at this time, stating a simple truth in landscape design which our Western schools have since profited by. Here landscape becomes "pattern" in the sense that it is an element in good decoration always.

In the opinion of the more enlightened Japanese lovers of art, this series represents the height of Hiroshige's power—therefore of any such power of which human life has made a record.

These scenes comprise the whole of Japanese life, in every imaginable aspect where life out-of-doors bears any relation to life indoors, or where human interests as they then existed in the human figure of the time touched in any way the nature-environment it really understood and naturally worshipped.

In this entire collection it is only fair to say that there are *no* inferior prints. All of them, without

exception, are superior examples in splendid first state, and most of them perfect untrimmed specimens of their kind—peerless examples of this art and craft. They are all untouched in every way, it having been deemed best not even to stretch or press them, nor to mend any wormholes that might be in them. Any such holes are disregarded in describing the condition of the print. If desired they can easily be filled by an expert, leaving no trace.

Any example disappointing its purchaser as to condition as described may be returned, and the purchase price will be refunded. This holds good also as to any reasonable suspicion which a purchaser may consider to attach to a print as in any slightest manner tampered with.

It is assumed that the purchasers of such specimens as are presented here will be familiar with the technical matters relating to the prints. Only a characterization of the subject and references to the nature of the print as a specimen of its kind as seen by the collector, will be made, as so many times in so many places this dry matter has been already fully recorded.

1. See footnote 1 in "In the Cause of Architecture: Purely Personal."
2. *Hosoye* refers to a long, narrow print, about 13 × 6", a common format for actor prints.

IN THE CAUSE OF ARCHITECTURE I:
THE ARCHITECT AND
THE MACHINE

The editor of The Architectural Record, M. A. Mikkelsen, was sympathetic to Wright's work and mission. In 1926 he commissioned the architect to write a series of articles under the title used in 1908 and 1914, "In the Cause of Architecture." Mikkelson began publishing the series in the May 1927 issue, and he offered to pay Wright five hundred dollars for each of the five articles. Mikkelsen extended the commission to include another nine articles for the next year. These earnings brought Wright a total of seven thousand dollars during a time when he was especially financially pressed. There was little or no architectural work coming to his office, and the stock market crash of October 1929 led to the cancellation of his most significant contract, the San Marcos-in-the-Desert resort hotel—a loss of a potential commission of forty thousand dollars.

From the beginning of his work on these articles, Wright felt that he was engaged in his most important writing to date. He wrote to Mikkelson:

> Herewith is the 2nd article in the series.[1] Contrary to expectation this needs no illustration. As you will see, it is an important clearing the way for what follows and is indispensable. It is no negligible article—because in it matters that have confounded architects for centuries are made a little clearer. It is the best and most important thing I have written, I think, and ought to whet the appetite for what is to come.
>
> There will be plenty of illustrations before we are through.
>
> Tell me frankly always what you think of what I do. It helps. . . .[2]

Some additional articles, intended for the series, were not published in the Record, but Wright kept on writing because he wanted to incorporate the entire series into a book. Aware of this desire on Wright's part to make a book of the articles, Mikkelsen wrote to him:

> It is understood that you are to have the right later on to reproduce in book form the five articles about to appear in The Architectural Record under the general title In the Cause of Architecture.
>
> We shall be very glad indeed to see them in book form with an acknowledgement of the

fact that they appeared originally in The Architectural Record.

No doubt you will want to add other material and possibly use illustrations in the book.

I am convinced that the book will have a profitable sale but I do not think we should undertake to publish it for you. As publishers we are equipped to reach the architectural profession but not to reach the general public and the book will have a much wider sale if it is handled by Knopf or some other house which specializes in book publishing.[3]

Mikkelsen was indeed pleased with the series as the articles came in: "I am delighted with the article on 'The Logic of the Plan.' It is interesting, suggestive, and sound—the sort of gospel which, through you, I am eager to present to the architectural profession."[4]

The series opens with Wright's view of the machine as beneficial or destructive, depending upon how it was to be understood and used. He addresses the issue of the machine in the twentieth century just as he had more than twenty-five years earlier in his famous Hull House paper, "The Art and Craft of the Machine." Paralleling a finer understanding of machine methods, his articles explore the various materials on hand in the building industry: stone, brick, wood, steel, reinforced concrete, sheet metal, and glass. These he later refers to as "the tools in the tool box" at the disposal of designer and builder. Reinforced concrete, steel, and glass he especially qualifies as "the miracles of our modern era." Imagination, plan, form, beauty, and style also are featured. Wright believed that the average architect was unconscious of creative design and also unconscious of the nature of materials. Architecture across the nation attested to these two conditions, and Wright was fighting to open the eyes of architects to better solutions. These articles formed a vehicle for his warnings. They were addressed to the profession, but Wright also wanted to reach the American public.

Two years after the articles appeared, Wright prepared a mock-up for a book tentatively titled Creative Matter in the Nature of Materials. *He edited some of the texts, selected illustrations, and designed the format, but nothing came of his plans to publish the book, and the mock-up now resides in the Frank Lloyd Wright Archives as an unfinished project.*

As with his 1901 paper, "The Art and Craft of the Machine," Wright went back to these articles several times during his life, worked on them, revised them, and amplified them. But they appear here as he first published them.[Published without illustrations in The Architectural Record, May 1927]

1. "What Styles Mean to the Architect."
2. Letter from Frank Lloyd Wright to M. A. Mikkelsen, September 30, 1927. The Frank Lloyd Wright Archives.
3. Letter from M. A. Mikkelsen to Frank Lloyd Wright, March 15, 1927. The Frank Lloyd Wright Archives.
4. Letter from M. A. Mikkelsen to Frank Lloyd Wright, August 31, 1927. The Frank Lloyd Wright Archives.

THE MACHINE IS THE ARCHITECT'S TOOL—WHETHER HE likes it or not. Unless he masters it, the Machine has mastered him.

The Machine? What is the machine?

It is a factor Man has created out of his brain, in his own image—to do highly specialized work, mechanically, automatically, tirelessly, and cheaper than human beings could do it. Sometimes better.

Perfected machines are startlingly like the mechanism of ourselves—anyone may make the analogy. Take any complete mechanistic system and compare it with the human process. It is new in the world, not as a principle but as a means. New but already triumphant.

Its success has deprived Man of his old ideals because those ideals were related to the personal functions of hands and arms and legs and feet.

For feet, we have wheels; for hands, intricate substitutes; for motive power, mechanized things of brass and steel working like limited hearts and brains.

For vital energy, explosives or expansives. A world of contrivance absorbs the inventive energy of the modern brain to a great extent and is gradually mastering the drudgery of the world.

The Machine is an engine of emancipation or enslavement, according to the human direction and control given it, for it is unable to control itself.

There is no initiative will in machinery. The man is still behind the monster he has created. The monster is helpless but for him—

I have said monster—why not savior?

Because the Machine is no better than the mind that drives it or puts it to work and stops it.

Greed may do with it what it did with slaves in "the glory that was Greece and the grandeur that was Rome"—only do it multiplied infinitely. Greed in human nature may now come near to enslaving all humanity by means of the Machine—so fast and far has progress gone with it.

This will be evident to anyone who stops to study the modern mechanistic Moloch and takes time to view it in its larger aspects.

Well—what of it! In all ages Man has endured the impositions of power, has been enslaved, exploited, and murdered by millions—by the initiative wills back of arms and legs, feet and hands!

But there is now this difference—the difference between a bow and arrow and gunpowder. A man with a machine may murder or enslave millions, whereas it used to take at least thousands to murder millions. And the man behind the machine has nothing on his conscience. He merely liberates an impersonal force.

What is true of the machine as a murderer is just as true of it as a servant.

Which shall it be? It is for the creative artist to decide—For no one else. The matter is sociological and scientific only in its minor aspects. It is primarily a matter of using the machine to conserve life, not destroy it. To enable human beings to have life more abundantly. The use of the machine can not conserve life in any true sense unless the mind that controls it understands life and its needs, as *life*—and understands the machine well enough to give it the work to do, that it can do well and uses it to that end.

Every age and period has had its technique. The technique of the age or period was always a matter of its industrial system and tools, or the systems and tools were a matter of its technique. It doesn't matter which. And this is just as true today.

This age has its own peculiar—and, unfortunately, unqualified technique. The system has changed. The Machine is our normal tool.

America (or let us say Usonia—meaning the United States—because Canada and Brazil are America too)—Usonia is committed to the Machine and is Machine-made to a terrifying degree. Now what has the mind behind and in control of the Machine done with it to justify its existence, so far? What work suited to its nature has been given it to do? What in the way of technique has been developed by its use that we can say really serves or conserves Life in our country outside mere acceleration of movement?

Quantity production?—Yes. We have ten for one of everything that earlier ages or periods had. And it is worth so far as the quality of life in it goes, less than one-tenth of one similar thing in those earlier days.

Outside graceless utility, creative life as reflected in "things" is dead. We are living in the past, irreverently mutilating it in attempting to modify it—

creating nothing—except ten for one. Taking the soul of the thing in the process and trying to be content with the carcass or shell or husk—or whatever it may be, that we have.

All Man-made things are worthy of life. They may live to the degree that they not only served utilitarian ends, in the life they served but expressed the nature of that service in the form they took as things. That was the beauty in them and the one proof of the quality of life in those who used them. To do this, love entered into the making of them. Only the joy of that love that gives life to the making of things proves or disproves the quality of the civilization that produced them.

See all the records of all the great civilizations that have risen and fallen in course of Time and you may see this evidence of love as joy in the making of their things. Creative artists—that is workmen in love with what they were making, for love of it— made them live. And they remain living after the human beings whose love of life and their understanding of it was reflected in them, are thousands of years dead. We study them longingly and admire them lovingly and might learn from them—the secret of their beauty.

Do we?

What do we do with this sacred inheritance? We feed it remorselessly into the maw of the Machine to get a hundred or a thousand for one as well as it can do it—a matter of ubiquity and ignorance—lacking all feeling, and call it progress.

Our "technique" may therefore be said to consist in reproduction, imitation, ubiquity. A form of prostitution other ages were saved from, partly because it was foolish to imitate by hand the work of another hand. The hand was not content. The machine is quite content. So are the millions who now have as imitations bearing no intimate relation to their human understanding, things that were once the very physiognomy of the hearts and minds—say the souls of those whose love of life they reflected.

We love life, we Usonians as much as any people. Is it that we are now willing to take it in quantity too—regardless of inferior quality and take all as something canned—long ago?

One may live on canned food quite well—But can a nation live a canned life in all but the rudimentary animal expressions of that life? Indefinitely?

Canned Poetry, Canned Music, Canned Architecture, Canned Recreation. All canned by the Machine.

I doubt it, although I see it going on around me. It has its limits.

We must have the technique to put our love of life, in our own way, into the things of our life, using for our tool the Machine, to our own best advantage—or we will have nothing living in it at all—soon.

How to do it?

Well! How does anyone master tools? By learning the nature of them and, by practice, finding out what and how they do, what they do best—for one thing.

Let architects first do that with the Machine. Architects are or must be masters of the industrial means of their era. They are, or must be—interpreters of the love of life in their era.

They must learn to give it expression in the background for that life—little by little, or betray their office. Either that or their power as normal high priests of civilization in a Democracy will never take its place where it is so badly needed. To be a mason, plasterer, carpenter, sculptor, or painter won't help architects much—now.

They may be passing from any integral relation to life as their architecture, a bad form of surface decoration superficially applied to engineering or buildings would seem to indicate and their function go to something other and else. An embarrassment of riches, in the antique, a deadly facility of the moment, a polyglot people—the necessity of "ready-made" architecture to clothe the nakedness of steel frames decently or fashionably, the poisonous taste of the period; these alibis have conspired with architects to land us where we all are at the mercy of the Machine. Architects point with pride to what has happened. I can not—I see in it nothing great—at least nothing noble. It is as sorry a waste as riches ever knew. We have every reason to feel ashamed of what we have to show for our *"selves"* in any analysis that goes below the skin.

A kind of skin disease is what most architecture is now as we may view it today. At least it never is organic. It has no integrity except as a "composition." And modern artists, except architects, ceased to speak of "composition" long ago.

Fortunately, however, there is a growing conviction that architecture is something not in two dimensions—but with a third and that third dimension in a spiritual sense may be interpreted as the integral quality in the thing or that quality that makes it integral.

The quality of *life* in man-made "things" is as it is in trees and plants and animals, and the secret of character in them which is again "style" is the same. It is a materialization of spirit.

To put it baldly—Architecture shirks the machine to lie to itself about itself and in itself, and we have Architecture for Architecture's sake. A sentimental absurdity. Such "Architecture" being the buildings that were built when men were workmen—and materials and tools were otherwise—instead of recognizing Architecture as a great living Spirit behind all that—a living spirit that left those forms as noble records of a seed time and harvest other than ours, thrown up on the shores of Time, in passing. A Spirit living still only to be denied and belied by us by this academic assertion of ours that they are that spirit. Why make so foolish an assertion? I have asked the question in many forms of many architects, in many places, and always had to answer myself. For there is no philosophy back of the assertion other than a denial or a betrayal—that will hold together. Instead there is a doctrine of Expediency fit only for social opportunists and speculative builders or "schools." There is no other sense in it.

The Machine does not complain—it goes on eating it all up and crying continually for more.

Where is more coming from? We have already passed through nearly every discovered "period" several times forward and gone backward again, to please the "taste" of a shallow present.

It would seem, now, time to take the matter seriously as an organic matter and study its vitals—in a sensible way.

Why not find out what *Nature* is in this matter. And be guided by principles rather than Expedients? It is the young man in architecture who will do this. It is too late for most successful practitioners of today to recover from their success. These essays are addressed to that young man.

IN THE CAUSE OF ARCHITECTURE II: STANDARDIZATION, THE SOUL OF THE MACHINE

[Published without illustrations in The Architectural Record, *June 1927]*

JOHN RUSKIN AND WILLIAM MORRIS TURNED AWAY FROM the machine and all it represented in modern art and craft. They saw the deadly threat it was to all they loved as such—and eventually turned again to fight it, to the death—their death. They are memories now. Pleasant ones. They did not succeed in delaying destruction nor in constructing anything. They did, however, remind us of what we were losing by using the machine or, as they might have said, letting the machine use us.

Repetition carried beyond a certain point has always taken the life of anything addressed to the living spirit.

Monotony kills.

Human feeling loves the vigor of spontaneity, freshness, and the charm of the unexpected. In other words, it loves life and dreads death.

The Machine Ruskin and Morris believed to be the enemy of all life. It was and is so still, but only because the artist has shirked it as a tool while he damned it; until now he has been damned by it.

Standardization as a principle is at work in all things with greater activity than ever before.

It is the most basic element in civilization. To a degree it is civilization itself.

An oriental rug, lustrous, rich with color and light, gleaming with all the brilliant pattern opulent oriental imagination conceived, has a very definite basis of standardization in warp and woof. In the methodical stitches regularly taken with strands of woolen yarn, upon that regular basis of cotton strings, stretched tight, lies the primitive principle of standardization. Serving the imagination full well.

Standardization here serves the spirit well—its mechanics disappear in the glowing fabric of the mind—the poetic feeling of the artist-weaver with love of beauty in his soul.

Standardization should have the same place in the fabric we are weaving which we call civilization—as it has in that more simple fabrication of the carpet. And the creative artist-mind must put it into the larger more comprehensive fabric.

How?

Not so simple.

This principle of standardization has now as its tool or body—the Machine. An ideal tool compared to which all that has gone before is as nothing.

Probably Gutenberg's invention of movable types was the first great advent of the machine in any sweeping form.

The blessing of that invention is obvious as is the curse that came with it.

The body of the book became volatile, almost infinite—and mind failed to keep up with it. Trash inundated the civilized world and streams of printed pages became wrapping paper to fill packing cases, light fires, and blow unheeded about the gutters of the world.

A deluge. And yet the book lives. There are a thousand writers for one in earlier eras and mostly worth one-thousandth part as much. "Shifting type" was the principle of standardization at work. The machine is the "press," that we have today serving it. What happened here in printing has happened to nearly everything in our lives. Happened or is happening or soon to happen with similar but more disastrous results, quantity at expense of quality—with always the blessing that comes from it, making available to the poor and needy a cheap or debased form of what was once rare and precious. I am speaking of fine art from the architect's standpoint.

So we see in the Machine the forerunner and ideal agent of Usonian Democracy such as it is. A Democracy sentimental and unsound, but that is another and longer story.

We see in this old force a new agency hard to control. A force once released into the world—never to be stopped until everything in it once precious and valuable for its own sake in its intimate relation to former good or great life has been fed to the dogs, or swine, speaking bitterly. But meantime raising the opportunities for "having things" the world over with a chance of turning the dogs, or swine, into more human beings.

And, honestly let it be said, of putting all human beings perhaps at the mercy of swine and dogs.

This is where the creative artist steps in: to bring new life of the mind to this potent agency: new understanding that will make living more joyous and genuine by abolishing the makeshift, showing up imitation for the base thing it is—saving us from this inglorious rampage and rapine upon antiquity. There is no artist conscience, it seems, in all this. The artist is like a hungry orphan turned loose in a bakeshop. The creative artist is not in it.

That ancient honor of the race, creative art, can not be dead. It needs only awakening. No wonder it lies all but moribund floating in the "deluge" at the mercy of the current of ubiquity, rushing toward—well, let us hope, toward the great peace of the great ocean.

This principle of standardization then, is no detriment to art or artist. It has always existed. And like any principle has its uses and its abuses.

How foolish therefore to take a prevalent abuse of any thing for the thing itself?

An artist is sentient. He is never fooled by brains or science or economics. He knows by feeling—say instinct—right or living, from wrong or dead.

He may not, however, have the technique to make his "knowing" effective and so remain inarticulate. But it is his duty to know, for his technique is what makes him serviceable to his fellows as artist. Acquiring the technique of the Machine as the tool of standardization, mastering the nature of both, is the only thing now that will make him the living force necessary to salvage the flotsam and jetsam of the "deluge," or, let it all go and begin over again.

Begin another era: the modern era of the machine with all it implies, economically making life more joyous and abundant as a matter of quality—as well as quantity.

Standardization apprehended as a principle of order has the danger of monotony in application.

Standardization can be murderer or beneficent factor as the life in the thing standardized is kept by imagination or destroyed by the lack of it.

By the "life" in the thing, I mean the *integrity* of the thing (we are talking of the things of art and craft) in the sense of the third dimension—as I have already tried to explain it.

The "life" in the thing is that quality of it or in it which makes it perfectly *natural*—of course that means organic. And that simply means true to what made it, as it was made, and for what it was made. That would be the *body* of the "thing." A matter of good sense.

New opportunities have come, not to hand but to the mind.

This may not seem specific. But it is a point of view necessary to the understanding of the experiences which follow. For in that spirit the experiments were made and the results judged as good or bad that will appear as I write.

The first study of importance in this connection is, of course, the nature of *materials*.

It is impossible to do anything intelligently to or with something you know nothing about. To know intimately the nature of wood, paper, glass, sheet metal, terra-cotta, cement, steel, cast iron, wrought iron, concrete, is essential to knowing how to use the tools available to make use of those materials, sensibly or artfully.

So let us glance at these more staple materials. We will find certain properties in all that standardization will serve well; and other properties, too, that standardization carried too far, will kill.

The principle of standardization, applied, may be said to be a matter of knowing by a *study* of the nature of whatever we apply it to—when to quit.

Let us begin with a short study of wood.

What is wood?

A workable, fibrous material got from trees in almost any length, certain breadths and thicknesses, now standardized. They may be had in almost any color or texture, as trees are growing, in great variety all over the world. Different woods vary in characteristics, made known by use in all ages. To it man has had recourse for nearly every need. He has made of it a part, of entirely, in one form or another, nearly everything he uses. It may be polished or painted or stained to bring out its grain which is the great characteristic of its beauty. It may be sawed or cut to bring this beauty to the surface in various ways. It was once laborious to hand-saw and cut and smooth it. Machines now do all that better. Machines cut veneers so cheaply and so thin and so wide they may be applied like wallpaper to broad surfaces. Machines cut rotary veneers from the curling surface of the log in any width, unwinding the surface with a cut of the grain unknown before. Really, this property of wood has been liberated and made available in beautiful sheets, so beautiful in surface that it is folly to mold it and join it and panel it painfully any more as before.

It may be used in broad, simple, plastic ways now even more cheaply than in laborious joinery with its tendency to go to pieces because it was all in pieces.

Much more could be said. Here is enough to indicate new possibilities of design in machined wood.

Inlaid lines are characteristic too—slender inlaid decorative purflings or battens in between wide, plain, broad, etc., etc.

Plastic treatment, now you see, instead of *constructed* ones or "structuralities."

There are infinite possibilities here. And in making wood into furniture, clean straight line effects, as delicate as may be, are characteristic of the machine. A limitation that makes the nature of wood very beautiful as it appears within these limitations of form.

Wood carving usually did violence to the nature of wood. It tended to mutilate and destroy it.

The machine can inlay, fret, and bring up the beauty of wood in plastic treatments more true to the nature of the wood. Why not then, forget ancient models that are especially made to suit freedom of the hand? The nature of wood was overwrought and lost in three out of five of such models anyway. But here the beauty that is wood lives above standardization, if the architect sees it and uses it in this new "plastic" sense.

Let us take glass.

Glass was once a delightful substance in itself. It is now chiefly a perfect "clarity" or nothing very delightful.

Such clearness in polished glass as we have is new in the world. We may have great polished surfaces for reflections, leaving openings as though nothing closed them—limpid surfaces playing the same part in all interiors that water plays in the landscape. We have lost a substance but found a freedom infinitely precious to the designer of buildings. This is the mechanical plate glass of the machine. New opportunities here. Imagine a few.

There is electro glazing to introduce the element of pattern into the clear glass in delicate straight lines in bewildering delicacy and variety.

The mind must enter now to take the place of

what, in the antique, was adorable as a natural quality of the glass itself. The scene has shifted, but we are still better off, in glass.

We can make colored glass for the painter to use as pigment in his hand, but it is now a lesser interest. We have limpid surfaces, true reflections, and unobstructed vision due to the machine.

And there is steel, a new thing under the sun. And the most significant material of this age. The one that has done most harm to the established order—or Pseudo-Classic.

IN THE CAUSE OF ARCHITECTURE III: STEEL

[Published without illustrations in The Architectural Record, *August 1927]*

STEEL IS THE EPIC OF THIS AGE.

Steel has entered our lives as a "material" to take upon itself the physical burden of our civilization.

This is the Age of Steel. And our "culture" has received it as ancient Roman culture received the great gift of the masonry arch. For centuries the Romans pasted the trabeated Greek forms of their "culture" on the arch in front as architecture, while the arch did the work behind.

Finally the noble virtue of the arch overcame the sham culture of the period and came forth and lived as a great and beautiful contribution to mankind.

Steel is still smothered in aesthetic gloom, insulted, denied, and doomed by us as was the masonry arch by the Romans. Inherent virtue will triumph here, too, in the course of time. So much wasted time!

This stupendous material—what has it not done for Man?

What may it not yet do for him with its derivatives and associates as the glare of the converters continues to mount into the sky, day and night.

Now, ductile, tensile, dense to any degree, uniform and calculable to any standard, steel is a known quantity to be dealt with mathematically to a certainty to the last pound; a miracle of strength to be counted upon!

Mathematics in the flesh—at work for man!

A mere plastic material, thin and yet an ultimate rigidity, rolled hot or rolled cold to any desired section of any strength unlimited in quantity; or, continuously night and day, drawn into thin strands of enormous strength and length as wire—enough to wind the world into a steel-covered ball; or, rolled in any thickness into sheets like paper, cut by the shears into any size.

A rigidity condensed in any shape conceivable, to be as easily bored, punched, planed, cut, and polished, too, as wood once was. More easily and cheaply curved or bent or twisted or woven to any extent and the parts fastened together. A material that in the processes already devised not only takes any shape the human brain can reduce to a diagram but can go on producing it until the earth is covered with it—and there is no escape from it. No, none!

For it is cheap.

Cheaper in its strength and adaptability than anything man ever knew before—thousands of times over.

But it has it in its nature to change its volume with changes of temperature.

It has a fatal weakness.

Slowly it disintegrates in air and moisture and has an active enemy in electrolysis. It is recovering

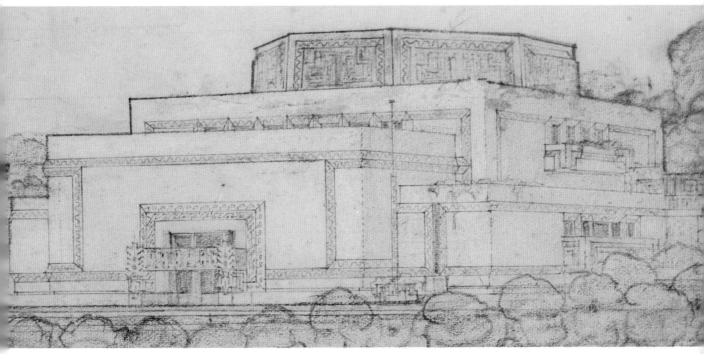

Theater for Aline Barnsdall (Project). Los Angeles, California. 1915–1920. Perspective. Color pencil and pencil on tracing paper, 23 x 7".
FLLW Fdn#2005.003

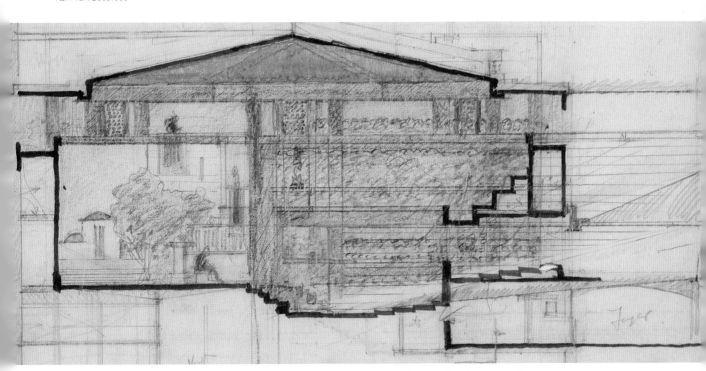

Theater for Aline Barnsdall (Project). Los Angeles, California. 1915–1920. Cross Section. Pencil and color pencil on tracing paper, 17 x 18". FLLW Fdn#2005.031

from this weakness. It is only fair to say that it may become, soon, immune. Then, what?

Meanwhile, owing to its nature it may be plated with other metals or protected by coverings of various sorts or combined with them. In itself it has little beauty, neither grain, nor texture of surface. It has no more "quality" in this sense than mud. Not so much as sand. It is a creature wholly dependent upon imaginative influences for "life" in any aesthetic sense at the hand of a creator.

So is terra-cotta. So is concrete, although both these friable materials have certain internal possibilities of texture and color.

So also relatives of steel have beautiful permanent surfaces—bronze, brass, silver, gold, aluminum, copper, tin, and zinc and others. It would be interesting to write about them all.

But the weaknesses of steel are not fatal to beautiful use, nor is the lack of individuality in texture other than an opportunity for the imagination.

Yet, how or where is steel evident in our life as a thing of beauty in itself? In tools? Yes, in knives and saws and skates: in hardware. In engines, in the rails of the railroad, in the locomotive, the submarine, the torpedo boat, the aeroplane. In bridges? Yes, but only where the engineer was inspired and allowed his stresses and strains to come and go clean in the members, innocent of any desire or intent on his part to "ornament" them. Used honestly by engineers, steel has something of the beauty of mathematics.

Remember, however, that music is but sublimated mathematics. And the engineer is no more capable of giving steel structure the life of "beauty" it should have than a professor of mathematics is capable of a symphony in music.

The principles of construction which find in steel a medium that will serve with safety and economically in various designs as a support for enormous loads to span wide spaces, or supporting enormous loads to enormous height, are, as long as they are really kept scientific and clean, showing as such, the best work we have to show.

And it is much.

But it is not the architect who can show it.

When the architect has dealt with it what has he done? The skyscraper and lied about it. The modern Cathedral, lifeless, dummy, supported from within to appear "lifelike" without. Anything you wish to name as architecture will be likewise.

Anything you may name as engineering where architects cooperated will be similar, probably.

An exception here and there is now manifest, already late. This era is fast and furious in movement. But all movement is not progress. Architecture has not progressed with steel. "Architecture" has all but died of it while architects were singing their favorite hymns and popular Christmas carols to the medieval antique.

Incredible folly! "Tower" Buildings, East River bridges, St. John the Divine's, States' Capitols, and all. How all of them mock integrity! Wherein lies the artist grasp of the "masters" who design such structures?

Had Bach or Beethoven made music the mathematics of which would be like the principles of construction in such edifices, what would such music sound like? Pandemonium, requiring hideous grimaces and falsities of tone and absurdities of concatenation with no rhythm, obvious or occult, outrage to the mind. Inconceivable!

For the principles of construction now find in steel because it is a strictly calculable material of miraculous strength, ideal expression as the sinews and bones of structure.

The architect has been satisfied to leave the mathematical sinews and bones unbeautiful, although serviceable as such, and content to hang garments over them rented from some costumers or not even that—pawed from the scrap heap of antiquity.

It is superstition or plain ignorance to believe these sinews and bones incapable of beauty as such—if such, to be clothed with a flesh that will be living on them, *an expression of them!*

Is it reasonable too to go further and say "sinews and bones?" Yes, but not as in the human frame, but as a new world of form in themselves capable of being beautiful in a new sense, so devised in construction that flesh is unnecessary.

Why should not the structural principle be expressed artistically as well as scientifically for its own sake in this ideal material? Expressed with a knowledge of rhythm and synthesis of form that a master musician would bring to his mathematics? Can we not imagine a building to be serviceably beautiful and beautifully serviceable as it is naturally made—in steel? Glass is all that is needed really after we have honestly insured the life of the steel.

And, added to this immense possibility, here enters a vital modern probability:

Steel is most economical in tension; the steel strand is a marvel, let us say, as compared with anything the ancients knew, a miracle of strength for its weight and cost. We have found now how to combine it with a mass material, concrete, which has great strength in compression. The coefficient of expansion and contraction of both materials is the same in changes of temperature. The more bulky material protects the slighter material from its enemy, disintegration. The heavier material, or protector, strangely grows stronger as it grows older. Permanent "flesh" if we care to so regard it.

A valuable partnership in materials in any case more congenial to the architect than steel alone for he can do more richly with flesh and sinews than he can with sinews and bones, perhaps. Certainly, if regarded as such by him.

Here we have reinforced concrete, a new dispensation. A new medium for the new world of thought and feeling that seems ideal: a new world that must follow freedom from the imprisonment in the abstract in which tradition binds us. Democracy means liberation from those abstractions and therefore life, more abundantly in the concrete. This is not intended as a pun. It happens to be so literally, for concrete combined with steel strands will probably become the physical body of the modern, civilized world. Here again and especially has the machine liberated the creative architect.

And he prefers his bonds!

The old structural limitation that took form as masonry, lintels and arches, "natural" posts and beams, is all gone. There is in their place a science of mathematics applied to materials of marvelous new properties and strength, here to the architect's hand instead—"mathematics materialized at work for man."

What are we, as architects, going to do with it? For as yet, we have done nothing with it on principle. We have merely "made shift." Architects have avoided an open break with the powers that be, on the ground of impotence, only by psalm singing and caroling in the name of tradition. But, enough.

Here in addition to the possibility of steel alone, is a perfect wedding of two plastic materials. A wondrous freedom! Freedom worthy of ideal democracy. Astounding! That upon so simple a means such a vast consequence to human life depends. But so it does. And just so simple has the initiation of far-reaching changes brought by evolution always been.

The limitation of the human imagination is all that ties the hands of the modern architect except the poison in his veins fostered by "good taste" for dead forms.

His imagination now must devise the new cross sections for the machine more suitable for use in harmoniously framing steel. Rivets have interesting effects as well as facts. Steel plates have possibilities combined with posts and beams. And now there is electric welding to make the work more simple and integral. Posts may become beautiful, beams too. The principle of the "gusset" has a life of its own, still. Strangely, here is plastic material delivered by the Machine in any rigid structural form to be fastened together as members in a structural design.

The design may emphasize the plastic as structural or the structural as plastic. What that means in detail is a liberal education in itself. It must be had by the young architect. He will have to go to work at it himself.

And again, easier to comprehend are the new forms brought to hand by reinforced concrete.

First among them is the slab—next the cantilever—then the splay.

To be able to make waterproof, weatherproof slabs of almost any size or continuity is a great simplification. A great means to a great end. To be able to make these slabs so they may be supported beneath as a waiter supports his tray on the fingers of his upraised arm, leads to another marvelous release, a new freedom.

This is the economic structural principle of the cantilever. A new stability as well as a new economy.

Gordon Strong Planetarium (Project). Sugar Loaf Mountain, Maryland. 1924. Perspective. Color pencil and pencil on tracing paper, 31 x 20". FLLW Fdn#2505.039

Steel Cathedral (Project). New York City. 1926. Elevation. Pencil on tracing paper, 31 x 23". FLLW Fdn#2602.003

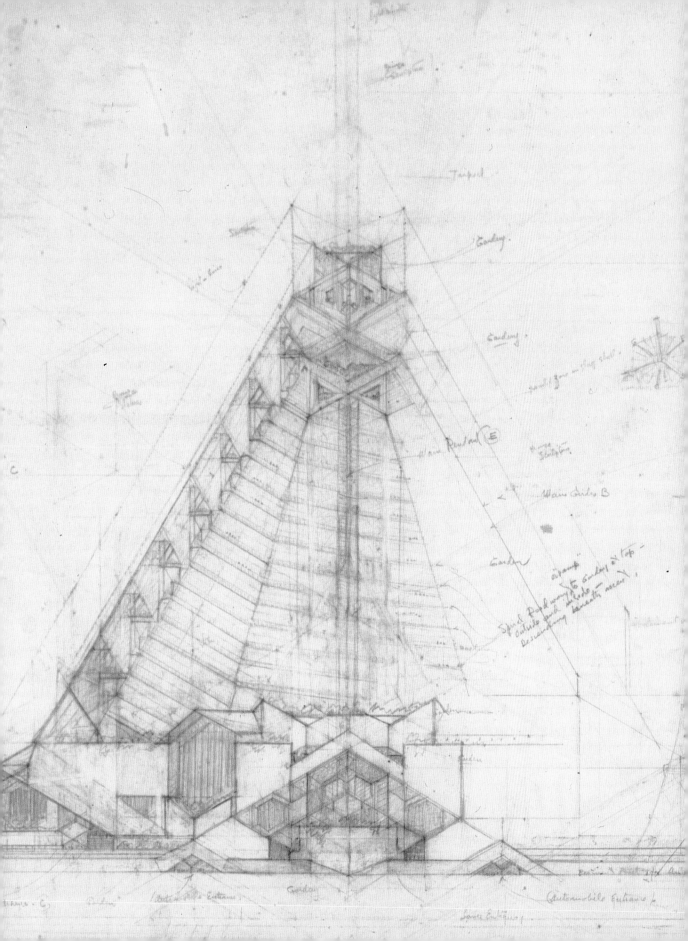

The most romantic of all structural possibilities is here.

And last, there is the splay or sloping wall, used as a slide from wall into projections or from floors into walls or used in connection with the cantilever slab. It may be used as an expression of form in itself for protection or light. For economy it may be useful as support in both cases and enhance the plastic effect of the whole.

There is nothing in architecture ready-made to meet these sweeping new "freedoms."

What a release is here! The machine brought it in the ubiquitous ductile steel strand with its miraculous strength and the fortunate wedding of that strength with poured concrete.

What a circumstance!

Here, "young men in architecture," is your palette. The "foyer" of your new world.

Let us of the former generation see you at work on it, in it for all you are worth.

And here again, the password is the word "plastic." "Structuralities" as such must be forgotten. If you will take paper and fold it and bend it, or cardboard sheets and cut them and fit and arrange them into models for buildings, you will see the sense of the new structure in its primitive aspect. And then after this superficial external view, get inside and make the whole line as one plastic entity—however the slabs tend to separate or fall to themselves.

And never lose sight of the fact that all in this new world is no longer in two dimensions. That was the old world.

We are capable of a world now in three dimensions; the third, as I have said before, interpreted as a spiritual matter that makes all integral—"at one."

How life may be blessed by the release this simple development of its viewpoint will bring to mankind.

Paintings and sculpture for use to enrich and enhance the work, still live. They now live a detached life as things apart, for and by themselves. It is a pity, for they can never thrive in that separate life.

Unfortunately, there is a conviction in certain quarters—if it amounts to a "conviction"—chiefly European—that ornamentation is untrue to the Machine in this, the Machine Age. That the use of ornamentation is a romanticism and therefore inappropriate.

The contrary is the case.

But it is true that ornamentation in the old sense as an "applied" thing, as something added to the thing superficially, however cleverly adapted or "composed" is dead to this new world.

Ornamentation in the plastic sense is as characteristic of the thing we call the Machine as ornamentation in the old sense was a characteristic feature of "The Renaissance"; more so, because it is the imagination living in the process and so woven into the life of the thing. A matter of the "constitution" of the thing. The trace of human imagination as the poetic language of line and color must now live *in* the thing so far as it is natural to it. And that is very far.

IN THE CAUSE OF ARCHITECTURE IV: FABRICATION AND IMAGINATION

[Published without illustrations in The Architectural Record, *October 1927]*

TIME WAS WHEN THE HAND WROUGHT. TIME IS HERE WHEN the *process* fabricates instead.

Why make the fabrication a lie or allow it to "become one when we try to make it "beautiful?" Any such lie is an abuse of Imagination.

All Man has above the brute, worth having, is his because of Imagination. Imagination made the Gods—all of them he knows—it is the Divine in him and differentiates him from a mere reasoning animal into a God himself. A creative being is a God. There will never be too many Gods.

Reason and Will have been exalted by Philosophy and Science. Let us now do homage to Imagination.

We have suspected it and punished it and feared it long enough.

Imagination is so intimately related to sentient perception—we can not separate the two. Nor need do so.

Let us call Creative-Imagination the Man-light in Mankind to distinguish it from intellectual brilliance. It is strongest in the creative-artist. A sentient quality. To a degree all developed individuals have this quality, and to the extent that it takes concrete form in the human fabrications necessary or desirable to human life, it makes the fabrication live as a reflection of that Life any true Man loves as such—Spirit materialized.

The Machine is an obedient, tireless fabricator of a nonsentient product. A shaper and drawer of steel, a weaver of fabrics—"casting" forms continually in every material solvent by fire or water.

So the study of the process is as important as the study of the Machine. It is another phase of the Machine and in the method of the process too lies the opportunity for the artist. Unless he understands it what can he do with it—to qualify its product—from within? To modify it externally is not enough. He has been on the surface, as intimately related to its nature as a decalcomania on a tin box cover is to the Nature of the thing going on inside. He has been a decorative label when he has been at all.

Let us, then, get inside.

We will find all the magic of ancient times magnified—Aladdin with his wonderful lamp had a poor thing relatively in that cave of his. Aladdin's lamp was a symbol merely for Imagination. Let us take this lamp inside, in the Architect's world.

Where begin? With mechanistic processes like weaving? printing? stamping? Or with casting? Or with plastic, chemicalized materials like concrete, plastering, steel making, glass making, paper making, ceramics?

One must serve for all. Then let us take one that is both a chemical-process and casting—concrete.

Concrete is a plastic material but sets so slowly

as yet that molds or so-called "forms" are used to give it *shape*. It must be held, until it hardens sufficiently, to hold the shape desired.

Ordinarily in itself it has no texture unless the mold leaves it on the surface. It is, however, possible to use fine colored-gravel or crushed-marble or granite in the mixture so the superficial-cement (retarded in setting by some substance like soap applied to the interior surfaces of the "forms") may be easily washed away, leaving the hard gleaming aggregate exposed in almost any color or texture.

All composite materials like concrete have possibilities of bringing out the nature of the mixture in some kind of surface treatment, and the materials may be variously composed in the substances, mixed to secure these effects of texture and color desired in the finished product.

But, mainly, concrete is still a mass material taking form from molds, erroneously called "forms."

The materials of which the molds themselves are made, will, therefore, modify the shape the concrete naturally takes, if indeed it does not wholly determine it.

Unity Temple at Oak Park was entirely cast in wooden boxes, ornamentation and all. The ornament was formed in the mass by taking blocks of wood of various shapes and sizes, combining them with strips of wood, and, where wanted, tacking them in position to the inside faces of the boxes.

The ornament partakes therefore of the nature of the whole, belongs to it. So the block and box is characteristic of the forms of this temple. The simple cubical masses are in themselves great concrete blocks.

The design makes a feature of this limitation as to form as they are grouped to express the great room within.

Here is a building, a monolith in mono-material, textured as described above, left complete as it came from the molds—permanent architecture.

The whole is a great casting articulated in sections according to the masses of concrete that could safely be made to withstand changes of temperature in a severe climate.

It is a good record of this primitive period in the development of concrete building when it was necessary to pour the material into boxes to "set it" into shape.

It is a "natural" building therefore, in a transition-period of the development of the use of concrete.

I say a period of transition because concrete is essentially a plastic material, sometime to be used as such; used as a plastic material by plastering upon cores or upon steel fabrications. The resultant form may then take the shapes characteristic of drifted snow or sand or the smooth conformation of animals perhaps—as they become finished buildings.

But at the present time there comes a less cumbersome and a cheaper because less wasteful method than the molds on a large scale that built Unity Temple. It was necessary then to build a rough building complete in wood as a "mold" into which the temple could be cast.

Now, in this easier more plastic method, standardization enters as the *unit-system*.

A unit-mass of concrete, size and shape determined by the work intended to be done and what weight a man can reasonably be expected to lift and set in a wall, is fixed upon. This in order to avoid the expensive larger molds—say, the slab block we make 16" × 16" × 2½" thick.

Mechanical steel or aluminum molds are made in which to precast the whole building in a small "unit" of that size. Grooves are provided in the edges of the slab-blocks so a lacing of continuous steel rods may be laid in the vertical and horizontal joints of the block slabs for tensile strength. The grooves are as large as possible so they may be poured full of concrete after each course of blocks is set up, girding and locking the whole into one firm slab. Here ultimately we will have another monolith *fabricated* instead of *poured* into special wooden molds. The molds in this case are metal, good for many buildings, and take the impress of any detail in any scheme of pattern or texture imagination conceives. The whole building "precast" in a mold a man can lift.

Here the making of the structural-unit and the process of fabrication become complete synchronized standardizations. A building for the first time in the world may be lightly fabricated, complete, of mono-material—literally woven into a pattern or design as was the oriental rug earlier referred to in "Standardization": fabrication as infinite in color, texture, and variety as in that rug. A certain simple technique larger in organization but no more complex in execution than that of the rug-weaving, *builds* the building. The diagrams and unit molds are less *simple*. They have much study put on them, and organization becomes more than ever important.

When Machine-Standardizing enters, all must be accurate, precise, organized.

The Machine product can stand no slovenly administration for it can make good no mistakes.

The limitations of both process and material are here very severe, but when these are understood and accepted we may "weave" an architecture at will—unlimited in quality and quantity except by the limitation of imagination.

Several mechanical molds may be thrown into a Ford and taken where gravel and sand abound. Cement is all else needed, except a few tons of ¼" commercial steel bars, to complete a beautiful building. This—and an organization of workmen trained to do one thing well.

The ground is soon covered with slab blocks, the block-stuff curing in moisture. After that, it is all a matter of reading the architect's diagrams, which is what his plans now become. They are not tediously figured with haphazard dimensions any longer. They are laid out by counting blocks, corner blocks, and halfblocks; so many blocks wide, so many high, and showing where specific blocks go is like counting stitches in the "woof" and threads in the "warp." Building is a matter of taking slab-block stitches on a steel warp.

So, a livable building may be made of mono-material in one operation!

There is an outer shell and an inner shell separated by a complete air space.

The inner walls, floors, and ceilings which this inner shell becomes are the same as the outside walls, and fabricated in the same way at the same time.

Windows? Made in the shop, standardized to work with the slab-block units. Made of sheet metal finished complete and set in the walls as the work proceeds.

Piping? Cut to the standard unit-length in the shop and set into the hollow spaces. Plastering? None. Carpenter work? None. Masonry? None. "Form" work? None. Painting? None. Decorations? All integral, cast into the structure as designed with all the play of imagery known to Persian or Moor.

The process of elimination which *standardization* becomes has left only essentials. Here is a process that makes of the mechanics of concrete building a mono-material and mono-method affair instead of the usual complex quarreling aggregation of processes and materials: *builds* a building permanent and safe, dry and cool in summer, dry and warm in winter. Standardization here effects economy of effort and material to the extreme, but brings with it a perfect freedom for the imagination of the designer who now has infinite variety as a possibility in ultimate effects after mastering a simple technique.

I give here only one instance of many possibilities in this one material.

What precisely has happened?

Well, one consistent economical imperishable whole instead of the usual confusion of complexities to be reduced to a heap of trash by time.

A quiet orderly simplicity and all the benefits to human beings that come with it.

A simple, cheap material everywhere available, the common stuff of the community—here made rare and exquisite by the Imagination.

Imagination conceives the "fabric" of the whole. The "unit" is absorbed as agreeable texture in the pattern of the whole. Here, too, is certainty of results as well as minimum of costs assured to the human being by free use of the Machine, in perfect control. The whole now in human scale and thoroughly humane. Here is true technique. The technique of a principle *at work*; at work in every minor operation with this material—concrete. Here the material is affected by a process suited to the result desired to such an extent that Architecture may live in our life again in our Machine Age as a free agent of Imagination.

Copper, glass—all materials are subject to similar treatment on similar terms according to their entirely different natures.

The forms and processes will change as the material changes—but the principle will not. In the case of each different material treated the expression of the whole would become something quite different with new beauty. So comes a true variety in unity in this, the Machine Age.

Coition at last. The third dimension triumphant.

The sickening monotony achieved by a two-dimensional world in its attempts to be "different" mercifully ended, perhaps forever.

True variety now becomes a *natural consequence;* a *natural* thing. We can live again and more abundantly than ever before. Differently, yet the same.

Such harmony as we know in the Gothic of "Le Moyen Age" is again ours—but infinitely expanded and related to the individual Imagination, intimately, and therefore to the human being as a unit of scale.

Is Machine-Standardization a hindrance? No, a release.

Boundless possibility, and with that comes increase of responsibility. Here, in the hand of the creative-artist, in *fabrication* in this sense, lies the whole expression, character and style, the *quality*, let us say, in any spiritual sense, of modern life.

The integrity of it all as an *expression* is now a matter of the creative-artist's Imagination *at work.*

Where is he? And if *he* is, may he be trusted with such power? Yes, if he has the Gift. If he is "God" in the sense that "man-light" lives in him in his work.

But should he fall short of that, if he is faithful, looking to principle for guidance, he is sufficiently disciplined by the honest technique of fabrication to be sure to produce steady quiet work.

Inspiration cannot be expected in any total fabric of civilization. It may only be expected to inspire the whole and lay bare the *sense of the thing* for others.

The whole is safe when discovered principle is allowed to work! Going *with* Nature in the use of Imagination may seem little different from going against Nature—but how different the destination and the reward!

It has been said that "Art is Art precisely in that it is not Nature," but in *"obiter dicta"* of that kind the Nature referred to is nature in its limited sense of material appearances as they lie about us and lie to us.

Nature as I have used the word must be apprehended as the life-principle constructing and making appearances what they are, for what they are, and in what they are. Nature inheres in all as *reality.* Appearances take form and character in infinite variety to our vision because of the natural inner working of this Nature-principle.

The slightest change in a minor feature of that "Nature" will work astounding changes of expression.

When the word Nature is understood and accepted in this sense, there is no longer any question of originality. It is natural to be "original" for we are at the fountainhead of all forms whatsoever.

The man who has divined the character of the ingrown sense-of-the-pine, say, can make other pine trees true to the species as any that may continually recur in the woods; make pine-tree forms just as true to the species as we see it and as we accept it as any growing out-of-doors rooted in the ground.

But, principles are not formulas. Formulas may be deduced from principles, of course. But we must never forget that even in the things of the moment principles live and formulas are dead. A yardstick is a formula—Mathematics the principle. So, beware of formulas, they are dangerous. They become inhibitions of principle rather than expressions of them in nonsentient hands.

This principle understood and put to work, what would happen to our world? What would our world be like if the Nature-principle were allowed to work in the hands of creative imagination and the *formulae* kept where it belongs?

★*Note: the chemicalization of concrete or cement is too well-known to need any attention here.*

IN THE CAUSE OF ARCHITECTURE V: THE NEW WORLD

[Published without illustrations in The Architectural Record, *October 1927]*

THE NEW WORLD? A DANGEROUS TITLE.

But for a sense of humor in this old one there would be no new one. Length and breadth—with just enough thickness to hold them together for commercial purposes we have had in the old world and all *that* implies in Art and Philosophy.

The new world begins to be when the little "thickness" we have had in the old one becomes *depth* and our sense of depth becomes that sense of the thing, or the quality in it that makes it *integral*—gives it integrity as such. With this "quality" the new world develops naturally in three dimensions out of the one which had but two.

The abstractions and aesthetic lies of a canned pictorial-culture crumble and fade away, worn out and useless.

"Institutions" founded upon those abstractions to serve that culture, crumble. And Architecture now belonging to, and refreshing as the forests or prairies or hills, the human spirit is free to blossom in structure as organic as that of plants and trees. Buildings, too, are children of Earth and Sun.

Naturally we have no more Gothic Cathedrals for the busy gainful-occupations. No more Roman or Greek Sarcophagi for the sacred Banking business. No more French châteaux for Fire-Engine houses. No more Louis XIV or Louis XV or Louis XVI or any Louis at all, for anything at all!

The Classics? A fond professorial dream.

The Periods? Inferior desecration.

Picture-Postcard Homes? Museum relics affording much amusement.

The Skyscraper—vertical groove of the landlord? Laid down flatwise. A trap that was sprung.

Churches? We fail to recognize them.

Public buildings? No longer monuments.

Monuments? Abolished as profane.

Industrial buildings? Still recognizable for they were allowed to be themselves in the old world.

Commercial buildings, industrial, or official? Shimmering, iridescent cages of steel and copper and glass in which the principle of standardization becomes exquisite in all variety.

Homes? Growing from their site in native materials, no more "deciduous" than the native rock ledges of the hills, or the fir trees rooted in the ground, all taking on the character of the individual in perpetual bewildering variety.

The City? Gone to the surrounding country.

The landlord's exploitation of the herd instinct seems to be exploded. That instinct is recognized as servile and is well in hand—but not in the landlord's hand.

A touchstone now by way of the human mind lies in reach of human fingers everywhere to enable the human being to distinguish and accept the quick and reject the dead!

It would seem after all, that this "new world" is simply a matter of being one's *self.*

Beech trees are welcome and allowed to be beech trees because they are beeches. Birches because they are birches. Elms are not oaks and no one would prefer them if they were, or get excited about making them so if they could.

Nor are evergreens Christmas trees.

Materials everywhere are most valuable for what they are—in themselves—no one wants to change their nature or try to make them like something else.

Men likewise—for the same reason: a reason everywhere working in everything.

So this new world is no longer a matter of seeming but of *being.*

Where then are we?

We are in a corner of the twentieth century emerging into the twenty-first—and the first Democracy of *being* not seeming.

The highest form of Aristocracy be it said the world has ever seen is this Democracy, for it is based upon the qualities that make the man a man.

We know, now, the tragedy of a civilization lying to itself. We see the futility of expecting in hope, that a culture willing to deceive itself could or would know how to be sincere with others—or allow them happiness or know happiness itself.

What an inglorious rubbish heap lies back there in the gloom of that duodimensional era! In that "Period" of superficial length and breadth with just enough "thickness" to make them hang together—for commercial purposes!

The "Period" of Fashion and Sham in which the "Picture" was the "cause" and not the consequence.

And the rubbish heap gradually grew back there, useless, as the great simplicity of an Idea that was in itself an integrity rose to smite the Sham for what it was and proclaim, in fact, the Freedom we then professed.

SHAM and its brood—inbred by the ideals of "the classic" and its authority in education—

fostered that duodimensional world beyond its ability to perform; educated it far and away beyond its capacity for life.

Character is Fate and invariably meets it. That Old World was ripe for the rubbish heap and went to its destruction by the grinding of universal principles, grinding slow, nor yet so exceedingly fine. For the awful simplicity of the Nazarene saw this "new world" at hand more than two thousand years ago. And here we are, two centuries later, only beginning to see it for ourselves.

Beginning to see it prepared by this simple enrichment of our selves in this *sense* of the "within" for our outlook. Beginning to understand and realize that the "Kingdom on Earth as it is in Heaven" of which He spoke was a Kingdom wherein each man was a King because Kingdom and King consisted of that quality of integrity of which, for lack of a better term, I have tritely spoken as the third dimension. That all of the Beyond is within, is a truism.

And just so simple, although at the time less obvious, is the initiation of all great evolutionary changes whatsoever.

But this simple first principle of being that is now at work for some strange reason came late and last.

Why?

We who have walked the Earth in eager search for the clear wine of Principle, tortured and denied or instead offered polluted water to quench an honest thirst, would like to know—why?

Were the Greeks poison? For us—yes. The Romans? More so.

Back there in the two-dimensional era we lived bewildered in a Roman-world—Romantic!

Not for nothing were we Romantic and did we speak a composite language corrupted from the Romance languages.

The honest Celt or Gaul or Teuton was corrupted by the Graeco-Roman corruption of the finer ancient culture of the Hellenes.

The Anglo-Saxon sanctified and recorrupted the corruption, and polished sophistries, imprisoning abstractions, became recipes for good life in the name of the Good, the True, and the Beautiful.

Hypocrisy for all cultivated men became as necessary as breathing and as "natural."

In order to be Beautiful—it became imperative to *lie*!

In order to *be* it became necessary to *seem*.

Art was a divorce from Nature.

"Nature" became the world of appearances round about us in our industrial life and all aspects of other individuals in relation to those appearances.

In the "Democracy" of the nineteenth century we witnessed the triumph of the insignificant as the fruit of the lie. A triumph by no means insignificant.

Some few unpopular individuals inhibited the "classic" in their education in that era, being afraid of it—seeing what it did to those who yielded to it, how it embalmed them in respectability and enshrined them in impotence. Seeing how it cut them off from Life and led them by the intellect into a falsified sense of living.

The precious quality in Man—Imagination— was shown the enticing objects man had made and shown them as so many "objectives." Therefore Imagination was offered patterns to the eye, not truths to the mind; offered abstractions to the Spirit not realities to the Soul. This was "Education."

To turn away from all that meant then, owing to the supreme psychology of the herd, well—what it has meant.

Since one need no longer turn from reality to be respectable, all sacrifices in former worlds are made a privilege, something to have enjoyed.

For the scene has shifted. The burden—there is no burden like artificiality—has lifted.

Art having been *"artificiality"* for centuries has come through its terrible trial, hard put to it by the Machine—which stripped it to the bone and lives.

It is living now because the Artifex survived the Artificer.

The Man has survived the Mime.

Be comforted—my young architect!

The "pictorial" still lives, for what it is, extended in this our new Usonian world, but as "consequence" not as "cause."

All we were given of love for the picturesque in gesture, form, color, or sound—gifts to the five senses—is realized. Appearances are expanded into a synthesis of the five senses—we may call it a sixth if we please—and all become manifest materialization of Spirit.

Appearances are now a great assurance. A splendid enrichment of Life. The Pictorial is merely an incident not an aim, nothing in itself or for itself or by itself; no longer an *end* sought for its own sake.

The picturesque? Therefore it is a by-product inevitably beautiful in all circumstances, from any and every point of view.

What wrought this miracle?

NATURE gradually apprehended as the principle of Life—the life-giving principle in making things with the mind, reacting in turn upon the makers.

Earth-dwellers that we are, we are become now sentient to the truth that living on Earth *is* a materialization of Spirit instead of trying to make our dwelling here a spiritualization of matter. Simplicity of Sense now honorably takes the lead.

To be good Gods of Earth *here* is all the significance we have here. A God is a God on Earth as in Heaven. And there will never be too many Gods.

Just as a great master knows no masterpiece, and there are no "favorite" trees, nor color, nor flowers; no "greatest" master; so Gods are Gods, and all are GOD.

Be specific? I hear you—Young Man in Architecture.

Shall I too paint pictures for you to show to you this new world?

Show you "pictures" that I might make?

Would you not rather make them for yourself?

Because any picture I could make would not serve you well.

A specific "picture" might betray you. You might take it for the thing itself—and so miss its merely symbolic value, for it could have no other value.

This new world so far as it lives as such is conditioned upon your seeing it for yourself—out of your own love and understanding. It is that kind of world.

As another man sees it, it might entertain you. Why should you be "entertained?"

His specific picture, the better it might be the more it might forestall or bind you. You have had enough of that.

For yourself, by yourself, within yourself, then, visualize it and add your own faithful building to it, and you cannot fail.

We are punished for discipleship—and, as disciples, we punish the thing we love.

Who, then, can teach? Not I.

It too is a gift.

Already I have dared enough. Try to see—in work.

Idealism and Idealist are the same failure as Realism and Realistic. Both the same failure as Romance and Romantic.

Life is. We are.

Therefore we will loyally love, honestly work and enthusiastically seek, in all things—the one thing of Value—Life.

It is not found in pictorial shallows.

IN THE CAUSE OF ARCHITECTURE I: THE LOGIC OF THE PLAN

[Published with six illustrations in The Architectural Record, *January 1928]*

PLAN! THERE IS SOMETHING ELEMENTAL IN THE WORD itself. A pregnant plan has logic—is the logic of the building squarely stated. Unless it is the plan for a foolish fair.

A good plan is the beginning and the end, because every good plan is organic. That means that its development in all directions is inherent—inevitable.

Scientifically, artistically to foresee all is "to plan." There is more beauty in a fine ground plan than in almost any of its ultimate consequences.

In itself it will have the rhythms, masses, and proportions of a good decoration if it is the organic plan for an organic building with individual style—consistent with materials.

All is there seen—purpose, materials, method, character, style. The plan? The prophetic soul of the building—a building that can live only because of the prophecy that is the plan. But it is a map, a chart, a mere diagram, a mathematical projection before the fact, and, as we all have occasion to know, accessory to infinite crimes.

To judge the architect one need only look at his ground plan. He is master then and there, or never. Were all elevations of the genuine buildings of the world lost and the ground plans saved, each building would construct itself again. Because before the plan is a plan it is a concept in some creative mind. It is, after all, only a purposeful record of that dream, which saw the destined building living in its appointed place. A dream—but precise and practical, the record to be read by the like-minded.

The original plan may be thrown away as the work proceeds—probably most of those for the most wonderful buildings in the world were, because the concept grows and matures during realization, if the mastermind is continually with the work. But that plan had first to be made. Ultimately it should be corrected and recorded.

But to throw the plans away is a luxury ill-afforded by the organizations of our modern method. It has ruined owners and architects and enriched numberless contractors. Therefore, conceive the building in the imagination, not on paper but in the mind, thoroughly—before touching paper. Let it live there—gradually taking more definite form before committing it to the draughting board. When the thing lives for you—start to plan it with tools—not before. To draw during conception or "sketch," as we say, experimenting with practical adjustments to scale, is well enough if the concept is clear enough to be firmly held. It is best to cultivate the imagination to construct and complete the building before working upon it with T square and triangle.

Working on it with triangle and T square should modify or extend or intensify or test the conception—complete the harmonious adjustment of its parts. But if the original concept is lost as the drawing proceeds, throw all away and begin afresh. To throw away a concept entirely to make way for a fresh one—that is a faculty of the mind not easily cultivated. Few have that capacity. It is perhaps a gift—but may be attained by practice. What I am trying to express is that the plan must start as a truly creative matter and mature as such. All is won or lost before anything more tangible begins.

The several factors most important in making the plans—after general purpose scheme or "project" are:

2nd—Materials
3rd—Building methods
4th—Scale
5th—Articulation
6th—Expression or Style

In the matter of scale, the human being is the logical norm because buildings are to be humanly inhabited and should be related to human proportions not only comfortably but agreeably. Human beings should look as well in the building or of it as flowers do.

People should belong to the building just as it should belong to them. This scale or unit-of-size of the various parts varies with the specific purpose of the building and the materials used to build it. The only sure way to hold all to scale is to adopt a unit-system, unit-lines crossing the paper both ways, spaced as predetermined, say 4'-0" on centers—or 2'-8" or whatever seems to yield the proper scale for the proposed purpose. Divisions in spacing are thus brought into a certain texture in the result; ordered scale in detail is sure to follow.

A certain *standardization* is established here at the beginning, like the warp in the oriental rug. It has other and economic values in construction. I have found this valuable in practice even in small houses. Experience is needed to fix upon the proper size of the unit for any particular building. Trained imagination is necessary to differentiate or syncopate or emphasize, to weave or play upon it consistently.

Scale is really proportion. Who can teach proportion? Without a sense of proportion, no one should attempt to build. This gift of sense must be the diploma Nature gave to the architect.

Let the architect cling, always, to the normal human figure for his scale and he cannot go so far wrong as Michelangelo did in St. Peter's in Rome. St. Peter's is invariably disappointing as a great building, for not until the eye deliberately catches a human figure for purpose of comparison does one realize that the building is vast. All the details are likewise huge and the sense of grandeur it might have had if the great masses were qualified by details kept to human scale—this effect of grandeur—is lost in the degradation of the human figure. A strange error for a sculptor to make.

The safest practice in proportion is not to attempt to allow for "perspective," stilting domes as he did, changing pitches of roofs as many do, and modifying natural lines and masses to meet certain views from certain vantage points as the Greeks are said to have done, but to make the constitution of the thing right in itself. Let the incidental perspectives fall when and how they will. Trust Nature to give proper values to a proper whole. The modifications she may make are better than any other. There is something radically wrong with a scheme that requires distortion to appear correct.

In the matter of materials. These also affect scale. The logical material under the circumstances is the most natural material for the purpose. It is usually the most beautiful—and it is obvious that sticks will not space the same as stones nor allow the same proportions as steel. Nor will the spacing adjustable to these be natural to made-blocks or to slabs or to a plastic modeling of form.

Sticks of wood will have their own natural volume and spacing determined by standards of use and manufacture and the nature of both.

A wood plan is slender: light in texture, narrower spacing.

A stone or brick plan is heavy: black in masses, wider in spacing.

Combination of materials: lightness combined with massiveness.

A cast-block building: such massing as is felt to

H.J. Ullman House (Project). Oak Park, Illinois. 1904. Perspective. Pencil on tracing paper, 19 x 11". FLLW Fdn#0411.002

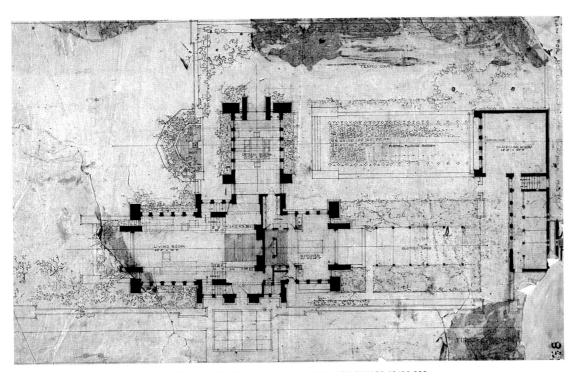

H.J. Ullman House (Project). Oak Park, Illinois. 1904. Plan. Ink on paper, 28 x 18". FLLW Fdn#0411.008

Charles E. Ennis House. Los Angeles, California. 1923. Perspective. Pencil and color pencil on tracing paper, 40 x 20". FLLW Fdn#2401.003

be adequate to the sense of block and box and slab; more freedom in spacing.

The purely or physically plastic structure: center line of thin webbing with a flesh-covering on either side; unit-system may be abandoned.

Then there are the double-wall constructions requiring great skill in spacing so that the interior shell will work simply with the outer shell. And there are as many others as there are combinations of all these.

But the more simple the materials used—the more the building tends toward a mono-material building—the more nearly will "perfect style" reward an organic plan and ease of execution economize results. The more logical will the whole become.

A wood plan is seen in the plan for the Coonley house at Riverside and in the plan for "D101 house."

A cast-block and slab building: the plan for Unity Temple at Oak Park.

Brick plans: the plan for the D. D. Martin residence in Buffalo, and the Ullman house in Oak Park, Illinois.

A steel-and-glass plan for a skyscraper, concrete supports and floor slabs: this plan will be used later in this series to illustrate another article.

The purely "plastic" structure may be seen in the "Einstein Tower" by Mendelsohn and buildings by European Modernists.

A double-wall construction, in this case of precast blocks, is seen in the Ennis house at Hollywood.

A thin concrete slab-structure: the merchandise building in Los Angeles.

In the matter of building methods. These methods too are meantime shaping the plan. In the Coonley house—the 4'-0" unit works with 16" centers as established in carpenter practice for the length of laths, the economical spacing of studs and nailing-bearings, standard lumber lengths.

In Unity Temple—the only limit was the mass of concrete that could withstand the violent changes of climate and remain related to human scale and easy construction. The box and blocks, however, determine the shape of every feature and every detail of the features, as it was all cast in "boxes."

So a unit suitable for timber construction was adopted as the false-work in which its cast was made of lumber. Multiples of 16", syncopated, was the scale adopted.

In the Martin house, brick was used. Brick lends itself to articulation in plan and is an easy material to use architecturally. Bricks naturally make corners and the corners are easily used for play of light and shade. The Martin house is an organized brick-pier building. It is when assembling groups of piers in rhythmical relation to the whole that brick comes out best according to its nature. A 7'-9" unit reduced by minor mullions to 3'-9", was used, in the horizontal only. There are other views of brick as legitimate as this one, to be used according to the individual "taste" of the designer. The broken masses of textured walls, for instance.

In the steel-and-glass building there are no walls. The method yields best to suspended screens, shop-fabricated. A mechanized fabric enters here to give the form and style that is Architecture. The structural supports and floor-slabs in this case happen to be concrete. They could be protected steel as well. Planned on a 4'-0" unit, emphasis on alternate verticals. No emphasis on horizontals.

In the precast-block building, the method of building wholly determines the form and style. This is a mono-material structure planned on multiples of 16 inches square, both horizontal and vertical. No emphasis.

The slab-building is an expression of another method. Cast-slabs, set sidewise and lengthwise, and flatwise, making everything, as may be seen in the result planned on multiples of 7'-0".

Concerning articulation. The Ennis house will serve to illustrate the principle which, once grasped, is simple.

In the building, each separate portion of the building devoted to a special purpose asserts itself as an individual factor in the whole.

The dining room associated with terraces is one mass. The living room with bedroom attached, another mass standing at the center on a terrace of its own—the dominating feature of the group.

Mr. Ennis's bedroom, semidetached and used as a study or office, is another and terminal mass.

At the rear is the kitchen unit, a subordinate mass. All are connected by a gallery passing along the group at the rear. Finally the terrace wall ends in a detached mass to the rear of the lot—the garage and chauffeur's quarters.

A little study will show how each separate room makes its own characteristic contribution to the whole mass.

The completed whole crowns the end of a high ridge in Hollywood and is a precast slab-block building woven together with steel.

These articulations are as obvious in the plan as in the perspective. The Coonley house is similarly articulate.

Articulate buildings of this type have their parallel in the music of Bach particularly, but in any of the true form-masters in music.

It may be readily seen that in this particular direction lies infinite variety in expression. The sense of it is fundamental in any architectural release.

In the matter of expression and style.

As a matter of logic in the plan, it is easy to see there can be none except as the result of scale, materials, and building method. But with all that

American Ready-Cut System Houses. Milwaukee, Wisconsin. 1917. Model D101. Perspective. Ink on paper, 28 x 12". FLLW Fdn#1506.123

properly set, there is the important human equation at work in every move that is made. The architect weaves into it all his sense of the whole. He articulates—emphasizes what he loves.

No matter how technically faithful his logic may have been to his scale and materials and method—over and above all that, living in the atmosphere created by the orchestration of those matters, hovers the indefinable quality of style. Style emanating from the form, as seen by the man himself. And while it speaks to you of all those important matters, it leaves you imbued by dignity, grace, repose, gaiety, strength, severity, delicacy, and of

rhythmical order, in a musical sense, as the master wills—just as music does. Usually you hear music as you work. But not necessarily.

So every true building is of the quality of some man's soul, his sense of harmony and "fitness," which is another kind of harmony—more or less manifest in the fallible human process.

And his building will nobly stand, belonging to its site—breathing this message to the spirit quite naturally, so long as his work was well done or the course of human events does not inundate or human ignorance willfully destroy his building.

IN THE CAUSE OF ARCHITECTURE: PURELY PERSONAL

Wright *used the title* "In the Cause of Architecture" *for more than simply the collection of his articles that appeared in* The Architectural Record *during 1927 and 1928. The title became for him a general heading for several other writings pertaining to the state of architecture in America and to the new influences from France, Germany, and Holland. "Purely Personal" and "Composition as a Method in Creation" are examples of such statements. "Purely Personal" was later modified and edited by Wright to appear as book reviews of Le Corbusier's* Towards a New Architecture *and of Fiske Kimball's* American Architecture. *But the original draft, printed here for the first time in its entirety, includes more material, much of it strident and sometimes raw.*

Referring to Le Corbusier, Wright points out that the so-called surface and mass of the stark, skeleton-like forms coming from abroad were nothing more than a derivation of his own style in early works such as the Larkin Building, Unity Temple, and the Coonley house. [Unpublished essay, 1928]

MR. HITCHCOCK'S ARTICLES IN THE *RECORD,* ON "MODER- nity in Architecture," are the immediate occasion of a desire to interrupt this series and utter a few harsh, vain things. Also, there is the newly translated book by Le Corbusier, Fiske Kimball's *History of American Architecture,* and "ditto" by Tallmadge to add rage to the urge.

"Ists" and "isms" offend, now as ever. What a "New Traditionalist" may be, none may exactly know. Mr. Hitchcock says I am one. Monsieur Corbusier is, by the same Hitchcock token, the leader of the "*New* Pioneers."

Why "New?" A pioneer is a pioneer, *n'est-ce pas?*

A pioneer by Nature is ever new, and tradition is ever old?

However that may be found to be, all Monsieur Hitchcock has to say or can see done "Towards a New Architecture" was here at home in our own country, at work with Mr. Sullivan in his field and with myself in mine more than twenty-five years ago.

To say this is ungracious to the critic—perhaps inhospitable to foreign architects—but true. And there is worse to follow. The Corbusier formula was at work here, there, and then in three dimensions while our critic claims for but two—"surface and mass."

New "pioneering" pronouncements now reach us with éclat, as discovery, in a style as stark as a gas-pipe railing at the edge of one of the "New" cantilever porches.

Le Corbusier, at least, is no sentimentalist, but he is an aesthete!

These continental discoveries affect our provincial "historians" with all the charm of French novelty. . . ."*Toujours L'etranger!*" for them.

But, the two products, "surface and mass," which, as elements, constitute the Architecture of the "New" pioneering were the skeleton products of the ideas that built the Larkin Building in 1904, Unity Temple in 1906, and the Coonley House in 1907. So what can our critic do about it?

The affirmation of "rejection" may be seen in those buildings; and refreshing enough, at the time, the buildings were for that single reason, if for no other. At that time—it was the Larkin Building, Buffalo, versus the Flatiron Building, New York City.

"New" pioneering has either ignored this landmark or grasping the motif clearly enough has thought the statement of the theme then insufficiently "stark." Perhaps the expression of the principle involved was insufficiently "stark" to be very sensational now. But one may not stop with surface and mass even when one has discovered them and, as happens but seldom, got both on straight and refuses for the time being to go further into Architecture.

I have gone further. Since it is becoming an issue of the hour, let us get the matter historically right, inasmuch as our own local historians choose to ignore facts unfamiliar, distasteful, or disturbing to their preconceived and embalmed ideas. . . .The so-called "New" may lose itself today in work, in ideas, and ideas in the work of Louis Sullivan in his field, and of myself in mine, done long ago. That work was pioneering neither "New" nor "Old"; just pioneering, that's all, groundbreaking and sound. The pioneers, being in rough country, apparently succeeded only in breaking ground for the "new strangers" groundbreaking now.

Notwithstanding the personal matter I've just raised, I should be content were France—our fashion-monger—in this school of "surface and mass" to again set a fashion among us for a generation or two—as seems likely. Lean, hard plainness, mistaken for simplicity, has the quality of simplicity to a re-

freshing extent, where all is fat or false. It is aristocratic, by contrast. I say this fashion would be good for what ails these United States in Architecture, this cowardly, superficial artificiality. Any transient influence in the right direction is welcome.

But, I shall continue to resent "eers," "ists," or "isms" and particularly resist the "ist."

All that yet lives in Architecture, is still quietly alive in my work, "in exile," and living there as a sound skeleton in a sound body.

I will wear no label.

Were the "eer" to be given the letter S for prefix, the honor would be declined in the circumstances as worthless.

The organic elements of building are wholesome, I find. The proper organs of expression should be appropriately in place, all of them, before we may have Architecture. Were the planes revealed by stripping my buildings to mere surface and mass, they would startle the "New" by unsuspected resemblance to their recent "discoveries." The "New" delights in surface effects, but discovers the "skeleton" necessary and can see it wholly lacking in their present-day Architecture as it was wholly lacking in ours before the pioneers I've mentioned.

Now, a good skeleton in Architecture is indispensable, but only for the purpose of a sound body. So I have been working with these organic developments that contribute to the sound body, believing the poetry of Architecture, therefore the art of Architecture is to be inherent in surface and mass only when both are organically related to the constitution of the whole: yes and when they become a further development of the constitution of the whole. Here enters the element of the third dimension about which I have talked too much to have been understood.

An emotional being imbued with much sentiment, I am therefore called names—a "New Traditionalist" for one. Soon I shall be called an "Old Sentimentalist."

Indeed, that I suspect, is what the local historians already mean when they refer to me as a "Romanticist." At any rate, unashamed, I am searching for this poetic development that I call the sound body of Architecture. I suggest to the "New" pioneers to marry their surface and mass effects to this body, when novelty of "discovery" wears off.

The "American Classic," according to Fiske Kimball, cared nothing at all about any such marriage. Mr. Kimball mistakes the predominance of "the Classic"—that divine disregard of consequences to human life in America—for "triumph." A common enough mistake.

To the real pioneers, it was an unfortunate but a sadly accepted fact that the commercial machine owing to its deadly facility, in these United States, would have to find ready-made Architectural clothes to wear for some time. The necessary outfit was discovered at the Columbian Fair and has served as may be seen. But never for one moment during the thirty-four years since the needed garments first began to be borrowed has there been a doubt in my mind that the practical expression concealed by such cheap expedient would slowly emerge to eventually render the expedient unnecessary and absurd. Any true organic expression of underlying practical Nature is of slow growth. But it is sure growth. One may look within and already see transplanted forms, dying or dead. What little we have built out of our soil on principle will not die. It is all the "Architecture" we have; as always before on Earth where Architecture is the record of human life. Such building survives and is the ultimate triumph.

Towards a New Architecture declares "surface and mass" the chief characteristics of Architecture with which the Architect has to deal. So, the "New" proceeds to superficially play with those two by-products as though they were elements, ignoring the essential element that alone can guide either surface or mass to life. That element is depth.

Depth: That quality of "the third dimension," is all important.

Without it there is no great Architecture, Old or New.

Without sense of it there is no progress. Nothing happens. The "New" pioneers are without it and so making another kind of picture building by leaving off all the ornament, so-called. Shallow too. I will admit the omission temporarily refreshing and to be following in the right direction, less silly than Fiske Kimball's "American Classic." Applied ornamentation is not "ornament," it is a disease.

The "Cause of Architecture" is long and suffers much twisting by many and various twisters.

Our time is fleeting, but the great spirit of Architecture is nearer home because of actual pioneers, "New Pioneers" and "New Traditionalists," and out of each other comes something else, or whichever way round historians would like to have it.

But must "History" impose upon the credulous "New eers" and "New ists" in order to effect only another "ism"?

I respect and admire Otto Wagner, Berlage, Gropius, Olbrich, Oud, Widjeveld, Dudok, Mendelsohn, Mallet-Stevens, Perret, Le Corbusier, and a score of their peers and compeers—all fine earnest men at work. We are one family in a great cause. I welcome their advent here in this country where Louis Sullivan lies "defeated" and I am reported "in exile," by which I suppose is meant as good as dead—or worse.

But I am not *of* them.

Such as I am, I am myself.

But such as I am, I am for them as they are for me, such as they are, here where we are weary of stylish iniquity and iniquitous "styles." Or, to change the figure, where all is fat and no skeleton, except an occasional one like the skeleton of the skyscraper, now the personal triumph of Manhattan's commercial machine over architects.

It seems to me that "America," so far as it concerns a spirit, is more abroad than at home in this large matter of Architecture. And this is what Mr. Hitchcock's views indicate.

To a local historian, erstwhile of the "Prairie School"—in my own Middle West that label is now exchanged for another. Another critic, Tallmadge enumerates, in my name, a small category of moderate virtues of perception and judgement in Architecture.

I got them out of myself.

But he generously hands them over to the Japanese, informing his gentle reader that I was taught these virtues by the Japanese, whereas the truth is, once for all, I knew nothing of Japanese Architecture until I first saw it in 1906[1]. And they now know little or nothing of such virtues as he ascribes to them when he hands me over to them.

All must derive somehow from somewhere or from somewhere to somehow before our somebodies will let us join the tribe?

Why is it an historian's business to deal in deception to explain his victim's or subject's existence?

A critic should know that sympathies are not tendencies. Likenesses spring up spontaneously around the world, but with different purpose and meaning. Why be deluded by such and delude others?

Is this form of deception the historians' necessity just because he, too, must make some discovery or lose his rendezvous with Fame!

Anyhow, such "History" as is being written in the provinces will let no Architect live his own life, on his own merits.

Are you an architect? Then you are Mayan, Japanese, Bhutanese, or a New Pioneer or an Old or New Traditionalist. You belong to this or that great-little or little-great school or you unwisely founded one. Never would they give you credit for being clever—harsh enough to have avoided founding one when you have done so—choosing to remain free.

So it is the business of a historian cross-eyed, cockeyed, or blind to classify and pigeonhole you according to whatever light he has in him at the time.

Such history is more and more a perfidious freak of journalism.

Would it be too much to ask of my fellows in Architecture—marked copy to Historians—to allow me to remain just A Natural Architect, practicing, as near as I am able, a Natural Architecture?

But not just a Nature-Architect. This I humbly ask!

No—just a Natural Architect in his Native Land—wherever that land may extend. It seems, now to extend very far.

1. Wright's dating is not always accurate. His first trip to Japan was actually in 1905. He had also attended the 1893 Columbian Exposition in Chicago, at which the Japanese had built and furnished a pavilion in traditional styles.

IN THE CAUSE OF ARCHITECTURE: COMPOSITION AS METHOD IN CREATION

In direct contravention of the Renaissance method of making architectural forms by way of "composition," Wright here urges the architect to study the "geometry at the center of every Nature-form we see"—not to be simply "looking-at" nature, but looking into nature, grasping the principles at work, and then building forms that are not imitative but creative. This essay is one of his clearest espousals of the principles of study, design, and proper use of materials and the machine. [Unpublished essay, 1928]

"COMPOSITION" IN ARCHITECTURE IS, I HOPE, DEAD. Of course it always was dead but it has worn the look of life, and since the Renaissance it was all the method we had in Architecture. The Renaissance liberated painting—and sculpture and the literal reigned supreme—literature was its Art. Then, it was, I think, architects who began to "compose" buildings because they could no longer create them. Thus, "composition" was born.

Nothing is created by composition except superficial reactions of a merely picturesque character.

The decorator by Nature of his superficial office must compose, but the architect disposes of what the decorator composes whenever he enters into the Nature-spirit of Architecture and truly builds.

To "compose" is only to arrange. It is a secondary order of merit—to which we have had and always will have enough performances. As a "method" of creation it is barren. As method, "composition" is

taught—perhaps because it is something that can be taught, whereas creation must be wooed.

I have listened to painters, sculptors, and architects prate of "composition" until sick of the word and I contemptuous of them.

Composition literally is 2 plus 2 equals 4 minus 3 equals 1 times 1 equals 1. The kaleidoscope does as much in the field of pattern. The kaleidoscope then is the true virtuoso when it comes to composition? The ideal "composer?"

Composition is a tidy means to makeshift but is no true means to a great end.

The only method worth an architect's time is growth. An architect must "grow" his building from his motif, so that his building is just as natural an expression of thought and feeling directing power toward ultimate purpose as is any tree or any engine for that matter.

There is a life-principle expressed in geometry at the center of every Nature-form we see. This integral pattern is abstract, lying within the object we see and that we recognize as concrete form. It is with this abstraction that the architect must find himself at home before Architecture can take place. The essential-abstract is the architect's proper concern before all else.

Now what is this abstract concern?

A little book by Hokusai I found in Japan fifteen years ago had the answer. Hokusai analyzed with his T square, triangle, and compass any and every natural object one could think of, first giving the geometrical pattern on which depended the expression of each. Then, by a few free relevant strokes, he would make it the realistic object as we commonly see it. So slight sometimes were the necessary additional touches as to seem miraculous and to make realism seem ridiculous. Foliage, human beings, dogs, landscape, waves, trees, streams, mountains— everything and anything transformed itself from squares, circles, angles, lines, by a touch a child could give.

This hidden form-world is inherent in all forms. This form world is the architect's world. His thought must penetrate that world. In that interior world his lot is cast.

Great Chinese artists and especially the great Japanese artists of the Momoyama period[1] understood that inner realm, lived in it and loved it with such success that a Korin or a Sotatsu[2] is incomparable abstraction today in that very realm, although they never took the subject matter very far away from appearances. Even so, they have no counterparts in the West. They were interpreters of unsuspected concordances and rhythms in imaginative effects that arrested and delighted their fellows.

Sympathetic craftsmen were waiting and skillfully adapted these new discoveries and treatments of elemental form, hitherto unseen, applying them to various metals, textiles, wood and lacquer, paper, and glass until new life of the spirit came to the eyes as music comes to the ears to make Japanese life still more true to Nature. Materials were themselves subject to the same insight—the same method.

Here was integral method: true creative method that did not compose but developed, that got to the geometric heart of the object and got new

forms born out of it, where the mind of the Artist was touched by that form whatever it might be. No "composition" here. Composition remained for those who came after and took the things these artists did and began to arrange and rearrange them in the vain endeavor to make other things live from them. That is what and when composition is "for."

These lesser men, unable to go to the source, were adapters and modifiers, "composers" instead of creators.

Therefore, why should an architect any longer compose?

Why should he continue to be deceived by appearances? Why not now see as artists alone see the essential in abstract form as a source of form suggestion? This imaginative substance is the material to use with the Machine if it is to be successful as a tool in sentient artist hands and ever greatly serve humanity.

Realism, now, is as dead as realistic. The Machine killed both while seeming to exaggerate it.

Machine-made mimicry and mummery have had their day and much overtime—notwithstanding the novelty "Art and decoration" may stage and restage for superficial entertainment. Let us learn to see within, at least far enough within to grasp essential pattern in all created things. And, there, method in creation will come freely to him who sees thus, in the abstract. As a preliminary, study the geometry that is the idea of every form, a fern, a snail, a tree, or a fish. Certain natural objects yield their secret more readily than others because they are nearer to their origins, more primitive. Take for analysis, therefore, the more simple things—at first.

Then take for analysis the texture of the trees and learn to indicate these textures each in turn.

Learn the essential-pattern that makes the oak to the mind's eye and distinguishes it from the essential-pattern that makes the pine.

Then for exercise make new trees of unknown species. Try, after this, the curling vine, flowing water, curving sand.

Then try the flowers, butterflies and bees. . . .

A chrysanthemum is easy.

A rock or a rose is difficult.

And I do not mean to take the obvious, surface

effects that differentiate each—but to go within each to find the essential geometry of pattern that gives each character. That is proper study for any architect who would find method and be competent to develop integral-ornament.

Try this direct method regardless of "second hand" and gradually discipline your power to see.

Get patiently to the point where you naturally see this element of pattern in everything. Make it your favorite "intrigue." It is fascinating.

How much richer this vision will make your world you can have no idea until you develop this disciplinary power to see. Your world soon becomes manifold to you, rich with unsuspected significance, infinite in variety, story imbued with principle.

Once this essential Nature-pattern is mastered in the abstract, try to connect it up as form with what function it may have had. You may discover even this by search.

Learn the reasonableness, admire and appreciate the wisdom that cast the form for what it is and you will see that it is what it is because of what it has to be. Learn to see why it is what it is. That is the study of Architecture, at least—proper studies for an architect.

And I promise you a habit of thought arises from such eye-minded exercises to make constructive effort natural, "design" spontaneous.

Things of themselves begin to proceed from generals to particulars—they begin to build of themselves, to develop, emerge, and take inevitable form, forcing nothing, imposing not at all. Lying never.

Deception in this Nature-realm is unthinkable because it is stupid because it is unnatural. There is destiny inherent in every chosen motif and it finds destiny anew in your hands guided by imagination to your heart's desire.

How many buildings look cut from one piece in point of character? Style?

How rare to see any building whatsoever that is all one building!

Published in the *Record* continually are buildings very charmingly a dozen different buildings all essentially inharmonious although skillfully brought together as one. In such buildings we have *collection*, not *creation*. Again—composition.

Almost never may we see a thorough entity—instead we see a feature in this feeling and a feature in that, added to other features and parts that are, again, something else. These are the symptoms of "composition" always: discords forced for effect or softened by the slur—with due sense of the picturesque.

Any of the accepted architectural masterpieces of the time, the place, and the hour analyzed may be seen to be at least several if not seven or more distinctly different things arranged together—showing clearly how the structure was not born but arbitrarily made.

And novelties we see listed and praised by critics today as "modernistic" are really only a decorator's attempt at building. An attempt to gratify the decorator's instinct to see the "decor" finally triumphant as Architecture.

In "modernistic" buildings we may see some sense of plain surface, the surfaces proportioned and cut to shape for their own sake—and usually put upon it, or within it, or beside it—a startling mass of brilliant decoration—to get the contrasts that are "decorative" whether concerned with construction or not so concerned. This is comparatively easy. Sometimes charming. But not Architecture.

These matters are merely "decoration" profiting by the new simplicity-lie. There is method here, but not the method of creation. Rather "pose" and not of the method of the crystal, nor of the rose: the method of the *mise-en-scène*—not the method of creation.

Such buildings do not grow.

Such buildings happen. They are made.

In them "composition" still composes. Clever decoration often—these buildings, but—no sense of construction—no product of abstraction such as their frankly decorative attributes themselves often have to show in themselves.

The decor-architect has succeeded in his abstractions only where and as they may be *applied* as such.

"Appliqué" is his world.

"Appliqué" is his method.

He is "appliqué-architect" and "appliqué" is his building.

In many modern structures may be seen the triumph over Architecture of "Art and Decoration." Modernistic but not new, they are not yet modern Architecture. Nor until the abstraction finds proper use as method and motif for true building and the pattern of the building becomes the constitution of construction itself, and the simple source of its colorful imaginative features, as well, will we have the nobility of Architecture.

When the architect's mind is disciplined by this power to see in the abstract the very patterns of steel construction itself, as discovery for its own sake, we will have opened a new life to building. The steel skeleton is a novelty just now and certain architects are just discovering that bones have effects, with painful results to the beholder. To skin the bones is therefore Architecture for the moment.

But this, too, is a more serious endeavor than "make-up"—certainly—or make-believe.

But the method of creation is, no less, still to come in this effort.

Only as the principle of construction—cantilever, hanger, post, or beam finds expression in natural pattern (yes, young man in Architecture, all these elements of Architecture have "pattern") and not until that pattern becomes a plastic, rhythmic fabric consistently adapted to human needs with complete repose—not until then will any "modern" architectural crusade result in Architecture. It will be the usual masquerade.

We are now, A.D. 1928—at the two extremes.

"Art and Decoration" insisting upon make-up: its own.

The bone-yard, insisting upon the skeleton-articulate.

The one "school" claiming French painting as parent, gaily disposing of the matter with surface and mass.

The other school painfully rattling the bones ignored by the first, and, in the name of the Machine, turning the matter inside-out, putting barren boxes on top of stark posts: so glassing them in that one may see that they are boxes on top of posts and make no mistake about it whatever.

And this for the moment seems to be our development in Architecture.

It may be a beginning.

Beautifully dressed, the first, for the sake of the dress!

Stark, naked "necessity" the other, for the sake of the necessity!

Dear "pioneers"—"New" or Old.

The Machine needs no compliments from you! Instead the Machine needs honest work to do, work not got from you merely by way of your exposing its bones: no, no more than on its "face," it needs a more becoming "make-up."

Lay lipstick and rouge aside.

Drag no skeletons to light to murder repose. It is useless—unless to convict the murderer of murder.

Let us simply practice the method that builds a building naturally, significant as an entity perfected by the Machine, but not for the Machine nor as a Machine. Never will "Art and decoration" nor the sensational rattling of skeletons take the place of such Architecture, unless the people of Usonia have no vision. Perhaps it would be fairer to say, unless they fail their own vision.

The abstraction which the Machine can best perfect as architectural pattern may be found by no ists nor any isms.

Therefore build Nature-patterns in terms of such materials as best suit our human-nature, this and our Architecture will be the greater for the Machine. The Machine will have found its master in the architect, in his hand the key to a New world. We will then have buildings not only modern but New.

---

1. The Momoyama period, 1574–1614.
2. Tawaraya Sotatsu (?–1645?), a Kyōto artist, was one of the greatest of the Rimpa school painters.

IN THE CAUSE OF ARCHITECTURE II: WHAT "STYLES" MEAN TO THE ARCHITECT

[Published with three illustrations in The Architectural Record, *February 1928]*

IN WHAT IS NOW TO ARISE FROM THE PLAN AS CONCEIVED and held in the mind of the architect, the matter of style may be considered as of elemental importance.

In the logic of the plan what we call "standardization" is seen to be a fundamental principle at work in architecture. All things in Nature exhibit this tendency to crystallize—to form and then conform, as we may easily see. There is a fluid, elastic period of becoming, as in the plan, when possibilities are infinite. New effects may, then, originate from the idea or principle that conceives. Once form is achieved, that possibility is dead so far as it is a creative flux.

Styles in architecture are part and parcel of this standardization. During the process of formation, exciting, fruitful. So soon as accomplished—a prison house for the creative soul and mind.

"Styles" once accomplished soon become yardsticks for the blind, crutches for the lame, the recourse of the impotent.

As humanity develops there will be less recourse to the "styles" and more style—for the development of humanity is a matter of greater creative power for the individual—more of that quality in each that was once painfully achieved by the whole. A richer variety in unity is, therefore, a rational hope.

So this very useful tendency in the nature of the human mind, to standardize, is something to guard against as thought and feeling are about to take "form"—something of which to beware—something to be watched. For, overnight, it may "set" the form past redemption and the creative matter be found dead. Standardization is, then, a mere tool, though indispensable, to be used only to a certain extent in all other than purely commercial matters.

Used to the extent that it leaves the spirit free to destroy it at will—on suspicion, maybe—to the extent only that it does not become *a* style—or an inflexible rule—is it desirable to the architect.

It is desirable to him only to the extent that it is capable of new forms and remains the servant of those forms. Standardization should be allowed to work but never to master the process that yields the form.

In the logic of the plan we see the mechanics that are standardization, this dangerous tendency to crystallize into styles, at work and attempting to dispose of the whole matter. But if we are artists, no one can see it in the results of our use of it, which will be living and "personal," nevertheless.

There is a dictum abroad that "Great Art" is impersonal.

The Universal speaks by way of the Personal in our lives. And the more interesting as such the deliverer is, the more precious to us will that message from the Universal be. For we can only understand the message in terms of ourselves. Impersonal matter

"Hollyhock House" for Aline Barnsdall. Los Angeles, California. 1917. FLLW Fdn FA#1705.0087

is no matter at all—in Art. This is not to say that the manner is more than the matter of the message—only to say that the man is the matter of the message, after all is said and done. This is dangerous truth for weak-headed egotists in architecture who may be in love with their own reflections as in a mirror.

But why take the abuse of the thing for the thing itself and condemn it to exalt the mediocre and fix the commonplace?

All truth of any consequence whatsoever, is dangerous and in the hands of the impotent—damned. Are we, therefore, to cling to "safe lies?" There is a soiled fringe hanging to every manful effort to realize anything in this world—even a square meal.

The Universal will take care of itself.

Let us tune up with it, and it will sing through us, because of us, the song man desires most to hear. And that song is Man.

The question is now, how to achieve *style*, how to conserve that quality and profit to the fullest extent by standardization, the soul of the machine, in the work that is "Man." We have seen how standardization, as a method, serves as guide in the architect's plan, serves as a kind of warp on which to weave the woof of his building. So far, it is safe and may be used to any extent as a method, while the

"idea" lives. But the process has been at work in everything to our hand that we are to use with which to build. We can overcome that, even profit by it, as we shall see. The difficulty is that it has been at work upon the man for whom we are to build. He is already more or less mechanized in this the Machine Age. To a considerable extent he is the victim of the thing we have been discussing—the victim, I say, because his ideas are committed to standards which he now willfully standardizes and institutionalizes until there is very little fresh life left in him. To do so is now his habit and, he is coming to think, his virtue.

Here is the real difficulty and a serious one.

What fresh life the architect may have is regarded with distrust by him, suspected and perhaps condemned on suspicion, merely, by this habituate who standardizes for a living—now, and must defend himself in it. The plan-factory grew to meet his wants. Colleges cling to the "classic" to gratify him. His "means" are all tied up in various results of the process. He is bound hand and foot, economically, to his institutions and blindfolded by his "self-interest." He is the slave of the Expedient—and he calls it the Practical! He believes it.

What may be done with him?

Whatever was properly done would be to

"undo" him, and that can't be done with his con- sent. He cannot be buried because it is a kind of living death he knows. But there are yet living among him those not so far gone. It is a matter of history that the few who are open to life have made it eventually what it is for the many. History repeats itself, as ever. The minority report is always right— John Bright pointed to history to prove it.[1]

What we must work with is that minority— however small. It is enough hope, for it is all the hope there ever was in all the world, since time be- gan, and we believe in Progress.

These slaves to the Expedient are all beholden to certain ideas of certain individuals. They tend to accept, ready-made, from those individuals their views of matters like style and, although style is a simple matter, enough nonsense has been talked about it by architects and artists. So "Fashion" rules with inexorable hand. The simple unlettered Amer- ican man of business, as yet untrained by "looted" culture, is most likely, in all this, to have fresh vi- sion. And, albeit a little vulgar, there, in him, and in the minority of which we have just spoken, is the only hope for the architectural future of which we are going to speak.

The value of style as against standardized "styles" is what I shall try to make clear and, to il- lustrate, have chosen from my own work certain examples to show that it is a quality not depending at all upon "styles," but a quality inherent in every organic growth—as such. Not a self-conscious product at all. A natural one. I maintain that if this quality of style may be had in these things of mine, it may be had to any extent by Usonia, did her sons put into practice certain principles which are at work in these examples as they were once at work when the antique was "now." This may be done with no danger of forming a style—except among those whose characters and spiritual attainments are such that they would have to have recourse to one anyway.

The exhibition will become complete in the course of this series. The immediate burden of this paper is properly to evaluate this useful element of standardization with which the architect works for life, as in the "logic of the plan," and show how it may disastrously triumph over life as in the "styles" in this matter that confronts him now.

This antagonistic triumph is achieved as the consequence of man's tendency to fall in love with his tools, of which his intellect is one, and he soon mistakes the means for the end. This has happened most conspicuously in the architectural Renais- sance. The "re-birth" of architecture. Unless a mat- ter went wrong and died too soon there could be no occasion for "re-birth." But according to architects, architecture has been in this matter of getting itself continually re-born for several centuries until one might believe it was never properly born, and now thoroughly dead from repeated "re-birth." As a matter of fact, architecture never needed to be born again—the architects who thought so did need to be; but never were.

A few examples may serve to show "architec- ture" a corpse, like sticking a pin into some member of a cadaver. Such architectural members for in- stance as the cornice—pilasters and architraves, the façade, and a whole brain-load of other instances of the moribund.

But architecture has consisted of these things. And architecture before that had the misfortune to be a nonutilitarian affair—it was a matter of decorat- ing construction or sculpturing, from the outside, a mass of building material. At its worst it became a mere matter of constructing decoration. This con- cept of architecture was peculiarly Greek. And the Greek concept became the architectural religion of the modern world and became so, strangely enough, just when Christianity became its spiritual convic- tion. The architectural concept was barbaric, unspir- itual—superficial. That did not matter. Architecture was "re-born" in Florence on that basis and never got anywhere below the surface afterward, owing to many inherent inconsistencies with interior life as life within, lived on. I am talking of "Academic" architecture.

Of the three instances we have chosen, the cor- nice would be enough to show—for as it was, the other two were, and so were all besides. We are now attacking the standard that became standardized.

It was a standard that, to the eye, had grace and charm but to the mind had, never, organic integrity.

"Hollyhock House" for Aline Barnsdall. Los Angeles, California.1917. FLLW Fdn FA#1705.0090

It was "exterior" as thought, however exquisite the refinement and refreshing the play of light and shadow, or enticing the form—or seductive the nuances of shade. It could live only on the surface and thrive as a "cult." It was aristocratic as such. Sometimes an applied, studied elegance, it was often a studious refinement. But it had no interior vitality to inform new conditions and develop new forms for fresh life. The cornice, a constructed thing, constructed as a form for its own sake, became fixed as the characteristic architectural expression of this culture. The cornice was a gesture—a fine gesture, but an empty one. What original significance the cornice had was soon lost. It had come by way of the eaves of a projecting and visible roof. It stayed for "the look of the thing" centuries after its use and purpose had gone. It was said to be "a thing of beauty." It became the last word in the "language" of approved form, regardless of interior significance. And it hangs today in the eye of the sun, as dubious an excrescence as ever made shift. It has said the last word for "exterior" architecture. For the cornice has all but disappeared, and with it disappears a horde of artificialities no nearer truth.

Another concept of building enters in this coming era.

The building is no longer a block of building material dealt with, artistically, from the outside. The room within is the great fact about the building—*the room* to be expressed in the exterior as *space enclosed*. This sense of the *room* within, held as the great *motif* for enclosure, is the advanced thought of the era in architecture, and is now searching for exterior expression.

This is another conception of architecture entirely. It is probably new under the sun.

Here we have a compelling organic significance instead of seductive imposition of elegance.

Architecture so born needs no "re-birth." It will work out its own destiny at all times, in all places, under all conditions—naturally.

It will not fail of style.

This concept is a minority report in this democratic era. But it is the natural one for that era, because it is consistent with the nature of the highest spiritual and ethical ideal of democracy.

To make clear to the young architect this "interior" initiative, which is now his, is necessary to any comprehension on his part of the opportunity that is now to his hand in what may rise from his plan.

Once this interior viewpoint is grasped, his own nature will gather force from the idea and, with experience, become truly potent as a creative factor in modern life concerns.

"What significance?" This should be the question through which everything in the way of "form" should be sifted in imagination before it is accepted or rejected in his work.

Contrived elegancies the weary world has obediently borne and worn and regretfully cast aside in plenty, with undefined but inextinguishable hope.

But expressions of human life, rooted in that life, to grow and beneficently expand in human thought, compelled by our principle as great trees grow in their soil and expand in the air according to their interior principle, beguiled by the sun—that is what the world needs and what democracy must have. This is the very meaning of democracy, if it is ever to have any meaning.

The word "democracy" is used far from any such interior significance as yet. But once born into the soul and mind of American youth, this sense of architecture will grow fast and become strong as only law is strong, however weak man-made laws may ever be and pusillanimous his "enforcements."

To show this ideal at work in concrete form it is unnecessary to arouse animosity or give pain by illustrations of the falsity of the old conception, or, to be fairer, let us say the superficial character of that concept.

If we show the principle at work in certain new buildings—and it may be seen there, clearly—we will have no occasion to molest tradition or dissect the forms that are now sacred. We may leave all decently in their shrouds where architects, urged by the idea of "re-birth" have, for centuries past, wantonly refused to leave them.

Beyond what has been said of architectural members we will not go. We will go forward and then whoever will, according to his disposition, at his leisure, may look backward.

"Hollyhock House" for Aline Barnsdall. Los Angeles, California. 1917. FLLW Fdn FA#1705.0015

Apropos of "style"—let us take—say—Unity Temple.

Style I have said was a quality of the form that character takes, and it becomes necessary to explain what character means.

Any consistent expression of an organic entity, as such; any animal, tree or plant has "character" we may observe. In varying degree, this character may appeal to us as beautiful. It may even be what we call "ugly" and possess the *character* which is the secret of *style*.

Character is one of our strong words. It is loosely applied to any manifestation of force. Properly, it is used to signify "individual significance."

To be insignificant is to have no "character." Observe that we may use the word "character" for "style" and the word "style" for "character" with no great inconsistency. The words are not interchangeable, but applicable to either case. Character is the result of some inward force taking consistent outward shape taking *form* consistent with its nature. The *exterior* any initial life-force naturally takes, reveals "character."

Character then is the significant expression of organic-entity. Yes, but—

That sounds complicated—let's try again—

Character, like style, is the quality of "being" one's self or itself. That—too—but again incomplete.

Character is the result of nature-expression of the soul or life-principle of anything "organic" whatsoever—to the degree that the idea or life-impulse achieves consistent form to our senses—to that degree will "character" be evident.

Character then is not only fate—

As a final definition we may say that *"character" appears to be nature's "art."*

We may observe it in the smooth, dark green watermelon, its swelling alchemy of pink flesh maturing in the sun, its multitude of black seeds, as we see its polished oval lifted above the surrounding tracery of gray-green vines—or in the garter snake darting its forked tongue from among the fretted leaves. How similar may be the markings, the "decoration" of both!

What, then, if all style must have character and all character has style—is the difference between character and style? Well—the difference is the difference between Truth and Beauty—both are forms of the same thing and inseparable from each other in any final analysis as the light ray is inseparable from its source. But we may enjoy the light, ignorant of its source, and speak of it—for that purpose we have the word style. Or we may look to the source, ignoring its consequences. To speak of that we have the word character.

Style is a consequence of character.

The serpent has "style." Bees as well as butterflies. So has the scarab that tumbles its ball of cow-manure in the hot sun of the dusty road. The white crane, the horse, the rat, every flower, any tree—even human beings, when they are natural—have it, because they are genuine. They have *character*. Buildings often have it when they too are genuine, not posing as "architecture." The rear of the New York Public Library has something of this quality of style, while the front has only "styles." The Woolworth Building would have had it to a degree but for professional Gothic prejudices and predilection. The Suspension Bridge from New York to Brooklyn has it. Some aeroplanes have it and some steamships: by no means all of them. Many grain elevators, steel plants, engines have it, and occasionally an automobile. The Wainwright Building of Saint Louis by Adler and Sullivan, as a tall building, had it. There are many tall buildings, now, that are stylish to some degree but all more or less marred by "styles." Unity Temple, for a shameless instance, has style without prejudice or predilection. How did it get it? First by directly acknowledging the *nature* of the problem presented and expressing it with a sense of appropriate shape and proportion in terms of the *character* of the materials and the process of work that was to make the building. It does this consciously and sensibly, all in its own way, simply because there never is any other way.

Let us follow this building through the thought that built it, from the beginning when Dr. Johonnot, the Universalist pastor, called and said he had always admired the little white church with a steeple as seen in the "East" and wanted something like that—follow its evolution to final *form*.

1. John Bright (1811–1889), English orator and statesman.

IN THE CAUSE OF ARCHITECTURE III:
THE MEANING OF
MATERIALS—STONE

[Published without illustrations in The Architectural Record, *April 1928]*

THE COUNTRY BETWEEN MADISON AND JANESVILLE, Wisconsin, is the old bed of an ancient glacier drift. Vast, busy gravel pits abound there, exposing heaps of yellow aggregate, once, and everywhere else, sleeping beneath the green fields. Great heaps, clean and golden, are always waiting there in the sun. And I never pass without emotion—without a vision of the long dust-whitened stretches of the cement mills grinding to impalpable fineness the magic-powder that would "set" it all to shape and wish, both, endlessly subject to my will.

Nor do I come to a lumberyard with its city-like, gradated masses of fresh shingles, boards and timbers, without taking a deep breath of its fragrance—seeing the forest that was laid low in it and the processes that cut and shaped it to the architect's scale of feet and inches—coveting it, *all*.

The rock ledges of a stone quarry are a story and a longing to me. There is suggestion in the strata and character in the formations. I like to sit and feel it, as it is. Often I have thought, were great monumental buildings ever given me to build, I would go to the Grand Canyon of Arizona to ponder them.

When, in early years, I looked south from the massive stone tower in the Auditorium Building where I was pencil in the hand of a master—the red glare of the Bessemer steel converters to the south of Chicago thrilled me as the pages of the *Arabian Nights* used to do—with a sense of terror and romance.

And the smothered incandescence of the kiln! In fabulous heat baking mineral and chemical treasure on mere clay—to issue in all the hues of the rainbow, all the shapes of Imagination and never yield to time—subject only to the violence or carelessness of man. These great ovens would cast a spell upon me as I listened to the subdued roar within them.

The potter's thumb and finger deftly pressing the soft mass whirling on his wheel, as it yielded to his touch; the bulbous glass at the end of slender pipe as the breath of the glassblower and his deft turning, decided its shape—fascinated me. Something was being born.

Colors[1]—in paste or crayon—or pencils— always a thrill! To this day I love to hold a handful of many-colored pencils and open my hand to see them lying loose upon my palm, in the light.

Mere accidental colored chalkmarks on the sunlit sidewalk, perhaps, will make me pause and "something" in me hark back to "something" half remembered, half felt, as though an unseen door had opened and distant music had—for an instant, come trembling through to my senses.

And in the sense of earth—deep-buried treasure there—without end. Mineral matter and metal-stores folded away in the veins of gleaming quartz—gold and silver, lead and copper, and tawny iron ore—to yield themselves up to roaring furnaces and flow to the hands of the architect—all to become pawns in the play of the human mind.

And jewels! The gleam of mineral colors and flashing facets of crystals. Gems to be sought and set—to forever play with light to man's delight—in neverending beams of purest green or red or blue or yellow—and all that lives between. Light!—living in the mathematics of form to match with the mathematics of sound.

Crystals are proof of nature's architectural principle.

All this I see as the architect's garden—his palette I called it—to humble the figure.

Materials! What a resource!

With his "materials"—the architect can do whatever masters have done with pigments or with sound—in shadings as subtle, with combinations as expressive—perhaps outlasting man himself.

Stone, wood, pottery, glass, pigments and aggregates, metals, gems—cast in the industrious maw of mill, kiln, and machine to be worked to the architect's will by human-skill-in-labor. All this to his hand, as the pencil in it makes the marks that disposes of it as he dreams and wills. If he wills well—in use and beauty sympathetic to the creation of which he is creature. If he wills ill, in ugliness and waste as creature-insult to creation.

These *materials* are human-riches.

They are Nature-gifts to the sensibilities that are, again, gifts of Nature.

By means of these gifts, the story and the song of *man* will be *wrought* as, once upon papyrus, and now, on paper it is written.

Each material has its own message and, to the creative artist, its own song.

Listening, he may learn to make two sing together in the service of man or separately as he may choose. A trio? Perhaps.

It is easier to use them solo or in duet than manifold.

The solo is more easily mastered than the orchestral score.

Therefore, it is well to work with a limited palette and more imagination, than it is to work with less imagination and more palette.

So—work wherever possible in mono-material, except where the use of sympathetic extra-materials may add the necessary grace or graceful necessity desirable—or unavoidable.

Each material *speaks a language* of its own just as line and color speak—or perhaps because they do speak.

Each has a story.

In most Architectures of the world, stone has suffered imitation of the stick. Even in the oldest cultures like Chinese civilization, great constructions of stone imitate wood posts and beams in joinery—imitate literally great wood towering of poles and posts, beams, richly carved to imitate the carvings of the wooden ones that preceded them and could not endure. Undoubtedly the stick came first in architecture—came long before the stone. The ideas of forms that became associated with ideas of the beautiful in this use of wood took the more enduring material ignorant of its nature and foolishly enslaved it to the idea of the ornamented stick.

Stone is the oldest of architectural materials on record, as to form, except as the stone itself embodies earlier wood forms. So from Stonehenge to Maya masonry—the rude architecture of the Druid-Bards of whom Taliesin was one, down the ages to the intensely implicated and complicated tracery of the Goths—where stone-building may be said to have expired—stone comes first.

THE STORY OF STONE

Stone, as a building material, as human hands begin upon it—stonecraft—becomes a shapely block.

The block is necessarily true to square and level, so that one block may securely rest upon another block and great weight be carried to greater height.

We refer to such masses, so made, as masonry.

The stone may show a natural face in the wall, or a face characteristic of the tool used to shape

Imperial Hotel. Tokyo, Japan. 1916. FLLW Fdn FA#1509.0057

"Taliesin," Frank Lloyd Wright Residence and Studio. Spring Green, Wisconsin. 1925. FLLW Fdn FA#1403.0028

it—or be flatly smoothed. Sometimes honed or polished.

The walls take on the character of the surface left by the mason's use of his tools.

The character of the wall surface will be determined also by the kind of stone, by the kind of mason, the kind of architect. Probably by the kind of building. But, most of all, by the nature of the stone itself, if the work is good stonework.

Stone has every texture, every color, and—as in marble—also exquisite line combined with both—intensified clear down the scale until we arrive at what we call "precious" stone—and then on to jewels.

But most building stone—as Caen-stone, say—is a clear negative substance, like a sheet of soft beautiful paper, on which it is appropriate to cut images, by wasting away the surfaces to sink or raise traces of the imagination like a kind of human writing, carrying the ideology of the human race down the ages from the primitive to the decadent.

Other stone is hard and glittering; hard to cut. By rubbing away at it with other stones, the surface may be made to yield a brilliant surface, finally [sic] polished until its inner nature may be seen as though looked into, as in a glass—transparent.

Most marble is of this character. And granite.

"Taliesin," Frank Lloyd Wright Residence and Studio. Spring Green, Wisconsin. 1925. FLLW Fdn FA#2501.0866

The very nature of the material itself becomes its own decoration.

To carve or break its surface, then, is a pity—if no crime.

Stones themselves have special picturesque "qualities" and were much cherished for their "qualities" in China and Japan. Perhaps these Orientals love stones for their own sake more than any other people. They seem to see in them the universe—at least the earth-creation, in little—and they study them with real pleasure and true appreciation.

The Byzantine mosaics of colored stone are a cherishing of these qualities, too. These mosaics on a large scale gave beautiful stone results—fine

stonework—good masonry.

But stone is a solid material, heavy, durable, and most grateful for masses. A "massive" material, we say, so most appropriate and effective in simple architectural masses, the nobler the better.

The Mayas used stone most sympathetically with its nature and the character of their environment. Their decoration was mostly *stone-built*. And when they carved it the effect resembled naturally enriched stone surfaces such as are often seen in the landscape.

The Egyptians used stone—as the Chinese used stones—with real love and understanding.

The Greeks abused stone shamefully—did

not understand its nature at all except as something to be painted or gilded out of existence. Before they painted it, they fluted and rolled and molded it as though it were wood—or degraded it far lower.

Polished sophistication is not at home with stone.

The Roman architects had no feeling about stone whatever. Their engineers did have—but there were few large stones.

They cut these prizes into wooden cornices to please the architects, and invented the arch to get along with small stones for construction.

The Goths made most of stone. But stone became for the Gothic imagination a mere negative material which they employed supremely well in a structural sense.

Stonecraft rose highest in the Gothic era.

But they, then, set to work and carved the beautiful construction elaborately and constructed carving in the spirit of the construction to an extent never before seen in the world. No arris was left without its molding. It was as though stone blossomed into a thing of the human-spirit. As though a wave of creative-impulse had seized stone and, mutable as the sea, it had heaved and swelled and broken into lines of surging, peaks of foam—human-symbols, images of organic life caught and held in its cosmic urge—a splendid song!

The song of *stone*?

No—because stone was used as a negative material neither limitations respected nor stone nature interpreted. In wood the result was pretty much the same as in iron or in plaster, in the hands of the Goths.

But as a building material it was *scientifically* used. And such stone was usually chosen as had little to say for itself and so not outraged much by such cutting to the shapes of organic life—as it was subjected to, by them.

We may say the stone was not outraged—but neither was it allowed to sing its own song—to be *itself*. Always nearer that, by them, than anywhere else since archaic times.

But it was not the *stone* that inspired the Cathedrals of the Middle Ages nor invited them. It limited them.

Had it not been so—what would they have been like? Was Gothic architecture because of stone or regardless of it?

But that is going far afield for subtle matter and casting the shadow of doubt upon one of the most beautiful spectacles of the triumph of the human spirit over matter.

A greater triumph will be man's when he triumphs through the nature of matter over the superstition that separates him from its spirit.

And that is where he is now in his industrial world as he faces stone, as an architect. As he sees stone in the story recorded by the buildings on the earth—there is not so much to help him now.

To "imitate" would be easy but no man's way.

His present tool, the Machine, can clumsily imitate but without joy or creative impulse behind it when imitation is its menial office. As a mass-material he can now handle stone better and cheaper than ever before, if he allows it to be itself—if he lets it alone for what it is.

Or if—sympathetically—he brings out its nature in his use of it. The Chinese did this in the way they cherished and developed the natural beauties of jade—lapis lazuli—crystal—malachite and cornelian, quartz—and other great stones as well.

Man has done this with his machine when he has sawed the blocks of marble and, opening them into thin slabs, spread them, edge to edge, upon walls as facings revealing and accenting its own pattern and color.

He has done this when he planes it and lays it up in a straight-line mass for its own sake, with the texture characteristic of his tools.

He has done this when he takes the strata of the quarry and lays it in like strata, natural edges out—in his walls. He has done this when he makes mosaic of stones and lays them in simple, stone-patterns in color, for whole buildings—stone brocade.

He does this, when, inspired by the hardness and brilliance of the granite, his Machine can now render so well, he makes his ultimate form as simple and clearly hard in mass and noble in outline when finished.

He may even introduce alternate and contrasting materials qualifying broad masses harmonious with stone qualities in horizontal bands or rich masses. Whenever, in his designs, he allows the natural beauty of the stone, as stone, to speak its own material-language, he has justified his machine as an artist's tool. And the nobility of his work will compensate for the loss of the imitations of organic-forms-of-life in the material itself—an imitation that used to be architecture.

Interpretation is still his.

So it will be seen again, as always, that if he now works *with* stone in this sense, using the new power which the machine has given him over it, he will gain a spiritual integrity and physical health to compensate him for the losses of the storyful beauties of that period, since passed, when a building, so far as its *architecture* was concerned, was a block of ornamentally sculptured stone.

It would take a volume to fully illustrate the story that is here written—a mere sketch in bare outline.

In each of the materials we have named there is treasure enough to make Aladdin's cave a mean symbol of an architect's riches, were each architect confined to only *one*.

Aladdin's lamp was a symbol for Imagination.

With this lamp the architect may explore the riches of the deep caves where treasure is waiting for him. And, through him, the human race waits too; for the key that unlocks the man-made door is hanging at his belt—still—though rusty with disuse and the lock itself now stiff with rust and lack of proper oiling.

Let him take his microscope and see the principle that "builds," in nature, at work in stone. Geometry the principle, busy with materials—producing marvels of beauty to inspire him. Read the grammar of the Earth in a particle of stone! Stone is the frame on which his Earth is modeled, and wherever it crops out—there the architect may sit and learn.

As he takes the trail across the great Western Deserts—he may see his buildings—rising in simplicity and majesty from their floors of gleaming sand—where organic life is still struggling for a bare existence: see them still, as the Egyptians saw and were taught by those they knew.

For in the stony bonework of the Earth, the principles that shaped stone as it lies, or as it rises and remains to be sculptured by winds and tide—there sleep forms and styles enough for all the ages, for all of Man.

1. The next seven paragraphs of the original manuscript for the essay on stone as a building material were deleted from the publication of the April 1928 issue of *The Architectural Record*. Observations such as "Light—living in the mathematics of form to match with the mathematics of sound. Crystals are proof of nature's architectural principle" proclaim Wright's deep reverence for nature, including the minerals of the earth and precious stones.

IN THE CAUSE OF ARCHITECTURE IV: THE MEANING OF MATERIALS— WOOD

[Published with five illustrations in The Architectural Record, *May 1928]*

FROM THE FANTASTIC TOTEM OF THE ALASKAN—ERECTED for its own sake as a great sculptured pole, seen in its primitive colors far above the snows—to the resilient bow of the American Indian, and from the enormous solid polished tree trunks upholding the famous great temple-roofs of Japan to the delicate spreading veneers of rare, exotic woods on the surfaces of continental furniture, wood is allowed to be wood.

It is the most humanly intimate of all materials. Man loves his association with it, likes to feel it under his hand, sympathetic to his touch and to his eye. Wood is universally beautiful to Man. And yet, among higher civilizations, the Japanese understood it best.

They have never outraged wood in their art or in their craft. Japan's primitive religion, "Shinto," with its "be clean" ideal, found in wood ideal material and gave it ideal use in that masterpiece of architecture, the Japanese dwelling as well as in all that pertained to living in it.

In that architecture may be seen what a sensitive material, let alone for its own sake, can do for human sensibilities.

Whether pole, beam, plank, board, slat, or rod, the Japanese architect got the forms and treatments of his architecture out of tree-nature, wood-

wise, and heightened the natural beauty of the material by cunning peculiar to himself.

The possibilities of the properties of wood came out richly as he rubbed into it the natural oil of the palm of his hand, ground out the soft parts of the grain to leave the hard fiber standing—an "erosion" like that of the plain where flowing water washes away the sand from the ribs of stone.

No Western peoples ever used wood with such understanding as the Japanese did in their construction—where wood always came up and came out as nobly beautiful.

And when we see the bamboo rod in their hands—seeing a whole industrial world interpreting it into articles of use and art that ask only to be *bamboo*—we reverence the scientific art that makes wood *theirs*.

The simple Japanese dwelling with its fences and utensils is the *revelation* of wood.

Nowhere else may wood be so profitably studied for its natural possibilities as a major architectural material.

Material here fell into artistic hands—a religious sentiment protecting it, in all reverence for simplicity.

Sometimes in the oak-beamed and paneled

Lake Tahoe Summer Colony (Project). Lake Tahoe, California. 1922. Perspective. Pencil and color pencil on tracing paper, 15 x 22".
FLLW Fdn #2205.001

rooms of Old England, when "carpentry" was re-strained, oak was allowed to be something similar as is seen in oak-timbering of the Middle Ages. In the veneering of later periods the beauty of wood came out—but the carpenter-forms of the work invariably did violence to the nature of wood. The "cabinetmaker" had his way with it.

Woodwork soon became what we learned to call carpentry; more or less a makeshift. Paneling was its sum and substance where the pilaster would not stick nor the cornice hang.

All wooden joinery of the periods, soon or late, fell to pieces, and interruption by too many ingenious "members" frittered away wood-nature in confusion or in contortions of an ingenious but false or inferior "taste."

Outside primitive architectures, sympathetic use of wood in beautiful construction would be found far north or far south—among the Norsemen, or among the South Sea Islanders.

Because of wood we have—the carpenter.

The carpenter loved wood in feeble ways—but he loved his tools with strength and determination. He loved his tools more. Good wood is willing to do what its designer never meant it to do—another of its lovable qualities—but therefore it is soon prostitute to human ingenuity in the makeshift of the carpenter. Wood, therefore, has more human outrage done upon it than Man has done, even upon himself.

It has suffered more—far more than any of the materials in our category.

Where and when it is cheap and, so, becomes too familiar as it nearly always does in a new country, it soon falls into contempt. Man's longing for novelty tries to make it something else. To the degree that the carpenter-artist has succeeded in doing this—one might think—is he the artist-carpenter.

In his search for novelty, wood in his hands has been joined and glued, braced and screwed, boxed and nailed, turned and tortured, scroll sawed, beaded, fluted, suitably furbelowed, and flounced at the carpenter's party—enough to please even him. By the aid of "modern" machines the carpenter-artist got it into Eastlake composites of trim and furniture, into Usonian jigger porches and corner-towers eventuating into candle-snuffer domes or what would you have; got it all over Queen Anne houses outside and inside—the triumph of his industrious ingenuity—until carpentry and millwork became synonymous with butchery and botchwork.

Queen Anne! What murder!

And even now—especially now—in the passing procession of the "periods" I never see orderly piles of freshly cut and dried timber disappearing into the mills to be gored, and ground, and torn, and hacked into millwork without a sense of utter weariness in the face of the overwhelming outrage of something precious just because it is by nature so kind, beneficent, and lovely.

Man has glorified the Tree in the use he made of the Stick—but that he did long before the Louis or the Renaissance got by way of Colonial and Eastlake—or was it Westlake—to Queen Anne; and then by way of the triumphant Machine to General Grant-Gothic and the depths of degradation that soon came in the cut-and-butt of the fluted "trim," with turned corner-block and molded plinth-block.

This latter was the fashion in woodwork when I found the uses of wood I shall describe.

Machinery in that era was well under way and ploughed and tore and whirled and gouged in the name of Art and Architecture.

And all this was so effectually and busily done that the devastation began to be felt in the "boundless" Usonian forests. Conservative lumbermen took alarm and made the native supply go a little further by shrinking all the standard timber sizes first one-eighth of an inch both ways—then a little further on one-eighth inch more both ways—now still a little further—until a stud is become a bed slat, a board kin to a curling veneer.

All standardized sticks great and small are shrinking by a changing standard to meet the deadly facility which the Machine has given to man's appetite for useless *things*.

Usonian forests show all too plainly terrible destruction and—bitter thought—nothing of genuine beauty has Usonia to show for it.

The darkness of death is descending on wood by way of unenlightened architecture.

The life of the tree has been taken in vain as

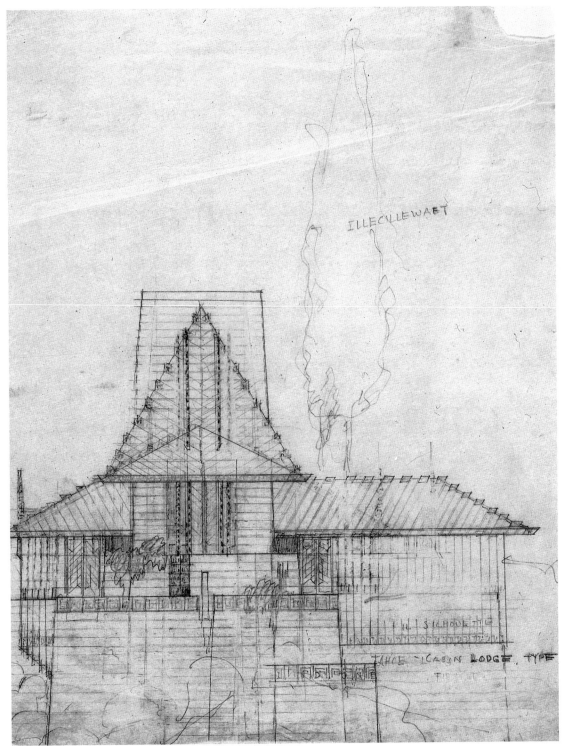

ILLECILLEWAET

Lake Tahoe Summer Colony (Project). Lake Tahoe, California. 1922. Elevation. Pencil and color pencil on tracing paper, 14 x 16".
FLLW Fdn #2205.022

the stick, the substance of the shapely stick, to become imitation-à-la-mode; the precious efflorescent patterns of wood, to be painted out of sight; its silken textures vulgarized by varnish in the misshapen monstrosities of a monstrous "taste."

The noble forest has become an ignominious scrap heap in the name of Culture.

The Machine, then—was it—that placed this curse on so beautiful a gift to man? So friendly a material—this brother to the man—laid thus low in murder.

No.

Unless the sword in the hand of the swordsman murdered the man whose heart it ran through.

The Machine is only a tool. Before all, the man is responsible for its use.

His ignorance became devastation because his tool in callous hands became a weapon effective beyond any efficiency such hands had known before, or any sensibilities he ever had. His performance with his Machine outran not only his imagination which, long since, it vanquished, but the endurance of his own sensibilities as human.

No. Blame the base appetite the Machine released upon the forest, for its devastation. Blame the lack of imaginative insight for the scrap heap we have now to show for the lost trees of a continent—a scrap heap instead of a noble architecture.

What should we have had to show were it otherwise? Vain speculation. What may we have to show for what is left—if base appetite becomes enlightened desire and imagination awakes and sees.

Well—we may have the nobility of the *material* if nothing else.

We may have simple timber construction, at least overhead, as a scientific art, free of affectation. The wood let alone as wood or as richly ornamented by hand in color or carving.

We may have satin-boarded wainscots—polished board above polished board, the joints interlocked by beaded insertion, so that shrinkage is allowed and the joint ornaments the whole in harmony with its nature, individualizing each board. We may have plaster-covered walls banded into significant color surfaces by plain wood strips, thick or thin, or cubical insertion, wide or narrow in surface.

We may have ceilings rib-banded in rhythmical arrangements of line to give the charm of timbering without the waste.

We may use flat wood-strips with silken surfaces contrasting as ribbons might be contrasted with stuffs, to show what we meant in arranging our surfaces, marking them by bands of sympathetic flat-wood.

We may use a plastic system of varying widths, weights of finely marked wood rib-bands to articulate the new plastic effects in construction never dreamed of before. The flat-strip came so easily into our hands, by way of the machine, to give us—the "backband" that follows all outlines even in an ordinary dwelling, by the mile, for a few cents per foot.

We may compound composite-slabs of refuse lumber glued together under high pressure and press into the glue, facings of purest flowered wood veneer on both sides—making slabs of any thickness or width or length, slabs to be cut into doors, great and small, tops thin or thick—preserving the same flower of the grain over entire series or groups of doors as a unit.

We may miter the flowered slabs across the grain at the edges of the breaks to turn the flowering grain around corners or down the sides and thus gain another plastic effect from the continuity of the flowering.

We may economically split a precious log into thin, wide veneers and, suitably "backed," lay each to each, opening one sheet to lay it edge to edge with the sheet beneath it, like the leaves of a book so the pattern of the one becomes another greater pattern when doubled by the next.

We may cross-veneer the edges of top-surfaces so that the grain of the top carries the flower unbroken down over the ends as it does on the sides.

There is the flat fillet (it happens to be true to wood) to "talk" with—if one must "explain."

We may use the plain-spindle alternating with the thin flat-slat or square or round ones in definite rhythms of light and shade—allowing the natural color and marking of the wood to enrich and soften the surface made by them as a whole. With this we may bring in the accent block.

We have the edgewise and flatwise-strip or

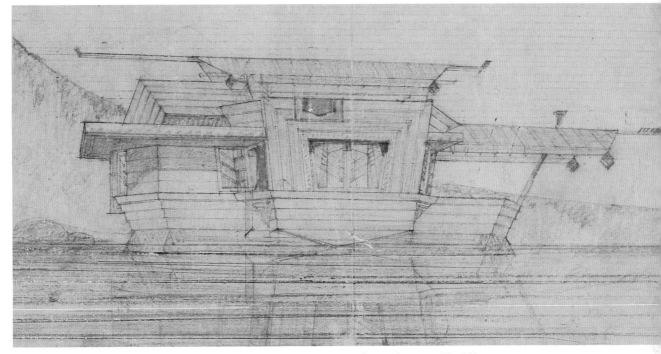

Lake Tahoe Summer Colony (Project). Lake Tahoe, California. 1922. Perspective. Pencil on tracing paper, 13 x 10".
FLLW Fdn#2205.004

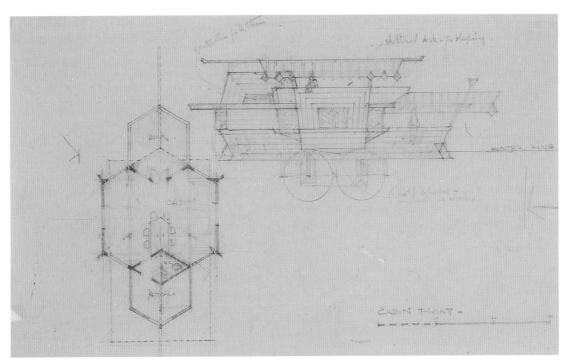

Lake Tahoe Summer Colony (Project). Lake Tahoe, California. 1922. Plan and elevation. Pencil on tracing paper, 13 x 10".
FLLW Fdn#2205.008

cubical stick and accent-block to "ingeniously" combine into screens for light filters or for furniture.

These treatments all allow wood to be wood at its best and the machine can do them all surpassingly better than they could be done by hand—a thousand times cheaper.

Thanks to the machine we may now use great slabs compounded under heat and pressure, where rotary-cut veneers unrolled from a log in sheets ten feet long and as wide as the circumference of the log will yield, in thicknesses of one-thirty-second of an inch, wood wallpaper. And we may lay these sheets, against various compounds, on ceilings—with any manipulation of the efflorescence, now exaggerated by the rotary cut, but still true to wood, and do this to any extent.

The finer properties of wood have been emancipated by the machine.

Observe that, naturally, all these are *plastic* effects. That is, used for the sake of the surfaces and lines of their "wood quality" in contrast to other materials. Carving has a small place in the grammar of these effects, except as an "insert."

There is always the limiting frame or border, constricting surfaces—the most obvious of all uses to which wood is put. And there is always a use of the solid wood stick to be made into honest furniture. There is the wooden frame to be overstuffed for deep comfort—wood showing only at extremities. In light stick-furniture wood combines well with plaited rattan or raffia.

In other words the beauty of wood as silken-texture or satin-surfaces upon which nature has marked the lines of its character in exquisite drawing and color qualifying flat-surfaces and rib-bands of infinite delicacy, in all variety—because we work *with* the machine, understanding wood, is more liberally ours.

Another opportunity is wood-inlay. There is the chequered turning of the grain to crossgrain in the same wood.

There are the patterns of inlay in contrasting woods.

There are the cunningly cut, denticulated or machined strips to be inlaid between boards or used as edging flat surfaces of veneer: the denticulations

to be picked out by polychrome in transparent bright stains, perhaps.

There is the whole gamut of transparent color stains from brilliant red, green, yellow, and blue, to all hues in between, to aid and intensify or differentiate these uses of wood.

And for exterior work there are characteristic board-and-batten effects—horizontal, vertical, diagonal or checkered, got out of planks or boards with surfaces rough from the saw to be color-stained or allowed to weather.

There are roofs boarded lengthwise of the slope, likewise inlaid between the joints but with properly devised ornamental copper flashing to come up over the edges and the ends.

There are brilliantly decorative treatments of poles, free-standing as the Alaskan totem stood, or in rows, horizontal or vertical. Palisaded walls.

There are combinations of the slender pole and square-stick and the spindle-rod, alternating with the slat or the board in endless rhythmic variety.

All these undressed-wood, plastic treatments, are much the same as for inside work, allowing wood to be wood but coarser in scale with an eye to weathering in the joinery.

And finally after we have exhausted the board and machined inlaid-batten, and the spread of the figure of the wood-flowering over flat surfaces, and the combinations of the following back-band and the varying rib-band—the spindle-stick, the flat-slab and the rod, the marking-strip and the accent-block, the ornamental-pole—rectangular timbering ornamentally planked, the undressed, interlocking boards on walls and roof slopes—then—

We have combinations of all these. A variety sufficient to intrigue the liveliest imagination for as long as life lasts—without once missing the old curvatures and imaging of organic-forms; the morbid twists and curious turns, the contortions imposed on wood in the name of the "Styles" *mostly* using wood as a makeshift—or, if not, as something other than wood.

A most proper use of wood, now that we must economize, are these treatments using marking-bands or plastic-ribbons, defining, explaining, indicating, dividing, and relating plaster surfaces. It is economy in the material, while keeping the feeling of its beauty. Architectural articulation is assisted and sometimes had alone by means of the dividing lines of wood.

In these plastic treatments—using wood gently banded or in the flat allowing its grain and silken surface even in the spindle screens to assert itself and wood-quality to enter into effect of the whole, we have found the Machine a willing means to a simple end. But for the Machine this free plastic use of wood either in rib-bands or extended flowered surfaces would be difficult, uncharacteristic, and prohibitive in cost.

Moreover this is true conservation of wood because in these effects it is used only for its qualities as a beautiful material. The tree need no longer be lost.

In these papers we are not speaking of "building" as a makeshift, but of building as the Art of Architecture. And while all building, as things are, cannot be Architecture but must make shift—Architecture should hold forth such natural ways and means for the true use of good materials that, from any standpoint of economical realization of the best the material can give to structure,

Architecture would put mere building to shame. Stupid waste characterizes most of the efforts of mere builders, always—even, or especially, when building for profit.

Wood grows more precious as our country grows older. To save it from destruction by the man with the machine it is only necessary to use the Machine to emancipate its qualities, in simple ways such as I have indicated, and satisfy the man.

There is no waste of material whatever in such uses, either in cutting up the tree or adapting the cutting to the work done when it is of the character described. The Machine easily divides, subdivides, sands, and polishes the manifold surfaces which any single good stick may be made to yield by good machine methods.

Wood can never be wrought by the machine as it was lovingly wrought by hand into a violin for instance, except as a lifeless imitation. But the beautiful properties of wood may be released by the Machine to the hand of the architect. His imagination must use it in true ways—worthy of its beauty. His *plastic* effects will refresh the life of wood, as well as the human-spirit that lost it—as inspiration—long since.

IN THE CAUSE OF ARCHITECTURE V: THE MEANING OF MATERIALS— THE KILN

[Published with four illustrations in The Architectural Record, *June 1928]*

I SEE TANG GLAZES AND SUNG SOFT-CLAY FIGURES FROM Chinese tombs in my studio as I write—a few of the noble Tang glazed horses that show Greek influence—and Han pottery. Some fragments of the Racca blue-glazed pots and the colored tiles of the Persians in Asia Minor—"the cradle of the race"— Egyptian vessels and scarabs.

It appears from a glance the oven is as old as civilization at least—which is old enough for us.

Our interest is not archaeological but architectural and begins with a lump of peculiarly pliable clay in the hand of the man who wants to make something useful and at the same time beautiful out of it—at the time when he knows he can bake it hard enough to make it serviceable. Then it all begins to grow rapidly in the experimental search for different clays. The grinding of minerals, to make paste for a flux to pour over the vessels to make them impervious and beautiful—and the legion of earnest chemical experiments that followed. The research of devoted craftsmen for several hundred centuries have laid up treasure and all but lost it but for a specimen or two—times without number.

The remains are a fascinating record of man's creative endeavor on his earth. A record that tells more of him probably than any other—for in it we find not only pottery and building but painting, sculpture, and script intimately related to the life of all the peoples who have inhabited the earth since cave dwellers built their fires.

All the materials we know, seem at one time or another in a state of flux. Fire is father-creator to them all—below ground. Light is mother-creator to all that rise in air out of the ground. Back to Fire again goes that which Fire made to be fused with man's creative power into another creation—that of his use and beauty.

Anything permanent as a constructive material comes into man's hands by way of Fire, as he has slowly learned to approach in "degrees" the heat in which his globe of earth was formed—and courage to set what he has himself made, again at its beneficent mercy. He knows much. But Fire knows more and has constant surprises for him.

He will never exhaust them all—nor need to.

He has the Brick.

He has the Tile.

He has the Pot and Bowl.

He has the Vase.

He has the Image.

He may color them all—forever so far as he knows—with the hues of nature and qualify each according to any or all the sensibilities he has—

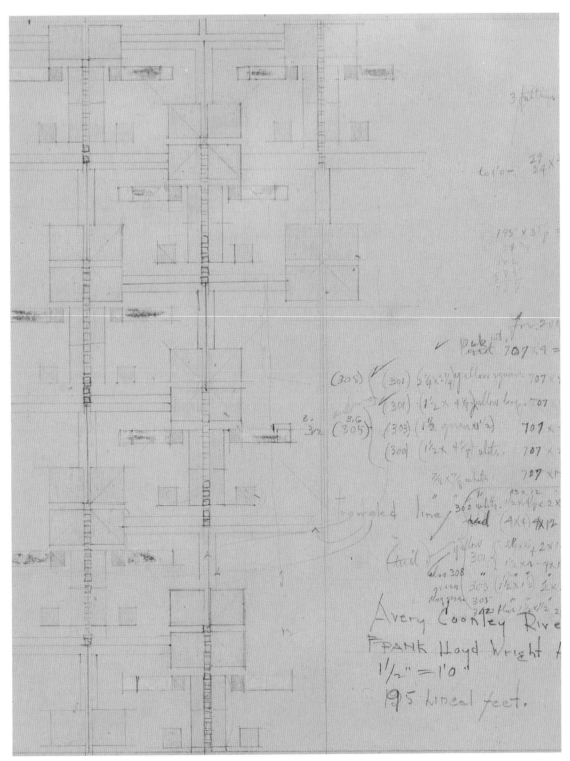

Avery Coonley House. Riverside, Illinois. 1908. Tile patterns. FLLW Fdn#0803.010

taught by the qualities he loves in the work of Nature all about him.

We have hitherto been speaking of "natural" materials. The natural material here is of earth itself. But to produce this material known as ceramics, another element, that of the artificer, has entered with Fire.

This product should therefore be nearer man's desire—molded, as it is, by himself. His creation is seen in it. What he has sensed of the story of his creation, he has put into it.

He sees as he is and this record will tell us what he sees, how he sees—as he sees it.

He has seen nothing, he is not himself. He is the imaginative geometrical tracery of the Persian and Moor and the noblest brick buildings man has ever erected. He is the noble sculpture and pottery of the Han dynasty in China, as well as the Satsuma and Nabeshima of Japan. His is the story painted on the pots and bowls of Greece no less than the flowered plaques of Byzantium or upon the utensils of the Indian cliff dweller.

His sense of form he took from those forms already made as his natural environment. In his striving for excellence in quality he was taught what to love by stone, leaf, and mold and flower—the book of "trees," the mosses and mists and the mosaics of foliage in the sun. Especially in China where his sense of Nature was profound did he learn from them. When he was at his best, he interpreted what he saw.

When he was inferior, he imitated it.

But always, superior or inferior, he was its reflection in his ceramics as in a mirror.

And in spirit looking away from himself, his eyes fixed on Gods as God or God as Gods—fashioning and firing and building as he himself was burning, all the while, better than he *knew*.

What has man to show for the Brick? I should offer the brick buildings of Asia Minor—Persia.

What he has to show for his Tile? Wherever Persian or Mohammedan influence was supreme.

What he has to show for the Pot and Bowl? Chinese pottery.

What he has to show for his Vase? The Grecian urn.

To show for his Image? Those of Egypt, Greece, and China.

The modern contribution to ceramics as building material is "terra-cotta." A poor name for an important material—but so it is named. I suppose "earthenware" seemed inadequate or not specific.

And it is the greatest opportunity for the creative artist of all the materials he may choose. It is, of course, burned clay in any color or glaze for entire buildings—pottery buildings! Earthenware on a great scale.

Modern terra-cotta has known but one creative master—only one—Louis H. Sullivan.

He is dead. His work in terra-cotta will live long after him. His was the temperament and the imagination that naturally found in this impressionable material the ideal medium for his genius. Terra-cotta lives only as it takes the impression of human imagination. It is a material for the modeler. It is in the architect's hand what wax is in the sculptor's hand.

After the material takes shape, the surface treatments are all a matter of taste. They are limitless in quality and style.

And the chief business of terra-cotta has been to imitate stone. It would imitate anything else as readily—with gratitude—it seems. It is the misfortune of anything impressionable to be called upon to give imitations. Mimicry is all too human. To imitate is the natural tendency of men. Not man.

But Louis H. Sullivan's exuberant, sensuous nature and brilliant imagination took terra-cotta—and it lived. It no longer asked permission of the Styles. It was *itself* because it was Louis H. Sullivan. In it this master created a grammar of ornament all his own. And notwithstanding certain realistic tendencies, an original style of ornamentation out of the man, astonishing in range, never lacking virility.

Into the living intricacy of his loving modulations of surface, "background"—the curse of all stupid ornament—ceased to exist. None might see where terra-cotta left off and ornamentation came to life. A fragment of Sullivanian terra-cotta—were we at some remote period of time to be excavated—would be found with a thrill. It would mean that a man lived among us at a dead time in Art.

Midway Gardens. Chicago, Illinois. 1913. FLLW Fdn#1401.0029

The Sullivanian motif was efflorescent, exvolute, supported by tracery of geometric motives—bringing up the clay in forms so delicate and varied and lively that no parallel in these respects exists.

We may see, for once, how completely a negative material can be appropriately brought to life by the creative artist. It is reassuring.

Is there in architectural history another man who out of himself not only created an exuberant type of beautiful architectural relief but furnished it forth, always consistent in style, in amazing variety that could not have ended but with his death? Even toward the last of his life, enfeebled, disillusioned,

but indomitable, he drew with all his old-time freshness of touch a series of beautiful designs that show no falling off in power whatever—even in spontaneity.

His ornamentation was the breath of his life. Clay came into his hand, that both might live on forever.

Because, now that we know what terra-cotta can be, and how it can be, we shall never be satisfied to see it degraded to imitation again—nor satisfied to see it imitating him.

Taught by him, we should learn how to use it. If not so well as he, at least on principle for its own sake as he did. His sense of Architecture found a fullness of expression in the plastic clay. Few architects ever find any such expression in any medium whatsoever.

Terra-cotta should revere him as its God, sing his praises but, better than that, be true to his teaching, which would mean more to him than psalms in his praise and his statue in the hills.

In the terra-cotta or pottery of earthenware building we may have today the sum and substance of all the kiln ever gave to architecture.

Modern methods have made the complete terra-cotta building, inside and outside, as definite a possibility as was the Han vessel in its time or the Greek vase. But—who would look upon it in its present state after Sullivan left it, as a work of Art?

It cannot live either on its own texture or color—to any great extent. And as for its design? It is a mendicant feeding on crumbs from the table of the styles.

Why? Is it because Sullivan is dead? Did this most valuable of modern achievements in "material" die with him, as it never really lived until he came?

No. Materials never die. This material is only asleep, waiting for some master to waken it to life.

Here, young man in Architecture, is a golden opportunity quite boundless so far as imagination goes. Rescue the royal beggar from penury and slavery.

Where is the pottery building beautiful in form and texture and color—as such?

Why are there not thousands cleaning themselves in the rain, warming themselves in the sun—growing richer with age instead of dingy and sad and old? Why do they look cheap and soon stale?

Just because there are no good pottery designs for good pottery buildings—so how can the pottery be good with no more inspiration than that?

A neglected minion of the Machine!

By way of terra-cotta we have here arrived at the matter of Ornament. Because terra-cotta chiefly lives by virtue of the human imagination in ornamentation.

As we intend to discuss ornament by itself on its merits later, let us say now that true ornament is

of the thing, never on it. The Material develops into its own ornamentation by will of the master. He does not impose forms upon it. He develops it into forms from the within which is characteristic of its nature if he is "the master."

We may see this in Sullivanian terra-cotta. The only limit to Sullivan's treatment was the degree to which the substance of the pliable clay would stay up between the thumb and finger and come through the fire. Background disappeared but surface was preserved. There was no sense of background, as such, anywhere. All was of the surface, out of the material. So no sense of ornament as *applied* to terra-cotta, because terra-cotta became ornament and ornamented itself.

Terra-cotta was this master's natural medium because his sense of beautiful form was the subtle fluctuation of flowering surface, songlike, as found in organic plant-life—the music of the crystal is seen as a minor accompaniment only.

The tones of the main theme are those of organic efflorescence—*growth* as it is performed by plant species. This idea of growth was the theme—invariably—which he glorified.

He created a "species" himself—and kept on creating others.

This procedure of Growth intrigued his imagination—inspired him. "Organic" was his God-word, as he traced Form to Function.

When, I suggested, as I once did, that quite as likely the function might be traced to the form, he disposed of the heresy—by putting it on a par with the old debating school argument as to which came first, the Hen or the Egg. His interpretation was to him the Song-of-Creation and he never tired of singing it. As it was visible to him in the growth of the plant he saw it in all—as indeed it may be.

Think of this when you see his synthetic motifs in his sentient terra-cotta.

And realize that there are ways of making a pottery building, the joints of the material becoming unit-lines in the pattern of the whole—which he, the pioneer, touches upon but was called away before realization or called away *to* realization—who knows?—and imagine the glorious marvel of beauty it might be.

I remember going to Palermo some years ago to see the mosaics of Monreale.

I had just got into the Cathedral-square and lifted my eyes to that great work when to the left I saw—or did I see it—for some moments I thought I dreamed—there against the sky—no not against it, of it, literally of the sky was a great dome of pure Racca blue.

I forgot the Cathedral for quite some time in the wonderful blue dome so simple in form—a heavenly thing. I have never recovered from it. And that effect was "Ceramic." Why not Terra-Cotta? The old qualities in color; firing can not be dead!

To illustrate a simple use of brick I refer for noble examples to Ispahan, Sārí, Vera-min, Āmol, Samarkand, Bokhara, and, of course, tile and pottery as well. Unfortunately I have little brickwork to my credit. I have chosen a few examples that show the walls solidified by emphasis of the horizontal joint, and examples showing the brick-pier and mass as I feel it to be natural in brick construction today. Brick is the material we in Usonia know and love best. We probably have brought brick-making to a pitch of perfection never existing in the world before at any time. And we use it, on the whole very well. Not only is the range inexhaustible in texture and color and shape, but the material itself is admirable in quality.

Together with it go all those baked-clay, vitreous, hollow bricks and hollow tiles which are probably the most useful of all materials in building in our climate.

Usonian tiles and mosaics do not reach the quality of ancient or even contemporary materials of this na-

ture. There is enough good material, however, to warrant a more general use which would inevitably cause it to grow better—and our day needs this development.

The nature of the mosaic either of stone, glass, or ceramics is a truly architectural medium—useful in this era of the Machine and lending itself to plastic treatment with no insult to its nature. I should like to see whole buildings clothed in this medium.

Our pottery is imitative. We have had Teco, Rookwood, and other types—all deserving experiments with something of originality in most of them. But none proceeding on principle to develop style, but of the nature and character of the process.

The "vessel" does not inspire us, it seems, as it did earlier people. Perhaps because we know no such need of it as they knew. I have chosen some natural "vessels" to show the help nature generously offers in the matter, to mention only one humble resource.

The Usonian Image, likewise the Vase, is tentative when not openly imitative. We seem to have little or nothing to say in the clay figure or pottery vase as concrete expression of the ideal of beauty that is our own. No sense of form has developed among us that can be called creative—adapted to that material. And it may never come. The life that flowed into this channel in ancient times apparently now goes somewhere else.

A few natural forms found in the Champlain clays seem interesting to me in this connection.

Again our subject remains in barest outline—for to go adequately into this most human and important feature of all Man's endeavor to be and to remain beautiful, the "kiln" would exhaust interesting volumes.

IN THE CAUSE OF ARCHITECTURE VI: THE MEANING OF MATERIALS— GLASS

[Published with five illustrations in The Architectural Record, *July 1928]*

PERHAPS THE GREATEST DIFFERENCE EVENTUALLY BETWEEN ancient and modern buildings will be due to our modern machine-made glass. Glass, in any wide utilitarian sense, is new.

Once a precious substance limited in quantity and size, glass and its making have grown so that a perfect clarity of any thickness, quality, or dimension is so cheap and desirable that our modern world is drifting toward structures of glass and steel. Had the ancients been able to enclose interior space with the facility we enjoy because of glass, I suppose the history of architecture would have been radically different, although it is surprising how little this material has yet modified our sense of architecture beyond the show windows the shopkeeper demands and gets.

How that show window plagued the architect at first and still teases the classicist! It has probably done more to show the classicist up as ridiculous than any other single factor.

The demand for visibility makes walls and even posts an intrusion to be got rid of at any cost. Architecture gave up the first story but started bravely above the glass at the second, nothing daunted and nothing changed. The building apparently stood in midair. Glass did it.

Crystal plates have generally taken the place of fundamental wall and piers in almost all commercial buildings; and glass, the curse of the classic, as an opportunity for the use of delicate construction of sheet metal and steel, is a tempting material not yet much explored. As glass has become clearer and clearer and cheaper and cheaper from age to age, about all that has been done with it architecturally is to fill the same opening that opaque glass screened before, with a perfect visibility now, except for the use to which the shop-man demands that it be put. The shop! That is where glass has almost come into its own. We have yet to give glass proper architectural recognition.

What is this magic material, there but not seen if you are looking through it? You may look at it, too, as a brilliance, catching reflections and giving back limpid light.

But it is what it is today because it may be seen through perfectly while it is an impenetrable stop for air currents, when due allowance is made for its fragility. When violence is done to it, it may be shattered, but a precious feature of the material is that it does not disintegrate.

I suppose as a material we may regard it as crystal—thin sheets of air in air to keep air out or keep it in. And with this sense of it, we can think of uses to which it might be put as various and beautiful as the frost designs upon the pane of glass itself.

Susan Lawrence Dana House. Springfield, Illinois. 1900. Ceiling light. Courtesy of the Illinois Historic Preservation Agency. Photography by Albert Lewis. © 1992 Albert Lewis and Julie L. Sloan

Samuel Freeman House. Los Angeles, California. 1924. FLLW Fdn FA#2402.0011

Glass has been servile in architecture beyond the painting done with it in cathedral windows. It has been a utilitarian affair except when used for candelabra, chandeliers, or knobs—excepting only the mirror.

The sense of glass as the crystal has not yet to any extent entered into the poetry of architecture. It is too new, for one thing. For another thing, tradition did not leave any orders concerning it. It is strictly modern. Therefore, let us try to understand what it is. The machine has given to architects, in glass, a new material with which to work. Were glass eliminated now from buildings, it would be, so far as our buildings have gone, only like putting our eyes out. We could not see out or see into the building. We have gone so far as to make it the eyes of the building. Why not now combine it with steel, the spider's web, spin the building frame as an integument for crystal clearness—the crystal held by the steel as the diamond is held in its setting of gold—and make it the building itself?

All the diversity of color and texture available in any material is not only available but imperishable in glass. So far as deterioration or decay is concerned, it is possible now to preserve the metal setting for an indefinite period. And it is the life of this setting alone that would determine the life of the building. It is time to give attention to that setting.

Shadows have been the brushwork of the architect when he modeled his architectural forms. Let him work, now, with light diffused, light refracted, light reflected—use light for its own sake—shadows aside. The prism has always delighted and fascinated man. The Machine gives him his opportunity in glass. The machine can do any kind of glass—thick, thin, colored, textured to order—and cheap. A new experience is awaiting him.

Then why are modern cities still sodden imitations of medieval strongholds? Black or white slabs of thick glass have already gone far as substitutes for marble slabs. They could easily go farther for their own sake, in walls of buildings. Glass tiles, too, are not uncommon. Nor are glass mosaics an unusual sight.

All these uses together would form an incomparable palette for an architect. The difficulty is,

Samuel Freeman House. Los Angeles, California. 1924. FLLW Fdn FA#2402.0034

architects are bound by traditional ideas of what a building must look like or be like. And when they undertake to use new materials, it is only to make them conform to those preconceived ideas.

Every new material means a new form, a new use if used according to its nature. The free mind of the natural architect would use them so, were the unnatural inhibition of that freedom not imposed upon all by a false propriety due to the timidity of ignorance.

The Persian, the Egyptian, and the Moor had most insight concerning the mathematics of the principle at work in the crystal. The Persian and the Moor were most abstract; the Egyptian was most human.

All knew more of the secrets of glass than we do—we who may revel in it unrestrained by economic considerations of any kind, and who understand it not at all, except as a mirror.

As a mirror, the vanity and elegance of the French brought glass into architectural use. Their brilliant salons, glittering with cut-glass pendants and floral forms blown in clear and colored glass, were something in themselves new in architecture. The very limitation of the size of the sheet available gave a feature in the joint that adds rather than

Susan Lawrence Dana House. Springfield, Illinois. 1900. Entryway with statue. Courtesy of the Illinois Historic Preservation Agency. Photography by Albert Lewis. © 1992 Albert Lewis and Julie L. Sloan

Susan Lawrence Dana House. Springfield, Illinois. 1900. Foyer fountain. Courtesy of the Illinois Historic Preservation Agency. Photography by Albert Lewis. © 1992 Albert Lewis and Julie L. Sloan

detracts from the charm of the whole effect of their work.

But now the walls might disappear, the ceilings, too, and—yes—the floors as well. A mirror floor? Why not? In certain cases. Nicely calculated effects of this sort might amplify and transform a cabinet into a realm, a room into bewildering vistas and avenues: a single unit into unlimited areas of color, pattern, and form.

The Mirror is seen in Nature in the surfaces of lakes, in the hollows of the mountains, and in the pools deep in shadow from the trees; in winding ribbons of the rivers that catch and give back the flying birds, clouds, and blue sky. A dreary thing to have that element leave the landscape. It may be as refreshing and as beautifying in architecture, if *architecturally* used. To use it so is not easy, for the tendency toward the tawdry is ever present in any use of the mirror.

But to extend the vista, complete the form, multiply a unit where repetition would be a pleasure, lend illusion and brilliance in connection with light effects—all these are good uses to which the

architect may put the mirror. As a matter of fact he never uses plate glass in his windows or indoors inside his buildings that he does not employ the same element in his architecture that the limpid pool presents in the landscape—susceptible to reflections. And this opportunity is new. It is a subtle beauty of both exterior and interior, as may be readily seen in the effect of the exterior if a poor quality of cylinder glass be substituted for polished plate glass. Perhaps no one other change in the materials in which any building is made could so materially demoralize the effect of the whole as this substitution.

In the openings of my buildings, the glass plays the effect the jewel plays in the category of materials. The element of pattern is made more cheaply and beautifully effective when introduced into the glass of the windows than in the use of any other medium that architecture has to offer. The metal divisions become a metal screen of any pattern—heavy or light, plated in any metal, even gold or silver—the glass a subordinate, rhythmical accent of any emotional significance whatever, or vice-versa. The pattern may be calculated with reference to the scale of the interior and the scheme of decoration given by, or kept by, the motif of the glass pattern.

I have used opalescent, opaque, white, and gold in the geometrical groups of spots fixed in the clear glass. I have used, preferably, clear primary colors, like the German flashed glass, to get decorative effects; believing the clear emphasis of the primitive color interferes less with the function of the window and adds a higher architectural note to the effect of *light* itself. The kindersymphony in the windows in the Coonley playhouse is a case in point. The sumac windows in the Dana dining room another. This resource may be seen in most of my work, varied to suit conditions. This is a resource commonly employed in our buildings but usually overdone or insufficiently conventionalized. Nothing is more annoying to me than any tendency toward realism of form in window glass, to get mixed up with the view outside. A window pattern should stay severely "put." The magnificent window painting and plating of the windows of the religious edifice is quite another matter. There the window becomes primarily a gorgeous painting—painting with *light* itself—enough light being diffused to flood the interior dimly. This is an art in itself that reached its height in the Middle Ages. Probably no greater wealth of pictorial color effect considered as pure decoration exists in the world than in the great rose windows and pointed arches of the Cathedral.

But, the glass and bronze building is the most engaging of possibilities in modern architecture. Imagine a city iridescent by day, luminous by night, imperishable! Buildings—shimmering fabrics—woven of rich glass—glass all clear or part opaque and part clear—patterned in color or stamped to form the metal tracery that is to hold all together to be, in itself, a thing of delicate beauty consistent with slender steel construction—expressing the nature of that construction in the mathematics of structure, which are the mathematics of music as well. Such a city would clean itself in the rain, would know no fire alarms—nor any glooms. To any extent the light could be lighting seems to come more easily and reduced within the rooms by screens, a blind, or insertion of opaque glass. The heating problem would be no greater than with the rattling windows of the imitation masonry structure, because the fabric now would be mechanically perfect—the product of the machine shop instead of the makeshift of the field.

I dream of such a city, have worked enough on such a building to see definitely its desirability and its practicability.

Beauty always comes to and by means of a perfect practicability in architecture. That does not mean that the practicability may not find idealization in realization. On the contrary. Because that is precisely what architecture does and is when it is really architecture. Architecture finds idealization in realization or the reverse if you like.

Then, too, there is the lighting fixture—made a part of the building. No longer an appliance nor even an appurtenance, but really architecture.

This is a new field. I touched it early in my work and can see limitless possibilities of beauty in this one feature of the use of glass. Fortunately this field has been more developed than any other. The sense of integral lighting seems to come more easily and naturally because there was no precedent to impede progress. And it is now with the lighting feature, so will it soon be a disgrace to an architect to have left anything of a physical nature whatsoever, in his building unassimilated in his design as a whole.

Integral lighting began with this ideal in mind in my work thirty-one years ago, as may be seen in the playroom ceiling and in the dining room ceiling of my former house in Oak Park. Also, in the ceiling of my studio library in that building. Perhaps it might be said to have begun earlier than that in the Auditorium by Adler and Sullivan where the electric lights became features of the plaster ornamentation. The lights were not incorporated, but they were provided for in the decoration as accents of that decoration.

Glass and light—two forms of the same thing!

Modern architecture is beckoned to a better reckoning by this most precious of the architect's new material. As yet, little has been done with it but the possibilities are large.

This great gift of glass is of the machine—for today mechanical processes are as much the Machine as any other of its factors.

IN THE CAUSE OF ARCHITECTURE VII: THE MEANING OF MATERIALS— CONCRETE

[Published with four illustrations in The Architectural Record, *August 1928]*

I AM WRITING THIS ON THE PHOENIX PLAIN OF ARIZONA. The ruddy granite mountain-heaps, grown "old," are decomposing and sliding down layer upon layer to further compose the soil of the plain. Granite in various stages of decay, sand, silt, and gravel make the floor of the world here.

Buildings could grow right up out of the "ground" were this "soil," before it is too far "rotted," cemented in proper proportions and beaten into flasks or boxes—a few steel strands dropped in for reinforcement.

Cement may be, here as elsewhere, the secret stamina of the physical body of our new world.

And steel has given to cement (this invaluable ancient medium) new life, new purposes, and possibilities, for when the coefficient of expansion and contraction was found to be the same in concrete and steel, a new world was opened to the Architect. The Machine in giving him steel-strands gave concrete the right-of-way.

Yet three-fourths of the dwellings here are of wood and brick brought from great distances and worked up into patterns originated, east, thirty years ago. The "houses" are quite as indigenous as a cocked hat and almost as deciduous; one-half the cost of the whole—freight.

The Indian did better in the adobe dwelling he got from Mexico and built in the foothills. Even the few newer concrete buildings imitate irrelevant "styles"—although more relevant Mexico is coming north at the moment, to the rescue, in little ways. So funny, they will be architectural comedy ten years later.

It is only natural that the Architect, at first, should do as he has always done—reproduce badly in the new material the forms of the old Architecture or whatever he had instead, which were probably, themselves reproductions, as false.

Let us frankly admit that these human processes of thought move more by habit and indirection than by intellectual necessity and attach to the established order with tenacity worthy of a nobler thing.

The Architect, by profession, is a conservative of conservatives. His "profession" is first to perceive and conform and last to change this order.

Yet gradually the law of gravitation has its way, even with the profession: natural tendency in even so humble a thing as a building material will gradually but eventually force the architect's hand and overcome even his "profession."

Then after it has had its way, will come its sway, so that when a newer material condition enters into life, it, in turn, will have just as hard a time of it, until "the nature of the thing," by gravity, conquers "professional resistance" once more: a resistance compounded of ignorance, animal fear, and self-interest.

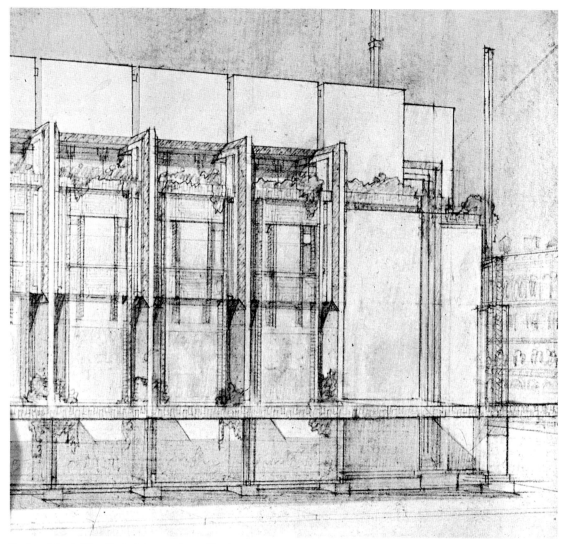

Merchandising Building (Project). Los Angeles, California. 1923. Detail of perspective. Pencil on tracing paper, 27 x 18". FLLW Fdn#2203.001

The literature of concrete, as a conglomerate, now fills libraries. Its physical properties are fairly well understood.

Aesthetically it has neither song nor story.

Nor is it easy to see in this conglomerate a high aesthetic property, because in itself it is amalgam, aggregate, compound. And cement, the binding medium, is characterless in itself. The net result is, usually, an artificial stone at best, or a petrified sand heap at worst.

Concrete would be better named "conglomerate," as concrete is a noble word which this material fails to live up to. It is a mixture that has little quality in itself.

If this material is to have either form, texture, or color in itself, each must artificially be given to it,

Previous pages: **Doheny Ranch Resort (Project). Los Angeles, California. 1923. Perspective: typical residence. Pencil and color pencil on tracing paper, 22 x 18".** FLLW Fdn#2104.006

by human imagination.

Thus it is one of the insensate brute materials that is used to imitate others.

"Concrete"—so called—must submit to the "artistic" at the hands of any parlor-architect or interior desecrator and, consequently seldom have life of its own worthy a substance so obedient and useful.

As a material it is its misfortune to project as wooden beams, travel molded as cornices. Yet it will faithfully hang as a slab, stand delicately perforated like a Persian faience screen or lie low and heavily in mass upon the ground. Again, unluckily, it will stand up and take the form (and texture too) of wooden posts and planks. It is supine, and sets as the fool, whose matrix receives it, wills.

When, and as, he has made up his mind to his "*taste*" it will set into whatever shape may be, and will then go to work with steel strands for sinews and do mighty things. When aged it becomes so stubborn that it would cost more to remove the structure often, than the ground upon which it stands might be worth.

Surely, here, to the creative mind, is temptation. Temptation to rescue so honest a material from degradation. Because here in a conglomerate named "concrete" we find a plastic material, that as yet has found no medium of expression that will allow it to take plastic form. So far as it is now used it might be tallow, cast iron, or plaster, poured into molds and at the mercy of their shape.

Therefore its form is a matter of this process of casting rather than a matter of anything at all derived from its own nature. Because it is thus, universally, at the mercy of demoralizing extraneous influences, it is difficult to say what is "concrete" form and what is not.

But certain truths regarding the material are clear enough. First, it is a mass-material; second, an impressionable one as to surface; third, it is a material which may be continuous or monolithic within certain very wide limits; fourth, it is a material that may be chemicalized, colored, or rendered impervious to water: it may be dyed or textured in the stuff; fifth, it is a willing material while fresh, fragile when

still young, stubborn when old, lacking always in tensile strength.

What then should be the Aesthetic of Concrete?

Is it Stone? Yes and No.

Is it Plaster? Yes and No.

Is it Brick or Tile? Yes and No.

Is it Cast Iron? Yes and No.

Poor Concrete! Still looking for its own at the hands of Man.

Perhaps the term "concrete" popularly meaning conglomerate, in this connection, denotes it the mongrel, servile as such, destined to no more than the place of obedient servant in the rank of materials.

Terra-cotta, the fanciful, however, though less artificial, is not much more fortunate in character and makeup. The two materials have much in common. Terra-cotta having the great advantage of standing up to be modeled and becoming indestructible, colorful, and glazed when fired, a comparatively expensive process.

The chief difference between stone and concrete lies in the binding medium which, in the case of stone, is of the stone itself—a chemical affinity.

In the case of concrete it is a foreign substance that binds the aggregate. There is little or none other than a mechanical affinity in concrete.

But for this difference concrete would be, in fact, a true natural stone. And taking this difference for granted it is more truly an artificial stone than it is anything else; the nature of the artifice enabling the artificer to enter at the time the mixture is in a state of flux, to give it whatever shape he may desire.

Yes, artificial stone it is that concrete usually becomes.

But the essential difference between stone and concrete is still unconsidered. And that essential difference is the plasticity of the material itself as distinguished from natural stone which has none at all.

I should say that in this plasticity of concrete lies its aesthetic value. As an artificial stone, concrete has no great, certainly no independent, aesthetic value whatsoever. As a plastic material—eventually becoming stone-like in character—there lives in it a great aesthetic property, as yet inadequately expressed.

Overleaf: **Charles Ennis House. Los Angeles, California. 1924. Photograph by Julius Shulman**

To design a concrete pattern for a casting that would feature this flow of the material might be possible and so allow its plastic nature to come through the process into artistic expression, thus distinguishing concrete from stone. I have seldom seen it done unless by accident. Of course, where the material is tamped relatively dry or beaten into molds there is no such problem.

There is another plastic possibility in treatment. The material *en masse* may be printed, "goffered," while fresh and wet, as the printer's die embosses his paper—and such effects had as may be seen in stone where fossil remains of foliage or other organic forms, either cameo or intaglio, are found in it. And this treatment would be nearer to its nature, aesthetically, than is any casting whatsoever.

The pre-cast slab, rolled to small thickness but large in size, is a means common to all materials that set hard from a flux and absorb reinforcement. But there is little or nothing in that treatment to distinguish concrete from sheet steel or glass or plaster.

The slab may be made smaller, be printed with design appropriate to the material, and be knit together with steel laid in wide grooved joints and the whole poured and locked together into a thin slab, and express the nature of the material itself no more than it would express terra-cotta or glass or metal, except as the feeling of the design and mass, as a whole, reflected it.

Most usefully then, probably, in this mechanical era, concrete is another passive or negative material depending for aesthetic life almost wholly upon the impress of human imagination. This element of pattern, however it may mechanically be made to occur, is therefore the salvation of concrete in the mechanical processes of this mechanical age, whenever it rises as a material above the mere mass into which it may naturally be thrown on the ground and where it serves as such better than any other material.

Of course, always there is the interior content or aggregate of the concrete to work up in various ways, giving texture and color to the block, slab, or mass. These treatments are too familiar to require much comment, and are all useful to qualify the material, but of no great significance in the broad question of finding the aesthetic interpretation that will best express the nature of concrete considered as a material.

These expedients all partake of the nature of stone and bring concrete still nearer as artificial stone, the sole advantage of the concrete being that it may be formed in place, in great size, by small means, by way of accretion—whereas stone must be got out, expensively cut, transported, and lifted to place in bulk.

Thus concrete becomes the ideal makeshift of this, the vainglorious Makeshift Era.

There never was a more "inferior" building material than was the old concrete block; unless it was ungalvanized sheet iron. The block was cheap imitation and abominable as material when not downright vicious. Every form it undertook it soon relegated to the backyard of aesthetic oblivion.

Several of the illustrations show what that self-same degraded block may become with a little sympathy and interpretation, if scientifically treated.

Herein the despised thing becomes at least a thoroughbred and a sound *mechanica*l means to a rare and beautiful use as an architect's medium, as the "block" becomes a mere mechanical unit in a quiet, plastic whole. And this mechanical use of concrete as a *mechanical* material has only just begun. In it, alone, is a medium for an "Architecture"—humble as it is before Imagination enters.

And there remain to be developed those higher uses—non-mechanical, plastic in method, treatment, and mass—to which I have referred, working naturally with color into truly plastic beauty.

IN THE CAUSE OF ARCHITECTURE VIII: SHEET METAL AND A MODERN INSTANCE

[Published with five illustrations in The Architectural Record, *October 1928]*

THE MACHINE IS AT ITS BEST WHEN ROLLING, CUTTING, stamping, or folding whatever may be fed into it.

Mechanical movements are narrowly limited unless built up like the timer of a Corliss engine or like a linotype.

The movements easiest of all are rotary, next, the press or hammer, and the lift and slide works together with either or both. In these we have pretty much the powers of the "Brute." But infinite are the combinations and divisions of these powers until we have something very much like a brain in action— the Robot itself, a relevant, dramatic conception.

The consequences may well be terrifying when man's volition is added to these brute powers. This volition of man's, deprived of soul, may drive these powers to the limit of human endurance, yes—to the ultimate extinction of the humanity of the race.

Commerce, as we have reason to know, has no soul.

Commercial interests left to themselves would soon write their own doom in the exploitation of their own social life. They would soon cease to reproduce. They would fail to reproduce because the elements of commerce are those of the machine— they lack the divine spark necessary for giving life. The margin of profit, piling up into residue, is inert, inept, impotent.

The Machine itself represents this margin of profit in the physical body of our modern world: a profit, inept, inert, impotent.

The question propounded in these papers and the continual haunting reference in all of them— "What is this interpreter of life, the Architect, going to do about it?"—is again insistent here. For in sheet metal there is opportunity to give life to something the Architect seems to despise, while forced to use it because it is cheap. He avails himself of it as a degraded material. In the building trade, we find cornices, gutters, downspouts, watersheds, in lead, zinc, and tin, iron, and copper, everywhere. Imitations too in these materials, of every other material, are everywhere.

But where may sheet metal be seen used as a fine material for its own sake?

Oh yes, occasionally. But why not "everywhere." It is the one "best thing" in modern economy of materials brought by the Machine. Building trades aside, we now make anything at all of sheet metal—kitchen utensils, furniture, automobiles, and Pullman coaches. And in flashings and counter flashings or roofing it is keeping nearly all the citizens of America dry in their homes at the present moment.

Copper is easily king of this field, and what is true of copper will be true also of the other metals in some degree, with certain special aptitudes and properties added or subtracted in the case of each.

Back of this sheet-metal tribe, literally, we have the light-rolled steel section for stiffening any particular sheet-metal area in all particular cases whatsoever. All "spread" materials need reinforcement. Metal sheets no less than concrete slabs.

In the building trades we have had recourse to these metal fabrics in the cheapest and most insulting fashion, in buildings where the architect has either never been seen, or has been set aside. Sheet metal is prime makeshift to his highness the American jerry-builder.

Roofs seem to be the building problem naturally solved by sheet metal, as it may be stamped into any desired form, lock seamed, and made into a light, decorative, and permanent watershed. It is possible to double the thicknesses in long panels or channels, sliding non-conducting material between them and lock-seaming together the continuous slabs thus made so that they lie together like planks on the roof framing, finished from below as from above. Each slab is a natural water channel.

The machinery at work in the sheet-metal trades easily crimps, folds, trims, and stamps sheets of metal as an ingenious child might his sheets of paper. The finished product may have the color brought up in surface treatment or be enameled with other durable substances as in enamel color glazing or plating or by galvanizing the finished work may be dipped and coated entire. But copper is the only sheet metal that has yet entered into architecture as a beautiful, permanent material. Its verdigris is always a great beauty in connection with stone or brick or wood, and copper is more nearly permanent than anything we have at hand as an architect's medium.

But now that all metals may be rolled into sheets and manipulated so cheaply—combinations of various metals may be made as any other combination of materials may be. And will be.

The Japanese sword guard shows how delightful these properties of metal become when contrasted and harmonized in the hands of a master-artist. A collection of these mighty little things in art and craft should be the *vade mecum* of every metal student or worker. In fact it seems that upon metals the Japanese, and before them the Chinese, have lavished much of their genius and have excelled from the making of a keen cutting-blade that would hold its edge against blows on steel to inventing subtle texture-treatments in iron for all decorative purposes.

Leaving the precious metals in a category by themselves, these sympathetic treatments of various humble metals are most significant for us who, as masters of metal production, are committed to it in our industries, though we have developed the beauty of it in use not at all.

In previous ages, beyond the roofer's use of lead in roofing and water-leads and the blacksmith's wrought iron as seen in gates and lanterns, there has been little use made of metal by architects, excepting such occasional use of bronze as Ghiberti made in his famous doors. But Ghiberti was a sculptor, not an architect, or his doors would, probably, have been wood elaborately ironed in the mode.

I believe the time is ready for a building of sheet copper wherein the copper may be appropriate carriage for glass only. What would such a building be good for and what would it be like?

Why should we have such buildings? This architect will try to answer in his own fashion.

Since first meeting, thirty years ago, James A. Miller, a sheet-metal worker of Chicago, who had intelligent pride in his material and a sentiment concerning it (designing a house for himself at one time, he demanded a tin-floored balcony outside his bedroom window in order that he might hear the rain patter upon it), I have had respect for his sheet-metal medium.

At that time I designed some sheet-copper bowls, slender flower holders, and such things, for him, and fell in love with sheet copper as a building material. I had always liked lead, despised tin, wondered about zinc, and revolted against galvanized iron as it was then used in Chicago quite generally as a substitute for granite.

Miller Brothers in addition to other offices of that factory were then interested in sheet-metal window sash and frames—especially in skylights and metal doors.

We had contempt for them because they were made to imitate wooden sash. The doors too were made up in wood and covered with metal, the result being an imitation in metal of a wood-paneled door. It was usually "grained" to complete the ruse.

National Life Insurance Company (Project). Chicago, Illinois. 1924. Perspective. Pencil on tracing paper, 24 x 18". FLLW Fdn# 2404.005

No one thought much about it one way or another. The city demanded these mongrels as fire-stops in certain places under certain conditions and that was that.

They were not cheap enough in those days—forcing the material as it was forced in this imitation work—to offer much incentive to bother with the problem.

But see how the matter has since grown up! We need no statistics to add to the evidence of our eyes wherever we go, which may see that what is left of the architectural framework of the modern world after concrete and steel have done with it will be in some form or other, sheet metal.

Twenty-seven years ago, under the auspices of Jane Addams, at Hull House, Chicago, an Arts and Crafts society was formed, and I then wanted to make a study of the Machine as a tool at work in modern materials. I invited Mr. Miller, Mr. Bagley, Mr. Wagner to come to the tentative meeting to represent respectively sheet metal, machined marble work, and terra-cotta. I wanted them there with us to tell us what we as artists might do to help them. At that time, to put the matter before the proposed society, I wrote (and read) the "Art and Craft of the Machine," since translated into many languages.

It was useless. As I look back upon it I smile, because the society was made up of cultured, artistic people, encouraged by University of Chicago professors who were ardent disciples of Ruskin and Morris. What would they want to see, if they could see it in such a programme as mine?

It all came to nothing—then—although next day's *Tribune,* in an editorial, spoke of "the first word said, by an artist, for the machine." I suspect Miss Addams of writing it herself. Ever since my stand taken there, however, the matter has grown for me, and, if not for them, it is all about them now in nearly everything they use or touch or see, still needing interpretation today as much as it was needed then.

But to get back from this reflection to this sheet-copper and glass building which has eventually resulted from it.

I have designed such a building.

It is properly a tall building.

It is a practical solution of the skyscraper problem because the advantages offered by the material and method add up most heavily in their own favor where they can go farthest—either up or crosswise.

Standardization here may come completely into its own, for standardization is in the nature of both sheet-metal process and material. It may be again seen that the life of the imagination awakens its very limitations to life.

The exterior walls, as such, disappear—instead are suspended, standardized sheet-copper screens. The walls themselves cease to exist as either weight or thickness. Windows become in this fabrication a matter of a unit in the screen fabric, opening singly or in groups at the will of the occupant. All windows may be cleaned from the inside with neither bother nor risk. The vertical mullions (copper shells filled with non-conducting material) are large and strong enough only to carry from floor to floor and project much or little as shadow on the glass may or may not be wanted. Much projection enriches the shadow. Less projection dispels the shadows and brightens the interior. These protecting blades of copper act in the sun like the blades of a blind.

The unit of two feet both ways is, in this instance, emphasized on every alternate vertical with additional emphasis on every fifth. There is no emphasis on the horizontal units. The edge of the various floors being beveled to the same section as is used between the windows, it appears in the screen as such horizontal division occurring naturally on the two-foot unit lines. The floors themselves, however, do appear, at intervals, in the recessions of the screen in order to bring the concrete structure itself into relief in relation to the screen as well as in connection with it.

Thus the outer building surfaces become opalescent, iridescent copper-bound glass. To avoid all interference with the fabrication of the light-giving exterior screen, the supporting pylons are set back from the lot line, the floors carried by them thus becoming cantilever slabs. The extent of the cantilever is determined by the use for which the building is designed. These pylons are continuous through all floors and in this instance exposed as pylons at the top. They are enlarged to carry electrical, plumbing, and heating conduits, which branch from the shafts, not in the floor slabs but into piping designed into visible fixtures extending beneath each ceiling to where the outlets are needed in the office arrangement. All electrical or plumbing appliances may thus be disconnected and relocated at short notice with no waste at all in time or material.

Being likewise fabricated on a perfect unit system, the interior partitions may all be made up in sections, complete with doors, ready to set in place and designed to match the general style of the outer wall screen.

These interior partition-units thus fabricated may be stored ready to use, and any changes to suit tenants can be made overnight with no waste of time and material.

The increase of glass area over the usual skyscraper fenestration is only about ten percent (the margin could be increased or diminished by expanding or contracting the copper members in which it is set), so the expense of heating is not materially increased. Inasmuch as the copper mullions are filled with insulating material and the window openings are tight, being mechanical units in a mechanical screen, this excess of glass is compensated.

The radiators are cast as a railing set in front of the lower glass unit of this outer screen wall, free enough to make cleaning easy.

The walls of the first two stories, or more, may be unobstructed glass—the dreams of the shopkeeper in this connection fully realized.

The connecting stairways necessary between floors are here arranged as a practical fire escape forming the central feature, as may be seen at the front and rear of each section of the whole mass, and though cut off by fireproof doors at each floor, the continuous stairway thus made discharges upon the sidewalk below without obstruction.

The construction of such a building as this would be at least one-third lighter than anything in the way of a tall building yet built—and three times stronger in any disturbance, the construction being balanced as the body on legs, the walls hanging as the arms from the shoulders, the whole, heavy where weight insures stability.

But of chief value, as I see it, is the fact that the scheme as a whole would legitimately eliminate the matter of "architecture" that now vexes all such buildings, from field construction, all such elements of architecture "exterior" or interior becoming a complete shop-fabrication—assembled only in the field.

The shop in our mechanical era is ten to one, economically efficient over the field, and will always increase over the field in economy and craftsmanship.

The mere physical concrete construction of pylons and floors is here non-involved with any interior or exterior, is easily rendered indestructible, and is made entirely independent of anything hitherto mixed up with it in our country as "Architecture." In the skyscraper as practiced at present the "Architecture" is expensively involved but is entirely irrelevant. But here it is entirely relevant but uninvolved. Also the piping and conduits of all appurtenance-systems may be cut in the shop, the labor in the field reduced to assembling only, "fitting" or screwing up the joints being all that is necessary.

Thus we have, literally, a shop-made building all but the interior, supporting posts and floors, which may be reinforced concrete or concrete-masked steel.

In this design, architecture has been frankly, profitably, and *artistically* taken from the field to the factory—standardized as might be any mechanical thing whatsoever, from a penny-whistle to a piano.

There is no unsalable floor space in this building created "for effect," as may be observed.

There are no "*features*" manufactured "for effect."

There is nothing added to the whole merely for this desired "effect."

To gratify the landlord, his lot area is now salable to the very lot-line and on every floor, where ordinances do not interfere and demand that they be reduced in area as the building soars.

What architecture there is in evidence here is a light, trim, practical commercial fabric—every inch and pound of which is "in service." There is every reason why it should be beautiful. But it is best to say nothing about that, as things are now.

The present design was worked out for a lot three hundred feet by one hundred feet, the courts being open to the south.

There is nothing of importance to mention in the general disposition of the other necessary parts of the plan. All may be quite as customary.

My aim in this fabrication employing the cantilever system of construction, which proved so effective in preserving the Imperial Hotel in Tokyo, was to achieve absolute scientific utility by means of the Machine—to accomplish—first of all—a true standardization which would not only serve as a basis for keeping the life of the building true as architecture, but enable me to project the whole, as an expression of a valuable principle involved, into a genuine living architecture of the present.

I began work upon this study in Los Angeles in the winter of 1923 having had the main features of it in mind for many years. I had the good fortune to explain it in detail to "lieber-meister," Louis H. Sullivan, some months before he died.

Gratefully, I remember—and proudly too—"I have had faith that it would come," he said. "This Architecture of Democracy—I see it in this building of yours, a genuine, beautiful thing. I knew what I was talking about all these years you see. I never could have done this building myself, but I believe that, but for me, you could never have done it."

I am sure I should never have reached it, but for what he was and what he did.

This design is dedicated to him.

IN THE CAUSE OF ARCHITECTURE IX: THE TERMS

[Published with four illustrations in The Architectural Record, *December 1928]*

ENOUGH, BY NOW, HAS BEEN SAID OF MATERIALS TO SHOW direction and suggest how far the study of their natures may go. We have glanced at certain major aspects of the more obvious of building materials only, because these studies are not intended to do more than fire the imagination of the young architect and suggest to him a few uses and effects that have proved helpful in my own work. The subject has neither bottom, sides nor top, if one would try to exhaust "the nature of materials!" How little consideration the modern architect has yet really given them. Opportunity has languished in consequence and is waiting, still.

Perhaps these articles have been guilty of "poetic" interpretation now and then, turning these "materials" over and over in the hand. The imagination has caught the light on them, in them as well, and tried to fix a ray or two of their significance in the sympathetic mind.

Poetry, Poetic, Romantic, Ideal.

These words now indicate disease or crime because a past century failed with them and gave us the *language* of form—instead of the significant form itself.

So if we are not to fall into the category of "language" ourselves, I owe an explanation of the meaning of these words, for I shall continue to use them.

It has been common practice among artists to apply the terms qualifying one art to another art—say, those of Music to Architecture or vice versa. This may be done because certain qualities in each are common to all. It may be helpful to make comparisons between them to bring out particular significance, as our English vocabulary is poor at best in all the words we have with which to express shadings of qualities or of our feeling in dealing with qualities.

We can hack away at the thing with our body-terms and get the subject anywhere or nowhere except misunderstood.

Nor do we speak a common tongue in the use we have come to make of these main words. We may pack into each of them more or less, and differently than another would dream of doing, or could do. So it is well to clean them up—for now we are going to write about the uses and purposes of "materials" in creating this thing we name Architecture.

"Poetry of Form," for instance, is a phrase that will now make almost any sensible man sick.

The word "poetry" is a dangerous word to use, and for good reason. Carl Sandburg once said to me, "Why do you use the words 'poetry,' 'beauty,' 'truth,' or 'ideal' any more? Why don't you just get down to tacks and talk about boards and nails and barn doors?"

Good advice. And I think that is what I should do. But I won't, unless I can get an equivalent by doing so. That equivalent is exactly what I cannot get. Those words—romance, poetry, beauty, truth, ideal—are not precious words nor should they be *specious* words. They are elemental human symbols and we must be brought back again to respect for them by using them significantly if we use them at all, or go to jail.

Well, then—our lot being cast with a hod of mortar, some bricks, or stone or concrete and the Machine, we shall talk of the thing we are going to do with these things in the terms that are sensible enough, when we speak of the horsehair, catgut, fine wood, brass and keys, the "things" that make up the modern orchestra. By the way, that orchestra is New. Our possibilities in building with the Machine are New in just the same sense.

Although Architecture is a greater art than Music (if one art can be greater than another) this architect has always secretly envied Bach, Beethoven, and the great Masters of Music. They lifted their batons after great and painful concentration on creation and soared into the execution of their designs with a hundred willing minds—the orchestra—and that means a thousand fingers quick to perform every detail of the precise effect the Master wanted.

What a resource!

And what facility they were afforded by forms—they made them—moving according to mood from fugue to sonata, from sonata to concerto—and from them all to the melodic grandeur and completeness of the symphony.

I suppose it is well that no architect has anything like it nor can ever get it.

But as a small boy, long after I had been put to bed, I used to lie and listen to my father playing Beethoven—for whose music he had conceived a passion, playing far into the night. To my young mind it all spoke a language that stirred me strangely, and I've since learned it was the language, beyond all words, of the human heart.

To me, architecture is just as much an affair of the human heart.

And it is to architecture in this sense that we are addressing ourselves. We are pleading here in that cause.

What then, is "Poetry of Form"?

The term has become a red rag or a reproachful tag to architects at home and abroad. And, too, it is something that clients would rather not hear about. For all clients are, to some degree, infected by this contact with architects. And some of the best among them fall ill with Neo-Spanish that was itself Neo-Italian or some kind of Renaissance of the Renaissance, or linger along Quasi-Italian, or eventually die outright of Tudor or Colonial.

It is a new form of the plague—"this poison of good taste," as Lewis Mumford has precisely called it. This "poison" has cursed America for generations to come. And this happened to the good people who spoke the language of "Poetry of Form" and hopefully sought the "Romantic" when they became clients.

"Poetry of Form," in this romantic, popular sense, has not only cost wasted billions in money but has done spiritual harm beyond reckoning to the America of the future. But the fact remains that America wanted it and sought it. The failure is less significant than the fact.

So instead of speaking of "Poetry of Form" in buildings, perhaps, after all, we would do better to say simply the natural building, naturally built, native to the region.

Such a building would be sure to be all that "Poetry of Form" should imply, and would mean a building as beautiful on its site as the region itself.

And that word ROMANCE, Romantic or Romanza, got itself born in literature a century ago. Later Novalis and his kind chose the blue flower as its symbol. Their Romance was rather an escape from life than any realization of the idealization of it. As the word is popularly or commonly used today, it is still something fanciful, unlike life. At least it is something exotic. "Romance" is used as a word to indicate escape from the pressure of the facts of life into a realm of the beyond—a beyond each one fashions for himself or for others as he will—or may—dream.

But in music the Romanza is only a free form or freedom to make one's own form. A musician's sense of proportion is all that governs him in it. The mysterious remains just enough a haunting quality in a whole—so organic as to lose all tangible

Overleaf: **San Marcos-in-the-Desert, Resort Hotel (Project). Chandler, Arizona. 1927. Perspective. Pencil on tracing paper, 35 x 20".**
FLLW Fdn #2704.049

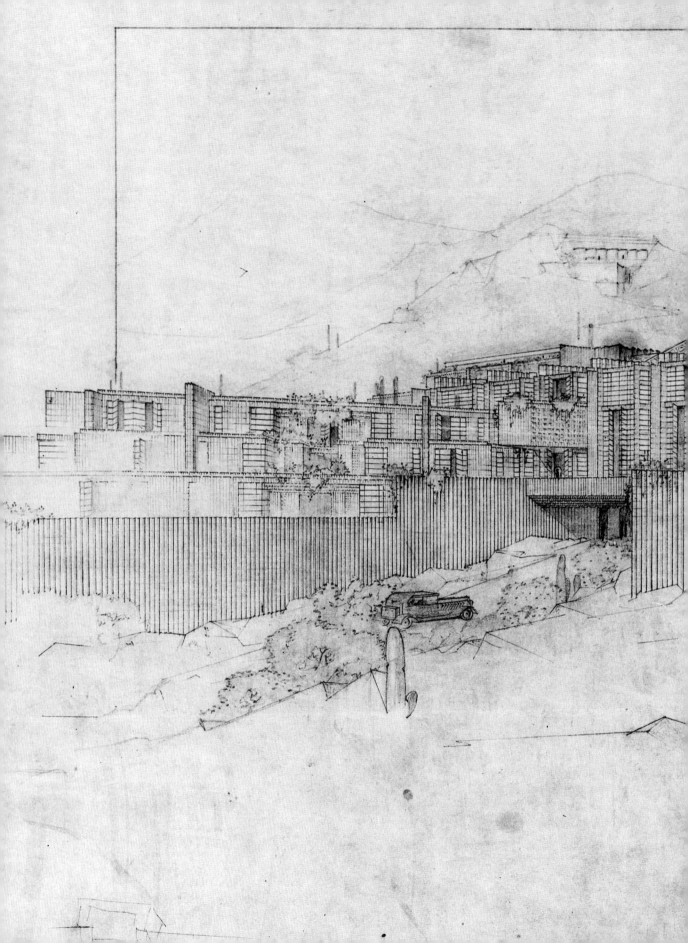

evidence of how it was made—and the organic whole lives in the harmonies of feeling expressed in sound. Translate "sounds and the ear" to "forms and the eye," and a Romanza, even, seems reasonable enough, too, in architecture.

And now that word IDEAL.

The IDEAL building? Why, only that building which is all one can imagine as desirable in every way.

And POETRY? Why, the poetry in anything is only the song at the heart of it—and in the nature of it.

Gather together the harmonies that inhere in the nature of something or anything whatsoever, and project those inner harmonies into some tangible "objective" or outward form of human use or understanding, and you will have Poetry. You will have something of the song that aches in the heart of all of us for release.

Any of these Arts called "Fine" are POETIC by nature. And to be poetic, truly, does not mean to escape from life but does mean *life raised to intense significance and higher power.*

POETRY, therefore, is the great potential need of human kind.

We hunger for POETRY naturally as we do for sunlight, fresh air, and fruits, if we are normal human beings.

To be potentially poetic in architecture, then, means—to create a building free in form (we are using the word Romanza), that takes what is harmonious in the nature of existing conditions inside the thing and outside it and with sentiment (beware of sentimentality)—bringing it all out into some visible form that expresses those inner harmonies perfectly, *outwardly,* whatever the shape it may take.

In this visible shape or form you will see not only what was harmonious in the existing conditions inside and outside and around about the building, but you will also see, in this sentiment of the architect, a quality added from the architect himself—because this ultimate form inevitably would be *his* sense of BEAUTY living now for you in these known and visible terms of his work.

These words—Poetry, Romance, Ideal—used in a proper sense—and I believe I have given them

proper expression and interpretation here—are indispensable tools in getting understood when talking of creation.

At any rate, I shall use them, always in the sense I have just given them.

And there is need of another term to express a new sense of an eternal quality in creation.

Need, really, of a new dimension?

Either a new dimension to think with or a new sense of an old one.

We have heard of the fourth dimension frequently, of late, to meet this need. Why a fourth dimension, when we so little understand the possibilities of what we already use as the three dimensions?

If we make the first two (length and width) into one, as really they are both merely surface, and then add the third (thickness) as the second, thus getting mass, we will have an empty place as third in which to put this new sense as the missing dimension I shall describe. Thus comes in the third dimension about which I have talked a good deal and written somewhat.

Or suppose we arrive at it another way by simply giving spiritual interpretation to the three dimensions we already use. Say length (the first dimension) becomes continuity, width (the second dimension) becomes that breadth of which we speak when we refer to the measure of some great man's mind or a great prospect. Then thickness (the third dimension) becomes depth and we give to that word, "depth," the meaning we give to it when we speak of the "profound," the organic, the integral—again we have the third dimension.

We reach the missing dimension either way, but reach it we must.

For it is necessary to find some term that will make it easy to express this missing quality in discussing creation and reaching within for understanding.

But why say fourth dimension when, by properly interpreting the three we already have and by giving them the higher significance which is theirs by nature, we may be spared the confusion of more mere numbers?

This, then, is what I mean by the third dimension. Either an interpretation of the physical third, an interpretation that signifies this quality of "at-one-ness" or integral nature in anything or everything. Or, arrive at it by naming the three dimensions as now used as actually but two, adding the third as a new concept of organic-integrity, or more properly speaking, as that *quality* that makes anything *of* the thing and never on it.

Thus came the new conception of architecture as interior space finding utilization and enclosure as its "*members*"—as architecture. The *within* is thus made concrete realization in *form*.

This is the *integral* concept of building for which I have pleaded, am still pleading, and will continue to plead, instead of the earlier one—beautiful but less great—in which a block of building material was sculptured, punctured, and ornamented into architecture.

In this matter of supplying the needed term as the third dimension I may be found guilty of making a language of my own to fit my necessity.

Perhaps that is true—although it seems obvious enough to me that the quality lacking in the thought of our modern world where creation is concerned, is simply expressed in this way. I should be thankful for a better, more evident expression of this subjective element.

If I could find it, I should be among the first to use it.

Until then I can only write and speak of this essence of all creative endeavor, objectively, as the third dimension. And here in this matter will be found the essential difference between what is only modern and what is truly new.

The pictorial age in which we live will no longer be satisfied to have the picture continue without this interior significance expressed in integral form. Two dimensions have characterized the work of the past centuries and two-dimensional thought and work is still modern, it seems. Is it too much to hope that the coming century will be one in which this element of the third dimension —this demand for organic significance—will characterize all the pictures that go to make up the main picture, which will be then tremendous with integrity and pregnant with new beauty?

Now, there are certain things as hard as nails, as pointed as tacks, as flat as a barn door that go to make up the technique of creation in this deepened, enlivened, more potential sense.

Since we now have materials in our hands to work with as elements, it is method that I now want to write about, believing that if I can make even the beginning of the matter of making true, significant buildings a little more clear, I shall have rendered real service. I would much rather build than write about building, but when I am not building, I will write about building—or the significance of those buildings I have already built.

The conception of the room *within,* the interior spaces of the building to be conserved, expressed, and made living as architecture—the architecture of the *within*—that is precisely what we are driving at, all along. And this new quality of thought in architecture, the third dimension, let us say, enters into every move that is made to make it—enters into the use of every material; enters the working of every method we shall use or can use. It will characterize every form that results naturally from this integral interpretation of architecture in its demand upon us for integrity of means to ends—for integrity of the each in all, and of the all in all in whatever we do—yes, from pig to proprietor, from a chicken-house to a cathedral.

One more word is indispensable to get the essence of this matter of creation visible on the surface.

That word is "PRINCIPLE."

In an earlier paper, there is an attempt to define character and to throw some light on the vexed matter of style!

Principle is the working scheme, or the scheme at work in character, style, integrity, truth, or beauty. It is not a motif but a means. We might say principle is the law that governs the production of any one or all of them.

The principle of anything is the law that works its being.

Natural law is principle, or the other way around, as you please. Our application of what we understand of principle is mostly expedient, seldom a genuine working of principle. That is all that is the matter with us. Principle is the tool with which the architect must consciously work to be a safe man or get great effects in his work.

He may be an artist—that is, he may be sentient to his fingertips and be merely artistic without this command of principle, or, let us say, without this noble submission to its command, never knowing the command when seen or heard or "sensed."

In command of principle or commanded by it, only so is the artist potential in creation.

This miserable assumption of virtues, though one has them not, may be expedient, but it is all the hell there is attached to this affair of getting spirit materialized in works that gratify supremely human desires—we might say, "getting the Beautiful born." And then have someone pop up and say with a sneer, "Yes, but what is beauty?" as though beauty were a commodity like soap, cheese or tobacco.

Well, yes. Here, in beauty, is another word to stumble over or mumble within this age of the pragmatic "expedient" which, after all, is only an experiment.

But, now we have them all in a row—Poetry, Romantic, Ideal, Beauty—faithful mistresses of principle which we may now name Truth. And "Integrity," "Character," "Style," are attributes, merely, of the working of the master—Principle.

What is Beauty? And Keats' "Ode to a Grecian Urn" answers—"Truth, Beauty—Beauty, Truth."[1]

Obviously, the gifted boy was right, but the nature of either is no nearer for his statement—in the case of the young architect who wants to build something that is both true and lovely. Before we get out of this, that word "love" and the word "joy" too, will get in, I feel sure. Here they are at this moment. Very well, let them in to the distinguished company they know so well. And then let us ask them for help.

"Art is the evidence of man's joy in his work," man has said. And that love is the motivating power in creation we all know by experience.

We are talking about creating or about creations, and this motivation, "Love," is essential to any conception of it—to any beginning of it.

Conceive, then, in love, and work with principle, and what men call Beauty will be the evidence of your joy in your work. After the purity and intensity of your desire or love, then, according to the degree that you have got command of Principle or willingly obey its commands, that materialization of spirit will appear in your work in earthly form—and men will call it Beauty.

Look about you at earthly forms! Trees, flowers, the reactions to one another of the elements in sky, earth, and sea. All are merely effects of the working of definite principles with definite "materials"—which are really only elements in the creative hand.

The "design" of this in the altogether is too large in pattern to be yet comprehended by man, yet for our purposes in all or in each, we may find the evidence we seek of method in creation.

Method in creation?

It is there most certainly. Principle is at work continually in this school for architects—working there with simple materials and never-failing *ideas* of form. The form is a consequence of the principle at work. It would seem that no proper excuse for "making" anything ugly need ever be accepted from an architect—with all this prima facie evidence surrounding him, evident even in his own fingers as he writes or draws. He may study forms, "types" constructed by the infallible working of interior principles in this common school. What escapes us is the original idea or ultimate purpose.

This urge to create the beautiful for love of the beautiful is an inheritance. Enough for us that because of the inheritance we have carved out for ourselves with imagination, this higher realm of Beauty.

With imagination, then, let us try to learn the method of working principle with such simple elements as are everywhere put into our hands as materials. Love in our hearts—passion, yes, is essential to success, as our motif.

Now having done our best to light up these words and discuss the relationship existing between them, we will go on to talk of those matters, as hard as nails, as pointed as tacks, as flat as a barn door, that are involved in the method—of creation.

Love no one can give. Assuming that inspiration is in the heart, we can show facts and performances with materials according to Principle that will be helpful to others in relation to method in creation.

---

1. Wright has misquoted Keats. The line reads: "Beauty is Truth, Truth Beauty."

TOWARDS A NEW ARCHITECTURE

[Published in World Unity, *September 1928]*

IN A STYLE AS STARK AS ONE OF THE GAS-PIPE RAILINGS AT the edge of one of his "new" cantilever porches, Le Corbusier, no sentimentalist, comes to us to tell us that this machine age has "surface and mass"—effects neglected in our architecture. He points to the clean lines and surfaces of the aeroplane, the ocean grey-hounds, and to certain machinery—having no other motif than to express in the simplest terms the nature of its necessity—as the "new" beauty. He is right.

"Styles," says he, are no more than the feather in madam's hat. His way of putting our own minority report.

France, our fashionmonger, has arrived at the psychological moment to set a fashion for us in architecture—to pull the plumes from the hat we call our "Classic," and maybe get the hat itself.

The fact that all Le Corbusier says or means was at home here in architecture in America in the work of Louis Sullivan and myself—more than twenty-five years ago and is fully on record in both building and writing here and abroad—has no meaning for him in this connection.

He was talking to France, but unwittingly he now speaks to us.

France the discoverer must "discover" these plain truths anew or have nothing to do with them. It is her habit. It has taken her quite up-to-now to recover from Art Nouveau. Germany, Austria, Holland, and Sweden must now smile to see this belated "discovery" by France.

In those countries, the matter for which Le Corbusier claims two dimensions has been at work all these years, while here in America it was at work in full three dimensions. True—a minority report it was, and still is. But as John Bright was fond of pointing to history to prove—the minority was always right.

What then will happen should a French fashion now be made of the minority report in American architecture? The truth will move on and be found elsewhere in another minority report to be "discovered" again at some future time as usual—but "progress" is ahead no less.

Our "American Classic" needs this dressing down, from the "abroad" it has itself aped and imitated. Therefore France will be more effective and convincing in this matter than anything anyone at home could say or do, especially as it comes just when Manhattan's commercial machine has triumphed over architects and compelled their cornice (our feathered hat) to go.

This testimony from the passing stranger applauds that triumph and not at all deplores the blow the machine dealt the classic. The machine is showing its strength. The feathered hat is already on askew. This fresh breeze blowing from abroad for some years past and now renewed from the cradle of liberty itself—well—hat and all is going to go. Our psychology in affairs of the arts is notorious.

And yet this pronouncement by Monsieur—what is it? Really it is essentially a plea for another kind of picture-building. It is only more appropriate now to leave off all the "trimming" and keep all severely plain.

In this matter of art, the Frenchman has seldom got inside. He has usually discovered the surface "effect" best suited to the time, the place, and the hour. It is no small virtue in him and has heaped honors upon his Nation.

But that "flair" is no longer good enough. In this matter of architecture, France may for once find herself behind. America's minority report already handed in—goes deeper and the French movement may soon lose its two dimensions—"surface and mass" within the three that characterize the American work. The third dimension we already have, to be added to the two of France, is depth.

It is this quality of depth that alone can give life or purpose to the other two dimensions and result in that integrity in architecture that makes the building no less organic than the tree itself.

"Surface and mass," which the talented Frenchman (true to the custom of his people since time began) declares the chief elements of architecture with which the architect has to deal are in reality not elements at all but products. Length, width, and thickness make after all but two dimensions—the superficial ones—until that third element as the quality of depth that makes all integral has entered—nothing has happened in Architecture beyond a refreshing semblance of simplicity.

A spiritual interpretation must be given to length, width, and thickness. Length considered as "continuity," width considered as "breadth," and thickness as "depth"—all to be made homogeneous.

We are learning to see from the outside the "effects" produced by such homogeneity and to desire them. We are beginning to hunger for them really. But we will not learn to produce them by studying them from the outside. We will get at them from "within" or we will create nothing. We will be giving an imitation of the more appropriate aspect of the thing we see—making more picture-buildings—adding another ist to effect only another ism—among so many gone down before.

But I wish everyone engaged in making or breaking these United States would read the Le Corbusier book. Universities especially should read it. And as for World Unity—it seems that insofar as this ideal of America is a spirit, America already, except for the minority report, is found much more abroad than at home in this great matter of Architecture. We are, by nature of our opportunity, time, and place, the logical people to give highest expression to the "New." We are the great thing in this sense. We fail to see it in ourselves because we have been imitating an old world that now sees in us, neglected, a higher estate than it has ever known in its own sense of itself.

So welcome, Holland, Germany, Austria, and France—what you take from us we receive from you gratefully. Had you not taken it, we as a nation might never have been aware of it, never, even, have seen it.

FISKE KIMBALL'S NEW BOOK

[Published without illustrations in The Architectural Record, *August 1928]*

I HAVE JUST FINISHED READING FISKE KIMBALL'S NEW BOOK on *American Architecture*—after admiring the slip-cover effectively showing the "Temple to Mammon."

The title of Mr. Kimball's book should have been *Architecture in America*. According to him American architecture has passed out and all we have left is what McKim, Mead, and White and the plan-factories—initiated by Daniel H. Burnham—have borrowed from Europe—the Classic—and have used to successfully conceal the ways and means by which it has its being.

I learned from the genial writer in the early chapters of his book, and enjoyed his glowing pages until I got to the matter of which I know considerable, beginning with the chapter, "What is Modern Architecture?" Here Fiske Kimball allows Nature quite enough rope to hang herself and awards the "victory" to the sophist Greek and his elegant abstractions in this—the Machine Age. He does this apparently with both eyes wide-open, quite gaily unconscious of the fact that he pleads the old mime of "Art for Art's Sake." Therein is he a good Greek.

There is no objection to anyone's doing this so well as Fiske Kimball does it, but, easy to see, he doesn't really believe it, as does no one else of his caliber today.

His real sympathies, all the while, are with us—Mr. Sullivan, the modern Europeans and myself. He writes much better and more sympathetically in his obituaries of Mr. Sullivan and of myself than of his triumphant bona-fide heroes of the "American Classic," which may only be, after all, his sentimentality getting the better of his generosity.

But, I think he served us best where he showed his "Two Poles of Modernism" side by side.

The synthetic Guaranty Building by Louis Sullivan alongside the pretentious Century Apartments in New York City. The one, thought-built. The other, taste-built, regardless of thought. The one a work of art, the other merely artistic. And let us accept this bold contrast as true but say, "the affirmation and negation of modernism" for the two can never stand on equal footing as "Poles."

The Guaranty is architecture.

The Century is picture-building.

Now, Fiske Kimball's book is a brief for picture-building when it arrives at third base and starts on the home run. It is shameless in this respect. The virtue of "a buccaneer glorifying theft in the face of the law"—has this book. Fiske Kimball is lawless.

The "American Classic" (that is a choice phrase of his) is lawless—without logic or philosophy, that is—and defiant of cause and effect. At best, it is what a very wealthy client of mine, president of a great company, accused me of some years ago. Visiting Taliesin, he looked about honestly delighted—astonished. He said, "I've heard a deal about this place, but hang it, I ain't heard the half." He looked out, looked in, and looked around and turning to me said suddenly, "after all there ain't nothing to it, is there? It's just 'taste,' ain't it?" Well—I plead not guilty. But there you have Fiske Kimball's brief for "American Classic." "It's just 'taste' ain't it?"

And then in the chapter, "Counter-Currents"—I feel, like Mark Twain, the "reports of my own death greatly exaggerated." But so knowing and generously kind is this chapter that I should not find fault with it.

Granting the Kimball re-assumption of "Art for Art's Sake"—that perennial mimicry—there are few errors of statement or judgement in this interesting book—that I could see. One was "from Richardson must also have come the first suggestion of the foliated ornament which Sullivan afterward developed so characteristically." This of course is oblique surmise.

I have drawings in my possession showing the gradual development of Sullivanian ornament from Beaux Arts days and John Edelman's influence down to the time I, myself, drew for him, and the unfoldment of the style is unbroken and consistent. It would have been the same had Richardson never lived.

But, too, along with others, I am glad Fiske Kimball wrote this book. I have heard many say they were glad he did, that it was needed and that he had done it well, as I think he has. But I am glad for a different reason. It shows me the weakness of his own position, and that he knows it. His is far too searching and clever a mind not to know it.

And some of the time while reading the book I wondered if in the disguise of "American Classic" he wasn't just befriending our true cause in Machiavellian style.

29

THE PLAN FOR THE ERECTION OF A MODEL BUILDING

The following article was intended to accompany the drawings for Saint Mark's Tower, an apartment build-ing Wright designed to be built near the church Saint Mark's in the Bouwerie. The text he wrote describes not only the type of structure to be constructed, but also the way in which the building would be financed: "Every dollar contributed paying for a dollar's worth of building—nothing paid for financing, holding, or agencies."

The Saint Mark's scheme was beautifully worked on in all details, but the Depression interrupted its construction. Twenty-seven years later, however, its design was used for the H.C. Price Tower in Bartlesville, Oklahoma. The Price Tower is partly residential and partly commercial, but the project implemented the principles espoused here. [Unpublished essay]

IT IS APPARENT THAT IF THIS DEPRESSION (OR IS IT compression?) is to end, a set of new and better ideas is needed to encourage enterprise.

In the field of architecture the old system of building was masterful and none too useful. The old system by which the building was financed was a makeshift and so wasteful that the wind and water in most "financed" buildings has left the investors with no buildings, and the bankers do not know what to do with the buildings on their hands by way of foreclosure.

We propose a type of building that is not wasteful and is more useful than the buildings now built, and we propose to build it by direct owner-ship, every dollar contributed paying for a dollar's worth of building—nothing paid for financing, holding, or agencies.

A trustee for funds and a syndicate is proposed composed of subscribers to the cost of construction in amounts from one hundred dollars to fifteen hun-dred dollars.

We propose a type of apartment building, eighteen stories high, standing free in a small green park, quadruple in plan, each apartment a duplex. Each apartment will be the equivalent in usable area and comfort of the usual five-room apartment and will be completely furnished except table and bedli-nen and tableware.

The structure is an economic balanced con-struction similar to the construction that saved the Imperial Hotel, [leaving it] unharmed in the earth-quake of 1923.

Only the core or inner shaft of structural con-crete and steel of this building will be built in the field. The visible and usable architecture and appur-tenance systems of the building will be assembled by way of shop-fabrication. By this means we are able to lighten and economize construction one-third

St. Mark's Tower (Project). New York City. 1929. Cut-away perspective, apartment interior. Pencil and color pencil on tracing paper, 34 x 12". FLLW Fdn#2905.032

and strengthen it. The total saving in usable area of building effected by conservation of space by the inclusion of integral metal furnishings; then light glass and metal screens substituted for the thickness of outer masonry walls and interior partitions; and the economies of the continuous slab in cantilever construction is more than one-third of the cost of equivalent net living space in present buildings. Also, at least another third of the cost of present structures goes into promotion and financing. So two-thirds of the cost of the buildings now in trouble could be saved in this new model built by the direct ownership we propose. But, as before stated, more than this the architecture of the building yields a happier living condition, more sunlight, more privacy, greater individuality, easier and more economical operation, greater distinction in the artistic effect of the apartment as a whole.

The accompanying drawings will help to explain and verify these statements. We can give subscribers to this scheme complete assurance that the cost of the building will not exceed the estimates herewith—and that instead of adding one more apartment building where too many already exist—this building opens the way to better living at less cost in greater harmony than can be had at any price in any of the present structures and therefore is a true incentive to continue building to improve conditions and relieve the present discouragement.

It needs no argument to convince anyone that new and constructive ideas in art or life cannot take place by appealing to the bank or broker. The banker is a banker because he hangs to the old order and is doomed to hang with it.

When this project is completed we will be able to come back to our subscribers with other schemes for better buildings, for better life—say the new theater, the appropriate moving-picture house, the gas station as a modern building that will grace our towns and not disgrace them. And many other enterprises.

By this way of trust and direct ownership, profitable, architectural exemplars may be built where by way of the old system they would only be killed as a matter of expediency.

Every subscriber to the building of this model will actually own his tangible and profitable share of the building without lien of any kind, except his share of taxes subject to the cooperative will of the syndicate as expressed by its own trustees.

St. Mark's Tower (Project). New York City. 1929. Perspective. Pencil and color pencil on tracing paper, 13 x 29". FLLW Fdn#2905.020

SURFACE AND MASS—AGAIN!

The European work in modern architecture at this time, 1929–1930, was being lauded in the United States under the heading the "International Style." Its pioneering practitioners were Le Corbusier, Walter Gropius, and Mies van der Rohe. Their architectural forms, lacking all ornament, were heralded by certain American critics as expressions of "surface and mass." But Wright considered their buildings bare, sterile, and boxlike—devoid of the third dimension, of what he termed the "depth dimension." He regarded this style to be as dangerous to the American architectural scene as imitative "period" buildings: "Architects who thought they were modern concentrated on the box and exposure of structure. Why should you always expose structure? I call it 'indecent exposure,'" Wright later wrote.[1]

In this article, however, he is not so much attacking the European architects as he is the American critics. In fact, in a letter to Lewis Mumford he refers to Mies, Gropius, and Le Corbusier in the context of an exhibition of his work and theirs: "I consented to join the affair [the 1932 exhibition at The Museum of Modern Art, New York] thinking I would be among my peers."[2]

Here, to defend his position regarding ornament, the machine, and "surface and mass," he cites examples of some of his own work: the Imperial Hotel in Tokyo and the Rosenwald School for Negro Children, in Tennessee. "I design a Negro schoolhouse in the South—make it theirs, in point of life and color—form too—departing, nowise, from integral building." He further describes his own home Taliesin, his prairie houses, and his work in both California and Arizona. When he was writing this article, his office was preparing the final working drawings for San Marcos-in-the-Desert and the attached residences for Cudney and Young, Chandler, Arizona. [Published in The Architectural Record, *July 1929]*

A TRUE ANNOUNCEMENT OF THE LAW OF CREATION, IF A man were found worthy to declare it, would carry Art up into the Kingdom of Nature and destroy its separate and contrasted existence.

A wise and noble countryman of mine said that.

I listened before entering an Architect's office and have faithfully worked to be worthy to make that declaration here where Architecture was the game of a rude and youthful people and not the labor of a wise and spirited Nation.

That effort now only well begun, Nature allows me to look in on many "post-mortems," in honor of those foregathered for the purpose. "History" proceeds to repeat itself, as ever—oblique surmise.

Edificer Cram[3] quotes, "No one who begins a cause is ever allowed to finish it," calling upon that same History as witness. It seemed to comfort him.

He was discussing with Artificer Tallmadge[4] the fate of the "Modern"—really modern-"ism." The Artificer lightly underwrote it for the next thirty years as a joke on Oak Park, if New York and

Paris "came in." The Edificer said it was dead already, he understood, and fervently hoped it was.

Nature will surprise and disgust both with that consummation we notice in her for both have betrayed her.

At the moment she has her eye on Douglas Haskell[5] and Russell Hitchcock.[6] Here come, eventually, valuable critics?

Yet, by way of the former, last November, I learn that by "weight" I am satisfactorily betrayed into the long grasp of Tradition. Well—insofar as Architecture may not be divested of the weight of organic nature, I plead guilty—the trees are guilty likewise.

Useless weight and ornament *are* sins.

I have sinned. Sometimes for a holiday. Sometimes betrayed by a happy disposition. Weekdays I seek lightness, toughness, sheerness, preferring them. Weekends I fall from grace.

Has machinery already made exuberance a sin?—poverty a virtue?

Meantime, my critics, although a pupil of Louis Sullivan, never have I been his disciple. He has himself gratefully acknowledged this publicly. Had I been his disciple I should have envied him and in the end have betrayed him.

Unjust then as untrue to quote from his autobiography—"The search for the rule so broad as to admit of no exception"—as mine when the "exception" still, as always, interests me most, as necessary to prove any rule both useful and useless. That trait enables most critics to fail to penetrate the variegated surface of what I've tried to do.

Do I make excursion into the feeling of an oriental race and—no lessening grasp upon organic Architecture—build their building by means of their own handicraft, dedicate the building to them as oriental symphony?

A wail! I have been false to the mode of the Machine I had proclaimed and championed.

Should I have proclaimed that "Mode"—now of Paris—from Tokio housetops by means of oriental *handicraft* no matter how false the circumstances? Not for a moment the Machine forgotten, but in abeyance while I took off my hat to the Japanese and destructive force, was conquered by integral building—showing that Architecture may be "symphonic" in more sound senses than one.

This exception proved many rules, but broke more and still confounds the critics.

I design a Negro schoolhouse in the South—make it theirs, in point of life and color—form too—departing, nowise, from integral building. The mode of the machine deserted, again, to be humane. This is license?

I build a home for myself in southern Wisconsin—a stone, wood, and plaster building, make it as much a part of my grandfather's ground as the rocks and trees and hills there are.

This Architect has "lapsed into the picturesque."

On Midwestern prairies I build, in three dimensions, houses that proclaim the prairie's quiet level—the third dimension evident as unbroken roofplanes likewise lying in similar repose—as human *shelter.*

The floor-planes too in evidence to give scale to the whole.

Well—"the Gothic has been put to bed on its side!"

The effort in California and Arizona? Harassed by vexation of industrial confusion, forced lying, handsore, and heart-sick with makeshift tools, I finally found simple mechanical means to produce a complete building that looks the way the Machine made it—as much so at least as any woven fabric need look. Tough, light but not "thin," imperishable, plastic—no necessary lie about it anywhere and yet, Machine-made, mechanically perfect. Standardization as the soul of the Machine here, for the first time may be seen in the hand of the Architect, put squarely up to Imagination, the limitations of imagination the only limitation of building.

Unhappily, my critics, having seen, must continue to see Egyptian, Mayan, Chinese, Japanese, Persian, Moorish. Not one motif of the sort can they fairly fix in these buildings for such were never in my mind.

Only because these desert buildings too are naturally elemental in form can they verify resemblance.

Did I prefer them lean—sun-defiant—ascetic? They might be so, *honestly,* and please my critics.

Here, in principle—as servant, not as master is the Machine.

But why should the product look like machinery?

Fountains of aesthetic invention and beauty in our Utopia are all but dried up. If, now, we make gospel of any "Mode" whatsoever—they *are* gone! Irrationally bound by cruel provincial judgments of Ismtown and Istville, we have known no freedom in Creative Art.

Are we so hidebound to this bondage that Mode can destroy in Architecture the very principle of Liberty proudly declared in our cherished Jeffersonian charter as essential to Life?

The Modern is. Was always, must always be. At this critical juncture it is at least thirty-two years old.

The New is ever Old—all shallow pretense aside, and will, repeatedly, seek to become the prisonhouse of a mode, beginning with the young.

Therefore, nothing is more vital in America at this psychological moment in her Architecture than active realization of what *living,* and that means, *organic* Architecture, would bring.

We've had little. Until yesterday we were insultingly careless of that little.

Europeans, only, valued and conserved it or we should now be helplessly prone to the "Modern" imported as French fashion and be, soon, sterile again for another thirty years.

We show signs of pique at such European conservation inclined to disprove the case rather than render thanks. Here is Douglas Haskell—Russell Hitchcock no less—in this ungracious act.

These young critics, I believe, love Architecture as a mysterious essence intrigued by the science and philosophy of the great Art.

They see in "surface and mass" abstractions of great and gifted Europeans "inspired by French painting," the Truth. But I know these abstractions repudiate the third dimension, ignoring depth of matter to get surface-effects characteristic of canvas and pigment as painting and not of Architecture—no, no matter howsoever stark begot with gas pipe, thin slabs, and naked steel work. These "materials" may now be used as "decoration" too. Witness the concoctions of wire, lead pipe, plumbing-fittings, brass keys, bits of glass, and wood—of this school? Sophisticated, ingenious, cleverly curious—they smell of the dissecting room—affect me as a morgue.

Rosenwald School for Negro Children (Project). Tennessee. 1929. Perspective. Pencil and color pencil on tracing paper, 26 x 13".
FLLW Fdn# 2904.001

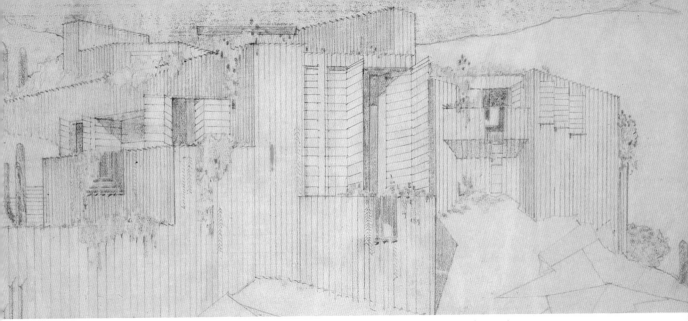

Ralph and Wellington Cudney House (Project). Chandler, Arizona. 1928. Perspective. Pencil and color pencil on tracing paper, 22 x 19". FLLW Fdn#2706.008

These artificially thin walls like cardboard, bent, folded, and glued together, are frankly, likewise dedicated *not to the Machine but to machinery!* Therefore they do not live.

The *lines* not the *spirit* of mechanical "mobilization," inspire their dry sophistication with a new "aesthetic" and for the moment a new simplicity-lie charms us afresh.

But why strive to divest organic nature of wholesome natural "weight" in vain endeavor to make houses seem to "fly" anywhere—even into the face of poverty?

Dear boys—do not spend too much too freely, that might be better kept did you make it yours.

We have here, no stranger—only a familiar in another guise with more guile than the folly we slept with yesterday—as much pose but with better breeding—a gesture of the right sort.

But a gesture seeking to ignore steps already faithfully, painfully, and soundly taken to establish here the *reality* thus begestured abroad. In order to prefer French painting as a more convenient parent?

Is this because it seeks to be a "movement," always, in Art, a damnable agency, and, that it may move as such must ignore too much?

"Poverty" is no Messiah, needs no prophets. Poverty is disease.

Know that at the very center of every true form of human-use or aesthetic-worth, whatsoever, stands *Nature*. The third dimension *naturally* distinguishes Architecture from Painting. By it we know, the one mind from the other.

Instead of this inner mastery of method and materials of sound-construction, with scientific surrender to utility, in behalf of plastic-simplicity—these "surface-and-mass" effects are no more organic than the "American Classic" of New York City or Los Angeles Tudor-Spanish.

Moreover, stark boxes blister the eyes by refusing the sun-acceptance trees, rocks, and flowers love.

Is this ignorance—impotence? Or merely empirical endeavor to force issue upon Nature?

Gracious, grateful, sun-acceptance comes by way of texture, pattern-integration, by way of human Imagination. To the eye it is what music is to the ear.

Buildings not knowing this, or, knowing, refusing it, as does a concrete sidewalk, are no more architecture than are buildings using ornament the way the "new" architects use surface and mass—that is to say superficially, for itself alone.

Such are the edifices of the Artificer or the artifice of the Edificers—not radical work of the Architect.

The nature of true Architectural ornament should not be foolishly mistaken and the abuse of the thing taken for the thing—preferring "Art and Decoration" per se, to come in commercially triumphant as substitute.

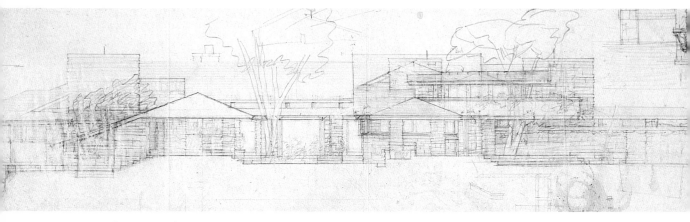

"Taliesin," Frank Lloyd Wright Residence and Studio. Spring Green, Wisconsin. 1925. Elevation. Pencil and color pencil on tracing paper, 36 x 22". FLLW Fdn#2501.041

Handicapped by depth of organic-endeavor and happy disposition I know well how difficult simple, integral things are in Architecture and believe in none otherwise.

I am seeking plastic-simplicity as Architect, not as Painter. No. Nor believing that because of the Machine the Architect has now become mere agent providing for Art and Decoration.

Therein seems the basis for radical difference between myself and the so-called cardboard house as "New." Were this vital element of the third dimension deducted from my work, what is now seen in the buildings endorsed by our critics as New would be found to be at least as Old as that work itself.

Nor could the varied group of buildings I have created have been produced by a "mannerist." The matter is too deep, the range too wide.

My concern here is not with the Asceticism of superficial surface and mass effects. That I respect as I would a monk's. Nor with its "Aesthetic"—which is legitimately mine. And we have in this "New" a "picture-house" more to my "taste" than any before. Were the country to choose it before those of our Edificer's, Artificer's, and Fashion mongers, it would choose well, but would have to choose again in course of time and have only its labor for its pains over another period of thirty years.

Poverty might get along with it. "Aristocracy" might, too, for a time—it lives on gestures of the sort from New York and Paris.

But we have a better choice.

In America, realizing Democracy implies *organic* architecture—buildings implicit with the same *organic-integrity* the aeroplane seeks and has not yet found and our great industrial endeavor seeks, mostly in vain. This quality is nearer in Architecture than in anything else if we will only seek it.

It is a surviving virtue of the skyscraper that it prepared us to see it.

Thirty years, at least, of performance has piled on sound precept until now this country need ask none how to build, from within, its own great buildings in noble, sane, sure way with all the joy of freedom from the prison house of any Mode. No longer creatively sterile but potent beyond anything ever known in this world, America would become, practicing *principles* of Organic Architecture, Art be carried up into the Kingdom of Nature and its separate and contrasted existence destroyed.

1. Frank Lloyd Wright, *An American Architecture,* edited by Edgar Kaufman, Jr. (New York: Horizon Press, 1955), p. 84.
2. Frank Lloyd Wright to Lewis Mumford, January 19, 1932.
3. Ralph Adams Cram (1863–1942), prolific architect and writer, was the most prominent of the Gothic Revival architects in the United States.
4. Thomas Eddy Tallmadge (1876–1940), after serving as draftsman for Daniel Burnham, opened his own practice in the Chicago area. His Prairie-style work was characterized by historical reference, which increasingly moved toward medievalism.
5. Douglas Haskell (1899–1979), an influential critic and editor, wrote a monthly architectural column for *The Nation* from 1930 to 1932.
6. Henry Russell Hitchcock (1903–1987), an architectural historian and critic, was one of the promoters (along with Philip Johnson) of the "International Style" in the early 1930s. Initially at odds with Hitchcock, Wright would later collaborate with him on *In the Nature of Materials* (1941).

THE LINE BETWEEN THE CURIOUS AND THE BEAUTIFUL

Wright's style in writing matured at a slower pace than his style as a builder. In architecture, as he predicted in 1908, his work would "grow more truly simple; more expressive with fewer lines, fewer forms; more articulate with less labor."[1]

Eventually the same striving for simplicity would result in his writings. Some of his earlier texts are verbose and difficult to read, sentences roam and are studded with idiosyncratic punctuation. Sometimes, however, an especially poignant passage, a shining thought, emerges with astounding clarity. This essay includes a particular example: "Beauty then, fundamentally, is the Order of the Natural, whether of mind or body, because we are Nature ourselves in this sense. The curious is a form of disorder in Nature."

Frequently it appears that writing, for Wright, was a kind of exercise, a rigorous training by which he was steadily seeking to better his expression of those ideas and to bring them home to the reader. [Unpublished essay]

AND PERHAPS WE SHOULD SAY ZONE INSTEAD OF LINE—THE twilight zone of the beautiful—the dawn zone of the curious.

The line is seldom surely drawn in our time by the educated individual. And yet, for the purposes of this paper let us keep it as a line. It is a line it would seem as a center of the zone. To teach the individual to draw the line in the proper place, and keep it there, as conditions change, is the great office of any University. A University is concerned primarily, I take it, not only with the widening of the horizon of a man's appreciation, but it is University-business to make the man a more sentient being where the beautiful is concerned, instead of one more susceptible to the curious, or one less continually mistaking the curious for the beautiful: this, it seems to me,

is the only office that makes the University an institution above a science observatory, a trade school, or the mere fact-dispensary of the factotum.

In the phrase "It is more curious than beautiful" lies the difference between sight and vision—all the difference between the developed individual and the undeveloped individual.

I am an architect—and because it is a subjective Art—especially in Architecture much confusion concerning the line may be seen everywhere. I find that even our so-called "best minds" will lapse into barbarism where the distinction is concerned without warning or apparent reason. Education it seems is no protection—and we have no recourse, except time to develop the defense. So, it would seem, as we look about us that something important in the development of the civilized being—was long ago lost, or has never yet been found. Perhaps it is peculiarly the misfortune of our Age, changed so ruthlessly and rapidly, to have been divorced from Nature by way of its progenitors. We have largely inherited confusion in respect to this civilized line— or line of civilization in our Machine Age, and the line has become so badly tangled for most worthy members of the body politic, that so far as the beautiful is concerned, they are impotent or incompetent, lost in the "cultural lag" or drowned in the tides of a new Order—God help them and us.

And I respectfully submit that this not only detracts from any value they may possess as cultured human beings, the essential recompense for having been born, but settles over our life in this era as a pestilential blight. By their betrayal of their era we will have been filched of the gift Life should bring as Life.

I now perceive too, that the same lack of discrimination—and it is the confusion of the curious and the beautiful that characterizes the Savage— may be seen as a dark place in those too sophisticated so-called "Modern" Artists to whom the sadistic or masochistic deformation of the flower, or the glorification of the *fleur de mal* is a result of a kind of *mal de mer* of the Soul. Or is it the violence of a deep despair of any integrity in Life—as significant?

I believe that this thrust at Life as abnormal is only the surrender to the curious raised to the ninth power. In the name of culture, the curious catering to senses or instincts gone wrong because they got on the wrong side of the line to make their living or gratify their curiosity as Artists or give vent to a rage or despair that is subconscious. They would no longer know how to get back again. Now the "middle of the road egotist" would not stand for this decadent Art a moment as seen so frankly . . . in pictures. But it is always difficult, not only for the layman to recognize the same characteristics or quality in different media: that is to say, see the same quality in Music, Sculpture, Drawing, Architecture—as the quality of character he carries around in himself, but no less difficult for the elect to see it. Anatole France was only annoyed by music—to him music was intolerable noise.

And just as long as this confusion exists in educated minds, and we have demoralization of the beautiful in the name of the ugly and glorification of the ugly in the name of the beautiful—we cannot justly feel ourselves to be highly civilized. Go to the movies for confirmation of this demoralization of the "Line." Listen in at the radio for more confirmation. Go to a Pie-club dinner for information and see how that organization amuses itself. See the "Shriner" or the "Knight" on parade. Look at the miles of strange houses, miles on miles of meaningless elaboration, merely curious in the name of Architecture. Sit down to four-fifths of the books written today. Nine out of ten people when you meet them—look over their dress and see how they have overlooked the "Line": the Line is everywhere obscure or lost— that, properly drawn, is the greatest safeguard and at the same time the most precious asset a civilization may have. Indeed, I believe, it is Civilization itself. So, the University that knows no better than to subscribe to and administer mediocrity and falsity in the very name of the beautiful or reasonable, may be known as themselves false, by their endorsements and preferences. Not for nothing are we given choice in this Life—such as it is. By their exercise of that gift you shall know them.

By what any of us have and hold, you may see what we are, and how we are better—than you may learn it from what we teach or by anything we say. The responsibility of any University is increased by the fact that by any known standards that hew to the line we are discussing not only the average man, a helpless impressionable bulk afloat upon a sea of ignorance, blown hither and thither by accepted "tastes," which are only the same ignorance as his own, capitalized as "Culture," but the University itself judged by its own choice apparently is as confused. The average Man does not know where he is. Ask him. The Universities do not know where they are—see them. And well, you may ask now—what is the beautiful? The great question asked in all past civilizations and the answers have always been disputed.

We of the Machine Age should raise the question in earnest and hope, but this question should be, above all others, the University Question. It should be the University who answers our question.

The answers, debated how they may be—ably defended by the University. It is already easy to see how in this Age the working of an eternal principle creates a new Order and how this new Order shines with a new countenance of Simplicity. You may see this countenance in the things we have accomplished, like the plane, the car, and the liner—yes, you may see it in our plumbing—see it in every home—see it in our utensils of every description. These utilitarian things, many of them appeal and sensibly appeal to us as beautiful. What gave them appeal? In this quest for the "Line" there is something there worth knowing. Something is working there which known as a process may help to establish the Line where it belongs in this Age at this distracted moment and enable our Civilization as such to have a clear life of its own to live. He must discover objectives in the line of a more natural culture that will yield more life and better life as direction comes clear. And this is not in Architecture alone but in every direction of our Culture.

It seems to me that our issue in that general direction is all muddled by mediocrity—political palliation of every weakness we have to some selfish ends, but more by the false standards of an archaeology as an impotent sentimentality that can only fill a house or a mind or a heart with the "antique." And let us add by history all out of drawing with Nature. Education is addled by the worship of the sophisticated abstraction. American Life is poisoned at the source by any assumption whatsoever that Culture consists in "classical education." Certainly any similar impotent belief transferred to the field that produced the machines of which we are so justly proud would have resulted in exactly none of them. We should have been rowing in triremes, driving chariots along the highways, living in unheated houses, and walking, as we might, to the ancestral privy. Our thinking would have been done for us. Tradition would naturally be our guide and counselor. I am not saying we might be as well-off—all values being relative in this thing we call Life. But we cannot have both—having the one, the other becomes perversion. We might thus be the happy tail-end of an old Civilization, but we are the Nose, like it or not, of a New one.

The tail may enjoy the life of the animal as much as the nose. But the fact is—were the tail where the nose ought to be and the nose where the tail ought to be—there would be little enjoyment for either, and the beast would want to give up the ghost.

And in this figure of transposition we may see the outrage of a first eternal Principle, that recognized as workable—enables us to begin to differentiate the curious from the beautiful. It is, simply that tail and nose properly where they belong—and Beauty has a chance to be. Tail and nose in the wrong place and we merely have the curious. Beauty then, fundamentally, is the Order of the Natural, whether of mind or body, because we are Nature ourselves in this sense. The curious is a form of disorder in Nature. In the degree that the disorder is extraordinary we are interested and, ourselves as we say—curious. The disorder may be so extraordinary that we become not only interested but excited, astonished, repelled, or attracted—perhaps entertained and probably—human Nature is like that—fascinated and eventually captivated.

Frequently seen over long stretches of time, associated by habit with our Life—by propinquity—we say, disorder as curious thus becomes to us the weaker among Order as beautiful. A stumbling block has then grown up upon the "path."

Habit of association or propinquity as we may see impresses upon sensibility all sorts of useless baggage or aesthetic garbage until the race, itself confused, lives distracted-divorced from the fountain of any clear Life fed by the springs of the beautiful until Life is no longer able to reproduce as Life. Especially now have the changes brought by new tools and materials confused our Civilization as a whole. A vast number of dead forms encumber Life as ghastly survivals for burial. To bury the dead is as essential to the health of the Spirit as it is essential to the health of the body. Any outgrown form, whether as creed or aesthetic, or philosophy as Culture, or as Art—is dead; to cling to the corpse is to be poisoned by it. A strange perversion takes place in our Culture: we willingly die in order that the dead may only seem to live; this futile living death grins at us all from nearly every scholastic or religious edifice today. In what we call the University this living death lays cold hands upon the imaginative fervor of Youth. This death in Life wherever you may go, and to such an extent that unless your eyes are very clear indeed and your natural senses wide awake, poisonous emanations—miscalled Culture—enter into the very air you breathe. A cultural perfume to permeate our nostrils today is more likely to be the odoriferous decay of these survivals for burial, than the breath of Life itself. This carbon monoxide of the Soul or else the utter indifference of nostrils atrophied by the long, slow poison of the insidious worship of the dead. Thus is Death in Life of the Spirit, the decay of the Beautiful. Our true Poets, such Artists as we have of the first rank, inspired teachers, and preachers, and the healthy instincts of Youth, these are the only existing forces at work to stay destruction by machine brutalities and corpses of dead traditions, check the spread of academic plague by proper burial of the dead, that we may get of the New safely born for fresh Life. It seems that new Ideas more appropriate to our Life can only come into action in the appointed and agonizing course of Birth and Death. The Spirit has not yet triumphed over this primal cause and effect. So, the first condition of any Life of the Beautiful is a clearing of the encumbered ground. With untainted air to breathe, let us take hold of fresh opportunity for unspoiled Life—begin to perceive the Beautiful is always a form of spiritual realization for the Individual perceiving it. Beauty in all forms is inspirational. Inspiration may abolish evils that philosophy, philanthropy, and science only palliate. The Life of the Mind being no wise different from the Life of the Body except as the thought differs from the act—that difference lies only in that a thought is an unrealized act, an act only a realized thought. But when the thought becomes an act it becomes the realization of others—no less. The Beautiful as image or Art may then be perceived as integral Order or the expression of internal harmony by all so-minded. The physical features of a true work of Art are the countenances of internal or organic simplicity as natural. Beauty is always atonement of this character in this sense. That is to say this expression of "one-ness" in the whole—of complete Order—therefore Form in Order with function, each and every part in Order with each, all parts and all related, according to Nature to the nature of the Whole. Therefore to distinguish this Order of the Beautiful from disorder as curious—take nothing for granted as appropriate in this sense.

1. "In the Cause of Architecture," *The Architectural Record*, March 1908.

ARCHITECTURE AS A PROFESSION IS ALL WRONG

Addressing the alarming state of architectural firms, Wright here condemns the growth and development of what he calls the "plan-factories":

> Great corporate enterprises are taking the place of individual enterprise—business interests like a man who will enter into their game, go to jail with them, or for them if necessary. A man who will play cricket and stay put.

This article of 1930 is but a continuation, in spirit, of Wright's 1900 essay "The Architect." Regardless of these warnings, the great plan-factories of the 1950s evolved into gigantic offices incorporating great numbers of employees: ad men, promoters, financiers, architects, draftsmen, and contractors. The glut of nondescript architecture, especially after the war, only proved Wright's accusation to be just. [Published without architectural illustrations in The American Architect, December 1930]

I HAVE NO SYMPATHY WHATEVER WITH THE VIEW ENTERtained by certain facetious young men in architecture—that the A. I. A. is made up of old gentlemen who catch cold easily, wear rubbers, carry umbrellas, and resent any innovation whatsoever as a personal affront. The A. I. A. of course, is the soul of the profession—or was. And the time was, I remember, when there were men in the profession—and the profession meant the A. I. A.—one knew and that one had to know.

What has become of the architect in this old sense?

Who and where they say they are, themselves, may be gleaned from city directories throughout the country—now ten, to one then. Nevertheless, the old-style practitioner as a "professional" is a "specimen," to be stuffed and exhibited soon. In no art gallery either, but in a museum for unnatural history; such is the gratitude of a great Republic.

Do you remember when editors were individuals in their own right—editors like Horace Greeley, Charles A. Dana, James Gordon Bennett, Marion Reedy, Henry Watterson, and many more? Today it is *The Times, The Sun, The Herald,* etc. If you do remember, you may also remember when architects were likewise, say Richardson, Louis Sullivan, John Root, "Old Man" Jenny, Dankmar Adler, "George B.," the aristocratic "R. M. H.," and Henry Hardenberg, idol of the Manhattan rich—Yes, and later Charles McKim, Stanford White, and many others.

Today it is "The Firm."

Today all is more or less in the style of Graham, Anderson, Probst, and White, etc., etc., etc.,

etc., to an extent, at least, showing clearly enough the tendency to organize the work of an architect into a business, alongside the hat, cap, and shoe business. We know who runs the business but, unless unpopularly curious, we no longer know who makes the designs.

The individual architect serves the business as best he can or the business will use his name and "lay him off"—unless the undertaker comes along, in time, to "lay him out."

So, "Be Businesslike or Bust" is no idle threat.

Promotion, Financing, Operating, Building—here are four departments of modern architectural practice unknown to yesterday's architect, who devoted his mind and extended his powers in the direction of making plans and writing specifications for a real building that he himself expected faithfully to superintend.

Well—Standardization, Mass-effort, Mass-production—they are here in architecture rampant for the masses, rampant in all else in machine-made Usonia.

More power to them all but more brains too, and—smile if you like—more heart. Having neither, they have no Style.

Forces are blind forever. Human interests affected by these forces are just as blind over long stretches of time, but not forever. Awakening comes before "the end," as it comes to the napper on the train who barely manages, by commotion, to get out on the station platform, "just in time," leaving his luggage to be sent back from down the line.

So I imagine it will be, with us, in architecture.

This tendency to commercialize, centralize, or organize and standardize is expedient, or it wouldn't be here. It is profitable or it wouldn't continue.

Certainly it is the end of the old order.

But the beginning of any new order the American people can afford to accept will scrap the commercial expedients now in use in architecture as makeshift, having once "got by."

In other words the old fellows are gone—"done in" by time and the circumstance we sometimes stupidly call Progress. But "The Firm" or the "Plan-Factory" that takes their place in the immediate present is no more than a passing make-shift while the country gets its eyes open and looks to itself.

Something important in the long run, more important than all else beside—the essentially human values—have been overlooked or deliberately left out. Important omission for this reason:

Man is going to conquer the Machine. The Machine is not going to conquer Man—even though in all this, it may seem to have him down. We see in all these makeshifts now in use in architecture the work of the minions of the Machine—Mechanization—Standardization—Merchandising. Sell it—or sink it and sink with it.

Machine overproduction glorifies salesmanship.

But soon, individuality will be doubly desirable and infinitely more treasured in America just because of this issue between the Man and the Machine, just as genius is now at a premium in Russia for reasons not so dissimilar as one might think, glancing superficially at the matter.

I don't know just what procedure is going to evolve from this convolute "Progress" to enable the man of ideas, technique-trained and adequate, to get those ideas into the form of practical, beautiful buildings for the human joy and use—tomorrow—where there is so little or none today.

Had I just one guess, I should say this man would have more in common with the composer-conductor of an orchestra. The orchestra, and therefore that office, is modern.

Modern industrial, and therefore economic affairs, are becoming daily more "orchestrated," meaning more dependent upon each other if not better correlated in this country. The characteristic building enterprise that is attractive to bond-holders today is attractive and successful most often on account of its size and importance. But, on account of its size and importance, it is now out of *individual* scale.

So the architect's employer today is more likely to be a corporation than any—except the extraordinary—individual. But more important, therefore, that this corporate aggregate, with its inherent weakness in initiative, and the mediocrity of its "committee decisions," center upon the architect competent to create. That can only mean upon the supreme individual, however he may be "hooked up" or "hooked in" to the corporate aggregation.

It becomes all the more important to insure performance of the "piece" or building *according to design,* as greatly conceived—details being more than ever consequential *as invention.* It is indispensable in fact, now, to have the conception natural to new material and economic methods. Lines of least resistance in industry must now be followed to maximum human benefits. Nor does that mean entirely biggest, immediate net profits to the landlord. In short, the architect being more important than ever, it is imperative today that he qualify for his job— "profession" or no "profession."

Qualifying would mean knowing industrial conditions well, knowing modern tools and methods even better, and knowing best of all their relation to the specific human-purposes of the building project. And here again, say, as the composer-conductor we have in mind knows his score, knows his instruments, knows his players, and knows their possibilities in relation to the human desire for music.

It is true that the modern architect on any creative basis, except in circumstances extraordinary, can no more be compounded of several men today than he could have been in the old order. Imagine several men together leading that orchestra!

Architecture today is a great orchestration of materials, methods, and men. The architect must be correlated to it all, but rise above it all. When he does so, Machine conditions will only have extended his opportunities, however he may choose to divide his responsibilities. A creative *"modern"* architecture would probably mean financial ruin to the architectural "Firm" as now organized, and certainly the end of the plan-factory. The plan-factory knows it, or will soon. The old triangle unluckily sponsored and fostered by the A. I. A.—"Owner, one; Architect, two; and Contractor, three"—that has formed the basis of professional architectural practice has proven about as satisfactory "service" as the triangle

that forms the prevalent pattern of the popular play or novel. It gives rise to the same demoralization.

The architect usually sits where the unlucky husband sits in the domestic triangle—as happily circumstanced. And the building comes out of the embroglio much as the illegitimate child.

The commissioned builder is too often a competitor of the commissioned architect, easier for the client to understand and therefore to depend upon, to the detriment of the real issue—the building—if the architect knows his work. Various other modifications of the triangle have arisen with serious drawbacks for the owner, architect, or contractor or all together.

No system will be sufficiently adequate for modern conditions that does not give to the architect complete control of his design and assures control by him until final completion of the building. Anything else in the way of "system" can not cope with modern conditions, however the architect may have made shift to stay with his conception in the past.

The old system was too often comparable to one (keeping our composer-conductor figure in mind) in which that conductor would be subject to the stupid ambition or avarice of his concert meister or his paymaster or perhaps even his piccolo player.

Great corporate enterprises are taking the place of individual enterprise—business interests like a man who will enter into their game, go to jail with them, or for them if necessary. A man who will play cricket and stay put.

"Business" wants a "safe-man" . . . as it calls him—meaning one, who, if he has to be bought, will not only *stay* bought, but like it, and believe in it for the sake of the by-products to which all are cheerfully resigned.

It doesn't matter how much of an architect this fellow is, if he can make a popular picture of his building.

The great corporation itself is the broker-builder and merely "uses" him.

Well then, and why not the great corporation actually the builder, as a matter of fact, and directed by a real architect—"profession" or no "profession"?

The A.I.A.—in the main an honorable institution— does not stand for corporate use of the architect as a tool. But the A. I. A. is an institution—therefore a refuge.

I have never joined the "Institute," not that it could make any difference to the Institute. The A. I. A. has a code of ethics. But some of its members, I found, did whatever they thought necessary so they might live. Wherever in practice I encountered an A. I. A., I found this so invariably true that I came to believe my own standard of conduct in selling my services and building my buildings was higher in practice if not in theory.

I recall at this point a signed-up professor of ethics—A. I. A.—who got to Tokio when I was doing my best to get work on the Imperial Hotel finished. This man hurried around to my oriental clients to tell them the whole thing "violated" the occidental ordinance and would come tumbling down on their heads the first shake of a quake.

"Holocaust" was his word—I remember. He wanted something done about it. Right away. He was ready to help do it. So from first to last, A. I. A. came to signify for me—Arbitrary Institute of Appearances.

IN ORDER TO BE MODERN

In this relatively short article, Wright truly summarizes all that he has been writing and building for the past three and a half decades. Here those ideas and precepts emerge more as a poetical assertion than as a formal essay. [Published in Architectural Progress, *December 1930]*

NO LONGER BUILD OR LIVE IN LITTLE DECORATED CAVERNS, Spanish, Colonial—or whatever: not even "Mediterranean."

Sense the enlarged means of today—by way of our new materials—demanding a new simplicity born in sunlight.

Believe that this new simplicity as countenance of the Machine Age will no longer be a box.

Know—my Architect—that cutting holes as windows or for doors in boxes or masses of masonry material has gone as far as it can go as Architecture.

Whence came the American motley? It came from rummaging to and fro in the "Styles" wherefrom to "decorate" these United States.

Hate the futile monotony in this popular depravity.

Rebuke senseless reiteration of such mincing lies—varying inflection in vain tricks of speech. So far as the language itself goes, nothing can be said but silly falsehood.

Free in spirit, grasp now the new order of the sunlit space, beautifully screened-in by glass and metal.

See the new order of the interior space—sunlit—as the reality of the building itself—and within, see—a higher Order of the Spirit.

Walls as solid walls are vanishing.

The heavy bulk of building material, sculptured how it may be, hollowed out as a cave—is disappearing with the fortification that protected the might of feudal Estate. No householder needs "box up" or "hole in" for protection as Master or Slave or as Lord or Serf.

In this Age of Democracy, then—live no longer like the Savage animal Man once was.

Master lightness—openness—as directly related to strength—the gift of steel in tension. John Roebling's brave Brooklyn Bridge heroically began a new era.

And we know, now, the perfect clarity in air to keep air out, or keep it in, and allow human vision perfect freedom to roam the sky or ground. This is glass as we have it in this Age—the gift of gifts.

And we know, too, the textile as a shimmering robe to clothe interior space, within the glass—to modify the relation of interior-space to sunlight—all the nuances of Nature entangled as texture or pattern in its meshes.

Modern Building now rises—brother to the trees: a shaft of light flashing in the sun: true sun-acceptance: indestructible fabric of light metal—woven in webs of turquoise, blue or green, gold or silver or the deep hues of bronze—or all together.

Or let the Building lie long, floating lazily upon the ledges: a streak of light. Or it may lie low upon the plain, a gaily colored ribbon of light, glass enmeshed in metal strands, as music is made of notes.

Why crawl more backwards to the Past—supine to all that wakes in this your own Age, sunk in stupid faith in scientific "fact" that one and one makes two?

Post and Beam, Weight and Mass, they are the one and one that make two *in* the Past of the Past.

Know instead why and how in Art, one and one may still make only one.

Architecture no longer needs nor knows the post as post, nor beam as beam—these two things Art, as Modern—makes one thing: a plastic Whole. And see by simple sense of such simple means—new countenance of truth. This—"the one plus one that still makes one"—makes "Modern."

Meantime—my Architect—see the Earth as a poignantly beautiful place for human Life, beautiful in all its expressions. Take joy in its beguiling, inspiring entertainment. Realize that only when Man, missing the Earth-message of beauty—harshly, clumsily, wastefully builds—is outrage done upon it and far more done upon himself.

Whenever and wherever Man has built, inspired by Nature in this sense, he has risen supreme to all about him, and more than ever, now he may make the atonement that in him lies, as Gift.

THE LOGIC OF CONTEMPORARY ARCHITECTURE AS AN EXPRESSION OF THIS AGE

A rchitecture is the triumph of Human Imagination over materials, methods, and men, to put man into possession of his own Earth," wrote Wright in "In the Cause of Architecture.

Indeed, "In the Cause of Architecture" in its entirety was but a further embellishment and explanation of this statement. [Published without illustrations in The Architectural Forum, May 1930]

I DO NOT LIKE THIS TITLE BECAUSE IT SEEMS TO ME EITHER too obvious or too ambiguous, but it is the Editor's and so I shall keep it. Is it logical to assume that this age may find Expression in contemporary architecture, that is to say, in an Architecture of its own? I wonder, because contemporary architecture in this age has neither logic nor expression. The Age has, so far, given itself away! But, is it logical that a contemporary architecture should express its own age?

Is the rising sun logical, Mr. Editor? It is natural, and that is better.

It is just as natural as that the sun should rise that contemporary architecture also rise to express its own "age"—in this instance—our own time. To express our own time would be to characterize our age for all time. An Architecture might be borrowed for this purpose, but only to stigmatize the age! An Architecture might be conceived and taught as something fine in itself, much admired as such, to no greater end than to sentimentalize and therefore stultify the age.

To no greater end, I say, because only contemporary Architecture could possibly express this age or has ever expressed any other age—such as the Architecture or the Age happened to be. What other Architecture could express the age except the architecture of the age itself?

Of course we may imagine an era wherein there was nothing architectural to express or there were no architects to express whatever there was, and recourse had to plan-factories, academies, and schools to supply the lack out of the world's stock to save the situation—so to say. And that would be about all the "contemporary" architecture that particular era or age would get—or deserve to get—as "expression"—even if that lack were ever so quickly and richly supplied and every fine thing that ever happened in ancient Architecture was externally applied as "Contemporary Architecture." That shame would really be the "logic of Contemporary Architecture" as an "expression of that age"—the expression of the fact that the age had no architecture of its own and had tried on at least 57 Varieties to find one ready-made to fit.

It is no exaggeration to say that the *expression* of this Machine Age has, so far, been waste and *repression*. How about the wasted timber resources—the lost trees of a new continent to merely rot or burn as "mill-work"? How about the butchery by machinery of every traditional form ever borrowed and worn to win the contempt of the civilized world, especially of the Beaux Arts—that was supposedly its advocate? How about neglect and insult by way of Traditions to great, new materials, and the separation in consequence of Engineering and Architecture: and the great change in human thought the ideal of Democracy represents; left without any interpretation in Architecture whatsoever?

Traditions had for us the vitality of inertia—the "vitality" of the ball and chain, instead of the inspiration of traditional forms loved only as an expression of the age to which they were "contemporary." That love would honor Tradition as distinguished from the abuse of traditions. And that love might have instructed us and saved our age for a great Architecture of our own. What made Traditional Architecture modern and living in its own age—that was the only business we had with Tradition in Architecture. And that was great business.

But twentieth-century America must pay a ghastly price for nineteenth-century grave-robbing in architecture, a price that staggers reason, and pay it all back for lack of a simple sense of Tradition that would allow America to live its own life and by so doing, greatly honor Tradition. Imitation may be the sincerest form of flattery, but whom have we flattered, and how—and, for what?

Creation knows Imitation only as a form of self-abuse. It takes creative imagination to see stone as stone, see steel as steel, see glass as glass, and to view traditions as Tradition. Perhaps that was too much to expect, but where, I ask, is there one honest, living word, Tradition as a vital force has been allowed to say for itself anywhere in this area prostitute to traditions, 2,000 miles north to south and 4,000 miles east to west, that is to say, the length and breadth of this great new ground of ours—let the climate rage or smile upon it how it may? If the

editor of *The Forum* will compile a list, I will take it up item by item and either convince myself or convict him.

This is the Machine Age as distinguished from all other ages; this is the age too, of steel and steam. Ours is the age of the individual, supreme as such, in a life that he can call his own. These great new needs in Art were the Architect's great opportunity. His great office consisted in the fact that Human thought is, here and now, stripping off old ideas like old garments, and such cutting, fitting, and trying on as we have done—to find ready-made to wear—all ends naturally in a mis-fit.

All are a mis-fit. But the age is still young and healthy. It seems at last to have shaken off the expedient-interest and be willing now to find the great urge to awaken the creative faculty that has been lying sterile, neglecting the wretched need of great imaginative interpretation in good work for four hundred and thirty-eight years.

If great Life is sure of great Art, and it is— how can America fail of great Life—once this confusion of ideas, arising perhaps from the Babel of tongues and the embarrassment of the riches of a great but antiquated inheritance passes—and the great immediate facts of the Life that is her destiny stand out clearly before her people?

For America's future none but the working of Principle is safe Tradition. The only precedent she can find worthy is Principle. If, now, modern architecture may be both Modern and Architecture, we realize great Architecture as greatest proof of human greatness as it ever was before and in all ages.

Architecture is the scientific art of making structure express Ideas.

Architecture is the triumph of Human Imagination over materials, methods, and men, to put man into possession of his own Earth.

Architecture is man's great sense of himself embodied in a world of his own making. It may rise as high in quality only as its source, because Great Art is Great Life!

Now what is the American Ideal of Great Life?

Liberty is the foreground, middle-distance, and future of that Life. Toleration and Liberty are the foundations of this Great Republic?

Notwithstanding all powerful threats—of a Machine Age—to this Ideal, why not the hope in American hearts that Liberty in Art will be the native offspring of Political Liberty?—And for a new people—a new Architecture!

The old culture itself, for nearly five-hundred years, miserably failed with the form-language of the human heart and mind in Architecture. The Renaissance was that failure and the pseudo-Renaissance in America was a tragic betrayal of such ideals as we are learning now to love to call "American."

The sense of Romance suffered most by the betrayal. But this sense is already shifting its circumference, therefore its horizon, as it has done before and will continue to do, for Romance is Immortal.

Industry in the Machine Age can only become a machine without it. Modern Architecture itself will become a poor, flat-faced thing of steel-bones, box outlines, gas-pipe and handrail fittings—as sun-receptive as a concrete sidewalk or a glass tank, without Romance—the essential Joy of Living as distinguished from Pleasure—alive in it.

Architecture without that Joy could inspire nothing but mediocre emulation and would degenerate to a box fit merely to contain the objects of Art and Decoration it should itself create and maintain.

Constructing architectural features and parts to give the decorative effect of simplicity is not good enough. It comes to just the same thing in the end as—America's disgrace—now.

Why should Architecture or objects of Art in the Machine Age, because they are made by Machines, resemble Machinery? Because they were so made might be the best of reasons why they should not. Nor is there good reason why Forms stripped clean of all considerations but Function and Utility should be admirable beyond that standpoint. They may be abominable from the human standpoint. Let us have no fear, therefore, of Liberalism in our Art of Architecture, nor in our Industries.

Romance, all great poets are agreed, is only Liberalism in Art. It never did apply to "make believe" or to constructing Architectural features and parts for ornamental effect, or to falsifying, or to degenerate to sentimentality except as it was betrayed by the Renaissance.

The taste for mediocrity grows by what it feeds upon, therefore the public of this Republic is more than ever likely to find the love of commonplace elegance that curses it, and that was gratified by the sentimentality of the ornamental, now replaced by a pleasure in the ornamentality of affected simplicity or a reaction toward the sterility of ornaphobia.

Yes, this Machine Age, especially now at the moment of awakening from damnation by senseless sentimentality, may be in danger of being sterilized—castrated by a factory-aesthetic.

The Machine is the brainless craftsman of a new freedom in social order. Untried and unqualified this "New" is a dangerous means to great realization in Architecture.

But—Scientists and Philosophers!—convention us no narrow *conventions*, New or Old, to rise up in middle-minds and get into selfish, meddling hands as *preventions* in this Modern World that—thanks to an Organic-Architecture—we are going to build upon fertile new ground. As Sons of Liberty we are going to build that New Freedom in Art upon ground fertilized by the Old—ground in which the carcasses of ancient Architecture lie rotting beneath our feet if Traditions are to die where and how and when they should die that Tradition may nobly live.

Until the dead past has buried its dead, Life is poisoned and itself dies of its own dead.

WHO SAID "CONSERVATIVE?"

Written sometime during 1930, the following three articles, although never published, reflect Wright's strong criticism of the architectural profession and of its so-called "conservative" element. Criticism of his "In the Cause of Architecture" series and the appearance of European modern architecture in the United States in publications and exhibitions prompted him to write "In the Cause of Architecture: Confession" (page 344). Here, he reiterates the significance of "The Nature of Materials," as he calls the The Architectural Record *essays, and defends his romantic and imaginative approach both to materials and to the machine. [Unpublished essay]*

ALL MY LIFE LONG I'VE BEEN HEARING THE POPULAR SONG of "the conservative" close to my ears, until the so-called "Conservative" would seem salt of the earth, savior of all, God-man of the social order.

Who sings this song?

Yes, of course—but I've seen through them. Long ago, in any work in the world, I discovered the man who calls himself the "practical man" to be merely a slave of the expedient. When this man speaks of the Practical, he means only the Expedient. And I've found that he cannot be trusted with an idea or an ideal. He will murder it in behalf of safety. His own safety, somewhere around, most likely.

And the so-called "Conservative," I suspect, is but an exaggerated form of that slave of the Expedient. He is too "practical" to be trusted.

These "practical" slaves of the Expedient do not even know what conservation means. They think it means holding tight, or sitting on the lid, or opposition to the "New" on general principles.

"Letting good enough alone" is the highest ideal of conservation most of them ever achieve because as a class they lack imagination. Very well—let's say their fear is the ballast in the hold of the ship, the sandbags of the balloon, the wooden plug in the bung-hole of the barrel, the paint on the post. In sociology, say, they themselves are the same as the law of gravitation in physics: nothing moves if they can help it unless by main-strength it can overcome them and get away with it. They are the watchdogs of property, the judges of the law—the policemen of the universe. Most of them are cowards, healthy, and weighing about 185 pounds apiece.

Were you to inform the wary gentlemen that no man less than truly radical could ever be genuinely conservative, they would have the Kiwanis or Rotarians on you, or the 100-percent Americans maybe.

But nothing is more true than that only the Radical can be genuinely a Conservative. Radical is a beautiful word. It means roots, has roots, is roots, and yet the so-called conservative sees it as red. He always sees red whenever the sound of the word falls on his ears, and looks to his securities.

The so-called conservative is not conservative at all. He is not even preservative.

In ninety-nine cases out of a hundred he is merely in the way of the true conservation of anything you may imagine—and provocative of disaster.

He is seldom worth his ride. And he will only ride anywhere.

It is my belief that any cause he espouses will leave off from sheer fatigue and stay right there where he is. Although he talks progress, staying right there where he is is what he means by it, for that is good enough and far enough for him.

The Majority is by nature conservative in this sheepish sense, and, though it cannot realize it, is itself only a stupid conspiracy against what it calls Progress. Progress, alone, is truly conservative and Progress is forever—for its very life, mind you in the charge of the radical minority—just as the thought the so-called conservatives are sitting and riding along upon today was, once.

No, Conservation is no function of the conservative, so-called.

Conservation is never so easy.

In the first place, conservation means keeping the "life" in whatever is subject to the conserva-tives' services. And, as the radical alone knows, life can't live without growing.

That is why most causes that have any life in them grow out of the hands of the would-be conservatives, or die there.

To be a conservative one must first know in what that very life of the matter consists, and how can that be known unless to the radical?

And then, conservation is understanding—the understanding that is a form of love, a sympathy necessary to keep this life in line of growth. It is only the true radical who will fight for that, and it is almost always necessary to fight and defeat the so-called conservative to preserve growth in this sense.

This would-be, so-called conservative is forever found clinging to dead forms after the life in them has fled, imagining himself, on honorable terms, the preserver of what he calls Tradition. Or he will be found sitting, snugly gilt, in favored places where it is hard for the radical conservative to reach him—as things are.

There the high-priest of "things-as-they-are" sits, with the thing he professes to love by the throat, about as truly conservative as a jealous husband.

Let us come back to the genuine Radical and learn to honor him as the true Conservative if we are ever going to have the sense of the word as significant as it should be for the proper ground-work of Democracy. False, or "so-called," conservation was born of narrow self-interest. It will take the life of anything. Especially will it take the life of the Democracy itself.

IN THE CAUSE OF ARCHITECTURE: CONFESSION

[Unpublished essay]

A SERIES OF ARTICLES UPON "THE NATURE OF MATERIALS" recorded in *The Architectural Record* of New York have not been satisfactory writing on the subject; that is to say, they have not been satisfactory to me. And although my editor has not complained, critics have referred to the articles as "poetic," in the style of Walt Whitman, or imaginative—meaning, I presume not specific enough in point of fact. My critics seem to think Architecture as a theme should be no other matter than a slab of sheet rock and a bucket of paint. As for its insides they seem to think, too, that the writer should categorize Watt, B.T.U., catalogue the siphon-jet versus the wash-down W.C. argue riveting versus welding—or is it even now welding versus riveting. The writer should "staccato," categorize the effect of the zoning law on our merchant marine, pay his diagrammatical respect to the traditions of the parking problem, or specify premature airports for the rapidly changing aeroplane. The writer should illustrate his writing by designs for slab-sided cardboard-houses he has not built, but designed to be handed over *à la mode* to "Art and Decoration" for beautifying, also *à la mode*. In short, the writer should 1-2-3-4-5 pigeonhole Architecture and tell all and sundry not so much what to do as tell sundry and all just how to do what. The new style writer does not write, he specifies. Thus Architects: Boulevard George, Avenue Gus & Co. Object: Jail. Purpose: Incarceration. Materials: Baked Mud and Cold Steel.

Color: Dun and dreary. Contractors: Pour's Pouring Corporation Ltd. Style: Modernistic. Method: Pour, pour and pour pseudo-classic washed behind the ears, then pour some more. Remarks: Boulevard George, Avenue Gus & Co., modernized overnight.

This is the rot of the Age, the decay of Imagination, the desire for the recipe:—Art aping Science—lacking a mind of its own. No longer inspire the Novice, No, take him.

Yes, recipes are wanted still. But any Man who has a recipe in the Art of Architecture, even commercial (Yes, it is the fine Art of Architecture I have been writing about) would indubitably be a quack, I believe. No matter, or rather that is just what is the matter, because the aspirant who would take any recipe even on trial, however categorical or enumerically specific, would either be a fool, a middle-of-the-road egotist, or perhaps some ego-maniac philosopher in the Science of Art—which comes to much the same thing after a few essays, I perceive. Perhaps I should not say "Fool" but say only "foolish," because a lie does not make a Liar, nor a foolish act make a fool, of course. But what is this desire to take a slide or a free ride down a shortcut or a chute to somewhere in particular that is really nowhere? See who is at the bottom and how. Are young Architects becoming so unimaginative as to derive little from the stimulus of general suggestion, however vital the suggestion may be? Or is it only the critic who feels for them and tries out this method? Are young architects to get by the appeal to Imagination to achieve performances "statistico" or aesthetics staccato? Does the Novitiate want formulae to use an Architecture as he uses his four foot rule—to create? Is the Novice to be so sunk in perfunctory fact before he starts that he cannot move except by rote? But I think I know this ailment. Science has gone wrong with this specifist, has "struck in." As a form of the natural abuse of scientific success, the specificator apes the scientific method. Perhaps some part of this specimen desire for the ready-made or the recipe (imagination aside) deserves pity, is nausea (nostalgia really) due to over-indulgence in the current abuse of high words, high words oversold by high-priests of American advertising—a religion that acknowledges salesmanship, only, as Divinity. In other words an inner-experience befitting this lean and statistical Specifite from his a to his izzard. Art is, in him seen, prostitute to the commercial, Expedient to make and sell goods; Architecture merely happens to be the goods. I confess that categorical common sense is far preferable to any sickening sentimental incense. But it is the common sense of the thing that has interested me in this effort in the direction of the nature of materials. But my appeal, is as always, only to the imagination. Writing up on a subjective theme, I use terms appropriate to the subject regardless of any evil association with these popular perverse influences corrupting the terms. I have thus refused to take the abuse of the thing for the thing.

Yes, I have written imaginatively of Materials, because that is the only way (by way of imagination) they can come alive in the human hand as Architecture. Imagination is just what is lacking in any treatment they receive from any source, especially from the Architect; imagination is just what is lacking in the mind of the specifex.

So far as I know there is nothing at all in our English language, such as I have been writing on the Nature of Materials. Nor, so far as I know is there anything in any other language—the matter was omitted even by my old Master, Louis Sullivan.

I admit that I have been "preaching." The tail end of a long line of Preachers going back to the days of the Reformation in England—could hardly do anything else. But, nevertheless, the gospel of Materials imaginatively preached is sound, sensible basis for all and any imaginative Architecture. That basic sense of Architecture is to me the real "meaning" of materials.

And I have advocated and described the proper use of the tools we have with which to work on the new materials we have. I have tried to interpret, not specificate, the machine: the machine as tools in general, the machine in terms of both process and materials. Eventually such exposition along these definite lines will be found helpful to those who may sincerely enter in, as Architects must enter soon, with imagination or America will have no true Architecture at all to live with above the scientific catalogue of the specifant.

It is quite easy to be explicit when dealing with only two dimensions—surface and mass, say—but any true Architecture for America can only mean Organic Architecture. When the third dimension enters as a quality (the quality of organic integrity essential to Architecture), the whole matter becomes less easy to write about, because the Spirit behind the Form then tries to speak. When the third dimension thus enters Architecture, the matter has been taken from the realm of the objective into the subjective realm. The matter is more living than ever before, but it is at the same time less obvious in words; it is at the mercy of ignorance, hence the Specifist—except as essential poetry may be felt by him who reads the words. Essential poetry is the burden, and at the same time the inspiration, of the third dimension as I have explained the term, and it is this, the third dimension—a matter of incisive imagination—which gives the articles whatever value they may eventually have. I say "eventually" because I have faith that Architecture with us (I mean all the world) is passing rapidly at the moment through a superficial phase as Surface and Mass Architecture, to emerge into a greater and deeper usefulness as Organic Architecture, therefore eventually emerge as a more deeply significant Architecture. It is only by way of superior Imagination that this may be achieved. Surface and mass effects of the European Schools, as I now see them, are only makeshift preparation for this deeper imaginative insight, because it seems to me to think in one dimension is first necessary to later thinking in two dimensions, and thought in two dimensions the condition of next reaching deeper thought in three dimensions. So, as a kindergarten exercise, this latest awakening in France may be helpful, following without giving credit, as it does antecedent exercises in Holland, Germany, Switzerland, and Austria. That is to say the French suffix may be a helpful American affix unless it merely becomes the fashion and even then such a fashion, would leave the public mind more receptive to an Organic Architecture, or to Simplicity as organic, because that public came to know Simplicity as an appearance, and to desire it even as such.

The whole progress of human thought is so painfully slower than any Thinker ever imagines it to be. The gentle carpenter, nearly two thousand years ago, thought his Ideal at hand, whereas were he to return today, he would find nearly every institution we cherish—the family, the state, the Arts—all founded on the Laws of the very Romans he thought to conquer. He would find his thought a small kernel buried deep in the mass, or a very still, small voice indeed. And yet the Mass has progressed in the line of that thought? So in this matter of Organic Architecture first actually preached in America by Louis Sullivan, progress has been made.

But for nearly thirty-two years, except for superficial emulation, the effort has remained at work in a little world of its own while an applied book-Architecture in our Country had right of way, supreme to buy the living with the dead.

But if you think we shall never have growth from within, as Architecture, reflect that such response as we see to even a Simplicity lie indicates appreciation and hunger for the appearance of Simplicity at least. That response may indicate too, in time, spiritual desire for the structural integrity that would make Simplicity a natural thing.

The deeper truths of being are also the truths of Architecture. Of their ultimate triumph there can be no doubt whatever. But meantime, some of us suffer, seeing the prodigal waste and selfish propaganda and pretentious specism on every hand—ourselves more and more exploited and wasted by it.

Even where the Ideal seems to have a free hand creatively, as in the Chicago World Fair Project for 1932, the New may be mimicked only to dishonor the Old.

So there is little to be done except write one's best thoughts (if one has thoughts) and, as may be, build that best thought whenever and however it can be built.

My editors left me free to write what I pleased, as I pleased, at a time when even writing was a blessing to me. I have enjoyed writing what I wrote. Enjoyment should be one indication of good work, although I believe the Novice as amateur often enough enjoys as much the thing he does for the sake of the thing itself. But believe the Veteran, too, enjoys seeing in words a reflection of a coherent Ideal that has worked in him during a lifetime of building Buildings.

In thus writing, I have tried to share what I know as well as what I feel concerning this Ideal with others—vainly probably. But, I should say, what I feel is more important than what I know or more important than anything anyone could specify. At least it is in the same imaginative spirit and with the same fervor as I have built that I have written.

Today here I am, curious as any spectator. Standing aside, I see in all forms of Art the subtle curves of the nude flesh stripped to the hard bone, without being interested to join in the stripping either as sadist or scientist, either in writing or building.

I believe the heart of this matter of the Modern to be wise, but not so much wise as sentient and more warmly merciful to humanity than the stripping would indicate, after all has been stripped and stark. Where we are condemned to standardization by machinery, all the more do we need human warmth and the quality poetic imagination, I say.

In getting proper new work done, elimination is no more than the preliminary condition of any sound Architecture now as it ever has been—but not any more now, the intermediate nor any final condition than ever before. The negation of the Protestant must become the affirmation that is catholic before America will have Architecture as Architecture.

I can have no sympathy whatever with the Idea that the Machine has made Imagination and individuality undesirable, if not impossible, in Architecture. I have no sympathy whatever with shallow effects that reduce the building itself to a box or skeleton or a little of both, and then reduces that little of both to a mere background to be placed again in the hands of a "liberated" art and craft for beautification. I cannot. I do not choose to see Architecture thus degraded, nor will I see the great depths of human riches it has contained because of this Machine Age, emptied into several minor vessels instead of being poured into the splendid one we call Architecture. Organization, correlation, coordination in any Architectural application are old, as Architecture is old, but characteristically modern. The machine makes them all natural, therefore indispensable, to our time. Then why not go a little further and realize, as a modern possibility, a building as a more harmonious entity in the name of Architecture? Instead of pouring the great consequence, Architecture into the several vessels of Sculpture, Painting, Decoration—minor vessels that originally poured into Architecture—why not pour them all back again to the greater Whole for the sake of the greater depth of harmony Life itself would gain? The Whole is greater than any Part. And I believe it is possible to bring Architecture sound and whole again as great Art when we imaginatively enter with depth of feeling for beauty upon the mastery of the Machine. Otherwise, the Machine will disintegrate the supreme essential factor in our greatness largely assisted by the so-called arts in a stupid modern commercial conspiracy against Art. Naturally enough, with this stupid conspiracy—either obvious or occult—I have no patience.

I see it as proper enough that the great city should disintegrate, break up into various centers. I see the decentralization as inevitable and desirable, and this because of certain distinct social advantages. But the Great Building cannot break up similarly without loss of the greatest human asset we have: the complete expression of the full power of the human soul by the native exercise of man's imagination. The man-built Great Buildings humanity possesses go further toward realization of the true greatness of man than anything else.

Nor will Man, I believe, ever give up that realization. Never by conscious decision will he lessen the cumulative force of his own Soul in this, or any other, supreme expression of himself as himself.

Such handicrafts as we have are broken up (or broken down) into special luxuries for the rich, or for the sentimentally aesthetic. We import it when we want it. Sculpture, where it ekes out a meager existence, is on its own, for what it may be worth—and that seems to be the portrait bust, a soldiers monument now and then, an occasional memorial relief, or some pretty figurines subsisting really as the portrait.

Painting too, on its own is with us as the easel picture, or is busy advertising or making a living illustrating—subsisting, too, on its own account chiefly as the portrait.

Textiles are where they are chiefly owing to dress, but rising in beauty.

Glass making, ceramics, are rising. Metalwork is seeking an opening and finding it.

All the crafts have shown willingness to rush in upon dying architecture, and are more or less quarrelling today over the spoils—naming themselves modern Architecture and wishing Architecture fully dead.

But would it not be better looking toward the future for them all to come in helpfully, as they now must come because instead of dying as expected, the Machine Age demands Architecture and the Architect. Both, therefore, will yet come alive and grow potent enough to weld them into the great entity they once were?

Until Architecture is risen again, Modern in this sense, there can be only a relatively inferior and merely snobbish Independence for all Arts and Crafts.

The Great Building—and a small one may be "great," as the great one may be "small"—is more essential to this Machine Age than it ever was to any other age. That it may be greater as Architecture than ever before, I believe as confession not as Profession.

But how slow it is in coming! What selfish confusion attends its progress! How mean and cruel are the provincial circumstances of its becoming! How painful this is to those loyal to its life! Only those who love Life in the guise of a noble civilization may know.

To love at all is to suffer. The more noble the Love or the more noble the Objective, the greater must be the suffering. That minor confession, however, is unnecessary as a matter of course. This minor confession is otherwise one of Joy. Joy to have been faithful notwithstanding during an Architect's full lifetime, truthful to a cause that now begins to have its own way with its enemies. To see successful falsehood and pretense turning about face, and with a smile, pretending to have been always friendly; to see the young already eager to hold that cause steadfast; to feel with the rueful Old sorry for them, but seeing justice lay them aside because their death is inexorably essential to life. In short, to see the beginning of the American Structure as that Organic Architecture of which I dreamed faithfully, even as a boy, then worked for as a youth side by side with a great master, and later fought for, almost single-handed, as a Man. A cause rising over the whole World triumphant, terrible in its destructiveness, because so great and beneficially constructive! This I confess with triumph and with gratitude. More difficult is the humility I would profess.

THE COMMERCIALLY DEGENERATE ARCHITECT

[Unpublished essay]

HE TALKS OF SALESMANSHIP.

He is "selling" himself to his client in order to sell his client.

He sells his client the kind of decoration—out or in—he thinks the client wants, or says he wants.

To do this he must have varieties to appeal to every taste—Medieval, Pseudo-Classic, Modernistic.

If these fail to land the prospect who has seen a house designed by—say, for instance one Frank Lloyd Wright—he will say—Ah, all right. You like that house? We will give you a Frank Wright house—and in a more business-like way than he would give you me.

Llewellyn—head of the Illinois A.I.A.—some years ago made these remarks and did the house. At La Grange, Illinois. And hundreds of others have done the same.

His idea of Architecture is a commodity.

A commodity in stocks—or if not then Madame we will get what you want.

He aims to please a customer—to get the job he has a system peculiar to himself.

He belongs to the club. His life is social. A golf-course and a locker are good tools—usually he has a young partner who can draw and "get out" the plans.

If he is a good performer and can "hold" the businessmen, he has several partners and a hundred men.

He is familiar with finance—connected with investment brokers and bankers who know he will stay in line.

A school of legitimate sharks swim in his shadow when he has grown big enough.

He swims in this shadow until he dies.

He invents nothing.

He contributes no ideas.

Ideas are anathema to him for he can't use them.

They clog his machinery.

INDEX

Page numbers in **bold** refer to illustrations.

From *Frank Lloyd Wright: Collected Writings*
Volume I

From the Introduction to the *Wasmuth Portfolio* (1910)

"Beauty, in its essence, is for us as mysterious as life. All attempts
to say what it is are as foolish as cutting out the head of a drum to
find whence comes the sound. But we may study with profit these
truths of form and structure, facts of form as related to function,
material traits of line determining character, laws of structure
inherent in all natural growth. We ourselves are only a product of
natural law. These truths, therefore, are in harmony with the
essence of our own being and are perceived by us to be good.
We instinctively feel the good, true, and beautiful to be
essentially one in the last analysis. Within us there is a divine
principle of growth to some end; accordingly we select as good
whatever is in harmony with this law."

From *The Meaning of Materials* (1928)

"Colors—in paste or crayon—or pencils—always a thrill! To this
day I love to hold a handful of many colored pencils and open my
hand to see them lying loose upon my palm, in the light.

Mere accidental colored chalkmarks on the sunlit
sidewalk, perhaps, will make me pause and something in me
harks back to something —half remembered, half felt—as though
an unseen door had opened and distant music had—for an instant,
come trembling through to my senses.

And in the sense of earth—deep-buried treasure there—
without end. Mineral matter and metal-stores folded away in the
veins of gleaming quartz—gold and silver—lead and copper, and
tawny iron ore—to yield themselves up to roaring furnaces and
flow to the hands of the architect—all to become pawns in the
play of the human mind. . . .

All this I see as the architect's garden—his palette I called
it—to humble the figure.

Materials! What a resource!"

ISBN 0-8478-1547-1

90000>

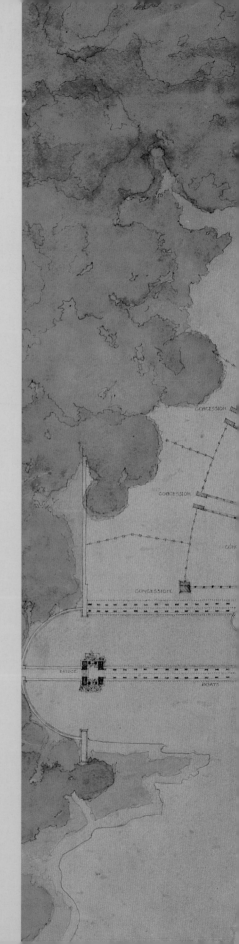